ANNUAL EDITIONS

Dying, Death, and Bereavement 09/10

Eleventh Edition

EDITORS

George E. Dickinson, PhD
College of Charleston

George E. Dickinson, Professor of Sociology at the College of Charleston, received his PhD in sociology from LSU in Baton Rouge and his MA in sociology and BA in biology from Baylor University. He came to the College of Charleston in 1985, having previously taught in Minnesota and Kentucky. The recipient of both NSF and NEH grants, Dickinson has been the author/co-author of over 70 articles in peer-reviewed journals, 10 invited papers/editorials in journals, and 18 books/anthologies (with Michael R. Leming), primarily on end-of-life issues (*Understanding Dying, Death and Bereavement* 6th ed., Wadsworth Publishers, 2007, and *Annual Editions: Dying, Death and Bereavement* 10th ed., McGraw-Hill, 2008). His research and teaching interest in end-of-life issues goes back to 1974 when he taught a course on death and dying and in 1975 when he began research on medical schools and physicians. He is on the editorial boards of *Mortality* (UK), the *American Journal of Hospice & Palliative Medicine* (US), and *The Journal of Multidisciplinary Healthcare* (New Zealand). He was the 2002 recipient of the Distinguished Teacher/Scholar Award and the 2008 recipient of the Distinguished Research Award at the College of Charleston and was given a SC Governor's Distinguished Professor Award in 2003. In 1999 he was a Visiting Research Fellow in palliative medicine at the University of Sheffield's School of Medicine (UK) and in 2006 at Lancaster University's Institute for Health Research (UK). Earlier, Dickinson did postdoctoral studies at Pennsylvania State University (gerontology), at the University of Connecticut (medical sociology), and at the University of Kentucky's School of Medicine (thanatology).

Michael R. Leming, PhD
St. Olaf College

Michael R. Leming is Professor of Sociology and Anthropology at St. Olaf College. He holds degrees from Westmont College (BA), Marquette University (MA), and the University of Utah (PhD) and has done additional graduate study at the University of California in Santa Barbara. He is the co-author (with George E. Dickinson) of *Understanding Dying, Death and Bereavement* 6th ed., Wadsworth Publishers, 2007, and *Annual Editions: Dying, Death and Bereavement* 10th ed., McGraw-Hill, 2008 and *Understanding Families: Diversity, Continuity, and Change,* Two Editions (Harcourt Brace, 1995). He is also the co-editor (with Raymond DeVries and Brendan Furnish) of *The Sociological Perspective: A Value-Committed Introduction* (Zondervan, 1989) and HYPERLINK "http://www.sagepub.com/book.aspx?pid=9608"*Handbook of Death and Dying,* 2 Edited Volumes (with Clifton D. Bryant, Charles K. Edgley, Michael R. Leming, Dennis L. Peck, Sage Publications, Inc. 2003).

Dr. Leming is the founder and former director of the St. Olaf College Social Research Center, former member of the board of directors of the Minnesota Coalition on Terminal Care and the Northfield AIDS Response, and has served as a hospice educator, volunteer, and grief counselor. For the past nine years he has directed the Spring Semester in Thailand program (HYPERLINK "http://www.AmazingThailand.org" www.AmazingThailand.org), affiliated with Chiang Mai University and open to American students. He and his wife are happy to live in Thailand during Minnesota's coldest months.

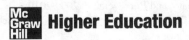

Higher Education

Boston   Burr Ridge, IL   Dubuque, IA   New York   San Francisco   St. Louis
Bangkok   Bogotá   Caracas   Kuala Lumpur   Lisbon   London   Madrid   Mexico City
Milan   Montreal   New Delhi   Santiago   Seoul   Singapore   Sydney   Taipei   Toronto

ANNUAL EDITIONS: DYING, DEATH, AND BEREAVEMENT, ELEVENTH EDITION

Some ancillaries, including electronic and print components, may not be available to customers outside the United States.

1 2 3 4'5 6 7 8 9 0 QPD/QPD 0 9

ISBN 978–0–07–812767–0
MHID 0–07–812767–X
ISSN 1096–4223

Managing Editor: *Larry Loeppke*
Production Manager : *Beth Kundert*
Developmental Editor: *Dave Welsh*
Editorial coordinator: *Mary Foust*
Editorial Assistant: *Nancy Meissner*
Production Service Assistant: *Rita Hingtgen*
Permissions Coordinator: *Shirley Lanners*
Senior Marketing Manager: *Julie Keck*
Marketing Communications Specialist: *Mary Klein*
Marketing Coordinator: *Alice Link*
Project Manager: *Joyce Watters*
Design Specialist: *Tara McDermott*
Senior Administrative Assistant: *DeAnna Dausener*
Senior Operations Manager: *Pat Koch Krieger*
Cover Graphics: *Maggie Lytle*

Compositor: Laserwords Private Limited
Cover Image: © Getty Images

Library in Congress Cataloging-in-Publication Data
Main entry under title: Annual Editions: Dying, Death, and Bereavement. 2009/2010.
 1. Dying, Death, and Bereavement—Periodicals. I. Dickinson, George E., and Leming, Michael R., *comp.* II. Title: Dying, Death, and Bereavement.
658'.05

www.mhhe.com

Editors/Advisory Board

Members of the Advisory Board are instrumental in the final selection of articles for each edition of ANNUAL EDITIONS. Their review of articles for content, level, currentness, and appropriateness provides critical direction to the editor and staff. We think that you will find their careful consideration well reflected in this volume.

Preface

In publishing ANNUAL EDITIONS we recognize the enormous role played by the magazines, newspapers, and journals of the public press in providing current, first-rate educational information in a broad spectrum of interest areas. Many of these articles are appropriate for students, researchers, and professionals seeking accurate, current material to help bridge the gap between principles and theories and the real world. These articles, however, become more useful for study when those of lasting value are carefully collected, organized, indexed, and reproduced in a low-cost format, which provides easy and permanent access when the material is needed. That is the role played by ANNUAL EDITIONS.

Dying, death, and bereavement have been around for as long as humankind, yet as topics of discussion they have been "offstage" for decades in contemporary American public discourse. In the United States, dying currently takes place away from the arena of familiar surroundings of kin and friends, with approximately 80 percent of deaths occurring in institutional settings such as hospitals and nursing homes. Americans have developed a paradoxical relationship with death: We know more about the causes and conditions surrounding death but have not equipped ourselves emotionally to cope with dying, death, and bereavement. The purpose of this anthology is to provide an understanding of dying, death, and bereavement that will assist in coping better with and understanding our own deaths and the deaths of others.

Articles in this volume are taken from professional and semiprofessional journals and from popular publications written for both special populations and a general readership. The selections are carefully reviewed for their currency and accuracy. Many of the articles have been changed from the previous edition through updating and responding to comments of reviewers. Most of the articles refer to situations in the United States, yet other cultures are represented.

The reader will note the tremendous range of approaches and styles of the writers from personal, first-hand accounts to more scientific and philosophical writings. Some articles are more practical and applied, while others are more technical and research oriented. If "variety is the very spice of life," this volume should be a spicy venture for the reader. Methodologies used in the more research-oriented articles range from quantitative (e.g., surveys/questionnaires) to qualitative (e.g., interviews/observation). Such a mix should especially be of interest to the student majoring or minoring in the social sciences.

These articles are drawn from many different periodicals, thus exposing the reader to a variety of publications in the library. With interest stimulated by a particular article, the student is encouraged to pursue other related articles in that particular journal.

This anthology is organized into six units to cover many of the important aspects of dying, death, and bereavement. Though the units are arranged in a way that has some logical order, one can determine from the brief summaries in the table of contents and the cross-references in the topic guide whether another arrangement would best fit a particular teaching situation. The Unit 1 is on issues in dying and death. Unit 2 takes a life-cycle approach and looks at the developmental aspects of dying and death at different age levels. Unit 3 concerns the process of dying. Unit 4 covers ethical issues of dying, death, and suicide. In Unit 5, the articles deal with death rituals and funerals. Finally, Unit 6 presents articles on bereavement.

Annual Editions: Dying, Death, and Bereavement 11/e is intended for use as a supplement to augment selected areas or chapters of textbooks on dying and death. The articles in this volume can also serve as a basis for class discussion about various issues in dying, death, and bereavement.

Annual Editions: Dying, Death, and Bereavement is revised periodically to keep the materials timely as new social concerns about dying, death, and bereavement develop. Your assistance in the revision effort is always welcome. Please complete and return the postage-paid article rating form at the back of the book. We look forward to your input.

George E. Dickinson
Editor

Michael R. Leming
Editor

Contents

UNIT 1 – Exam 1
Issues in Dying and Death

E+2

UNIT 2
Dying and Death across the Life Cycle

The concepts in bold italics are developed in the article. For further expansion, please refer to the Topic Guide.

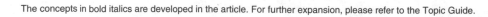

UNIT 3
The Dying Process

The concepts in bold italics are developed in the article. For further expansion, please refer to the Topic Guide.

UNIT 4
Ethical Issues of Dying, Death, and Suicide

UNIT 5
Funerals

The concepts in bold italics are developed in the article. For further expansion, please refer to the Topic Guide.

UNIT 6
Bereavement

The concepts in bold italics are developed in the article. For further expansion, please refer to the Topic Guide.

Correlation Guide

The *Annual Editions* series provides students with convenient, inexpensive access to current, carefully selected articles from the public press. **Annual Editions: Dying, Death, and Bereavement 09/10** is an easy-to-use reader that presents articles on important topics such as *the dying process, ethical issues of dying, suicide,* and many more. For more information on *Annual Editions* and other *McGraw-Hill Contemporary Learning Series* titles, visit www.mhcls.com.

This convenient guide matches the units in **Annual Editions: Dying, Death, and Bereavement 09/10** with the corresponding chapters in one of our best-selling McGraw-Hill Psychology textbooks by DeSpelder/Strickland.

Annual Editions: Dying, Death, and Bereavement 09/10	The Last Dance: Encountering Death and Dying, 8/e by DeSpelder/Strickland
Unit 1: Issues in Dying and Death	**Chapter 1:** Attitudes toward Death: A Climate of Change **Chapter 2:** Learning about Death: The Influence of Sociocultural Forces **Chapter 3:** Perspectives on Death: Cultural and Historical
Unit 2: Dying and Death across the Life Cycle	**Chapter 2:** Learning about Death: The Influence of Sociocultural Forces **Chapter 3:** Perspectives on Death: Cultural and Historical **Chapter 5:** Health Care: Patients, Staff, and Institutions
Unit 3: The Dying Process	**Chapter 4:** Death Systems: Mortality and Society **Chapter 5:** Health Care: Patients, Staff, and Institutions
Unit 4: Ethical Issues of Dying, Death, and Suicide	**Chapter 6:** End-of-Life Issues and Decisions **Chapter 12:** Suicide
Unit 5: Funerals	**Chapter 8:** Last Rites: Funerals and Body Disposition
Unit 6: Bereavement	**Chapter 9:** Survivors: Understanding the Experience of Loss

Topic Guide

This topic guide suggests how the selections in this book relate to the subjects covered in your course. You may want to use the topics listed on these pages to search the Web more easily.

On the following pages a number of Web sites have been gathered specifically for this book. They are arranged to reflect the units of this Annual Editions reader. You can link to these sites by going to *http://www.mhcls.com*.

All the articles that relate to each topic are listed below the bold-faced term.

Internet References

The following Internet sites have been selected to support the articles found in this reader. These sites were available at the time of publication. However, because Web sites often change their structure and content, the information listed may no longer be available. We invite you to visit *http://www.mhcls.com* for easy access to these sites.

Annual Editions: Dying, Death, and Bereavement 09/10

General Sources

An Introduction to Death and Dying
http://www.bereavement.org/

This electronic book was created to help those who grieve and those who provide support for the bereaved. Sections include Grief Theories, Death Systems, Ritual, and Disenfranchised Grief.

Yahoo: Society and Culture: Death
http://dir.yahoo.com/Society_and_Culture/Death_and_Dying/

This Yahoo site has a very complete index to issues of dying and a search option.

UNIT 1: Issues in Dying and Death

Agency for Health Care Policy and Research
http://www.ahcpr.gov

Information on the dying process in the context of U.S. health policy is provided here, along with a search mechanism. The agency is part of the Department of Health and Human Services.

Brain Injury and Brain Death Resources
http://www.changesurfer.com/BD/Brain.html

Visit this site to investigate the debate concerning brain death. When is someone dead? Go to the philosophy of life, consciousness, and personhood page to get specifics.

Growth House, Inc.
http://www.growthhouse.org

Growth House is a nonprofit organization working with grief, bereavement, hospice, and end-of-life issues, as well as pain, AIDS/HIV, suicide, and palliative care issues.

Mortality Rates
http://www.Trinity.Edu/~mkearl/b&w-ineq.jpg

This site contains a graphic representation of the U.S. death rates of different social groups to ascertain social inequities.

WWW Virtual Library: Demography and Population Studies
http://demography.anu.edu.au/VirtualLibrary/

A definitive guide to demography and population studies, with a multitude of important links, can be found here.

UNIT 2: Dying and Death across the Life Cycle

CDC Wonder on the Web—Prevention Guidelines
http://wonder.cdc.gov

At this Centers for Disease Control site, there are a number of papers on suicide prevention, particularly relating to American youth.

Children with AIDS Project
http://www.aidskids.org

This organization's role is to develop fuller understanding of children with and at risk of AIDS, including medical, psychosocial, legal, and financial issues. The mission of the organization is to develop local and national adoptive, foster, and family-centered care programs that are effective and compassionate.

Light for Life Foundation
http://www.yellowribbon.org

The Yellow Ribbon Program of the Light for Life Foundation provides educational material for American youth aimed at preventing youth suicide through the provision of easy access to support services.

National SIDS Resource Center
http://www.sidscenter.org/

The National Sudden Infant Death Syndrome Resource Center (NSRC) provides information services and technical assistance on SIDS and related topics.

Palliative Care for Children
http://www.aap.org/policy/re0007.html

The American Academy of Pediatrics maintains this page, which gives a model for providing palliative care for children living with a life-threatening disease or terminal condition.

UNIT 3: The Dying Process

American Academy of Hospice and Palliative Medicine
http://www.aahpm.org

This is the only organization in the United States for physicians that is dedicated to the advancement of hospice/palliative medicine, its practice, research, and education. There are also links to other Web sites.

Hospice Foundation of America
http://www.hospicefoundation.org

Everything you might need to know about hospice and specific information on the foundation is available at this Web site.

Hospice Hands
http://hospice-cares.com

An extensive collection of links to hospice resources can be found at this site. Try "What's New" to access the *ACP Home Care Guide,* a book whose goal is to support an orderly problem-solving approach in managing care of the dying at home.

National Prison Hospice Association
http://www.npha.org

This prison hospice association promotes care for terminally ill inmates and those facing the prospect of dying in prison.

Internet References

The Zen Hospice Project
http://www.zenhospice.org

The Zen Hospice Project organizes programs dedicated to the care of people approaching death and to increasing the understanding of impermanence. The project also runs a small hospice in San Francisco. There are links here to related information on the Web.

UNIT 4: Ethical Issues of Dying, Death, and Suicide

Articles on Euthanasia: Ethics
http://ethics.acusd.edu/Applied/Euthanasia/

This site covers biomedical ethics and issues of euthanasia in many ways, including recent articles, ancient concepts, legal and legislative information, selected philosophical literature, Web sites, and a search engine.

Euthanasia and Physician-Assisted Suicide
http://www.religioustolerance.org/euthanas.htm

This Web site covers Euthanasia in the United States, as well as status of euthanasia elsewhere in the world and recent developments.

Kearl's Guide to the Sociology of Death: Moral Debates
http://WWW.Trinity.Edu/~mkearl/death-5.html#eu

An Internet resource on the ethics of biomedical issues that includes issues of dying and death, such as euthanasia, is found here.

The Kevorkian Verdict
http://www.pbs.org/wgbh/pages/frontline/kevorkian/

This Web site from PBS features two thought-provoking interviews that explore the future for assisted suicide in the United States. What are the dangers and needed safeguards if it is legalized? How should we view Dr. Kevorkian's role in spotlighting this issue?

Living Wills (Advance Directive)
http://www.mindspring.com/~scottr/will.html

The largest collection of links to living wills and other advance directive and living will information is available at this Web site.

Not Dead Yet
http://www.notdeadyet.org/

The Americans with Disabilities organization uses this Web site to mobilize Americans against euthanasia and mercy killing. Information about the Hemlock Society is also available here.

Suicide Awareness: Voices of Education
http://www.save.org

This popular Internet suicide site provides information on suicide (both before and after), along with material from the organization's many education sessions.

UNOS: United Network for Organ Sharing
http://www.unos.org/

This Web site of the United Network for Organ Sharing includes facts and statistics, resources, and policy proposals regarding organ transplants.

Youth Suicide League
http://www.unicef.org/pon96/insuicid.htm

International suicide rates of young adults in selected countries are available on this UNESCO Web site.

UNIT 5: Funerals

Cryonics, Cryogenics, and the Alcor Foundation
http://www.alcor.org

This is the Web site of Alcor, the world's largest cryonics organization.

Funeral Consumers Alliance
http://www.funerals.org/

The Funeral Consumers Alliance is the only group that monitors the funeral industry for consumers regarding funeral guides, planning, and issues of social concern.

Funerals and Ripoffs
http://www.funerals-ripoffs.org/-5dProf1.html/

Sponsored by the Interfaith Funeral Information Committee and Arizona Consumers Council, this Web site is very critical of the funeral industry and specializes in exposing funeral home financial fraud.

The Internet Cremation Society
http://www.cremation.org

The Internet Cremation Society provides statistics on cremations, links to funeral industry resources, and answers to frequently asked questions.

UNIT 6: Bereavement

Bereaved Families of Ontario Support Center
http://www.bereavedfamilies.net/

The Self-Help Resources Guide at this site indexes resources of the Bereaved Families of Ontario Support Center along with more than 300 listings of other resources and information that are useful to the bereaved.

The Compassionate Friends
http://www.compassionatefriends.org

This self-help organization for bereaved parents and siblings has hundreds of chapters worldwide.

Practical Grief Resources
http://www.indiana.edu/~famlygrf/sitemap.html

Here are lists of Internet and print resources that are available for understanding and coping with grief.

Widow Net
http://www.widownet.org/

Widow Net is an information and self-help resource for and by widows and widowers. The information is helpful to people of all ages, religious backgrounds, and sexual orientation who have experienced a loss of a spouse or life partner.

UNIT 1

Issues in Dying and Death

Unit Selections

Key Points to Consider

- Why do we fear death? What can one do to overcome such a fear?

- What is a good death to you? What is a good death to one diagnosed with a terminal illness? Would the two definitions differ? If you had your choice, how would you like to die? Do you feel that most individuals around the world die in a way they would wish to die?

- What procedures are followed in handling a dead body in the intensive care unit of a hospital? What is the role played by nurses in such a situation?

- How are dying and death portrayed in the media, music, recreation, and humor? Are you aware of how often dying and death are a part of a television program, a movie, music, or are included in a joke? Why do you think that jokes about death are popular?

- Given the high cost of medications, how does one weigh the cost against the "worth" of life? Are a few more days/weeks of life really worth the high cost of such medications?

- How are bodies counted in times of war? How accurate are these "estimates?" Do you think that death counts of the "enemy" are overexaggerated? If yes, why?

Student Web Site

www.mhcls.com

Internet References

Agency for Health Care Policy and Research
http://www.ahcpr.gov

Brain Injury and Brain Death Resources
http://www.changesurfer.com/BD/Brain.html

Growth House, Inc.
http://www.growthhouse.org

Mortality Rates
http://www.Trinity.Edu/~mkearl/b&w-ineq.jpg

WWW Virtual Library: Demography and Population Studies
http://demography.anu.edu.au/VirtualLibrary/

Death, like sex, is a rather taboo topic. British anthropologist Geoffrey Gorer's writing about the pornography of death in the mid-twentieth century seemed to open the door for publications on the subject of death. Gorer argued that death had replaced sex as contemporary society's major taboo topic. Because death was less common in the community, with individuals actually seeing fewer corpses and being with individuals less at the time of death, a relatively realistic view of death had been replaced by a voyeuristic, adolescent preoccupation with it. Our modern way of life has not prepared us to cope any better with dying and death. Sex and death have "come out of the closet" in recent decades, however, and now are issues discussed and presented in formal educational settings. Baby boomers are aging and changing the ways we handle death. In fact, end-of-life issues are frequently discussed in the popular media, as evidenced by the recent popular television shows *Six Feet Under* and *Family Plots* and numerous documentaries and other drama series about hospitals and emergency rooms. Yet, we have a long way to go in educating the public about these historically taboo subjects.

We are beginning to recognize the importance of educating youth on the subject of dying and death. Like sex education, death education (thanatology, literally "the study of death") is an approved topic for presentation in elementary and secondary school curricula in many states, but the topics (especially death and dying) are optional and therefore rarely receive high priorities in the classroom or in educational funding. With the terrorist attacks on the United States, Spain, and England, the war in Iraq, and various natural disasters around the world, an increased interest on death and dying in the curricula could have a positive impact on helping to cope with these various mega death-related situations.

Many (most?) individuals have a fear of death. Just what is a "good death?" These topics are addressed in the articles entitled "Death, Dying, and the Dead in Popular Culture" and "Confronting Death: Perceptions of a Good Death in Adults with Lung Cancer." Different interpretations may occur for different social contexts as to what is a "good death."

What it the value of a human being? How do we measure this? Dan Brock's "How Much Is More Life Worth?" discusses the high cost of drugs in treating individuals with a terminal illness and asks if the financial cost of medications is really worth a few weeks or months of extended life.

What are the procedures that follow the death of an individual in an intensive care unit? Hans Hadders discusses these behind-the-scene rituals as performed by nurses in Norway.

© Thomas Hartwell/2003

Other issues discussed in this section include the determining of mortality in the war in Iraq, as presented in "Estimating Excess Mortality in Post-Invasion Iraq." How are "body counts" managed? Are civilians' lives lost distinguished from those of soldiers? The final article in this section is written by well-known British sociologist Tony Walter. Walter analyzes the sociology of death in the twenty-first century and shows how various disciplines have combined to develop this subfield within the social sciences.

Thanatological

Death, Dying, and the Dead in Popular Culture

KEITH F. DURKIN

Chg

Fulton and Owen (1987) have observed that for members of the generation born after World War II, individuals who generally lack firsthand experience with death, the phenomenon of death and dying has become abstract and invisible. Americans, like members of many other societies, attach fearful meanings to death, dying, and the dead (Leming and Dickinson 2002). Moreover, it is has frequently been suggested that the United States has become a "death-denying" culture. A number of scholars have documented the various ways in which Americans attempt to deny death (e.g., DeSpelder and Strickland 2002; Leming and Dickinson, 2002; Mannino 1997; Oaks and Ezell 1993; Umberson and Henderson 1992). For example, we have a societal taboo against frank discussions about death and dying. When we do refer to these topics, it is normative for us to use euphemisms, such as *passed away* or *expired*. Furthermore, in the United States death typically occurs in the segregated environments of hospitals and nursing homes, and we typically relegate the task of handling the dead to professionals, such as funeral directors.

Although the United States is a death-denying society, Americans may be said to have an obsessive fascination with death and death-related phenomena. As Bryant and Shoemaker (1977) observe, "Thanatological entertainment has been and remains a traditional pervasive cultural pattern both in the United States and elsewhere, and has become very much a prominent and integral part of contemporary popular culture" (p. 2). For instance, death, dying, and the dead "regularly appear in various informational and entertainment media" (Walter, Littlewood, and Pickering 1995:581). Accordingly, the mass media have become a primary source of information about death and dying for most Americans.

In this chapter, I explore the various manifestations of death, dying, and the dead in contemporary U.S. popular culture. This discussion is not intended as an exhaustive exposition of this topic; rather, I seek to address the more prominent examples of this phenomenon. These include portrayals of death, dying, and the dead on television, in cinema, in music, and in products of the print media, as well as in recreational attractions, games, and jokes. Additionally, I explore the social import of the presence of these thanatological themes in popular culture.

Television

Nearly every American household has at least one television set, and a large percentage have several. Death and dying are brought directly into homes via the medium of television. According to DeSpelder and Strickland (2002), in an average issue of *TV Guide,* approximately one-third of the listings "describe programs in which death and dying feature in some way" (p. 35). These topics appear in soap operas, crime dramas, mysteries, documentaries, and comedies. Many of the current top-rated shows, such as *ER* and *CSI,* prominently feature death and dying. The popular "reality" show *Survivor* deals with a type of symbolic death. In fact, death and dying are the most frequently appearing social topics even in religious television programming (Abelman 1987). Recently, the unique series *Six Feet Under,* the ongoing saga of a family that owns and operates a mortuary, has proven to be compelling for many viewers.

Many people have expressed tremendous concern about the amount of violent death featured on U.S. television. According to the National Institute of Mental Health, by the time the average American reaches age 16, he or she has seen 18,000 murders on television (Kearl 1995). It has been estimated that violent death "befalls five percent of all prime time characters each week" (Gerbner 1980:66). Violent death is not limited to prime-time programming, however. The cartoons that are featured on Saturday mornings contain an average of 20 to 25 violent acts per hour, and many of these acts result in the apparent deaths of characters (Wass 1995). However, unlike in reality, cartoon characters have their deaths "reversed with no serious consequences to their bodily functions" (Mannino 1997:29).

Death has also long been a mainstay of televised news programming, but with the advent of cable television and satellite broadcasting, death coverage has taken on a new dimension. The Gulf War of 1991 was a major news event, with live coverage of the battles as they occurred. An average of 2.3 million households tuned in daily to the O. J. Simpson trial, the so-called Trial of the Century (Durkin and Knox 2001). The funeral of Diana, Princess of Wales, was seen on television "by 31 million people in Britain and two billion worldwide" (Merrin 1999:53). The tragic terrorist attacks on the World Trade Center and the Pentagon on

September 11, 2001, were a media event that transpired on live television:

> Every major network, as well as many specialized cable networks (e.g., VH1 and MTV) featured live coverage of the events as they unfolded. According to Nielsen Media Research, 80 million Americans watched television news coverage on the evening of September 11th. . . . In the days following September 11th, there was around-the-clock coverage of the subsequent reaction to the attack, the rescue efforts, and the eventual military retaliation. (Durkin and Knox 2001:3–4) — natural dis – Haiti

Cinema

Thanatological themes have traditionally been, and continue to be, an extremely popular element of the cinematic enterprise. For instance, death and dying feature prominently in westerns and war movies. There have also been many successful film dramas about dying, including *Love Story, Dying Young, Stepmom, My Life,* and *Sweet November.* Death has even been the topic of comedies, such as *Weekend at Bernie's* and *Night Shift.* As Kearl (1995) notes, beginning in the 1970s, a popular motif "involved attacks on humanity by the natural order—frogs, bees, sharks, meteors, earthquakes, and tidal waves". A vast array of movies have featured "disastrous life-threatening phenomena such as diseases (e.g., AIDS, Ebola-like virus), massive accidents (e.g., airplane crashes, nuclear plant accidents) and natural disasters" (Bahk and Neuwirth 2000:64). Ghost movies (e.g., *Truly, Madly, Deeply* and *Ghost*) as well as thrillers such as *Flatliners* have used the near-death experience as a narrative focus (Walter et al. 1995).

Many movies have a decidedly morbid focus. Young people appear to be particularly fascinated by films that feature violent deaths (Leming and Dickinson 2002). Zombie films such as *Dawn of the Dead* and *Night of the Living Dead* not only feature the undead but have scenes containing gruesome acts of violence and murder. The notorious serial killer Jack the Ripper has been featured in a large number of films, including *Murder by Decree, A Study in Terror,* and *Man in the Attic* (Schecter and Everitt 1997). A number of recent films have portrayed the activities of murderers, including *Silence of the Lambs, Hannibal, American Gothic,* and *Natural Born Killers.* In the popular *Faces of Death* series, which appeared in video rental outlets in the mid-1980s, "actual death was displayed, with images of suicides, executions, and autopsies" (Kearl 1995:28).

One specific genre of horror film, the slasher movie, has become especially popular in recent years. According to Molitor and Sapolsky (1993):

> The genre can be characterized as commercially released, feature length films containing suspense evoking scenes in which an antagonist, who is usually a male acting alone, attacks one or more victims. The accentuation in these films is extreme graphic violence. Scenes that dwell on the victim's fear and explicitly portray the attack and its aftermath are the central focus of slasher films. (P. 235)

Slasher movies feature plenty of sex and large teenage body counts (Strinati 2000). Examples include *Halloween, Friday the 13th, Nightmare on Elm Street, Slumber Party Massacre,* and *Motel Hell.* In 1981, 25 slasher movies were ranked among the 50 top-grossing films of that year (Strinati 2000). The impact of slasher films has extended far beyond the cinema; for example, the mayor of Los Angeles proclaimed September 13, 1991, Freddy Krueger Day, in honor of the killer featured in the *Nightmare on Elm Street* film series (Lewis 1997).

Music

Historically, thanatological themes have been present in nearly all musical styles. For instance, folk songs about serial killers date back well into the 19th century (Schecter and Everitt 1997). Death-related themes are also present in many operas and classical musical pieces. These motifs have played a major role in the recording industry. Interestingly, one of the first recordings ever "produced for the Edison phonograph featured an actor reading the shocking confessions of H. H. Holmes, the notorious nineteenth-century "Torture Doctor" (Schecter and Everitt 1997:185). However, death became particularly prominent in the popular music of the so-called Baby Boom generation's teenage years (Kearl 1995). In the 1950s, a musical genre often referred to as "coffin songs"—songs featuring themes related to dying and grief (e.g., "Last Kiss")—became popular with young Americans (DeSpelder and Strickland 2002). The eminence of death-related motifs continues to this day. At times, this can assume remarkable configurations. For example, the funeral of Diana, Princess of Wales, produced pop artist Elton John's hit single "Candle in the Wind '97" (Merrin 1999), which is a lyrically rearranged version of an earlier John song about the dead movie icon Marilyn Monroe. Moreover, a large number of musicians have died in tragic and untimely fashion. Some examples include John Bonham, Kurt Cobain, Jimi Hendrix, Buddy Holly, Janis Joplin, John Lennon, Bob Marley, Keith Moon, Jim Morrison, Elvis Presley, Bon Scott, and Ritchie Valens.

The music that is popular with today's young people frequently has a morbid element that emphasizes death's destructive and catastrophic nature (Fulton and Owen 1987). Examples include songs about homicide, suicide, and extremely violent acts (Wass et al. 1988; Wass, Miller, and Redditt 1991). Many members of our society consider such topics to be particularly unsavory and antisocial, and, accordingly, a number of groups have been particularly vocal in their criticism of this music. For instance, as Wass et al. (1991) note, "A number of professionals, their representative organizations such as the American Academy of Pediatricians and the National Education Association, various child advocacy groups, including the Parent's Music Resource Center, and others have suggested that such lyrics promote destructive and suicidal behavior in adolescents" (p. 200).

The themes of death and destruction play an especially prominent role in two of the most popular styles of contemporary music: heavy metal and rap. Many heavy metal bands have names associated with death, such as Megadeath, Anthrax, Slayer, and Grim Reaper. Examples of heavy metal song titles include "Suicide Solution," "Highway to Hell," and "Psycho Killer." The band Guns N' Roses even recorded a cover version of the song

"Look at Your Game Girl," which was written by the infamous murderer Charles Manson (Schecter and Everitt 1997).

In rap music, the violent lyrics of artists such as Snoop Dogg, Dr. Dre, Eazy-E, and Puff Daddy have generated a great deal of controversy. In fact, one of the most successful rap recording companies is named Death Row Records. Examples of rap song titles include "Murder Was the Case," "Sex, Money, and Murder," and "Natural Born Killers." The song that rapper Eminem performed at the Grammy Awards in 2001, "Stan," describes a murder-suicide. Rap music came under national scrutiny after performer Ice-T released the song "Cop Killer." The murders of rap artists Tupac Shakur and Notorious B.I.G. in recent years have also served to enhance the deadly image of this style of music.

Print Media

Dying, death, and the dead are principal themes in much of American literature (Bryant and Shoemaker 1977). Westerns, war novels, mysteries, and true-crime books are exceptionally popular with readers. Violent death is a ubiquitous theme in popular fiction (Fulton and Owen 1987). Books about hospitals and doctors are also fairly successful (Bryant and Shoemaker 1977). Death and dying are even featured in children's stories (DeSpelder and Strickland 2002; Umberson and Henderson 1992). Newsmagazines frequently publish stories that deal with death and dying, often featuring these stories on their covers. Even comic books have featured the exploits of notorious serial killers (Schecter and Everitt 1997).

Reports of death and dying are common in daily newspapers. The deaths of ordinary people are usually reported only in brief obituaries, unless a person has died in some sensational fashion. Newspapers report the deaths of public figures such as politicians, celebrities, and musical artists in far greater detail (Walter et al. 1995). For instance, the *Seattle Times* ran a front-page feature on the death of rock star Kurt Cobain, complete with photos of the suicide scene (Martin and Koo 1997).

In general, newspapers tend to overemphasize catastrophic causes of death (Combs and Slovic 1979). As Walter et al. (1995) observe, those dramatic deaths that are "boldly headlined and portrayed in the news media are extraordinary deaths" (p. 594). The image of the burning World Trade Center towers was featured on the front pages of many newspapers on September 12, 2001.

Newspaper depictions of death and dying are not always so explicit, however. When Umberson and Henderson (1992) conducted a content analysis of stories about the Gulf War that appeared in the *New York Times,* they found a striking absence of explicit references to death. Instead, the stories frequently employed governmentally inspired euphemisms such as "collateral damage" when discussing death. Moreover, the stories repeatedly quoted State Department and military spokespersons who talked about efforts to keep casualties to a minimum.

One form of print media that scholars have traditionally overlooked is the supermarket tabloid. The weekly circulation of the six major tabloids (*Star, Sun, National Enquirer, National Examiner, Globe,* and *Weekly World News*) is about 10 million, with an estimated readership of about 50 million (Bird 1992). As Durkin and Bryant (1995) note, these publications are full of thanatological content. Articles about murders, accidents, celebrity health scares, and dead celebrities are common, as are stories about paranormal phenomena such are reincarnation, ghosts, and near-death experiences. Health advice regarding the prevention of life-threatening medical problems can be found in some tabloids. In fact, Durkin and Bryant report that the *National Enquirer* has "received an award from the American Cancer Society for medical stories that the paper provided" (p. 10).

Recreation

Aside from their presence in the media, dying, death, and the dead play an important role in the recreational activities of many Americans. As Bryant and Shoemaker (1977) note, many people show an "interest in, and morbid fascination with, facsimiles of the dead, the pseudo dead as it were" (p. 12). An example of this common fascination is the ever-popular wax museum. Also, the traveling museum exhibit of objects from King Tut's tomb was a nationwide sensation. In fact, actual dead bodies have sometimes been used for sideshow exhibits. According to Bryant (1989):

> For many years carnival concessionaires have displayed various kinds of odd bodies and curious corpses . . . because the public was fascinated with such unusual exhibits. A particularly morbid type of display that was common to carnivals was the exhibition of deformed fetuses in jars of formaldehyde, euphemistically known in the trade as "pickled punks." (P. 10)

In a somewhat similar vein, Bunny Gibbons, a sideshow exhibitor, displayed the "Death Car" of serial killer Ed Gein at county fairs throughout the Midwest (Schecter and Everitt 1997).

Some scholars have adopted the term *dark tourism* to refer to "the presentation and consumption (by visitors) of real and commodified death and disaster sites" (Foley and Lennon 1996:198). For example, since 1994, one of the more popular tourist attractions in Los Angeles has been the Brentwood condominium where Nicole Brown Simpson and Ronald Goldman were murdered (Schecter and Everitt 1997). Battlefields such as Gettysburg have traditionally been successful tourist attractions, as has the site of the assassination of President John F. Kennedy (Foley and Lennon 1996). During times of disaster, public safety officials often experience major problems in controlling curiosity seekers motivated by the chance to experience novel situations firsthand (Cunningham, Dotter, and Bankston 1986). Authorities have labeled this phenomenon *convergent behavior* (Bryant 1989).

Cemeteries and burial sites are also popular tourist attractions. For instance, the Forest Lawn cemetery near Hollywood is internationally known as the "cemetery of the stars" (Morgan 1968). Arlington National Cemetery in Virginia has millions of visitors annually (Bryant and Shoemaker 1977). As Frow (1998) reports, Graceland, the former home and burial site of music legend Elvis Presley, "is the object of both everyday pilgrimage and especially intense commemoration during the vigils of Tribute Week, culminating in the candle-lit procession around Presley's grave on the anniversary of his death" (p. 199). Merrin (1999) notes that when a telephone hot line was first opened for members of the public to order tickets to visit the grave of Princess Diana, it was "reported that up to 10,000 calls a minute had been attempted at peak times" (p. 58).

Games, a popular form of recreation, frequently contain thanatological themes. War toys and board games featuring characters like Casper the Friendly Ghost are popular with children. Video games such as *Mortal Combat* and *Duke Nukem* feature vivid images of violent deaths (see Funk and Buchman 1996). Several million copies of the *Ouija Board*, which is touted as a means of communicating with the dead, have been sold (Bryant and Shoemaker 1977). As Schecter and Everitt (1997) report, the thanatological themes in games can assume morbid dimensions:

> Though it is unlikely to become the next *Trivial Pursuit*, a board game called *Serial Killer* set off a firestorm of outrage when it was put on the market a few years ago. . . . [It] consisted of a game board printed on a map of the United States, four serial killer game playing pieces, crime cards, outcome cards, and two dozen plastic victims (in the possibly ill-advised form of dead babies). (P. 31)

Jokes

Humor is a mechanism that allows for the violation of taboos regarding the discussion of death-related topics (Mannino 1997). A vast array of jokes deal with death, dying, and the dead. Thorson (1985) identifies two major varieties of death humor. The first is humor associated with the body. This includes jokes about cannibalism, funerals, undertakers, burials, and necrophilia. The second type, humor associated with the personality, includes jokes about suicide, homicide, memories of the departed, grief, executions, deathbed scenes, last words, and the personification of death.

Some jokes about death, dying, and the dead involve what has frequently been referred to as gallows humor. This term originated "from the genre of jokes about the condemned man or helpless victim, and is often generated by the victims themselves" (Moran and Massam 1997:5). An excellent example is Freud's classic anecdote about a man who joked on his way to the gallows. Currently, gallows humor is conceptualized as more of a philosophical posture than a specific repertoire of jokes (Van Wormer and Boes 1997). This type of humor is intentional (Thorson 1985) and tends to express "a cynical, morbid focus on death" (Sayre 2001:677).

An especially violent and cruel strain of death humor spread through American popular culture in the 1980s (Lewis 1997) and is still popular today. AIDS jokes are the classic example of this type of humor, in which the common tactic is to "specify an out-group and make fun not only of death but also of dying people" (Thorson 1993:21). Moreover, many jokes are told about particular murderers and accused murderers (e.g., Jeffrey Dahmer and O. J. Simpson). Additionally, a variety of jokes circulate in relation to disasters such as the crash of ValuJet Flight 592 in Florida and the destruction of the space shuttle *Challenger* (see Blume 1986). Americans have also created macabre humor surrounding the Ethiopian famine, the Gulf War, and the mass suicide of the Branch Davidians. Such jokes "invite us to be amused by images of bodily mutilation, vulnerability, and victimization" (Lewis 1997:253). Controversial by its very nature, this insensitive type of humor is particularly offensive to many people (Thorson 1993); their responses ensure a dialectic, which increases the humor's entertainment value.

The Postself

Many of the manifestations of death and the dead in U.S. popular culture deal with what has been termed the *post-self*. This is especially true for deceased celebrities and other public figures. The postself is the reputation and influence that an individual has after his or her death. According to Shneidman (1995), this "relates to fame, reputation, impact, and holding on" (p. 455). The postself constitutes a form of symbolic immortality, whereby "the meaning of a person can continue after he or she has died" (Leming and Dickinson 2002:143). In essence, the deceased person continues to exist in the memories of the living (Shneidman 1995). On a cultural level, this functions symbolically to blur the bifurcation between the living and the dead (Durkin and Bryant 1995).

As Frow (1998) observes, the fame of dead celebrities sometimes assumes a pseudorcligious dimension in contemporary society: "A small handful of stars and public figures experience this adoration that raises them beyond the human plane . . . [such as] Elvis, Rudolph Valentino, Lenin, Stalin, Hitler, Mao, James Dean, Kurt Cobain, Bruce Lee, Che Guevara, and Evita Peron" (p. 199). Perhaps the most prominent example of this phenomenon in recent years is Princess Diana, whose tragic and untimely death has resulted in what has been characterized as the "Diana grief industry" (Merrin 1999:51). The devoted can buy Diana dolls, books, plates, videos, stuffed animals, key chains, ashtrays, T-shirts, towels, mugs, spoons, stamps, posters, and more. Although this phenomenon has certainly been highly profitable for a vast array of entrepreneurs, some people find it particularly distasteful. For instance, British Prime Minister Tony Blair has condemned the sale of Princess Diana collectibles as the tacky exploitation of Diana's memory (Merrin 1999).

Discussion

On the one hand, the contemporary United States is frequently described as a death-denying society. Numerous scholars have observed that recent generations of Americans lack the firsthand familiarity with death and dying that their ancestors had (e.g., Fulton and Owen 1987; DeSpelder and Strickland 2002; Leming and Dickinson 2002). Accordingly, many Americans express a great deal of death anxiety. On the other hand, many Americans also have an obsessive fascination with death, dying, and the dead (Oaks and Ezell 1993; Umberson and Henderson 1992). Nowhere is this paradox more apparent than in our popular culture. Television programming, movies, songs, the print media, games, jokes, and even recreational activities are fraught with thanatological content.

This seeming contradiction may be read at several levels, in that there are differential interpretations. The most obvious, albeit superficial, interpretation is that the United States is not as much of a death-denying society as many writers contend. A second explanation for the paradox is that our society is, indeed, a death-denying one, but our insulation from death causes us to crave some degree of information and insight concerning death, and we feed that craving through popular-culture depictions of death and dying. This situation would be not unlike the Victorian period in Great Britain and the United States, during which sexual Puritanism was an ideological mainstay of the value system, but nevertheless there was a significant demand for clandestine, salacious accounts of sex and sexual activity, such as smuggled "dirty" books from Europe.

Another interpretation of the contradiction between the death-denying nature of U.S. society and the saturation of death themes in the American mass media is that the treatment of death as entertainment and humor is simply an extension of, or another configuration of, death denial. By rendering death into humor and entertainment, we effectively neutralize it; it becomes innocuous, and thus less threatening, through its conversion and ephemerality in the media. This is, perhaps, the more compelling explanation.

Death is a disruptive event, not only for the individual who dies but for the larger social enterprise as well. Consequently, all societies must construct mechanisms to deal with death's problematic impacts (Blauner 1966). As Pine (1972) notes, the "beliefs and practices of the members of a society toward dying and death are largely dependent upon that society's social organization" (p. 149). Popular culture serves as a type of collective vision by which meanings are socially constructed, which in turn "greatly influences our norms, beliefs, and subsequent actions" (Couch 2000:25). It appears that the thanatological themes in U.S. popular culture function as a mechanism that helps Americans to deal with death. As Bryant (1989) notes, death, dying, and the dead "are traumatic and anxiety producing topics, and can be better confronted if they are socially neutralized" (p. 9).

Such social neutralization can help to assuage the disruptive impact of death and dying for the individual. This can occur in three related ways. First, in the context of popular culture, death, dying, and the dead are frequently reconceptualized into forms that stimulate something other than primordial terror. These phenomena may be considered fascinating, entertaining, and even humorous, depending on the social context. Bryant (1989) observes that when death is camouflaged in such a manner, "individuals can more comfortably indulge their curiosity about, and fascination with, such concerns" (p. 9). For instance, a visit to Elvis Presley's grave, to the site of the JFK assassination, to the spot where Nicole Brown Simpson and Ronald Goldman were murdered, or to the Forest Lawn cemetery near Hollywood might be considered part of a vacation. Moreover, many individuals find it thrilling to be frightened by horror and death at the movies (Leming and Dickinson 2002). Also, newspaper accounts of violent or accidental deaths may engender some voyeuristic, albeit convoluted, pleasure "or some macabre enjoyment in the misfortunes of others" (Walter et al. 1995:586). Similarly, many of the outrageous stories that appear in supermarket tabloids such as the *Weekly World News* and the *Sun* "appear to have no purpose other than catering to accident watchers" (Bird 1992:54).

Second, appreciation of many of the types of thanatological themes found in our popular culture requires some detachment on the part of the individual. Like spectators at professional wrestling matches, viewers of horror movies are required to suspend disbelief (Weaver 1991). Children or adolescents playing violent video games must detach themselves from the depictions of primal carnage occurring before their eyes. The quintessential example of this phenomenon is thanatological humor. Humor functions as a type of defense mechanism, allowing people to cope with the fear and anxiety associated with death and dying (Moran and Massam 1997; Oaks and Ezell 1993; Sayre 2001; Thorson 1993).

Enjoyment of this type of humor requires us to laugh at our own mortality (Thorson 1985). As Lewis (1997) notes, the appreciation of a so-called killing joke "calls for the adoption of a playful detachment from an act of violence or suffering" (p. 264).

Finally, some observers have argued that the tremendous amount of exposure to death, dying, and the dead that we receive through our popular culture may make us more accepting of these phenomena (Oaks and Ezell 1993). This saturated environment of thanatological concerns may function to inure individuals to death and dying, thus diluting or counteracting their anxiety about these phenomena (Bryant and Shoemaker 1977). Durkin and Bryant (1995) speculate that "the inordinate amount of attention afforded to thanatological themes in the tabloids may actually help to desensitize the reader" (p. 11). Similarly, Wass et al. (1991) suggest that the ubiquitous death-related themes in popular music might help adolescents confront their anxieties about these phenomena, given that death and dying are seldom discussed in the home or the classroom. — this last one is not so believable

Conclusion

The United States is commonly characterized as a death-denying society. Americans frequently attach fearful meanings to thanatological concerns, have taboos against frank discussions about death and dying, and relegate the task of handling the dead to professionals. Nonetheless, death, dying, and the dead occupy a prominent place in our popular culture. Thanatological themes appear frequently in television programming, cinema, the print media, jokes, and recreational activities. Dead celebrities also play an important role in our popular culture. These thanatological elements of popular culture function as a mechanism to help individuals deal with the disruptive social impacts of death and dying. They help us to redefine death as something other than a terror, and enjoyment of these themes requires some detachment on the part of the individual. It has also been argued that we may be more accepting of death, dying, and the dead because of our frequent exposure to these phenomena through our popular culture.

References

Abelman, Robert. 1987. "Themes and Topics in Religious Television Programming." *Review of Religious Research* 29:152–69.

Bahk, C. Mo and Kurt Neuwirth. 2000. "Impact of Movie Depictions of Volcanic Disasters on Risk Perceptions and Judgements." *International Journal of Mass Emergencies and Disasters* 18:63–84.

Bird, S. Elizabeth. 1992. *For Enquiring Minds: A Cultural Study of Supermarket Tabloids.* Knoxville: University of Tennessee Press.

Blauner, Robert. 1966. "Death and Social Structure." *Psychiatry* 29:378–94.

Blume, Delorys. 1986. "Challenger 10 and Our School Children: Reflections on the Catastrophe." *Death Studies* 10:95–118.

Bryant, Clifton D. 1989. "Thanatological Crime: Some Conceptual Notes on Offenses Against the Dead as a Neglected Form of Deviant Behavior." Paper presented at the World Congress of Victimology, Acapulco.

Bryant, Clifton D. and Donald Shoemaker. 1977. "Death and the Dead for Fun (and Profit): Thanatological Entertainment as Popular Culture." Presented at the annual meeting of the Southern Sociological Society, Atlanta, GA.

Combs, Barbara and Paul Slovic. 1979. "Newspaper Coverage of the Causes of Death." *Journalism Quarterly* 56:837–43.

Couch, Stephen R. 2000. "The Cultural Scene of Disasters: Conceptualizing the Field of Disasters and Popular Culture." *International Journal of Mass Emergencies and Disasters* 18:21–37.

Cunningham, Orville R., Daniel L. Dotter, and William B. Bankston. 1986. "Natural Disasters, Convergence, and Four-Wheel Drive Machines: An Emergent Form of Deviant Behavior." *Deviant Behavior* 7:261–67.

DeSpelder, Lynne Ann and Albert Lee Strickland. 2002. *The Last Dance: Encountering Death and Dying,* 6th ed. New York: McGraw-Hill.

Durkin, Keith F. and Clifton D. Bryant. 1995. "Thanatological Themes in the Tabloids: A Content Analysis." Presented at the annual meeting of the Mid-South Sociological Association, Mobile, AL.

Durkin, Keith F. and Kristy Knox. 2001. "September 11th, Postmodernism, and the Collective Consciousness: Some Sociological Observations." Presented at the annual meeting of the Mid-South Sociological Association, Mobile, AL.

Foley, Malcolm and J. John Lennon. 1996. "JFK and Dark Tourism: A Fascination With Assassination." *International Journal of Heritage Studies* 2:198–211.

Frow, John. 1998. "Is Elvis a God? Cult, Culture, and Questions of Method." *International Journal of Cultural Studies* 1:197–210.

Fulton, Robert and Greg Owen. 1987. "Death and Society in Twentieth Century America." *Omega* 18:379–95.

Funk, Jeanne and Debra D. Buchman. 1996. "Playing Violent Video and Computer Games and Adolescent Self Concept." *Journal of Communication* 46:19–32.

Gerbner, George. 1980. "Death in Prime Time: Notes on the Symbolic Functions of Dying in the Mass Media." *Annals of the American Academy of Political and Social Science* 447:64–70.

Kearl, Michael C. 1995. "Death in Popular Culture." Pp. 23–30 in *Death: Current Perspectives,* 4th ed., edited by John B. Williamson and Edwin S. Shneidman. Mountain View, CA: Mayfield.

Leming, Michael R. and George E. Dickinson. 2002. *Understanding Death, Dying, and Bereavement,* 5th ed. New York: Harcourt College.

Lewis, Paul. 1997. "The Killing Jokes of the American Eighties." *Humor* 10:251–83.

Mannino, J. Davis. 1997. *Grieving Days, Healing Days.* Boston: Allyn & Bacon.

Martin, Graham and Lisa Koo. 1997. "Celebrity Suicide: Did the Death of Kurt Cobain Influence Young Suicides in Australia?" *Archives of Suicide Research* 3:187–98.

Merrin, William. 1999. "Crash, Bang, Wallop! What a Picture! The Death of Diana and the Media." *Mortality* 4:41–62.

Molitor, Fred and Barry S. Sapolsky. 1993. "Sex, Violence, and Victimization in Slasher Films." *Journal of Broadcasting and Electronic Media* 37:233–42.

Moran, Carmen and Margaret Massam. 1997. "An Evaluation of Humour in Emergency Work." *Australasian Journal of Disaster and Trauma Studies* 3:1–12.

Morgan, Al. 1968. "The Bier Barons." *Sociological Symposium* 1:28–35.

Oaks, Judy and Gene Ezell. 1993. *Death and Dying: Coping, Caring and Understanding,* 2d ed. Scottsdale, AZ: Gorsuch Scarisbrick.

Pine, Vanderlyn R. 1972. "Social Organization and Death." *Omega* 3:149–53.

Sayre, Joan. 2001. "The Use of Aberrant Medical Humor by Psychiatric Unit Staff." *Issues in Mental Health Nursing* 22:669–89.

Schecter, Harold and David Everitt. 1997. *The A-Z Encyclopedia of Serial Killers.* New York: Pocket Books.

Shneidman, Edwin S. 1995. "The Postself." Pp. 454–60 in *Death: Current Perspectives,* 4th ed. edited by John B. Williamson and Edwin S. Shneidman. Mountain View, CA: Mayfield.

Strinati, Dominic. 2000. *An Introduction to Studying Popular Culture.* London: Routledge.

Thorson, James A. 1985. "A Funny Thing Happened on the Way to the Morgue: Some Thoughts on Humor and Death, and a Taxonomy of Humor Associated With Death." *Death Studies* 9:201–16.

———. 1993. "Did You Ever See a Hearse Go By? Some Thoughts on Gallows Humor." *Journal of American Culture* 16:17–24.

Umberson, Debra and Kristin Henderson. 1992. "The Social Construction of Death in the Gulf War." *Omega* 25:1–15.

Van Wormer, Katherine and Mary Boes. 1997. "Humor in the Emergency Room: A Social Work Perspective." *Health and Social Work* 22:87–92.

Walter, Tony, Jane Littlewood, and Michael Pickering. 1995. "Death in the News: The Public Investigation of Private Emotion." *Sociology* 29:579–96.

Wass, Hannelore. 1995. "Death in the Lives of Children and Adolescents." Pp. 269–301 in *Dying: Facing the Facts,* 3d ed., edited by Hannelore Wass and Robert A. Neimeyer. Washington, DC: Taylor & Francis.

Wass, Hannelore, M. David Miller, and Carol Ann Redditt. 1991. "Adolescents and Destructive Themes in Rock Music: A Follow-Up." *Omega* 23:199–206.

Wass, Hannelore, Jana L. Raup, Karen Cerullo, Linda G. Martel, Laura A. Mingione, and Anna M. Sperring. 1988. "Adolescents' Interest in and Views of Destructive Themes in Rock Music." *Omega* 19:177–86.

Weaver, James B. 1991. "Are Slasher Horror Films Sexually Violent?" *Journal of Broadcasting and Electronic Media* 35:385–92.

Dealing with the Dead Patient at the Intensive Care Unit

HANS HADDERS - social anthro - Norway
nurse - palliative care

Introduction

This paper limits its description to nurses' post-mortem work at the Intensive Care Unit (ICU). This work involves how nurses do the "last offices" *(stell)*, document death, and prepare the dead patient for the relatives "viewing of the deceased" (visning). This paper does not start the analysis of post-mortem care from a taken for granted vantage point of the biological body, the corpse, or the cadaver (see critique by Hallam *et al.,* 1999, p. 63ff). Instead, this paper will follow Mol's approach (2002), as described in her book *The body multiple: Ontology in medical practice*. The enacted objects, for example the dead patient or the dead body, will be described as these evolve and dissolve in the clinical contexts explored. Referring to the dead patient or the dead body as objects is not an analytical reductionism. Mol describes such ethnography as "praxiography" (Moll, 2002, p. 32f). Praxiography refers to and describes whatever ontology made present in the practice where it is constituted (see Timmermans, 2006, p. 53). The main focus of this analysis is not on representations, various perspectives, or social constructions of death and the dead, but on interventions and dealings with the dead (Mol, 2002, p. 152). Mol underscores that "*ontologies are brought into being, sustained, or allowed to wither away in common, day-to-day, sociomaterial practices*" (Mol, 2002, p. 6). The focal point of the description of medical practice in this paper is how the nurses deal with the dead patient. The term "dead patient" is common parlance among nurses. As such it constitutes a central ontological mooring throughout the nurses' post-mortem care. In order to illuminate the ethnographic field described below, this paper will begin with some reflections about death, social identity, and personhood.

This paper is partly based on tape-recorded semi-structured interviews with 27 nurses at the ICU of Trondheim University Hospital in Norway. On an annual basis, approximately 12–14% of the patients ($n = 80 – 90$) treated at the ICU die on this ward. The interviews took place in a secluded room in the near vicinity of the ICU, and the average duration of these interviews was approximately 30 minutes.[1]

A number of hospital procedure manuals have also served as a source of insight into how the nurses at the ICU undertake the care of the dead. Care of dead children (under 18 years old), of brain dead patients, and of organ donors has been excluded from this study. The reason for their exclusion from this study is that these cases, with all of their complexity, demand a study of their own. Such studies have already been undertaken by anthropologists (see, for example, Alnæs, 2001; Lock, 2002).

Death, Social Identity, and Persons

Within the social sciences there are several investigations of hospital dying and death which explore patients' social identity (Glaser & Strauss, 1966, 1968; Sudnow, 1967). In Chapter 7 of their work *Awareness of Dying* (1966), Glaser and Strauss comment on social identity and social death via their discussion of various clinical instances where American hospital personnel discount the awareness of their living patients. Examples of awareness discounting of patients given by Glaser and Strauss are for instance in connection with care of premature babies, hopelessly comatose, or senile patients (Glaser & Strauss, 1966, pp. 107–115). Such awareness discounting may amount to treating these patients as non-persons or socially dead. Glaser and Strauss also report instances when staff neglect general rules of decency and institutional instructions to treat the dead body with respect, as the staff become callous or pressed for time. However, in the last paragraph of Chapter 7, Glaser and Strauss also mention instances when health care personnel fail to discount awareness of the dead patients, temporarily treating the deceased as a sentient being during post-mortem care and as they arrange symbolic farewells for the relatives (Glaser & Strauss, 1966, p. 113f).

Sudnow's study *Passing on. The social organisation of dying* (1967) also investigates the professional management of death at an American hospital. In this work, Sudnow relates several instances of social death prior to biological death; "In dealing with comatose patients—a high proportion of County's critical ill population—personnel became accustomed to disattending the patient as a social object ..." (Sudnow, 1967, p. 88). Sudnow describes in detail how dying patients were treated as non-persons or produced as "pre-corpses" before their biological death in order to minimize staff contact with death: "Since predeath treatment as a corpse extends backward in time to include many comatose patients, there is, in actual practice, little distinction between the comatose and the dead" (Sudnow, 1967, p. 89). Mulkay (1993), who explores social death in Britain, defines the concepts of social death and social life as follows:

> The defining feature of social death is the cessation of the individual person as an active agent in others' lives . . . Social life is the obverse of social death and depends on the social continuation of the particular person, whether or not that person is biologically living (Mulkay, 1993, p. 32f).

In order to grasp better how the cessation or continuation of personhood may influence an understanding of the dead we need to look a little bit closer at some perspectives on personal identity and death.

Personal Identity and the Ontological Status of the Dead

In his discussion of medical ethics and the historical background to the Western view of moral obligations, physician and philosopher Raanan Gillon (2000) comments on Kant's and Lock's conception of a person.[2] Kant saw the rational willing agency which enabled individual moral judgment as the basis for what he called "persons" and "Locke saw the ability to think combined with self awareness over time as the essence of personhood" (Gillon, 2000, p. 50f). The Kantian and Lockean stances thus cannot, claims Gillon, grant personhood to living embryos, foetuses, comatose patients in persistent vegetative state, or to "brain dead" humans (Gillon, 2000). This paper will not enter into these and related complicated and intricate philosophical and ethical debates. However, from the perspectives of Kant and Locke, a "dead person," bereft of moral agency or consciousness, may seem like a contradiction in terms. For, presuming that a necessary condition for personhood is some sort or other of *self awareness* it follows by logical implication that the dead cannot be "persons". So, what may we mean, then, by talking about persons post-death?

The philosopher Lars Sandman starts his probing into this question by distinguishing between two possible and different views of the ontological status of the dead person, which he calls "the *religious view*" and "the *cessation view*" (Sandman, 2005, p. 16). According to the religious view, "death is not the absolute or total end of existence but a transformation into another form of existence or life" (Sandman, 2005). Sandman explains how the soul or person continues to exist in some form or other, with or without a resurrected body, or in some other life form (Sandman, 2005). Various aspects of personal identity beyond biological death have been carefully investigated cross-culturally by anthropologists, in part focusing on analysis of mortuary rituals and eschatological beliefs, typically in traditional and small-scale societies (see for example Cederroth *et al.,* 1988; Metcalf & Huntington, 1991; Robben, 2004). The common approach here among anthropologists is that the personal identity of the dead—whether in the form of a soul or an ancestor—is a social construction.[3]

When it comes to the second view of the ontological status of the dead person, "the *cessation view*," Sandman makes these comments:

> In this context it will be assumed that a (human) person is an entity with at least two necessary features—a living human physical body and consciousness. If either of these is lacking—that is, if the physical body is dead or if the living physical body (irreversibly) lacks consciousness—the person will be dead. Given the cessation view as to what post-death implies, that a person is dead will, in this context, mean the same as the person not existing (Sandman, 2005, p. 17).

Among contemporary ethical philosophers and psychologists, the so-called cessation view has been more prevalent—whether it is the cessation of individual agency, individual consciousness, or neurological activity in the brain—as a definition of human death (see Lizza, 1999).

Sandman sums up his probing of the two ways of perceiving the ontological status of the dead person by stating that from any of the two views he has presented, "the person is not coexistent with the physical body." The physical body, in this context, is but a remaining aspect of part of the former person, talked about only as the "remains" of that person (Sandman, 2005, p. 17). A possible alternative view of the ontological status of the dead person, left untouched by Sandman, is the phenomenological view of the dead person. To quote the words of Rom Harré (1979), from his work *Social being. A theory for social psychology,* to illustrate an example of his approach:

> There is a complex interaction between concept of agency, consciousness and physical death, which it is not part of my purpose to analyse. All that we need to notice is that with respect to the biological progress, an arbitrary point of closure is defined which is closely related to legal and other considerations. However, for ceremonial purposes a simulacrum of embodiment may be produced. For example, the body of a person may be embalmed and so decorated to seem to be alive, that is to seem to be still a member of a social world. Leave-takings may occur in which one of the participants is a corpse (Harré, 1979, p. 332).

It is the aspect of the "simulacrum of embodiment" of the social person in connection with the care of the dead body, the viewing of the dead patient, and the leave-taking by the relatives, that is of special interest here. Within this perspective the dead person may paradoxically be experienced as present and absent at the same time by the nurses and the relatives. The state of the deceased may be described as a presence of an absence or, alternatively, an absence of a presence (Hallam & Hockey, 2001). Now, at last, with these reflections of personhood, social identity, and ontology in mind, let us turn to the post-mortem work of the nurses at the intensive care unit.

Intimacy and the Personal Integrity of the Dead Patient

As far as possible, the practice is to move the dying patient into a single room on the ward as death draws near, in order to safeguard privacy for the patient as well as for the family. In some cases, when all smaller rooms are occupied, the death of the patient takes place behind closed curtains in the open ward. In these cases, as far as possible, the patient is moved to a single room afterwards for the last offices and the viewing by the family. Nurses dislike doing the post-mortem care behind curtains in the open ward. Several nurses told me that they do not like to be disturbed, rushed, or interrupted during the post-mortem care.

Whether it is stroking the hand by a relative or the act of washing the dying one by the nurse before death, it may not be very different to give similar attention to these acts after the death has occurred. Indeed, most nurses at the ICU ward told me that they undertake the act of washing the deceased in much the same manner as when washing the dying, carefully moving and supporting the body being washed. This attitude to the care of the dead is also mirrored in the recommendations of the hospital's procedural manuals for the last offices (stell); where it is stated that one should show respect and reverence towards the deceased during the care (Melheim, 2000). The deceased is cared for according to need, just as before the death took place. Thus the general attitude of respect paid towards the dead patient is not very different from the respect given to the dying patient, or to any patient in general. One nurse stated that it is an ethical imperative to treat the dead patient as a human person still present.

When the patient dies the nurse carefully closes the patient's eyes and props up the patient's jaw so that the mouth remains closed, creating a peaceful impression, as a patient in sleep. At the ICU, the washing of the dead patient often takes place within the first hours after the death, while the dead body may still be warm and more akin to the living body. Nurses remove soil, blood stains, and other signs of suffering from the dead body. While washing the dead patient the nurses cover the private parts of the patient with a towel, safeguarding the privacy and integrity of the deceased. Rubber gloves are used during washing according to need, as with any patient, alive or dead. Whether it is gentle washing, grooming with body lotion, or combing or shaving the dead patient, such acts of care can be understood as enhancing the affinity between the caregiver and the receiver of care.

Some nurses talk to the dead patient, informing them of what they will do next during the care, in the same manner as they would talk to a comatose patient. The practice of talking to comatose patients is partly based on the understanding that the comatose patients, though unconscious, may still hear what people say around them. This practice also helps the nurses to maintain the relational aspect of the care rendered. One nurse said she sometimes thought of talking to the dead patient as "a bit silly," since dead people do not hear, but she did so anyway. Another nurse who had worked several years at an oncology ward, where the practice of talking to the dead patient during the

post-mortem care is more common, had to reflect on whether this practice was proper or not after she had started to work at the ICU. This happened as she undertook her first washing of a dead patient together with another nurse at the ICU. When they had completed the care of the dead patient, the ICU nurse had remarked that she thought it was somewhat strange to talk to a dead patient. During the interview this oncology nurse, who had been socialized into talking to dead patients at the oncology ward, asked herself if this practice, in fact, may create confusion in relatives concerning the status of the dead patient. However, this nurse also mentioned that relatives themselves sometimes talk to the deceased, as they take part in the viewing of the deceased at the ICU. This nurse also asked herself where the line should be drawn; "shall we, kind of, treat all [dead patients] as if they are living right up to when they are shrouded . . . or should one . . . now the patient is actually dead, he cannot hear or see . . . is it less respectful not to explain what we do [to them] during the care . . ."

Where the relatives are concerned, it does not come as a surprise that a general longstanding relationship with the deceased person during life may linger on, and express itself in continued communication with the dead person after the clinical death has taken place. However, what may be more astonishing is the fact that the nurses, who generally have had a relatively brief contact with the patient in life, communicate with the dead during the post-mortem care. It seems as if the nurses often prefer to continue to relate to the dead patient as a person, in order to enable them to render what they perceive as a humane treatment of the deceased. Treating the dead patient as a person may also allow the nurses to cope with exposure to death.

In the manual concerning the death of a patient at Trondheim University Hospital, nurses are empowered to reach an agreement with the relatives if (a) the latter wish to wash or care for the deceased on their own, (b) or prefer to do so together with the nurses, (c) or just be present, or (d) absent themselves during the last offices (Melheim, 2000). The results of a recent investigation (Hadders & Torvik, 2003) of the relatives' participation in the last offices at the palliative ward at the hospital's oncology department show that relatives participated in 18% of the cases. (This investigation involved 244 cases. The oncology PMU department does not admit patients under the age of 18 years old.) In contrast to results from the palliative cancer ward, almost all nurses interviewed at the ICU reported that they never, or very seldom, ask relatives to participate in the last offices of the adult deceased, although some of the nurses would agree to let the relatives participate if they expressed a wish to do so. At the ICU, however, they had only a few instances in which relatives of adult patients had wished to participate in the last care of the dead patient. It is not uncommon that parents and relatives of children participate in the last offices. In these cases parents often dressed the children in personal clothing, something very rarely done to adult dead patients at the ICU. By contrast, at the palliative ward, relatives in 40% of cases included in the investigation decided to dress the adult deceased in personal clothing (Hadders & Torvik, 2003).

According to the ICU nurses, dead adults are generally left naked on the bed, under a clean white sheet, after they have

Diff cultures in ICU & oncology wards

been washed and cared for, in accordance with the wish of the pathology department. However, some nurses feel this to be inappropriate treatment of the dead patient, and accordingly dressed the corpse in a hospital nightshirt. Others feel that being dressed in a hospital shirt is not worthy enough. These nurses use a small sheet or a pillow cover, skilfully draping these over the dead person's shoulders and breast, covering the rest of the body with the bed sheet. Thus they create what looks like a ceremonial white death gown. Some of the nurses have adopted this practice from nurses that work in the oncology department, where this author has often observed this practice. One of the oncology nurses, who worked there when this practice was first introduced at the cancer ward, said she had learnt this way of draping the dead from an older nurse who worked within the residential geriatric care. The deceased is positioned as if in sleep, with the hands visible, folded and placed over the abdomen. The face and the hands, parts of the body associated with the living person, are thus made visible and prominent (Hallam *et al.,* 1999, p. 134f).

Why is the current trend to invite relatives to participate in the care of the dead, and to celebrate the social identity of the dead through private clothing, less prevalent at the ICU ward? There are many factors related to the care of the dead patient at this ward that are likely to create distance, aversion, and depersonalization of the deceased. Thus the nurses seem to be reluctant to invite relatives to participate at this time.

Distance, Aversion, and the Integrity of the Dead Body

Let us now turn to the nurses' descriptions of their care of the dead patient, and look at some quotations in which they describe some of these unpleasant factors. The aspects of the dead body which may result in distance and aversion are tied to visual, tactile, olfactory, as well as audible experience. The sight of a dead discoloured body with glazed staring eyes and a gaping mouth is unsettling. The limp and unresponsive body feels different than the living body. The dead body smells different. The dead body is conspicuously still and silent.

Several nurses describe how and why the washing and caring of the dead patient is a very special situation due to "lots of technical apparatus which the relatives may not understand." Another nurse explained why relatives may prefer to see the dead patient after the nurses have completed the washing and care; "it is better for them to see their own [deceased] without all these [technical] gadgets and the tube and all these things, there is so much apparatus. [Dead patients] almost 'drown' in gadgets . . ." Another nurse stated: "We try to arrange [the care of the dead] as respectfully as we can . . . I feel that the [actions with] least respect is when we pinch out equipment, tear and tug bandage; such things is the part of it, in a way, that are the least personal . . ." The same nurse described how all the technical equipment, via various catheters, tubes, and the like, perforate the body. During the care of the dead patient, when nurses remove this equipment, body fluid may leak out of the often oedematous, disfigured dead body. Several nurses point out how

the unpleasant task of rectum plugging is coped with through disengagement, focusing on the task and the body. The nurses are well aware of the importance of performing such unpleasant tasks well. Doing a good job is a way of paying respect to the deceased as well as to the relatives. In order to safeguard the wholeness of the deceased they have to breach the integrity of the dead body. Thus the nurses strive hard to stop bleeding and seepage, cleaning the dead patient, and arrange the body in the most favourable way, to prepare the deceased for viewing by the relatives at a later stage. One nurse said one reason why nurses at the ICU seldom dress adults in private clothing is that this is often practically difficult to, because of all of the extra body fluid. Another nurse recalled an incident where they had kept the relatives waiting for an extra 20 minutes before the viewing could take place, due to leakage of blood after pulling out a central venous catheter. All incidents described above are ample evidence as to why nurses may feel that it is difficult or improper to ask relatives to participate in the washing and care of the dead patient at the ICU. The facets of the post-mortem care described above also may create a distance between the nurse and the dead patient. Nevertheless, throughout this work the nurses remain reverent towards the dead body.

When it comes to irreverent behaviour towards the dead, several nurses report how they dislike any rough handling of the dead patient after death, be it by an escort or by a nurse, including moving the dead patient with haste and without reverence. The procedural manual demands that last offices always be done by two nurses working together, in order to safeguard a humane and careful handling of the dead patient's body (Melheim, 2000, p. 4). All nurses reported that this is also the way they prefer to do it in practice. In cases when the body of the deceased was large and heavy, three staff members took part in the last offices. Several nurses also mentioned a dislike of the thoughtless, irreverent tendency of some nurses to talk about irrelevant and banal issues while caring for the dead. One of the nurses preferred to speak in a somewhat hushed voice, in reverence of the dead patient. Another nurse related how she felt somewhat humble and reverent while doing the "last offices for a dead human being."

From the nurses' statements it is evident that in spite of the distancing factors of the care, they generally strive to safeguard the personal integrity of the defenceless dead patient. This kind of safeguarding is a general aspect of the nurses' care of any patient, whether alive, conscious, comatose, or dead. Throughout their work and care, the nurses often transgress the limits of personal integrity outlined by ordinary everyday social interaction (Lawler, 1991, pp. 155–176). Examples of this are the nurses licence to touch the patient, assist the patient in private body care, and even penetrate the patient's body while inserting catheters and lines, drawing blood samples, or administering injections. During post-mortem care when nurses come close to developing a callous and distant attitude, demeaning the patient and themselves of humanity, nurses often seem to strive to counteract this trend by treating their patients as human persons or as human remains. This behaviour can be illuminated by applying Goffman's dialectical terms deference and demeanour. Goffman used these terms to analyse how the moral order of a social group is maintained through social face-to-face inter-action (Goffman, 1956).[4] The rules of deference are the social norms guiding the conduct by which the nurse expresses respect for the patient's integrity, even while breaching it. The rules of demeanour define the conduct by which a persons signals to others that they are a respectable person, and thus worthy of earning the respect of others (Goffman, 1956). Deference and demeanour are inextricably linked to each other in practice, and it is only by an analytical abstraction that we may separate them (Goffman, 1956, p. 491ff). In the case of the nurses' dealing with the dead, it is paradoxically the nurses' responsibility to safeguard both positions in the dialectical dynamics between acts of deference and acts of demeanour. As commented above, nurses usually work in pairs during post-mortem care. This may help them to check their own conduct, as well as witness and check each others' conduct, vis-à-vis the dead.

The nurses generally speak of the deceased as the dead patient, the patient, or he/she. They also speak of the dead body, or the body. The term "corpse" (lik) is never used by the nurses, due to the implications of this designation, which is a complete separation between the dead person and the inanimate body, treating the dead patient as a thing or a piece of dead flesh. Throughout their work, even during the most technical and medical moments of care, the nurses seldom seem to lose contact with the human aspect of the dead patient. Jean-Paul Sartre says of this aspect of personhood and embodiment in his work *Being and Nothingness* (Sartre, 2001):

> . . . we can not perceive the Other's body as *flesh* as if it were an isolated object [a *this,* a thing] having purely external relations with other thises [things]. That is true only of a *corpse.* The Other's body as flesh is immediately given as centre of reference in a situation which is synthetically organized around it, and it is inseparable from this situation . . . Thus the Other's body is *meaningful* (Sartre, 2001, p. 320; italics in original).

Sartre's phenomenological perspective of a relational understanding of personhood tallies with the ICU nurses' descriptions of their experience of post-mortem care. However, throughout post-mortem care nurses seem to oscillate between poles of nearness and distance to the dead patient, experienced alternately as a sentient person or an inanimate body. One nurse described how she felt that her attitude towards the care of the dead was more reverent than the care for a comatose patient. The stressing of a "reverent attitude" in dealing with the dead patient can partly be explained in the nurses' need to counteract the experientially paradoxical aspects of being faced with someone who is both present and absent at the same time. However, the reverence for humanness involved during postmortem care is basically the same whether it is paid to a present person, or a former absent existence mirrored in the remains.

Mooney (2003) focuses on the difficulties nurses go through as they participate in post-mortem care for the first time. Mooney points out that the post-mortem care elicits emotions such as fear, anxiety, and sadness in the nurses, and that these emotions need to be coped with. The stressful and distancing aspect of post-mortem care for all nurses in general should

not be forgotten or underestimated; several other researchers also touched upon this aspect of postmortem care (Curtis & Rubenfeld, 2001; Lawler, 1991; Seymour, 2001; Sudnow, 1967; Timmermans, 1998; Wolf, 1988).

In her article *Encountering the dead body: Experiences of medical students in their anatomy and pathology training,* Sanner (1997) describes how respect and reverence is stressed during autopsy of a recently dead person, as well as in connection with dissections of depersonalized parts of the body, so called "preparations" (Sanner, 1997, p. 180). It is revealing to compare my research field—where the nurses' generally tend to focus on the human and whole aspects of the deceased—with Sanner's study. Sanner relates how the medical students cope with anxiety caused by the autopsy as follows:

> The opening [of the body] meant the transition from a human being to a corpse, an irrevocable destruction of a wholeness . . . The most common anxiety defence was to flee from wholeness to the parts, losing sight of the human and becoming involved with the structures or the "organ package." . . . During the autopsy, the face of the dead was usually covered by a towel, something most students saw as a relief (Sanner, 1997, p. 180ff).

Nevertheless, the medical students share the nurses' empathy for the dead body, but the impact of the incisions and manipulation of the dead body during autopsy result in distancing and depersonalization. The basic "superstructure of reverence" for human remains is the same among the two professional groups in their dealings with the dead (Sanner, 1997, p. 185ff). Sanner describes how the medical students' use of clean sheets and towels, and keeping the area surrounding the dissected body clean, represent a wish to pay respect to the dead (Sanner, 1997, p. 182). Such cleanliness tallies well with the nurses' way of respecting patients at the ICU.

The Shrouding, Identification, and Transport of the Dead Patient

In the Norwegian population it is not, unlike within Norwegian Muslim communities, a ritually or religiously prescribed action to shroud a dead body. In the hospital context, the shrouding of the dead patient is, on the whole, a practical matter undertaken by nurses in connection with transport and storage of the dead body. Another task allotted to nurses, parallel with that of shrouding, is the correct identification of the dead body, an act of juridical, medical, and personal importance. This identification is of importance due to a number of reasons. For example; the dead body may have to go through a medical autopsy later on as part of a further medical or forensic investigation, the dead person may later be "resurrected" for viewing at the hospital chapel, or at some other similar locality, involving a larger congregation of mourners, friends, and kin. Time and place of bio-medical death is taken down on the identification slip, together with the name of the dead patient and place of residence.

The shrouding or wrapping takes place after relatives have left the ward and the viewing by them has taken place. Many nurses find this act of covering the face of the deceased difficult or unpleasant. Almost all nurses at the ICU report that they cover the face last while shrouding. Several nurses relate how the act of covering the face constitutes a break in relating to the personhood of the deceased. These nurses point out that you do not shroud bodies and faces of sentient breathing patients. One nurse described an instance when a senior nurse instructed her to pull the shroud tighter around the dead patient's body, and fasten it with tape properly, in accordance with the routines and wishes of the escort personnel, to allow for uneventful transport to the morgue. As a result of identification with the deceased patient as sentient, this nurse even described how she felt that the act of shrouding took the breath out of *her* physically. Another nurse described how the act of covering the face of the deceased constitutes a definite closure of the patient's life. This nurse described the rendering of this solemn act as an honour. However, the ensuing sealing of the shroud with tape is loathed by the same nurse.

For practical reasons, nurses are supposed to use an extra strong sheet, especially designed and stored for the sole purpose of shrouding and transporting dead patients. This sheet is known as the *mors* sheet. But some nurses dislike this brown and what they perceive as an un-aesthetic sheet. The use of this dark sheet may create a feeling of further distance to the deceased during the act of shrouding. Several nurses at the oncology ward feel that this gloomy and dingy sheet is undignified, and refuse to use it. These nurses use a double set of ordinary white bed sheets for the purpose of shrouding the deceased. When used, the dark sheet is usually hidden under an ordinary white bed sheet while relatives view the deceased. It is not until the final act of shrouding, when the relatives have left the scene, that the dark sheet becomes visible. To abate the effect of the dark sheet, the hospital's head chaplain has suggested that a white cloth be used to cover the head of the deceased, to maintain the patient's dignity, before the covering of the face with the brown sheet. The use of such a face-cloth is routine among undertakers in Norway when they lay the deceased in the coffin. To my knowledge, no ward has as yet implemented this practice routinely at the regional hospital in question.

Some nurses describe how the dead patient becomes a "dead body" during the act of shrouding. This act may accentuate the experience of an absence of presence. Whereas the personal identity of the dead patient disappears during shrouding, nurses have to safeguard the juridical, medical, and personal identity of the deceased by the proper written identification tag attached to the dead body, as well as with a tag attached to the shrouded body. It is evident that to facilitate the proper shrouding of the dead patient the nurses have to fulfil several aspects of the post-mortem care (mentioned above), anchored in different sets of rationales. However, nurses feel that one of the more important aspects of the care of the dead, namely the safeguarding of the integrity of the dead patient, may become threatened during the act of shrouding, identification, and transport to the morgue.

Previously it was a common practice in Norwegian hospitals to attach the identity tag to one big toe of the deceased. This practice was most likely due to the placement of the dead bodies in the morgue, that is, with the feet turned towards the centre of the room. Thus, placing the tag on one big toe was practical if anyone needed to check the identity of the deceased. However, since the 1980s, nurses at the hospital have been increasingly critical of the tagging of the toe, due to the associations which this practice has for them. The nurses feel that this practice is a disrespectful way of marking the dead body, a treatment that they conceive as a depersonalization of the deceased, treating the dead one as a cadaver, a thing, or a packet to be transported. The most common tag used and tied to the toe is of the same type as that used for posting and shipping packages (a manila tag). The paper tag currently in use at the hospital in question is larger and designed only for the purpose of identifying the deceased patient. The current procedure manual instructs nurses to tie this identification tag to the left wrist, at the same part of the body where the living patient would wear an identification bracelet. It is also obligatory for nurses to place an identity tag to the head-end of the shrouded patient. The most common colloquial terms for the act of shrouding at the hospital are "packing the patient" *(packa in)*. The colloquial term "packing," bears witness to a more detached attitude. The term "shrouding" is less common, and perceived as somewhat old-fashioned word. The shrouded body is transported to the morgue by the escort on a hospital bed covered with a ceremonial bedspread, designed for this purpose only. However, it still happens that the contour of the dead body is hidden under additional bedding. Even if the body of the deceased is hidden from view during transport through the hospital corridors, the identity of the deceased is known to the escorts. The identity of the dead patient is obligatory information while ordering a transport via the escort electronic order system. The escorts have implemented this procedure in order to avoid transporting a dead acquaintance or friend unknowingly.

As we have seen, the covering of the face of the dead patient with cloth entails an ontological switch; a change from dead person to dead body or a corpse. For some nurses, the shrouding amounts to an unpleasant definite depersonalization of the deceased, whereas for the medical students in Sanner's study described above, the covering of the deceased face was a relief and a requisite for them during medical autopsy.

Mol (2002) points out that the cloth covering the face of the "corpse" during autopsy may serve the practical purpose of protecting the face from splashing blood, as well as serving the purpose of blocking out the personhood of the deceased. Later, the pathology assistant can skilfully shift the corpse back into its former personhood again, by carefully restoring and preparing the dissected body for a final viewing by the relatives (Mol, 2002, p. 126f). At times medical practices may be seamlessly aligned, whereas at other times there may be frictions between clinical practices. Mol underscores that "The ontology of medical practice is not *the* ontology of a *single* practice: there are as many frictions between objects enacted as there are between the practices in which their enactment takes place" (Mol, 2002, p. 150; italics in original).

Concluding Remarks

The main focus and locus for the post-mortem care is the body of the dead patient. The safeguarding of the integrity of the human body is the baseline for the nurses' post-mortem care at any time. The respect for the integrity of the personal body is an essential part of any nursing care in general. This respect is closely tied to the fact that during care work nurses often transgress the personal integrity of the patient, outlined by ordinary everyday social interaction (Lawler, 1991; Littlewood, 1991; Twigg, 2000). At the time of such transgressions during the post-mortem care the nurses oscillate between poles of nearness and distance to the dead patient, experienced alternately as a sentient person or an inanimate body. As we have seen, to what degree a nurse remains distant or near during the post-mortem care may depend on several factors. Such factors may also be tied to the existential or "ontological security" of the nurses themselves (Giddens, 1991, p. 36ff; Mellor, 1993, p. 12f). For example, if the nurse identifies closely with the dead person—in terms of age, gender or social position—this may result in a more detached attitude, in order to diminish anxiety and the existential threat that this particular death poses to the nurse themself. Thus it becomes clear that the personal integrity safeguarded during post-mortem care is the integrity of the dead as well as the integrity of the nurses themselves.

With this exposition of post-mortem care, this paper has tried to illuminate how the embodied personal identity is relevant in connection with reverence for the dead patient. One way of safeguarding the reverence for the dead patient is treating the dead patient as a social person. Thus, nurses may maintain the social life of the patient after bio-medical death. Treating the dead as if they were alive or sentient may also have to do with the nurses' avoidance of the "deathliness" of their work. Furthermore, the invitation of the relatives to participate in the last offices and to take leave of the dead patient through the viewing contributes to the personalized treatment of the deceased during the post-mortem care.

Traditionally, throughout the last century the nurse's duty to perform the last offices took place behind closed doors (Wolf, 1988, p. 118ff, 1991a, b). However, in the wake of the hospice movement and the greater focus on palliative care, these doors are opened and relatives of the deceased are more often invited in to participate (Clark, 1998; Clark & Seymour, 1999). For the family, caring for the body of the dead one may play an important part in the continuation of the social relationship with the deceased, at a time when this relationship is threatened. At the same time, the caring for the deceased may also help the relatives to confirm the loss of a loved one (Worden, 1991). One of the reasons often stated by health personnel for involving the family and relatives in a leave-taking event at this particular time and place is the motivation to alleviate the relative's suffering and to assist them in their bereavement and grief. This rationale is also included in the St. Olav hospital procedural manual for post-mortem care (Melheim, 2000, p. 1). The praxis of inviting the relatives to view the dead patient and relate to the dead body mirrors the "late-modern" tendency for the body to become a central locus for the modern person's self-identity (Giddens, 1991; Shilling, 1993, p. 1). Furthermore, involving the relatives at this time is also an outcome of the "late-modern" trend to celebrate the social identity of the dead one as he or she was while living (Hallam *et al.*, 1999; Seale, 1998; Walter, 1994, 1996, 1999).

Notes

1. I have also conducted field work at the ICU although I did not work there in my capacity as a nurse, as this would involve a conflict of roles. However, I have gained insight into the care of the dead from earlier experience while working and researching at Trondheim University Hospital's Palliative Medicine Unit (PMU) within the Department of Oncology and Radiotherapy. Since 2000, I have also been a contributor in a study of the routines carried out in connection with the death of a patient at the PMU (Hadders & Torvik, 2003).

2. For a detailed discussion of "the category of the person" cross-culturally, see Carrithers *et al.*, 1985.

3. The soul is, of course, an imprecise term, inadequate to cover the many nuances concerning vital essence, animation, or life principles dealt with by anthropologists in this connection. However, for the sake of convenience, I still use this term as a denomination for an imprecise eschatological field.

4. Leaning on Durkheim's work *The elementary forms of the religious life* (1954 [1912]), Goffman shows how secular social collectivity is cemented by the individuals' symbolic maintenance of their "sacredness" (Goffman, 1956, p. 473).

References

Aalnæs, A. H. (2001). *Minding matter: organ donation & medical modernity's difficult decisions*. Oslo: Department and Museum of Anthropology, Faculty of Social Sciences, University of Oslo.

Carrithers, M., Collins, S., & Lukes, S. (Eds.). (1985). *The category of the person. Anthropology, philosophy, history*. Cambridge: Cambridge University Press.

Cederroth, S., Corlin, C., & Lindström, J. (1988). *On the meaning of death; Essays on mortuary rituals and eschatological beliefs*. Uppsala: Almqvist & Wiksell International.

Clark, D. (1998). Originating a movement: Cicely Saunders and the development of St Christopher's Hospice, 1957–67. *Mortality, 3*(1), 43–63.

Clark, D., & Seymour, J. (1999). *Reflections on palliative care*. Buckingham and Philadelphia: Open University Press.

Curtis, J. R., & Rubenfeld, G. D. (Eds.). (2001). *Managing death in the intensive care unit*. Oxford: Oxford University Press.

Giddens, A. (1991). *Modernity and self-Identity. Self and society in late modern age*. Cambridge: Polity Press.

Gillon, R. (2000 [1985]). *Philosophical medical ethics*. Chichester: John Wiley & Sons.

Glaser, B. G., & Strauss, A. L. (1966). *Awareness of dying*. London: Weidenfeld and Nicholson.

Glaser, B. G., & Strauss, A. (1968). *Time for dying*. Chicago: Aldine.

14

Goffman, E. (1956). The nature of deference and demeanour. *American Anthropologist, 58,* 473–501.

Hadders, H., & Torvik, K. (2003). *Rutin eller ritual? Praxis och hållningar i rummet mellan levande och döda.Projektapport: "Evaluering av rutiner ved dødsfall.".* Oslo: Den Norske Kreftforening.

Hallam, E., & Hockey, J. (2001). *Death, memory & material culture.* Oxford: Berg.

Hallam, E., Hockey, J., & Howarth, G. (1999). *Beyond the body. Death and social identity.* London and New York: Routledge.

Harré, R. (1979). *Social being. A theory for social psychology.* Oxford: Basil Blackwell.

Lawler, J. (1991). *Behind the screens. Nursing, somology, and the problem of the body.* Melbourne: Churchill Livingstone.

Littlewood, J. (1991). Care and ambiguity: Towards a concept of nursing. In P. Holden & J. Littlewood (Eds.), *Anthropology and nursing* (pp. 170–189). London and New York: Routledge.

Lizza, J. P. (1999). Defining death for persons and human organisms. *Theoretical Medicine and Bioethics,* 20, 439–453.

Lock, M. (2002). *Twice dead. Organ transplants and the reinvention of death.* Berkeley: University of California Press.

Melheim, B. L. (2000). *Dødsfall (v. 1.1), EQS* [digital version of the procedure manual for a hospital death]. Trondheim University Hospital, Norway.

Mellor, P. (1993). Death in high modernity. In D. Clark (Ed.), *The sociology of death* (pp. 11–30). Oxford: Blackwell Publishing.

Metcalf, P., & Huntington, R. (1991) (second edition). *Celebrations of death, The anthropology of mortuary ritual.* Cambridge: Cambridge University Press.

Mol, A. (2002). *The body multiple: Ontology in medical practice.* Durham and London: Duke University Press.

Mooney, D. C. (2003). *Nurses and post-mortem care: A study of stress and the ways of coping.* Griffith University. Retrieved April 1, 2007, from http://www4.gu.edu.au:8080/adt-root/public/adt-QGU20030815.145040/

Mulkay, M. (1993). Social death in Britain. In D. Clark (Ed.), *The sociology of death: Theory, culture, practice* (pp. 31–49). Oxford: Blackwell Publishing.

Robben, A. C. G. M. (Ed.). (2004). *Death, mourning, and burial. A cross-cultural reader.* Oxford: Blackwell Publishing.

Sandman, L. (2005). *A good death. On the value of death and dying.* Maidenhead: Open University Press.

Sanner, M. A. (1997). Encountering the dead body: experiences of medical students in their anatomy and pathology training. *Omega,* 35(2), 173–191.

Sartre, J.-P. (2001 [1956]). *Being and nothingness. An essay in phenomenological ontology.* New York: Citadel Press.

Seale, C. (1998). *Constructing death. The sociology of death and bereavement.* Cambridge: Cambridge University Press.

Seymour, E. J. (2001). *Critical moments – death and dying in intensive care.* Buckingham: Open University Press.

Shilling, C. (1993). *The body and social theory.* London: Sage.

Sudnow, D. (1967). *Passing on. The social organisation of dying.* Englewood Cliffs, NJ: Prentice-Hall Inc.

Timmermans, S. (1998). Resuscitation technology in the emergency department: towards a dignified death. *Sociology of Health & Illness,* 20(2), 144–167.

Timmermans, S. (2006). *Postmortem. How medical examiners explain suspicious deaths.* Chicago and London: University of Chicago Press.

Twigg, J. (2000). Carework as a form of bodywork. *Aging and Society,* 20, 389–411.

Walter, T. (1994). *The revival of death.* London and New York: Routledge.

Walter, T. (1996). A new model of grief: bereavement and biography. *Mortality,* 1(1), 7–25.

Walter, T. (1999). *On bereavement. The culture of grief.* Buckingham: Open University Press.

Wolf, Z. R. (1988). *Nurses' work: The sacred and the profane.* Philadelphia: University of Pennsylvania Press.

Wolf, Z. R. (1991a). Nurse's experience giving post-mortem care to patients who have donated organs: A phenomenological study. *Scholarly Inquiry for Nursing Practice: An International Journal,* 5(2), 73–87.

Wolf, Z. R. (1991b). Care of dying patients and patients after death: patterns of care in nursing history. *Death Studies,* 15, 81–93.

Worden, W. (1991). *Grief counselling and grief therapy: a handbook for the mental health practitioner.* London: Routledge.

HANS HADDERS is a PhD research fellow at Department of Social Anthropology, Norwegian University of Science and Technology, Trondheim, Norway. Hadders has a background in nursing within palliative medicine. His major research focus is on rituals and routines at the time of death.

Acknowledgements—I am indebted to my supervisors Solrun Williksen, Lars Johan Materstvedt, Pål Klepstad, and the staff at the ICU at Trondheim University Hospital for support, guidance, and feedback during the undertaking of this study. Lars Johan Materstvedt and Solrun Williksen have also read, corrected, and commented on several drafts of this article. I also want to express my gratitude to Tony Walter for reading my text and supporting me with useful feedback. Thanks are also due to the editors and anonymous reviewers of *Mortality* for their lucid and useful feedback.

How Much Is More Life Worth?

Dan W. Brock

vastin, Genentech's monoclonal antibody that it proposes to offer at twice the dose (and twice the price tag) to treat breast and lung cancer, has already made billions of dollars for the company through its original use—treating colon cancer. Now, with a potential pool of hundreds of thousands more patients, financial analysts predict its United States sales alone could grow nearly sevenfold to $7 billion by 2009.[1]

Extremely expensive drugs are hardly new. The pharmaceutical companies have long argued that these prices are justified by the extraordinarily high costs of getting new drugs to market. They typically estimate those costs at $800 million, which is said to reflect both the high costs of the large clinical trials required by the FDA to establish safety and efficacy, as well as the fact that only a small minority of potential new drugs ultimately makes it to market. The patent system for pharmaceuticals is designed to encourage research and development of new drugs by protecting the returns from successful drugs. Since the marginal costs of producing new drugs like Avastin are typically tiny in comparison to their patent protected prices, pharmaceutical companies could not justify the very large costs of research and development unless the patents prevented other companies from producing and selling them at those marginal costs.

Drug prices raise many controversial issues. Is the $800 million figure typically cited by the industry accurate, or are the real costs substantially less? Does the patent system primarily encourage the development of biologically new compounds, or does it instead promote so-called "me-too" drugs? Why do—and should—Americans pay substantially higher prices for drugs than citizens of other developed countries? Such economic, legal, and political issues are of great importance, but they apply across the industry broadly.

What is apparently new with Avastin is the justification that Genentech has offered for its extremely high price. Instead of relying on the traditional cost recovery argument, which would be hard to sustain if the estimates of a $7 billion market by 2009 are anything near accurate, the company is appealing to a new rationale—namely, the inherent value of life-sustaining therapies. It has priced Avastin based on "the value of innovation, and the value of new therapies," according to Susan Desmond-Hellman, the president of product development at Genentech.[2]

What should we make of this argument? How should the economic value of a life-extending intervention be determined? Is that value a justified basis for setting the price of the intervention? We have less experience addressing that first question in this country because most insurance plans do not explicitly and openly give weight to costs in making coverage decisions. The Centers for Medicare and Medicaid Services (CMS) is explicitly foreclosed by law from taking account of cost-effectiveness in decisions about coverage of new interventions.[3] While this rule has been criticized (correctly in my view), so long as it remains in place CMS's decisions look only at whether a drug "is reasonable and necessary in the diagnosis or treatment of illness or injury,"[4] without regard to costs. Since many private insurance plans tend to follow CMS in their coverage decisions, they too fail to explicitly consider cost-effectiveness or the economic values assigned to life extension.

> **Only the combination of patent protection together with purchasers' failure to consider cost-effectiveness and to bargain with Genentech will enable it to sell Avastin at the proposed price.**

e can get some help if we look abroad. In the United Kingdom, the National Center for Clinical Excellence (NICE) is charged with evaluating new technologies (broadly construed to include new drugs) for coverage by the National Health Service. Cost-effectiveness is a principal criterion in their evaluations using quality-adjusted life years (QALYs) as the benefit measure. Although NICE denies using any strict cost per QALY threshold, an analysis of their decisions suggests a threshold of approximately $50,000 per QALY.[5] No simple inference that this is an appropriate threshold in the United States is possible, among other reasons because the United Kingdom spends less than half as much per capita on health care as does the United States. In this country the value of a statistical life typically used in evaluating safety and health regulations and programs is in the neighborhood of $6 million, and the cost per QALY threshold is around $100,000.[6]

How much does Avastin cost per QALY produced? In use for colon cancer it is taken on average for eleven months and adds five months to life. If we assume usage and benefits will be the same for lung and breast cancer, which of course they may not be, this comes to a bit over $230,000 per life year, before any quality of life adjustment. Since chemotherapy is usually continued along with Avastin and the unpleasant side effects of that treatment are substantial, any reasonable quality of life adjustment would certainly raise the cost per QALY of Avastin significantly above the cost per life year estimate of $230,000. All of these numbers and estimates are crude, but they are enough to suggest that the cost per life year or per QALY of Avastin in the treatment of breast and lung cancer will substantially exceed typical guidelines used in the evaluation of other medical and nonmedical programs that extend lives.

These rough guides for maximum costs per life year or per QALY are caps, barring special circumstances, on the justified costs of such programs. But that does not imply that it is always justified to charge these maximums. Suppose you see a stranger fall off a dock who calls for help because he can't swim. The fact that if you throw him a life ring and save him, he will experience thirty more QALYs than he would if he drowns now would not justify your charging him $100,000 per QALY, or $3 million to throw him the life ring. We have an ethical obligation to save others from loss of life when we can do so with little if any risk or cost to ourselves. Exploiting desperate circumstances to extract the full economic value of the benefit received would be wrong.

Genentech, however, is a for-profit corporation, not an individual moral agent. It might argue that it is entitled to charge whatever the market will bear for the products it develops; it has no specific obligations to patients to make its products available for less. Someone who owns a building or a piece of land has no obligation to sell for any less than the best price another is willing to pay. Likewise, if Genentech were to manufacture a drug not under patent, then it would be entitled to set the price for it, leaving the market to determine whether there were buyers and whether other producers can undercut its sales or drive down the price. In a competitive market, the price should settle at the costs of production plus a reasonable profit to the producer.

But of course the patent system for pharmaceuticals makes their market anything but competitive. As a matter of law, patents allow drug companies to charge whatever they can command, and in practice, the major purchasers of drugs in this country have limited or no ability to bargain for lower prices. That is not, however, an ethical justification for charging whatever the market will bear. Suppose we discover that Avastin combined with a very cheap older chemotherapeutic agent that is off patent is vastly more effective in the treatment of breast and lung cancer than previously thought—instead of extending life on average for five months, it extends life for five years, twelve times as long as originally thought. On Genentech's reasoning, they would now be justified in charging twelve times the $100,000 now proposed for the five months gain in life extension,

despite no increase in the costs of developing and producing the drug. But that surely is not ethically correct. Absent patent protection, Genentech would not be able to increase the price to reflect the increase in benefit. Other competitors would come into the market to sell it closer to the costs of production, which don't change when it is discovered to be far more beneficial than originally thought. Even with patent protection, insurers who could consider the drug's cost-effectiveness, either at the current proposed price or at the new higher price if it were found to be more effective, could reasonably deny coverage on grounds that it was not cost effective and exceeded their willingness to pay a limit of, say, $100,000 per QALY.

So there are two fundamental ethical problems with Genentech's defense of the price of Avastin. First, it greatly exceeds any of the usual standards for economic evaluation of life-extension. Even granting that it can justifiably be priced in terms of the economic value of extending life, it is very overpriced. Only the combination of patent protection together with purchasers' failure to consider cost-effectiveness and to bargain with Genentech will enable it to sell Avastin at the proposed price. Second, even the $100,000 standard should be understood as a cap on prices, not what is ethically justified regardless of the costs of development and production.

Drug companies' traditional justification for high drug prices—that they were needed to cover the very high costs of developing new drugs—is at least plausible in principle, even if controversies remain about what those costs really are. This new justification—that high prices reflect the value of extending life—does not stand up to even minimal scrutiny.

Notes

1. A. Berenson, "A Cancer Drug Shows Promise, at a Price That Many Can't Pay," *New York Times,* February 15, 2006.

2. Ibid.

3. S.R. Tunis, "Why Medicare Has Not Established Criteria for Coverage Decisions," *New England Journal of Medicine* 350 (2004): 2196–98.

4. M.R. Gillick, "Medicare Coverage for Technological Innovations—Time for New Criteria?" *New England Journal of Medicine* 350 (2004): 2199–203.

5. M.D. Rawlins and A.J. Culyer, "National Institute for Clinical Excellence and Its Value Judgments," *British Medical Journal* 329 (2004): 224–27.

6. W.K. Viscusi, "The Value of Risks to Life and Health," *Journal of Economic Literature* 31 (December 1993):1912–46; W.C. Winkelmayer et al., "Health Economic Evaluations: The Special Case of End-Stage Renal Disease Treatment," *Medical Decision Making* 22 (September-October 2002): 417–30.

DAN W. BROCK, "How Much Is More Life Worth?" *Hastings Center Report* 36, no. 3 (2006): 17–19.

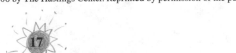

Confronting Death: Perceptions of a Good Death in Adults with Lung Cancer

Travonia Hughes et al.

Scientific and technological advancements coupled with conventional western medicine have extended life expectancy and changed the way many diseases are treated and how death is conceptualized along with the meanings assigned to it. It is not surprising that for many Americans death is regarded as a function of old age, a consequence of the failure of modern medicine to hinder or preclude the inevitable, or as a process that can be prevented, reversed, or prolonged.[1] Research findings suggest that contemporary attitudes towards death and dying reflect a degree of trepidation, fear, and denial.[2-4] Hooyman and Kiyak assert that individuals become uneasy when asked to comment on their views about death, particularly their own death and, *"this discomfort is shown even in the euphemisms people use—'sleep, pass away, rest'—instead of the word 'death' itself"* (p. 413).[1] In fact, to minimize the fear often associated with death, the term "good death" evolved out of the hospice movement. The term was originally used to describe the act of euthanasia. Terminally ill individuals experienced a "good death" if they actively participated in how, when, and where they chose to die.[5] It was not until the 1980s when researchers and clinicians began to focus on issues related to death and dying (eg, autonomy, palliative care, and dying with dignity) that the term "good death" moved beyond the confines of a synonym for euthanasia and was seen as a complex and individualized phenomena.

The meanings assigned to death and the characteristics of a "good death" are influenced by a number of factors including age, gender, patient/clinician role, and health status.[6-9] Researchers argue that there is no prevailing consensus of what a good death is. However, they do agree that the concept of a good death is both a dynamic and highly subjective process.[10-15]

Previous findings reveal that the characteristics of a good death differ among age groups,[3,16] men and women,[17] patients,[18] and clinicians.[19,20] Death is conceptualized by some as a multifaceted process and by others as a finite event.[18,21-23] However, the few studies of patients' perspectives on a good death are based on samples of fewer than 50 patients,[18,21,24] and most of these are not patients per se, but healthy older adults.[18,21] When patients are recruited to participate in studies, they have heterogeneous diagnoses, ages, and terminal stages.[24] Most studies have even greater sample heterogeneity, including perceptions of a good death from patients, surrogates, families, physicians, nurses, and other health care professionals. No studies have focused on a single group of patients having the same diagnosis and perhaps a more homogeneous view of a good death. Finally, most studies are strictly qualitative in nature and do not link patients' perceptions of a good death to any other psychosocial or demographic characteristics.

To this end, elements commonly used in the description of a good death and frequently emphasized in the literature include pain management, maintaining autonomy and control, establishing closure, acceptance and awareness of death, not being a burden to family members, strengthening relationships with family and friends, and being spiritually prepared to die.[5,19,24-27] Not surprisingly, a review of the literature revealed one of the most frequently cited elements of a good death among patients was pain management.[5,24,25,28] Pain management included freedom from physical pain and/or emotional distress. Some patients conveyed a desire to be as comfortable as possible, to be aware of their impending death, accept the inevitable, resolve relationship issues with family and friends to achieve closure, and achieve a satisfying level of spirituality.[5,24,25]

Much of the current literature emphasizes the need for more studies that examine the attributes of a good death from the perspective of the patient. Although major advancements in medicine and research have changed the way in which many diseases are diagnosed and treated, a major criticism of allopathic medicine is that it fails to recognize individual differences in treatment preferences, decision making, and end-of-life care. Thus, if care is to be delivered that meets the individual needs and preferences of patients and conforms to their subjective desires, then it is essential that patients' perspectives of a good death be acknowledged.[25] The purpose of this study was to examine perceptions of a "good death" in a convenience sample of patients diagnosed with lung cancer attending a multi-disciplinary cancer center in the United States.

Methods

Design

The study employed a cross-sectional design in which participants answered questions during a single individual interview at their convenience during a scheduled clinic visit.

Participants

Patients attending a multi-disciplinary treatment team clinic for lung cancer patients were approached by a staff nurse and asked if they were interested in talking to a researcher about the needs of lung cancer patients. Inclusionary criteria included a primary diagnosis of lung cancer, being cognitively intact, and age 18 or older. Patients who were interested in participating in the study were introduced to an investigator who explained the nature of the study, answered questions, and obtained informed consent. One hundred ninety eight patients were approached about the study; subsequently, 100 patients participated in the study (approximately a 50% recruitment rate).

Procedure

After obtaining informed consent the investigator read questions to obtain responses from individual participants. The investigator recorded participants' responses on a paper copy of the survey instrument. Data were subsequently entered in a data file and coded using SPSS v13.

Instrument

Demographic questions assessed age, gender, race, marital status, number of living children, education, income, employment status, and occupation. Questions were asked regarding the patients' smoking and treatment history. Treatment history questions included when patients first suspected a problem, made their first appointment with a physician and type of physician (general practitioner or specialist), miles traveled to the cancer center, date of their first appointment at the cancer center, when they began treatment, and what type of treatment(s) they had undergone. Psychosocial measures assessed respondents' coping,[29] spirituality and religious coping,[30] and life satisfaction.[31]

Participants were asked for their definition of a "good death" in an effort to identify the attributes of a "good death" from the perspective of patients diagnosed with lung cancer. Differences and similarities in the meanings given to a "good death" were examined by using an open-ended question that asked, "What in your opinion would be a good death?" Patients who gave an initial response were encouraged to offer any additional attributes of a good death that came to mind, and subsequently additional attributes were mentioned. All descriptions were recorded verbatim as the one word or a phrase that was used and were coded regardless of the order given.

Analyses

Content analyses allowed categorization of the one word or short phrases participants used to describe a good death. Frequencies for each theme were entered into the quantitative data file for further analyses. The Statistical Package for Social Sciences (SPSS version 13) was used for all analyses. Descriptive statistics were used to describe the sample and the frequency of responses given when study participants were asked to convey their personal opinion of a good death. Bivariate analyses (ie, *t* tests) identified demographic and psychosocial measures related to each major theme.

Results

Sample Characteristics

Forty-seven women and 53 men with a primary diagnosis of lung cancer participated in this study. Lung cancer patients did not differ in their demographic characteristics by gender. The overall sample consisted of 3 age groups, a young, middle-aged, and older adult group. The young adult group included 7 individuals (3 men and 4 women) aged 24 to 44 (mean = 37.14, SD = 7.36). The middle-aged group included 45 adults, comprising 22 men and 23 women, aged 45 to 65 (mean = 56.29, SD = 6.13). Finally, the older adult group was composed of 48 adults, including 28 men and 20 women, aged 66 to 85 (mean = 72.67, SD = 5.30). The majority of participants had less than a high school education (45%), followed by those who had completed high school (28%) or had attended college (27%). Participants generally had low incomes (69% less than $30,000) and most (64%) were married. There were no sex differences in patients' diagnostic or treatment histories. All patients had had lung cancer for less than 10 years, with 73% being diagnosed in the past 2 years. Most had started or finished treatment, although a few (11%) had not yet started treatment. Over half (60%) had some combination of chemotherapy, radiation, and/or surgical treatment, although almost a third (29%) had had only 1 type of treatment, predominantly surgery.

Common Attributes of a Good Death

When participants were asked what would constitute a "good death," 4 central themes emerged from the data: dying while asleep, death as pain-free, peaceful passing, and dying quickly (see Table 1). These 4 themes accounted for the bulk of all participants' comments. Although it would seem that these themes are closely related or perhaps synonymous, participants perceived them as distinct, listing them separately. Less frequently, participants mentioned concerns about family, their relationship with God, and dying free of regret.

Several interesting responses appeared only once in the data, that is, only 1 individual indicated that it was important for a good death. One woman wanted to "have made a difference," and having been a teacher, she probably had an impact on her students. A man contracting lung cancer earlier than many other participants specified that he wanted to be "unaware" of his death. In contrast to other participants mentioning their family, 1 married woman specified that she did *not* want her family around when she died. One man wanted to die free of financial worries. Finally, after specifying he'd prefer to be asleep and pain-free when he died, a retirement-aged man demonstrated how he used humor to cope with dying, quipping that his idea of a good death would be to be "shot by a jealous husband."

Table 1 Frequency of Participants' Themes Regarding Attributes of a Good Death

Theme	Number of Patients Mentioning the Theme (N = 100)
Asleep	84
Pain-free	74
Peaceful	27
Quick	16
With family around or cared for	12
With God	6
Free of regret	4
At home	3

Finally, bivariate relationships between the 4 most frequent themes (asleep, pain-free, peaceful, and quick), socio-demographic characteristics (age, sex, marital status, education, and income), and psychosocial characteristics were examined (coping, spirituality, religious coping, and life satisfaction). Only marital status was associated with mentioning having a peaceful death (x^2 [1, 100] = 4.57, P = .033) such that when mentioned, it was more likely from married participants versus nonmarried participants (14 vs 2, respectively). Participants' spirituality was associated with comments about being asleep (t [98] = 3.21, P = .002) and having a quick death (t [98] = 2.00, P = .048). Specifically, participants who indicated that a good death occurred when asleep were less spiritual than those who did not mention being asleep (mean = 4.1 vs mean = 3.4, on a 6 point scale), and participants mentioning a quick death were more spiritual than those who did not (mean = 3.9 vs mean = 3.5 on a 6 point scale). Religious coping was associated with preference for being asleep at death (t [98] = 2.68, P = .009) such that the participants using religious coping strategies were less likely to mention being asleep at death (mean = 1.2 vs mean = 1.0 on a 4 point scale).

Discussion

Few studies have examined the attributes of what would be considered a "good death" from the perspective of patients with a potentially fatal disease like lung cancer. Given that lung cancer is the number one cause of cancer-related deaths in the United States among men and women, and the survival rate for all lung cancers combined is an estimated 15%, it is not surprising that the current study's definitions regarding a good death would mirror those found in the end-of-life and palliative care literature.[32,33] A prevailing consensus among prior studies that have examined elements of a good death among those diagnosed with a terminal illness has been the absence of pain and suffering, the importance of family, and the sovereignty of religion.[20,34,35] The Institute of Medicine defines "good death" as "one free from avoidable distress and suffering for patients,

families and caregivers; in general accord with patients' and families' wishes and reasonably consistent with clinical, cultural and ethical standards" [p. 1] To this end, the experience of death is not confined to the dying patient but will directly affect members of his or her social network. Dobbins posits that the imminence and finality of death impresses upon the patient the need to seek closure for unresolved relationship issues in an effort to strengthen familial bonds and minimize the grieving process.[19]

In contrast to these perspectives, our study revealed that although lung cancer patients concur that the absence of pain is an important characteristic of a good death, family relationships and religious comfort are less likely to be mentioned. Although only 4 of the 100 participants were neither married nor had any living children, only 12 of 96 possible participants' comments concerned their families. Sixty percent of study participants were members of a church but only 6 (10% of church members) mentioned God in their comments. In addition, previous literature has suggested that patients wished to be aware of their pending death. Comments from our study participants suggest that they would prefer to be unaware (ie, asleep when they died). It is likely that, as lung cancer patients, our participants had already realized and accepted the likelihood of their deaths and thus resolved many of the issues previously cited in the literature.

In an effort to alleviate the fear and grief of death, patients often seek to redefine their relationship with God by achieving spiritual serenity. Prior study findings attest to the utility of religion and spirituality to transcend the anxiety, fear, and finality that is often associated with death.[6,7,36,37] In this study only 1 participant mentioned fear in his comments about a good death. Thus, it is possible that many in this sample of lung cancer patients had already resolved their fears through their religiosity and in doing so characterized their ideas of a good death differently. However, it is clear from our bivariate analyses that religiosity does play a role in preferences regarding being asleep at death and having a quick death. It is likely that having resolved one's relationship with God allows a patient to relinquish the need to be aware and in control at death. However, this speculation requires additional data for confirmation.

This study is not without its limitations. One major study limitation was the question used to examine perceptions of a good death. This question could have been expanded upon, and a series of follow-up questions could have been used to probe for additional elements and themes as they related to the construct of a "good death." Study findings will contribute to our understanding of the nature and meaning of a good death from the perspective of the patient as they reveal individual preferences regarding the dying process. In particular, lung cancer patients are in a unique position to comment on a good death. Their probable death, while not necessarily imminent, is more likely to occur than that of many other chronically ill patients.

Ultimately these and other study findings will guide end-of-life care decisions and improve patient treatment outcomes. The implications for health care professionals are clear. Patients primarily desire not to fully experience their own deaths. They would like to be asleep and pain-free, and perhaps having already resolved previous family or religious concerns they are more concerned with the peacefulness and speed of their own death.

References

1. Hooyman NR, Kiyak HA. *Social Gerontology.* Vol. 6. Boston: Allyn & Bacon; 2002.
2. Bassett J-F. Reaction time measures of death attitudes: examining the correlates of death anxiety and testing terror management hypotheses. *Dissertation Abstracts International: Section B: The Sciences and Engineering, 63*(6-B). Ann Arbor, MI: University Microfilms International; 2002.
3. Cicirelli VG. Personal meanings of death in older adults and young adults in relation to their fears of death. *Death Stud.* 2001;25(8):663–683.
4. De Masi F. *Making Death Thinkable: A Psychoanalytic Contribution to the Problem of the Transience of Life.* London: Free Association; 2004.
5. Kehl KA. Moving toward peace: an analysis of the concept of a good death. *Am J Hosp Palliat Med.* 2006;23(4): 277–286.
6. Ardelt M, Koenig CS. Role of religion for hospice patients and relatively healthy older adults. *Res Aging.* 2006;28(2):184–215.
7. Harding SR, Flannelly K, Weaver AJ, Costa KG. The influence of religion on death anxiety and death acceptance. *Ment Health Relig Culture.* 2005;8(4):253–261.
8. Hayslip B, Johnson CJ. *Death and Dying.* Washington, DC: Association for Gerontology in Higher Education; 2000.
9. Tomer A, Eliason G. Life regrets and death attitudes in college students. *Omega (Westport).* 2005;51(3):173–195.
10. Ardelt M. Effects of religion and purpose in life on elders' subjective well-being and attitudes toward death. *J Relig Gerontol.* 2003;14:55–77.
11. Bonner G, Gorelick PB, Prohaska T, Freels S, Theis S, Davis L. African American caregivers' preferences for life-sustaining treatment. *J Ethics Law Aging.* 1999; 5(1):3–15.
12. Chikako T. Changes in attitudes toward death in early and middle adolescence. *Japan J Devel Psych.* 2004;15:65–76.
13. Di-Mola G, Teresa-Crisci M. Attitudes toward death and dying in a representative sample of the Italian population. *Palliat Med.* 2001;15(5):372–378.
14. Fairrow AM, McCallum TJ, Messinger-Rapport BJ. Preferences of older African-Americans for long-term tube feeding at the end of life. *Aging Ment Health.* 2004;8(6):530–534.
15. McIntosh JL. Death and dying across the life span. In: Whitman TL, Merluzzi TV, White RD, eds. *Life-span Perspectives on Health and Illness.* Mahwah, NJ: Lawrence Erlbaum; 1999:249–274.
16. Blum CA. 'Til death do us part?' The nurse's role in the care of the dead. A historical perspective: 1850–2004. *Geriatr Nurs.* 2006;27(1):58–63.
17. Depaola SJ, Griffin M, Young JR, Neimeyer RA. Death anxiety and attitudes toward the elderly among adults: the role of gender and ethnicity. *Death Stud.* 2003; 27(4):335–354.
18. Vig EK, Davenport NA, Pearlman RA. Good deaths, bad deaths, and preferences for the end of life: a qualitative study of geriatric outpatients. *J Am Geriatr Soc.* 2002; 50:1541–1548.
19. Dobbins EH. Helping your patient to a "good death." *Nursing.* 2005;35(2):43–45.
20. Beckstrand RL, Calister LC, Kirchhoff KT. Providing a "good death": critical care nurses' suggestions for improving end-of-life care. *Am J Crit Care.* 2006;15:38–46.
21. Leichtentritt RD, Rettig KD. The good death: reaching an inductive understanding. *Omega (Westport).* 2000; 41:221–248.
22. Nenner F. A good death. *Am J Hosp Palliat Care.* 2002;19:356–358.
23. Pierson CM, Curtis JR, Patrick DL. A good death: a qualitative study of patients with advanced AIDS. *AIDS Care.* 2002;14:587–598.
24. Steinhauser KE, Christakis NA, Clipp EC, McNeilly M, McIntyre L, Tulsky JA. Factors considered important at the end of life by patients, family, physicians, and other care providers. *JAMA.* 2007;284(19): 2476–2482.
25. Mak JM, Clinton M. Promoting a good death: an agenda for outcomes research: a review of the literature. *Nurs Ethics.* 1999;6(2):97–106.
26. Singer PA, Martin DK, Kelner M. Quality end-of-life care: patients' perspectives. *JAMA.* 2007;281(2): 163–168.
27. Steinhauser KE, Clipp EC, McNeilly M. In search of a good death: observations of patients, families, and providers. *Ann Intern Med.* 2000;132:825–832.
28. Proulx K, Jacelon C. Dying with dignity: the good patient versus the good death. *Am J Hosp Palliat Med.* 2004;21(2):116–120.
29. Gottlieb BH, Rooney JA. Coping effectiveness: determinants and relevance to the mental health and affect of family caregivers of persons with dementia. *Aging Ment Health.* 2004;8(4):364–373.
30. NIA Working Group. *Multidimensional Measurement of Religiousness/Spirituality for Use in Health Research: A Report of the Fetzer Institute.* Kalamazoo, MI: Fetzer Institute; 1999.
31. Diener E, Emmons RA, Larsen RJ, Griffin S. The satisfaction with life scale. *J Pers Assess.* 1985;49:71–75.
32. Hanson LC, Danis M, Garrett J. What is wrong with end-of-life care? Opinions of bereaved family members. *J Am Geriatr Soc.* 1997;45:1339–1344.
33. Seymour J, Gott M, Bellamy G, Clark D, Ahmedzai S. Planning for the end of life: the views of older people about advance care statements. *Health Risk Soc.* 2002;4:279–303.
34. Bern K, Gessert C, Forbes S. The need to revise assumptions about the end of life: implications for social work practice. *Health Soc Work.* 2001;26:38–48.
35. Gold MF. Comfort, compassion, dignity mark end-of-life care. *Provider.* 2003;29:20–33.
36. Thorson JA, Powell FC. Developmental aspects of death anxiety and religion. In: Thorson JA, ed. *Perspectives on Spiritual Well-being and Aging.* Springfield, IL: Charles C. Thomas; 2000:142–158.
37. Cicirelli VG. Fear of death in mid-old age. *J Gerontol B Psychol Sci Soc Sci.* 2006;61(2):75–81.

From the University of Kentucky College of Medicine, Lexington, Kentucky.

The authors thank the Kentucky Lung Cancer Research Program for their grant support of The Comprehensive Support Protocol: Providing Psychosocial Assistance to Lung Cancer Patients and Their Families.

Address correspondence to: Mitzi Schumacher, Behavioral Science Department, University of Kentucky College of Medicine, Lexington, KY 40536; phone (859) 323-6075; e-mail: Mitzi.schumacher@uky.edu.

Estimating Excess Mortality in Post-Invasion Iraq

CATHERINE A. BROWNSTEIN, MPH AND JOHN S. BROWNSTEIN, PhD

There is no set formula for accurately tallying deaths from humanitarian crises. When a population becomes destabilized, estimation of mortality is likely to be severely challenged. In the case of a sudden traumatic event, such as a natural disaster affecting an otherwise stable population, health and human service agencies, though compromised, may well be able to facilitate an accurate assessment of deaths through the use of prospective registries of vital events.

In the event of a military invasion and ongoing war, however, the likelihood of obtaining good demographic data plummets. A death registry is unlikely to be developed or maintained, and as conditions deteriorate, it may become increasingly unlikely that bodies can be counted at all. In Iraq, there is also a strong cultural imperative that bodies be put to rest quickly, which may affect the ability to arrive at accurate estimates. Although sentinel populations are commonly monitored to rapidly estimate mortality in developing countries when a registry is not available, the impossibility of finding reliably representative populations in countries engaged in armed conflict and the absence of an accurate population count make it difficult to extrapolate from the rates at sentinel sites to produce reliable national estimates.

A more accurate option, but one that is more dangerous for researchers, is the household survey.[1] Even in nonemergency situations, the study design of the survey may be subject to under-reporting and may not accurately reflect rates of migration and fertility. Complex computations are required to account for variation among regions and subpopulations. During conflicts, an estimation of the death rate is further complicated by the difficulties involved in creating a valid sampling frame, the problem of reporting bias, and obstacles to accurate ascertainment of causes of death. Researchers often must risk their lives if they wish their estimates to accurately represent the population, and they must spend as much time in dangerous areas as in less dangerous ones to minimize bias.

In this issue of the *Journal* (pages 484–493) the Iraq Family Health Survey (IFHS) study group reports the results of a household survey conducted in Iraq in 2006 and 2007 for the purpose of estimating mortality between January 2002 and June 2006. The researchers divided the country into 56 mutually exclusive sampling strata and surveyed 9345 households in total (see map). Information on all deaths within a household was sought, in an effort to estimate overall and cause-specific rates of death. The group obtained an estimate of 151,000 violent deaths, with a purported 95% confidence interval of 104,000 to 223,000—a massive death toll—since the 2003 invasion. Violence was found to be the leading cause of death among Iraqi men between the ages of 15 and 59 years and a leading cause of death among Iraqi adults in general.

The results of this survey are most striking in comparison with those in two other reports: the Iraq Body Count Project[2] and a 2006 study by Burnham et al.[3] The IFHS authors note that their estimate is much lower than that reported in the study by Burnham et al., which yielded a point estimate of 601,027 violent deaths between 2003 and 2006. Since the latter tally was much publicized, the first response to the IFHS results may be disbelief; some will no doubt suggest that the findings are flawed. However, the Iraq Body Count arrived at an even lower total—47,668 (see graph).

How is it that these numbers vary so widely, given that there can be only one true answer? The IFHS study group does not directly address this question, but it deserves speculation. The probable cause is that the techniques used to obtain the estimates differ radically from one another. The Iraq Body Count collects details from every available distinct report for all identified incidents in which civilians were killed. Deaths are included if they appear in a minimum of two independent data sources, and they are cross-checked with media reports and with the records of hospitals, morgues, and nongovernmental organizations, as well as with official figures, to produce a credible record of known deaths and incidents (though as of December 21, 2007, credible single-source reports will now be recorded).[2] The Iraq Body Count doesn't include deaths of combatants—only those of civilians. Nor does it cover all possible non–English-language media outlets or incidents that are not covered by news reports. In other words, the Iraq Body Count's tally represents an undercount based on surveillance, not a survey, and should be treated as a reliable lower bound.

Meanwhile, there is ongoing discussion[4] about the validity of the study by Burnham et al. The survey methods have

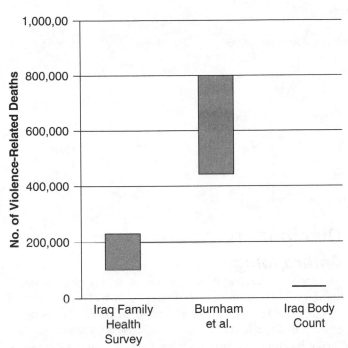

The ranges in studies by the Iraq Family Health Survey and by Burnham et al. represent 95% confidence intervals; data from the Iraq Body Count represent absolute minimum and maximum counts.

been scrutinized, and observers have put forward convincing arguments both that it does and that it does not overestimate mortality. One of the issues under debate is whether the clusters that were surveyed were nonrandomly distributed owing to "main-street bias" (an over-sampling of highly trafficked areas). What cannot be debated is that it was a much smaller study (1849 households in 47 clusters) than that conducted by the IFHS (9345 households in 1086 clusters).

Though the IFHS study group should be commended for its attempt to capture the highest-quality results, uncertainties remain. The survey design, in particular, is certainly open to criticism, and the authors honestly admit the shortcomings of their analysis. For example, sometimes it was problematic or too dangerous to enter a cluster of households, which might well result in an undercount; data from the Iraq Body Count on the distribution of deaths among provinces were used to calculate estimates in these instances. If the clustering of violent deaths wasn't accurately captured, that could also increase uncertainty.

The sampling frame was based on a 2004 count, but the population has been changing rapidly and dramatically because of sectarian violence, the flight of refugees, and overall population migration. Another source of bias in household surveys is under-reporting due to the dissolution of some households

after a death, so that no one remains to tell the former inhabitants' story. Mortality estimates that are derived from surveying deaths of siblings were also calculated, but this method may also be subject to such underreporting. However, the IFHS group's overall estimate of mortality does reflect uncertainty in the level of underreporting (20 to 50%) and the instability of the projected population during the post-invasion period (1 million to 2 million).

Under the current conditions in Iraq, it is difficult to envision a study that would not have substantial limitations. The circumstances that are required to produce high-quality public health statistics contrast starkly with those under which the IFHS study group worked. Indeed, it must be mentioned that one of the authors of the survey was shot and killed on his way to work.

We cannot begin to explore all the political implications of this work, which will no doubt shape international public opinion regarding the war in Iraq. What we can discuss, however, are the implications of this work for mortality-estimation research in areas in which violent conflict persists. The addition of this study and comparisons between it and others will permit a better understanding of the relationship between study techniques and mortality estimation that can, in turn, provide a basis for improved guidelines to decrease bias in future studies. When alternative data sources become available, the IFHS and the other surveys conducted to date will be verified or refuted, along with their survey techniques. The goal should be to ensure that decisions regarding epidemiologic methods for estimating mortality in high-risk populations are based on the best possible evidence; these estimates are critical for the effective implementation of humanitarian relief efforts.

Notes

1. Working Group for Mortality Estimation in Emergencies. Wanted: studies on mortality estimation methods for humanitarian emergencies, suggestions for future research. *Emerg Themes Epidemiol* 2007;4:9.

2. The Iraq Body Count Project. (Accessed January 2, 2008, at http://www.iraqbodycount.org.)

3. Burnham G, Lafta R, Doocy S, Roberts L. Mortality after the 2003 invasion of Iraq: a cross-sectional cluster sample survey. *Lancet* 2006;368:1421–8.

4. Giles J. Death toll in Iraq: survey team takes on its critics. *Nature* 2007;446:6–7.

MS. **CATHERINE A. BROWNSTEIN**, MPH is a doctoral student in the Department of Genetics at Yale University, New Haven, CT. DR. **JOHN S. BROWNSTEIN**, PhD is a faculty member in the Children's Hospital Informatics Program, Children's Hospital Boston, and an assistant professor of pediatrics at Harvard Medical School—both in Boston.

The Sociology of Death

Tony Walter[1] *sociologist*

Durkheim's *The Elementary Forms of the Religious Life* is famous for arguing that religion enables groups to gather together and symbolise their collective identity. What is often forgotten is that many of the aboriginal rites discussed by Durkheim were funeral rites. Durkheim therefore provides the basis for a sociology of death: 'When someone dies, the group to which he belongs feels itself lessened and, to react against this loss, it assembles. Collective sentiments are renewed which then lead men to seek one another and to assemble together' (Durkheim 1915, 339). A graphic example of this is the immediate response to 9/11, in which newspapers depicted suburban front lawns flying the stars and stripes. Several thousand are dead, but America lives on, and will not be defeated. It is precisely when groups—from families to nations—are depleted by death that they reconstitute themselves, symbolically and practically.

Less directly, Weber (1930) too privileged the human response to death; a particular form of afterlife belief, namely, the Puritan belief in predestination, was for him a key to the development of capitalism. In both Durkheim and Weber, death may be the end of an individual, but its associated rites and beliefs can be at the heart of the formation or development of society.

Berger (1969, 52) assumed that 'Every human society is, in the last resort, men banded together in the face of death'; we create social order in order to stave off the chaos and anomie brought by death. Willmott (2000, 656), however, argues that it is the other way around: ethnomethodology has shown that we create a sense of order through everyday social interaction, and this social order is disrupted by death. The grandest of grand theorists, Talcott Parsons, latterly showed an interest in American deathways (Parsons and Lidz 1967; Parsons et al. 1972), but generally sociologists after Durkheim ceased to make death central to their understanding of society. Scholars have researched social aspects of death, but these have been marginal to sociology, and in the USA sociology has become increasingly marginal to death studies. How, then, have the social sciences since Durkheim explored the relation between death and society? In the next section, I look at anthropology, history, sociology and psychology; a more comprehensive survey would need also to include religious studies, cultural studies and archaeology, along with non-empirical humanities such as philosophy, literature and music. Later in the article, I look at various debates and challenges in the sociology of death, and how to teach it.

Disciplinary Approaches
Anthropology

Anthropology has had most to offer, especially in understanding funeral rites (Robben 2004). Van Gennep (1960) and Hertz (1960), students of Durkheim, wrote in the early twentieth century in French about funeral rites (Davies 2000; Hockey 2002), but were not translated into English until 1960. Since then, they have greatly influenced anthropological research into ritual, notably via Turner (1977). Bloch and Parry argue, contra Durkheim, that society does not act in and for itself; rather, post-death rites provide an opportunity for creating society as an apparently external force (1982, 6). Árnarson (2007) has recently argued that bereavement counselling functions to regenerate the autonomous individual that is at the heart of contemporary society and politics, thus regenerating not just individuals but also the social order. So far, the anthropology of death (Conklin 2001; Danforth 1982; Metcalf and Huntington 1991) has largely focussed on traditional rural rather than modern urban societies, although Parry (1994) and Scheper-Hughes (1993) look at urban settings in developing countries. In the developed world, Davies (2002), Francis et al. (2005), Prendergast et al. (2006) and Suzuki (2001) represent welcome attempts by anthropologists to examine contemporary death practices, focussing on funeral, burial and cremation practices. Hockey (1990), Lawton (2000), McNamara (2001) and Kaufman (2005) look at the medical and institutional management of dying, Williams (1990) at illness and death among older people. Lock's (2002) comparative ethnography of transplantation in Japan and the USA provides a welcome hint of yet wider territory open to anthropological colonisation.

Most anthropological studies of death have been explicitly or implicitly functionalist. A major challenge comes from Holst-Warhaft (2000), an expert not in the social sciences but in comparative and classical literature. She argues that the passions aroused by grief can be so powerful as to destabilise the social order; political establishments therefore fear grief, and do their best to turn its passion into something dull and depressive. She also provides examples, such as Argentina's Mothers of the Plaza de Mayo and the AIDS quilt, when the power of grief has successfully challenged the social order. We have here, then, an embryonic politics of grief, a sociology of grief that takes conflict and power seriously. Other studies of grief in the context of political conflict include Verdery's (1999) analysis of how post-socialist governments use reburial as a political tool, and Merridale's (2000) analysis of how mourning the 50 to 60 million Russians whose post-1917 deaths were caused by the state or by war has shaped Russian society.

History

Historians, especially French historians, have also played a significant role in the social analysis of death. Philippe Ariès is remarkable for twice having painted a broad historical picture of a new field—first childhood (1962), then death (1974, 1983). His work has energised not only history, but also sociology. His negative portrayal of modern deathways, and his portrayal of the history of death as essentially a history of ideas, have been influential. Ariès sketched the development of four different mentalities over 1,000 years of European history, and how they impinged on ideas, beliefs and practices around death. Most other historical work, unlike Ariès, is period-specific and less obviously value-ridden, important examples being Stannard (1977), Farrell (1980), Laderman (1996, 2003) and Prothero (2001) on the USA; Gittings (1984), Jalland (1996), Houlbrooke (1998), Jupp and Gittings (1999) and Strange (2005) on the UK; and McManners (1981) and Kselman (1993) on France. Vovelle's (1983) important work, like Ariès, spans several centuries, but is yet to be translated into English (Kselman 2004). Finucane's (1996) history of ghosts and some edited collections, such as Whaley (1981), are wide ranging, both in time and place.

Sociology

That brings us to sociology, whose role in helping us understand the social reality of death has been decidedly patchy (Faunce and Fulton 1958). Warner (1959) produced a Durkheimian analysis of Memorial Day and of the American cemetery, and then the 1960s saw two landmark Californian hospital studies. Sudnow's (1967) study of the routine management of death in hospital is a classic work of ethnomethodology. Glaser and Strauss's study of communication in a cancer ward (1965, 1968) is the main empirical study in which their methodology of grounded theory (1967) was developed (Seale 1999). It is also, like Goffman's *Asylums* (1968), one of relatively few sociological research monographs that—by providing a mirror to existing institutional practice—prompted questioning and subsequent change in institutional practice. Influenced by the now unfashionable disengagement theory of old age (Cumming and Henry 1961), Blauner (1966) cogently argued that the impact made by a death depends on the social status and involvement of the deceased. The typical modern death, of an old person, no longer centrally involved in the key institutions of work or child-rearing, fails to disrupt the social order significantly, however great its psychological impact on a few individuals. Parsons (Parsons and Lidz 1967; Parsons et al. 1972) made similarly pertinent theoretical observations.

After that, it was pretty much all quiet on the Far Western sociological death front, although Lofland (1978) produced a lively analysis of what she calls the 'happy death' movement, Charmaz wrote a useful textbook (1980), Fox (1979) and Hafferty (1991) showed how witnessing autopsies and

conducting dissections help turn medical students into hardened doctors, and Christakis (1999) charted the uncertain science of medical prognosis. Gerontologists tended to forget that all old people die, although Marshall's *Sociology of Ageing and Dying* (1980) is a welcome exception. Fulton and Bendiksen's (1994) collection of mainly American pieces painted a picture of the limited sociological field. From the mid-1970s, North American academic publications on death overwhelmingly went down a psychological and medical path (e.g. Nuland 1994). Why the USA's early sociological lead in the field should have been lost is an intriguing question.

British sociology came to the field rather later. An early herald was anthropologist Geoffrey Gorer, who in 1965 conducted a sociological survey of attitudes to death and grief based on a representative national sample, a project still unique in any country. Like Ariès (1974) and Kubler-Ross (1970), this study is routinely cited around the world to this day. Marris produced an empirical study of widows (1958) and a theoretical social–psychological exploration of loss (1974) that stands the test of time. Given the medicalisation and hospitalisation of dying, medical sociology occasionally placed the dying and their medical attendants in their sights, but it was not till the 1990s that the sociology of death became identifiable through its own journals and conferences, and even these tended to be interdisciplinary. Key works include Armstrong (1987), Field (1989), Prior (1989), Clark (1993b), Walter (1994), Howarth (1996), Howarth and Jupp (1996), Seale (1998) and Hallam et al. (1999). Several works by Clark (e.g. Clark 1993a, Clark and Seymour 1999) and James and Field (1992), along with anthropologist Lawton (2000), have evaluated palliative care, significantly influencing practice. Much of this work originated in medical sociology, but fertile links were made with the sociology of religion, old age, the body and the media, not to mention links with anthropology and history—Britain was where the sociological death action was in the 1990s. Since then, there has been little new, with the exception of Kellehear (2007)—who is Australian. Howarth (2006) wrote the first book that may satisfactorily be used as a sociology of death textbook for British undergraduates. Overall, this body of British work looks largely at normal death in peaceful developed countries: absent are the violence, war and genocide that occupy journals of cultural studies and international relations.

Kellehear's (2007, 4–5) summary of the current state of the sociology of death is spot on. On the one hand, there are the intellectual musings of some senior sociologists such as Zygmunt Bauman (1992), cultural theorists such as Jean Baudrillard (1993) and psychoanalytic theorists such as Ernest Becker (1973) who make scant reference to empirical studies. On the other hand, empirical studies, of, for example, communication between nurses and cancer patients, are increasingly repetitive, insignificant and theoretically arid. And, whereas rites of passage have seen an integration of theory and data by anthropologists, and mourning has seen an integration of theory and data by psychologists, dying itself (rather than caring for dying patients) has been almost entirely untheorised—which is why Kellehear's attempts to do just that are welcome (1990a, 1996, 2007).

Psychology

Although the typical psychology undergraduate degree does not include courses concerning death, research into grief is conducted mainly by psychologists and psychiatrists. Here, we find a consistent project of developing models from theory, and interrogating each with data. From Freud (1984), through Bowlby (1979), Parkes (1996), Klass et al. (1996) to Stroebe and Schut (1999), theories have led to, and responded to, empirical research. Although Kubler-Ross's (1970) multi-million-selling *On Death and Dying* has been subjected to considerable criticism, it nevertheless linked data and theory, and was the more powerful for that.

The main limitations of the psychology of grief are that its subjects are overwhelmingly Western and white, and it sees grief largely as individual, rather than the product of social or even political processes (Small 2001). A few scholars, however, have attempted to use Western grief psychology to interpret mourning in other times (Rosenblatt 1983; Rosenblatt et al. 1976) and places (Conklin 2001), and there are some useful cross-cultural studies (Lifton 1968) and surveys (Eisenbruch 1984; Stroebe and Stroebe 1987, Chapter 3). In general, though, anthropology tells us about rituals in traditional societies, psychology about grief in modern societies. Since Marris (1958, 1974) and Gorer (1965), very few sociologists have looked at grief, recent exceptions being Walter (1999a) and Riches and Dawson (2000).

Death Studies

The late 1950s saw the emergence of North American death studies (Corr et al. 1999; Pine 1977, 1986), a field that attempts to be interdisciplinary but has been dominated by psychology. The main carriers for this have been, first, the journals *Omega* and *Death Studies*, which have reported rather too many uninspiring and unrepresentative surveys into death anxiety conducted by Midwestern psychology professors on their own students. Second, by the 1970s there were hundreds of American universities and colleges that offered a short undergraduate elective on death studies. These courses often entailed some humanities as well as the social sciences, and were very popular, but did not require sustained intellectual pursuit of any one discipline. Third, these modules have given birth to a number of interdisciplinary American textbooks, which include Corr et al. (1997); Fulton and Metress (1995); Kastenbaum (1995) and DeSpelder and Strickland (2002); some are by sociologists (Kearl 1989; Kamerman 2002; Leming and Dickinson 2002).

In the UK, the interdisciplinary journal *Mortality* was founded in 1996, with a somewhat different mix of disciplines, including history and religious studies, and with much more sociology than psychology. Britain has developed some interdisciplinary postgraduate degrees, for example, in 'death and society', 'death studies' and 'the rhetoric and rituals of death', but these attract tiny numbers compared to the many thousands of American undergraduates who opt for a small dose of death studies. Italy's new journal *Studi Tanatologici,* founded in 2006, provides a refreshing mix of disciplines, with articles in Italian, French and English.

Theory and Method in the Sociology of Death

Sociological work on death is as varied as sociology in general, although conflict perspectives are underplayed and Marxism markedly absent. Functionalism is clearly in evidence, especially in the study of rituals and funerals. Intriguingly, it has been non-sociologists who have highlighted conflict. The writer Jessica Mitford (1963) provided the main challenge to the 1950s social science assumption that funerals were functional for individual and society, arguing that they enabled a range of industries to exploit vulnerable families. I have already mentioned that Holst-Warhaft (2000), a scholar of classical literature, introduced the notion of grief as a political force. Interactionism influenced a number of American studies, such as Glaser and Strauss (1965), Charmaz (1980) and Lofland (1978), reflecting the intellectual fashions of the time. Habenstein's substantial studies of the funeral profession (Habenstein 1962; Habenstein and Lamers 1962) were influenced by his sociological mentor, Everett Hughes. More recently, some British work, for example, Armstrong (1987), Prior (1989) and Àrnarson (2007), has drawn on Foucault, while cultural studies publications, such as Noys (2005), draw on post-modern theorists such as Agamben (1998). There is also ample scope for social movement analysis (Lofland 1978; McInerney 2000).

More helpful, perhaps, is to differentiate idealist, cultural, structural and materialist perspectives in the sociology of death. Ariès's (1974) sketch of various historical mentalities has been highly influential, but sociological analysis needs to ground the evolution of ideas in social structure. Some sociological work has sidestepped this challenge, identifying instead various cultures of death (e.g. Walter 1999a). This has been particularly true of studies of ethnicity (Kalish and Reynolds 1981), which have been driven by the need of health and social care workers to know about how various ethnic groups do dying, funerals and grief. Kastenbaum's (1995) concept of a 'death system' is more systematic, but has generated surprisingly little empirical research. Walter (1994) attempted to root mentalities in social structure, the body, and systems of authority, but it was not until Kellehear's groundbreaking *Social History of Dying* (2007) that a fully materialist sociological theory of dying emerged. For Kellehear, how we die depends, ultimately, on the dominant mode of production, and he shows how and why that is, from the Stone Age to the globalised present.

Methodologically, although quantitative methods have dominated psychological research, sociological research into death and dying has been largely qualitative. This is true both of most of the classic studies and master's and doctoral theses being written today. Given that dying people have other matters preoccupying their minds and bodies, questions need to be raised about the ethics of an ongoing research industry that may tell us little new but that may be highly intrusive (Kellehear 1998). Seale stands out for the skill and competence with which he has chosen from the full range of methods those which are appropriate to the research question in hand, ranging from interviews to survey data to content analysis (1990, 1998, 2002).

Debates and Challenges
From Denial to Sequestration to Exposure

The notion that death is denied, or taboo, in modern society is a cliché still regularly heard in journalism and in everyday language. The notion of death having replaced sex as the taboo of the twentieth century goes back to Gorer (1955), while the notion of death denial is rooted in psychoanalysis, popularised by Kubler-Ross (1970) and Becker (1973). These ideas have been roundly criticised by sociologists (Blauner 1966; Kellehear 1984; Parsons and Lidz 1967) who have tried to develop more sociological analyses of the structural position in society of death, the dying and the grieving. Elias (1985) grounds avoidance of the dying or dead body within his historical theory of civilising processes. Several have pointed to death's medicalisation (e.g. Arney and Bergen 1984, Prior 1989), into which lay people are now thoroughly socialised: they talk of a loved one's death as a series of medical events and interventions, and are disturbed if no medical cause of death can be ascertained. Some sociologists (e.g. Walter 1994) see medicalisation as part of a recent process of secularisation that has eroded the religious frame within which death was previously seen. Kellehear (2007), however, sees the key process as professionalisation: both clerics and medics have highjacked knowledge of death away from the urban middle classes for at least two millennia.

Mellor and Shilling (1993) follow Giddens (1991) in suggesting that death, like madness and other fateful moments, has been sequestrated, put in a box, to protect society; death is hidden in public, although very present in private. Walter (1994), however, says the issue is somewhat different, namely, that public discourses, notably that of medicine, cannot easily link with private discourses of personal pain, spiritual anguish or family dynamics—although holistic palliative care attempts to do just that. Noys (2005) argues that modernity entails a drastic and naked exposure to death. His empirical evidence rests on extreme cases such as the Holocaust, HIV, refugees and confrontational avant-garde art, but he stands as a corrective to sequestration and medicalisation theorists who have ignored the many millions who face extinction unprotected by medicine or even citizenship. His challenge is taken up by Kellehear (2007): although comfortable middle-aged and student-aged Westerners may be insulated from death, this is not true of those many facing malaria, starvation, AIDS and, in the West, dementia in their nearest and dearest. Noys echoes the observations of some sociologists in the Cold War era: death had seemingly been banished by modern medicine, yet fear of the bomb hung over everyone. Today, it is arguably fear of global warming, terrorism and the dementia brought on by our medically induced long lives that worry even the affluent.

Death and the Media

Clearly death is very present in the mass media (Walter et al. 1995). Walter (2005) has argued that while medicine may be the practical tool for staving off death, it is the media that have replaced (or in the USA, augmented) religious attempts to generate meaning in the face of untimely death. Research has now been conducted to demonstrate how the media represent death, notably by Seale (e.g. Seale 2002), but also by Sofka (1997), Laderman (2000) and others. It is, of course, much easier to conduct content analyses of media texts than to investigate empirically how these texts are produced or received, although Armstrong-Coster (2001) has, on a small scale, done just this. Scholars operating within a cultural studies framework are much more willing than sociologists to publish their own 'readings' of media texts and to speculate on their meaning and, implicitly, their reception.

Closely connected to the mass media are two other phenomena. Watching a television documentary about Auschwitz and going there as a tourist are not the same but are clearly related. 'Dark tourism' 'is the act of travel and visitation to sites, attractions and exhibitions which has real or recreated death, suffering or the seemingly macabre as a main theme' (http://www.dark-tourism.org.uk/), and ranges from the display of human remains in exhibitions to battlefield, cemetery and Holocaust tourism, to the slavery heritage industry (Stone 2006). Dark tourism as a research field is largely populated by British tourism academics; input from scholars from other disciplines and countries would be of mutual benefit.

Also intertwined with the media is the rise of spontaneous shrines to victims of road accidents, murder and disaster and after celebrity deaths (Santino 2006). As with media studies in general, here we see two very different approaches. On the one hand, there is the careful collection of empirical data and the attempt to document how the phenomenon is changing; this is the approach of folklorists (e.g. Grider 2006) and several sociologists (e.g. Walter 1999b). On the other hand, there are cultural theorists who emphasise the cultural significance of the one mourned (Merck 1998; Kear and Steinberg 1999). Psychoanalytic interpretations abound, one of the most common being that, precisely because we did not personally know the dead celebrity, they become a blank slate upon which we may project our own fears and hopes; this is particularly true of murder and abduction victims about whom the public knew nothing beforehand. The first approach can be narrowly sociological, not recognising emotional dynamics (Brennan 2001); the second approach too often rests more on the analyst's pet theories than on empirical data.

Collective Memory

Most sociology of death looks at the ordinary deaths of ordinary people, which is perhaps fair enough because that is what happens to most modern Westerners. However, any understanding of death in today's world has also to recognise the reality of war, famine and genocide, which can shape individual and collective responses to life and death for generations. There are two bodies of scholarship here that need to be connected more closely with the sociology of death and with death studies.

The first is Holocaust studies, which have grown exponentially since the early 1990s, and now comprise a field of their own, drawing on the humanities and psychoanalysis as much as the social sciences (e.g. Young 1993; Langer 1995). Some scholars identify the Holocaust as specifically perpetrated against the Jews and therefore not generalisable to other genocides; others (Bauman 1989; Noys 2005) see it as very much the product of modernity. Meanwhile, studies of other mass killings, for example in Russia (Merridale 2000, Gheith 2007), are much less developed.

The second field is that of collective memory, one in which sociologists (Olick 1999) have been more prominent; many of their studies look at collective memory after traumatic events (Vinitzky-Seroussi 2002), not least war (Wagner-Pacifici and Schwartz 1991). The challenge is to link analysis of personal loss and grief, the subject of much research, with analysis of communal loss and grief (Erikson 1976; Holst-Warhaft 2000; Lifton 1968; Marris 1974); to link how deceased individuals become part of personal or family ancestry and identity (e.g. Klass et al. 1996) with how decimated generations become part of national identity (Edmunds and Turner 2002). Links could also be made with studies of migration, looking at how deceased first generation migrants become part of subsequent individual, family and community identity (Meyer 1993). The notion that bereavement can entail a continuing bond between mourner and deceased (Klass et al. 1996) needs to be expanded into research into how bereavement shapes subsequent generational and group identities. Goss and Klass (2005) suggest that this process underlies how the early Christians developed their collective mythology about their executed leader. Communal loss can shape history.

Contemporary Rites of Passage

Anthropologists have recently turned to look at funerals, burials and cremations in the contemporary world. A major question is the extent to which the classic theories of van Gennep, Hertz and Turner, developed in the context of tribal societies, illuminate death rituals in the modern world, and what other theories might be developed. Work in this area is being done in the Netherlands, by liturgists and scholars in religious studies as well as anthropology (Grimes 2000); sociologists have contributed rather little so far, though, see Kellehear (1990b).

Comparative Research - NEEDED!

Although there is both a popular and often academic assumption that modern ways of death may be contrasted with those of traditional societies, there are in fact wide variations in how all kinds of societies deal with the deaths of their members. In the modern urbanised world, for example, Americans, Irish and Japanese regularly view human corpses at the wakes of colleagues and neighbours; the English do not. Southern Europe does not have the English gothic fear of graveyards (Goody and Poppi 1994). Palliative care, premised on open communication between autonomous individuals, finds fertile soil in the English-speaking world, but struggles in family centred societies such as Italy (Gordon and Paci 1997) or collectivist societies such as Japan (Paton and Wicks 1996). Patterns of grieving vary widely by generation, gender and class (Stroebe 1998; Walter 1999a). Dying in many modern countries is largely medicalised, but 6 million Jews and up to 60 million Russians died in the twentieth century as a result of state action. Deaths from alcohol

afflict twenty-first-century Russia like no other nation (Seale 2000). Particular nations have particular histories and cultures of death (Merridale 2000; Noys 2005).

Such differences, however, are regularly ignored by sociologists of death. On the one hand, too many studies refer simply to America, England or Australia, with no interest in other societies. Consequently, we do not know whether the data and processes discussed are specific to that nation, or to modernity, or to cities, or what. On the other hand, too many studies refer to 'modern society', as though they are all the same, which in the area of death they manifestly are not. Global encyclopaedias describe death practices and beliefs in different societies (Matsunami 1998; Morgan and Laungani 2002–4) and religions (Badham and Badham 1987; Obayashi 1992), but rarely ask comparative questions as to why these might differ or how religion and culture interact to create variation—welcome exceptions being Wikan (1988) and Garces-Foley (2005). The only way, however, to get to the bottom of whether any particular response to death is Western, modern, urban, globalised or specific to a particular nation or cluster of nations (whether Anglophone, Scandinavian or ex-Soviet) is sustained comparative analysis. Rare examples of such work include Goody and Poppi (1994), Walter (2005) and Kellehear (2007). In the meantime, with no textbooks written comparatively, every current textbook is more or less useless for students in other countries—students simply cannot know what in the text applies to their country and what does not.

Attempts at evolutionary psychology, not least about grief (Archer 1999), are also in need of comparative research. Too often they rely on psychological data from modern Western humans, along with observations of other species. Given, however, that 99 per cent of human evolution occurred while we were hunter gatherers, it is vital that ethnographic data gathered over the past 150 years about remaining hunter gatherers be factored into evolutionary theories.

Disadvantaged Dying

An estimated 100 million people died of state-sponsored deprivation and violence in the first half of the twentieth century (Elliot 1972), yet they are at best marginalised, at worst ignored, by sociologists of death. Furthermore, social scientists know far more about communication with middle-aged cancer patients than with old people suffering from dementia; far more about premature bereavement than elderly bereavement; far more about counselling services frequented by middle-class clients than about working-class styles of coping; far more about adjustment to death and loss by privileged Westerners than by sub-Saharan Africans. Such are the biases that have dominated death studies. Researchers, like Western societies at large, have ignored their own elderly, their own poor, the poor half of the world, and those made stateless by exile or war—all of whom experience death and loss disproportionately often (Allen 2007; Kellehear 2007; Seale 2000). Scholars have theorised the consequences of the Holocaust for Jewish people today, but know very little about how the destruction of lives, homes and communities by terror, war, civil war and AIDS affects life today in Lebanon, sub-Saharan Africa, Cambodia or Tibet. Just as palliative care has made dying a less terrible event for Westerners dying of cancer but has made little impact outside the English-speaking world or with other diseases, so sociological knowledge about death and dying has similarly focused on death by cancer in the first world. Too much sociology of death has reflected parochial medical trends, rather than offering a mirror to global society. Extending the vision of the sociology of death should go hand-in-hand with sustained comparative research.

Teaching: Some Personal Reflections

My own experience of university teaching in England is that the sociology of death can be a very popular undergraduate second or third year option. Options are popular, it seems, if they refer to something that 20-year-olds can easily relate to (gender, the media) or perceive as exotic (criminology); sociology of death scores on both counts—the dead body and its management are mysterious, yet at the same time most students have aged relatives at or near the end of their lives. Death—like sexuality—is exotic yet familiar. It is also possible to make links with other sociological subfields, such as religion, the body, the media, medicine, professionalisation and industry. And it provides a classic way to show how something that is at root natural (our bodies eventually pack up and die) is also inherently social. In short, the sociology of death is an excellent vehicle for teaching sociology. By contrast, in some American electives, the teacher's aim is more humanistic, perhaps to enable students to consider their own mortality. That is not my aim as a teacher of sociology undergraduates.

The sociology of death should be an option, not compulsory. Some students either really do not want to think about mortality, or are having to struggle with terminal illness or bereavement and may not wish this to be a feature of their studies also. Such students actually often do choose to study it—I tell them to let me know if there is the occasional topic or class they would rather miss. More problematic, but quite common, is that mid-term one or two students report that, unexpectedly, their favourite grandfather has just died or their mother has just been diagnosed with breast cancer or—more rarely—that a housemate has just killed himself. Usually, students with close encounters report at the end of term that the sociology of death has helped them understand their own and others' practices, reactions and feelings. Another commonly reported response is that the sociology of death tends to distance the student from death itself—rather like the medical student studying anatomy.

I have also included euthanasia and controversies over human remains as topics within a large first year undergraduate class on Contemporary Social Issues. Students do not have the choice to opt out of these topics. However, they disproportionately choose exam questions on them; hence, it would seem they find sociological analysis of these topics more fascinating than disturbing.

I do not consider death studies a discipline. It has no distinctive theories or methods, that is to say, one's mind does not have to be disciplined in a way specific to death studies in order to study death, hence, the social study of death is best conducted by scholars trained in one or more existing disciplines, whether history, sociology, religious studies, English literature, archaeology, or whatever. I would therefore not wish to see an entire 3-year undergraduate programme in death studies: quite simply it does not provide basic training of the mind. At the Master's level, which in the UK means 1 year of study, I do not believe there is yet anything like enough in the *sociology* of death to occupy a year's curriculum. Master's programmes in this field are therefore multi-disciplinary, in which students—already trained in one discipline—face the challenge of integrating perspectives from different disciplines. Within British academia, sadly, institutional incentives or structures for inter-disciplinary teaching are limited.

Conclusion

The sociology of death has made some great leaps forward, notably in the USA in the 1960s and in Britain in the 1990s. It stagnated in the USA after the first leap, and is danger of stagnating in Britain after the second. The need, as in much sociology, is for empirically informed theory (too many senior intellectuals wander uninformed over the field) and for theoretically informed empirical research (too many doctoral dissertations are mindlessly empirical and derivative). And there needs to be sustained comparative work.

Sociologists need to engage with work done in cognate disciplines. As Dogan and Pahre (1990) observe, multi-disciplinary work is all but impossible. We no longer live in the Renaissance where one brilliant mind can encompass a dozen disciplines. It is hard enough for a scholar trained in one field really to grapple with work done in one other, let alone more than one, although some of the most fertile intellectual work has been done when scholars from two fields really work hard to relate to each other's thinking. In death studies, rare examples of scholars who work competently and creatively in more than one discipline include Douglas Davies (theology, anthropology, sociology), Bob Kastenbaum (psychology and sociology) and Paul Rosenblatt (psychology, anthropology, history), while Allan Kellehear, although clearly a sociologist, produced his social history of dying (2007) by engaging very directly with the work of historians and archaeologists.

I started with Durkheim and Weber. They showed how death is, or can be, one of the basic motors of society: death practices and beliefs profoundly affect society. Most of the work I have reviewed in this article, like Durkheim's other famous work on suicide (2002), looks at the relationship the other way around: society profoundly affects death practices and beliefs. What we therefore have today is a partially developed sociology of death practices and beliefs, but general sociology still proceeds largely as though no one dies. The glimpse Durkheim and Weber offered of society shaped by mortality has been substantially eclipsed, although Holocaust studies and research on collective memory remind us that death can still profoundly affect society. Although affluent sociologists may need to be reminded of this, millions of disadvantaged people around the world do not.

Note

1. Correspondence address: Social and Policy Sciences, University of Bath, Claverton Down, Bath, Somerset BA2 4PE, UK. Email: j.a.walter@bath.ac.uk.

References

Agamben, Giorgio 1998. *Homo Sacer: Sovereign Power and Bare Life.* Stanford, CA: Stanford University Press.

Allen, Chris 2007. 'The Poverty of Death: Social Class, Urban Deprivation, and the Criminological Consequences of Sequestration of Death.' *Mortality* 12: 79–93.

Archer, John 1999. *The Nature of Grief: The Evolution and Psychology of Reactions to Loss.* London, UK: Routledge.

Ariès, Philippe 1962. *Centuries of Childhood.* London, UK: Cape.

Ariès, Philippe 1974. *Western Attitudes toward Death: from the Middle Ages to the Present.* London, UK: Marion Boyars Publishers.

Ariès, Philippe 1983. *The Hour of Our Death.* London, UK: Penguin.

Armstrong, David 1987. 'Silence and Truth in Death and Dying.' *Social Science & Medicine* 24: 651–57.

Armstrong-Coster, Angela 2001. 'In Morte Media Jubilate: An Empirical Study of Cancer-related Documentary Film.' *Mortality* 6: 287–305.

Árnarson, Árnar 2007. '"Fall Apart and Put Yourself Together Again": The Anthropology of Death and Bereavement Counselling in Britain.' *Mortality* 12: 48–65.

Arney, William Ray and Bernard J. Bergen 1984. *Medicine and the Management of Living.* Chicago, IL: University of Chicago Press.

Badham, Paul and Linda Badham (eds) 1987. *Death and Immortality in the Religions of the World.* New York, NY: Paragon House.

Baudrillard, Jean 1993. *Symbolic Exchange and Death.* London, UK: Sage.

Bauman, Zygmunt 1989. *Modernity and the Holocaust.* Oxford, UK: Polity Press.

Bauman, Zygmunt 1992. *Mortality, Immortality and Other Life Strategies.* Oxford, UK: Polity Press.

Becker, Ernest 1973. *The Denial of Death.* New York, NY: Free Press.

Berger, Peter 1969. *The Social Reality of Religion.* London, UK: Faber.

Blauner, Robert 1966. 'Death and Social Structure.' *Psychiatry* 29: 378–94.

Bloch, Maurice and Jonathan Parry (eds) 1982. *Death & the Regeneration of Life.* Cambridge, UK: Cambridge University Press.

Bowlby, John 1979. *The Making and Breaking of Affectional Bonds.* London, UK: Tavistock.

Brennan, Michael 2001. 'Towards a Sociology of Public Mourning?' *Sociology* 35: 205–12.

Charmaz, Kathleen 1980. *The Social Reality of Death.* Reading, MS: Addison-Wesley.

Christakis, Nicholas 1999. *A Death Foretold: Prophecy and Prognosis in Medical Care.* Chicago, IL: Chicago University Press.

Clark, David and Jane Seymour (ed.) 1999. *Reflections on Palliative Care: Sociological and Policy Perspectives.* Buckingham, UK: Open University Press.

Clark, David (ed.) 1993a. *The Future for Palliative Care: Issues of Policy and Practice.* Buckingham, UK: Open University Press.

Clark, David (ed.) 1993b. *The Sociology of Death.* Oxford, UK: Blackwell.

Conklin, Beth A. 2001. *Consuming Grief: Compassionate Cannibalism in an Amazonian Society.* Austin, TX: University of Texas Press.

Corr, Charles, Kenneth Doka and Robert Kastenbaum 1999. 'Dying and Its Interpreters: A Review of Selected Literature and Some Comments on the State of the Field.' *Omega* 39: 239–59.

Corr, Charles A., Clyde M. Nabe and Donna M. Corr 1997. *Death and Dying, Life and Living* (2nd edn). Pacific Grove, CA: Brooks/Cole.

Cumming, Elaine and William E. Henry 1961. *Growing Old: The Process of Disengagement.* New York, NY: Basic Books.

Danforth, L. 1982. *The Death Rituals of Rural Greece.* Princeton, NJ: Princeton University Press.

Davies, Douglas 2000. 'Robert Hertz: The Social Triumph over Death.' *Mortality* 5: 97–102.

Davies, Douglas 2002. *Death, Ritual and Belief: The Rhetoric of Funerary Rites.* London, UK: Continuum.

DeSpelder, Lynne A. and Albert L. Strickland 2002. *The Last Dance: Encountering Death and Dying* (6th edn). Boston, MA: McGraw Hill.

Dogan, Mattei and Robert Pahre 1990. *Creative Marginality: Innovation at the Intersections of the Social Sciences.* Westport, CT: Praeger.

Durkheim, Emile 1915. *The Elementary Forms of the Religious Life.* London, UK: Unwin.

Durkheim, Emile 2002. *Suicide: A Study in Sociology.* London, UK: Routledge.

Edmunds, June and Bryan Turner 2002. *Generations, Culture and Society.* Buckingham, UK: Open University Press.

Eisenbruch, Maurice 1984. 'Cross-Cultural Aspects of Bereavement.' *Culture, Medicine & Psychiatry* 8 Pt 1: 283–309, Pt 2: 315–47.

Elias, Norbert 1985. *The Loneliness of the Dying.* Oxford, UK: Blackwell.

Elliot, Gil 1972. *Twentieth Century Book of the Dead.* London, UK: Allen Lane.

Erikson, Kai T. 1976. *Everything in Its Path: Destruction of Community in the Buffalo Creek Flood.* New York, NY: Simon & Schuster.

Farrell, James J. 1980. *Inventing the American Way of Death, 1830–1920.* Philadelphia, PA: Temple University Press.

Faunce, William and Robert Fulton 1958. 'The Sociology of Death: A Neglected Area of Research.' *Social Forces* 36: 205–9.

Field, David 1989. *Nursing the Dying.* London, UK: Routledge.

Finucane, Ronald 1996. *Ghosts: Appearances of the Dead & Cultural Transformation.* Amherst, NY: Prometheus Books.

Fox, Renée 1979. 'The Autopsy: Its Place in the Attitude-Learning of Second-Year Medical Students.' pp. 51–77 in *Essays in Medical Sociology: Journeys into the Field,* edited by Renée Fox. New York, NY: John Wiley & Sons.

Francis, Doris, Leonie Kellaher and Georgina Neophytou 2005. *The Secret Cemetery.* Oxford, UK: Berg.

Freud, Sigmund 1984. 'Mourning and Melancholia.' pp. 251–67 in *Sigmund Freud On Metapsychology* (Vol. 11). London, UK: Pelican Freud Library.

Fulton, Gere B. and Eileen K. Metress 1995. *Perspectives on Death and Dying.* Boston, MA: Jones & Bartlett.

Fulton, Robert Jr and Robert Bendiksen (eds) 1994. *Death and Identity* (3rd edn). Philadelphia, PA: Charles Press.

Garces-Foley, Kathleen (ed.) 2005. *Death and Religion in a Changing World.* New York, NY: M.E. Sharpe.

Gheith, Jehanne 2007. 'I Never Talked: Enforced Silence, Non-narrative Memory, and the Gulag.' *Mortality* 12: 159–75.

Giddens, Anthony 1991. *Modernity and Self-Identity.* Oxford, UK: Polity Press.

Gittings, Clare 1984. *Death, Burial and the Individual in Early Modern England.* London, UK: Croom Helm.

Glaser, Barney and Anselm Strauss 1965. *Awareness of Dying.* Chicago, IL: Aldine.

Glaser, Barney and Anselm Strauss 1967. *The Discovery of Grounded Theory.* Chicago, IL: Aldine.

Glaser, Barney and Anselm Strauss 1968. *Time for Dying.* Chicago, IL: Aldine.

Goffman, Erving 1968. *Asylums.* Harmondsworth, UK: Penguin.

Goody, Jack and Cesare Poppi 1994. 'Flowers and Bones: Approaches to the Dead in Anglo and Italian Cemeteries.' *Comparative Studies in Society and History* 36: 146–75.

Gordon, Deborah R. and Eugenio Paci 1997. 'Disclosure Practices and Cultural Narratives: Understanding Concealment and Silence around Cancer in Tuscany, Italy.' *Social Science & Medicine* 44: 1433–52.

Gorer, Geoffrey 1965. *Death, Grief, and Mourning in Contemporary Britain.* London: Cresset.

Gorer, Geoffrey 1955. 'The Pornography of Death.' *Encounter* 5: 49–52.

Goss, Robert E. and Dennis Klass 2005. *Dead But Not Lost: Grief Narratives in Religious Traditions.* Walnut Creek, CA: Alta Mira.

Grider, Slyvia 2006. 'Spontaneous Shrines and Public Memorialization.' pp. 246–64 in *Death and Religion in a Changing World,* edited by Kathleen Garces-Foley. Armonk, NY: M.E. Sharpe.

Grimes, Ronald 2000. *Deeply Into the Bone: Re-Inventing Rites of Passage.* Berkeley, CA: University of California Press.

Habenstein, R. 1962. 'Sociology of Occupations: The Case of the American Funeral Director.' pp. 225–46 in *Human Behaviour and Social Processes,* edited by A. Rose. London, UK: Routledge and Kegan Paul.

Habenstein, Robert W. and Williams M. Lamers 1962. *The History of American Funeral Directing.* Milwaukee, WI: Bulfin.

Hafferty, Frederic 1991. *Into the Valley.* New Haven, CT: Yale University Press.

Hallam, Elizabeth, Jenny Hockey and Glennys Howarth 1999. *Beyond the Body: Death and Social Identity.* London, UK: Routledge.

Hertz, Robert 1960. *Death and the Right Hand.* London, UK: Cohen & West.

Hockey, Jennifer 1990. *Experiences of Death.* Edinburgh, UK: Edinburgh University Press.

Hockey, Jennifer 2002. 'The Importance of Being Intuitive: Arnold van Gennep's The Rites of Passage.' *Mortality* 7: 210–7.

Holst-Warhaft, Gail 2000. *The Cue for Passion: Grief and Its Political Uses.* Cambridge, MA: Harvard University Press.

Houlbrooke, Ralph 1998. *Death, Religion and the Family in England 1480–1750.* Oxford, UK: Clarendon.

Howarth, Glennys and Peter Jupp (eds) 1996. *Contemporary Issues in the Sociology of Death, Dying and Disposal.* Basingstoke, UK: Macmillan.

Howarth, Glennys 1996. *Last Rites: An Ethnographic Account of the Work of the Modern Funeral Director.* Amityville, NY: Baywood.

Howarth, Glennys 2006. *Death and Dying: A Sociological Iintroduction.* Cambridge, UK: Polity Press.

Jalland, Pat 1996. *Death in the Victorian Family.* Oxford, UK: Oxford University Press.

James, Nicky and D. Field 1992. 'The Routinization of Hospice: Charisma and Bureaucratization.' *Social Science & Medicine* 34: 1363–75.

Jupp, Peter and Clare Gittings (eds) 1999. *Death in England.* Manchester, UK: Manchester University Press.

Kalish, Richard A. and David K. Reynolds 1981. *Death and Ethnicity: A Psychocultural Study.* Farmingdale, NY: Baywood.

Kamerman, Jack B. 2002. *Death in the Midst of Life.* Englewood Cliffs, NJ: Prentice Hall.

Kastenbaum, Robert 1995. *Death, Society and Human Experience* (5th edn). Boston, MA: Allyn & Bacon.

Kaufman, Sharon 2005. *And a Time to Die: How American Hospitals Shape the End of Life.* New York, NY: Scribner.

Kear, Adrian and Deborah L. Steinberg (eds) 1999. *Mourning Diana.* London, UK: Routledge.

Kearl, Michael 1989. *Endings: A Sociology of Death and Dying.* New York, NY: Oxford University Press.

Kellehear, Allan 1984. 'Are We a Death-Denying Society? A Sociological Review.' *Social Science & Medicine* 18: 713–23.

Kellehear, Allan 1990a. *Dying of Cancer: The Final Years of Life.* Chur, Switzerland: Harwood Academic.

Kellehear, Allan 1990b. 'The Near Death Experience as Status Passage.' *Social Science & Medicine* 31: 933–9.

Kellehear, Allan 1996. *Experiences Near Death: Beyond Medicine and Religion.* Oxford, UK: Oxford University Press.

Kellehear, Allan 1998. 'Ethical Issues for the Qualitative Researcher: Some Critical Reflections.' *Annual Review of Health Social Sciences* 8: 14–7.

Kellehear, Allan 2007. *A Social History of Dying.* Cambridge, UK: Cambridge University Press.

Klass, Dennis, Phyllis R. Silverman, and Steven L. Nickman (eds) 1996. *Continuing Bonds: New Understandings of Grief.* Bristol, PA: Taylor & Francis.

Kselman, Thomas 1993. *Death and the Afterlife in Modern France.* Princeton, NJ: Princeton University Press.

Kselman, Thomas 2004. 'Death in the Western World: Michel Vovelle's Ambivalent Epic *La Mort et l'Occident, de 1300 à nos jours.*' *Mortality* 9: 168–76.

Kubler-Ross, Elisabeth 1970. *On Death and Dying.* London, UK: Tavistock.

Laderman, Gary 1996. *The Sacred Remains: American Attitudes to Death, 1799–1883.* New Haven, CT: Yale University Press.

Laderman, Gary 2000. 'The Disney Way of Death.' *Journal of the American Academy of Religion,* 68: 27–46.

Laderman, Gary 2003. *Rest in Peace: A Cultural History of Death and the Funeral Home in Twentieth Century America.* Oxford, UK: Oxford University Press.

Langer, Lawrence 1995. *Admitting the Holocaust: Collected Essays.* Oxford, UK: Oxford University Press.

Lawton, Julia 2000. *The Dying Process: Patients' Experiences of Palliative Care.* London, UK: Routledge.

Leming, Michael R. and George E. Dickinson 2002. *Understanding Dying, Death and Bereavement* (5th edn). Forth Worth, TX: Harcourt.

Lifton, Robert J. 1968. *Death in Life: Survivors of Hiroshima.* New York, NY: Random House.

Lock, Margaret 2002. *Twice Dead: Organ Transplants and the Reinvention of Death*. Berkeley, CA: University of California Press.

Lofland, Lyn 1978. *The Craft of Dying: The Modern Face of Death*. Beverly Hills, CA: Sage.

Marris, Peter 1958. *Widows and Their Families*. London, UK: Routledge.

Marris, Peter 1974. *Loss and Change*. London, UK: Routledge.

Marshall, Victor W. 1980. *Last Chapters: A Sociology of Ageing and Dying*. Monterey, CA: Books/Cole.

Matsunami, Kodo 1998. *International Handbook of Funeral Customs*. Westport, CT: Greenwood Press.

McInerney, Fran 2000. 'Requested Death: A New Social Movement.' *Social Science & Medicine* 50: 137–54.

McManners, John 1981. *Death and the Enlightenment: Changing Attitudes to Death among Christians and Unbelievers in Eighteenth-Century France*. Oxford, UK: Oxford University Press.

McNamara, Beverley 2001. *Fragile Lives: Death, Dying and Care*. Buckingham, UK: Open University Press.

Mellor, Philip and Chris Shilling 1993. 'Modernity, Self-Identity and the Sequestration of Death.' *Sociology* 27: 411–32.

Merck, Mandy (ed.) 1998. *After Diana: Irreverent Elegies*. London, UK: Verso.

Merridale, Catherine 2000. *Night of Stone: Death and Memory in Russia*. London, UK: Granta.

Metcalf, Peter and Richard Huntington 1991. *Celebrations of Death: The Anthropology of Mortuary Ritual* (2nd edn). Cambridge, UK: Cambridge University Press.

Meyer, Richard (ed.) 1993. *Ethnicity and the American Cemetery*. Bowling Green, OH: Bowling Green University Press.

Mitford, Jessica 1963. *The American Way of Death*. London, UK: Hutchinson.

Morgan, John D. and Pittu Laungani 2002–4. *Death and Bereavement Across the World*. Amityville, NY: Baywood.

Noys, Benjamin 2005. *The Culture of Death*. Oxford, UK: Berg.

Nuland, Sherwin 1994. *How We Die*. New York, NY: Random House.

Obayashi, Hiroshi 1992. *Death and Afterlife: Perspectives of World Religions,* London, UK: Praeger.

Olick, Jeffrey 1999. 'Collective Memory: The Two Cultures.' *Sociological Theory* 17: 333–348.

Parkes, Colin M. 1996. *Bereavement: Studies of Grief in Adult Life* (3rd edn). London, UK: Routledge.

Parry, Jonathan P. 1994. *Death in Benares*. Cambridge, UK: Cambridge University Press.

Parsons, Talcott and Victor Lidz 1967. 'Death in American Society.' pp. 133–70 in *Essays in Self-destruction,* edited by Edwin Shneidman. New York, NY: Science House.

Parsons, Talcott, Renee Fox, and Victor Lidz 1972. 'The "Gift of Life" and Its Reciprocation.' *Social Research* 39: 367–415. pp. 123–54 reprinted in 1999. *The Talcott Parsons Reader,* edited by Bryan S. Turner. Oxford, UK: Blackwell.

Paton, Lee and Mark Wicks 1996. 'The Growth of the Hospice Movement in Japan.' *American Journal of Hospice & Palliative Care* 13: 26–31.

Pine, Vanderlyn 1977. 'A Socio-Historical Portrait of Death Education.' *Death Education* 1: 57–84.

Pine, Vanderlyn 1986. 'The Age of Maturity for Death Education: A Socio-Historical Portrait of the Era 1976–1985.' *Death Studies* 10: 209–31.

Prendergast, David, Jenny Hockey and Leonie Kellaher 2006. 'Blowing in the Wind? Identity, Materiality, and the Destinations of Human Ashes.' *Journal of the Royal Anthropological Institute* 124: 881–98.

Prior, Lindsay 1989. *The Social Organisation of Death*. Basingstoke, UK: Macmillan.

Prothero, Stephen 2001. *Purified by Fire: A History of Cremation in America*. Berkeley, CA: University of California Press.

Riches, Gordon and Pam Dawson 2000. *An Intimate Loneliness: Supporting Bereaved Parents and Siblings*. Buckingham, UK: Open University Press.

Robben, Antonius C. (ed.) 2004. *Death, Mourning, and Burial: A Cross-Cultural Reader*. Oxford, UK: Blackwell.

Rosenblatt, Paul 1983. *Tears, Bitter Tears: Nineteenth Century Diarists and Twentieth Century Grief Theorists*. Minneapolis, MN: University of Minnesota Press.

Rosenblatt, Paul, Patricia Walsh and Douglas Jackson (eds) 1976. *Grief and Mourning in Cross-Cultural Perspective*. Washington, DC: Human Relations Area Files Press.

Santino, Jack (ed.) 2006. *Spontaneous Shrines and the Public Memorialization of Death*. Basingstoke, UK: Palgrave Macmillan.

Scheper-Hughes, Nancy 1993. *Death without Weeping: The Violence of Everyday Life in Brazil,* Berkeley, CA: University of California Press.

Seale Clive 2002. 'Cancer Heroics: A Study of News Reports with Particular Reference to Gender.' *Sociology* 36: 107–26.

Seale, Clive 1990. 'Caring for People who Die: The Experience of Family and Friends.' *Ageing & Society* 10: 413–28.

Seale, Clive 1998. *Constructing Death*. Cambridge, UK: Cambridge University Press.

Seale, Clive 1999. 'Awareness of Method: Re-Reading Glaser and Strauss.' *Mortality* 4: 195–202.

Seale, Clive 2000. 'Changing Patterns of Death and Dying.' *Social Science & Medicine* 51: 917–930.

Small, Neil 2001.'Theories of Grief: A Critical Review.' pp. 19–48 in *Grief, Mourning and Death Ritual,* edited by Jenny Hockey, Jeanne Katz and Neil Small. Buckingham, UK: Open University Press.

Sofka, Carla J. 1997. 'Social Support "Internetworks", Caskets for Sale, and More: Thanatology and the Information Superhighway.' *Death Studies* 21: 553–74.

Stannard, David 1977. *The Puritan Way of Death: A Study in Religion, Culture, and Social Change*. New York, NY: Oxford University Press.

Stone, Philip 2006. 'A Dark Tourism Spectrum: Towards a Typology of Death and Macabre Related Tourist Sites, Attractions and Exhibitions.' *Tourism* 54: 145–60.

Strange, Julie-Marie 2005. *Death, Grief and Poverty in Britain, 1870–1914*. Cambridge, UK: Cambridge University Press.

Stroebe, Margaret and Henk Schut 1999. 'The Dual Process Model of Coping with Bereavement.' *Death Studies* 23: 197–224.

Stroebe, Margaret 1998. 'New Directions in Bereavement Research: Exploration of Gender Differences.' *Palliative Medicine* 12: 5–12.

Stroebe, Wolfgang and Margaret Stroebe 1987. *Bereavement and Health*. Cambridge, UK: Cambridge University Press.

Sudnow, David 1967. *Passing On: The Social Organisation of Dying*. Englewood Cliffs, NJ: Prentice Hall.

Suzuki, Hikaru J. 2001. *The Price of Death: The Funeral Industry in Contemporary Japan.* Stanford, CA: Stanford University Press.

Turner, Victor 1977. *The Ritual Process.* Ithaca, NY: Cornell University Press.

van Gennep, Arnond 1960. *The Rites of Passage.* Chicago, IL: University of Chicago Press

Verdery, Katherine 1999. *The Political Lives of Dead Bodies: Reburial and Postsocialist Change.* New York, NY: Columbia University Press.

Vinitzky-Seroussi, Vered 2002. 'Commemorating a Difficult Past: Yitzhak Rabin's Memorials.' *American Journal of Sociology* 67: 30–51.

Vovelle, Michel 1983. *La Mort et l'Occident, de 1300 à nos jours.* Paris, France: Gallimard.

Wagner-Pacifici, Robin and Barry Schwartz 1991. 'The Vietnam Veterans Memorial: Commemorating a Difficult Past.' *American Journal of Sociology* 97: 376–420.

Walter, Tony 1994. *The Revival of Death.* London, UK: Routledge.

Walter, Tony 1999a. *On Bereavement: The Culture of Grief.* Buckingham, UK: Open University Press

Walter, Tony (ed.) 1999b. *The Mourning for Diana.* Oxford, UK: Berg.

Walter, Tony 2005. 'Three Ways to Arrange a Funeral: Mortuary Variation in the Modern West.' *Mortality* 10: 173–92.

Walter, Tony 2006. 'Disaster, Modernity, and the Media.' pp. 265–82 in *Death and Religion in a Changing World,* edited by K. Garces-Foley. Armonk, NY: M.E. Sharpe.

Walter, Tony, Michoel Pickering and Jone Littlewood 1995. 'Death in the News: The Public Invigilation of Private Emotion.' *Sociology,* 29: 579–96.

Warner, William L. 1959. *The Living and the Dead: A Study of the Symbolic Life of Americans.* New Haven, CT: Yale University Press.

Weber, Max 1930. *The Protestant Ethic and the Spirit of Capitalism.* London, UK: Allen & Unwin.

Whaley, Joachim (ed.) 1981. *Mirrors of Mortality: Studies in the Social History of Death.* London, UK: Europa.

Wikan, Unni 1988. 'Bereavement and Loss in Two Muslim Communities: Egypt and Bali Compared.' *Social Science & Medicine* 275: 451–60.

Williams, Riley Jr. 1990. *A Protestant Legacy: Attitudes to Death and Illness among Older Aberdonians.* Oxford, UK: Oxford University Press.

Willmott, Hugh 2000. 'Death: So What? Sociology, Sequestration and Emancipation.' *Sociological Review* 484: 649–65.

Young, James 1993. *The Texture of Memory: Holocaust Memorials and Meaning.* New Haven, CT: Yale University Press.

Tony Walter has a BA in Sociology & Economic History from the University of Durham, and a PhD in Sociology from the University of Aberdeen. He was a freelance writer for many years, publishing books on religion, employment, welfare, landscape, and funerals, before becoming an academic, teaching first at the University of Reading and then the University of Bath where he is currently director of the MSc in Death & Society. In addition to those cited in this article, his books on the sociology of death include *Funerals: And How to Improve Them* (Hodder 1990), *The Eclipse of Eternity: A Sociology of the Afterlife* (Macmillan 1996), and (with Ian Reader) *Pilgrimage in Popular Culture* (Macmillan 1993). In the past 10 years, he has published research on belief in reincarnation, the concept of spirituality in health care, and the Body Worlds exhibition of plastinated cadavers. He has an ongoing research interest in mediations between the living and the dead. His website is at http://www.bath.ac.uk/cdas/peoplc/.

Acknowledgement—The author thanks Glennys Howarth and Allan Kellehear for their prompt and thoughtful comments on the first draft of this article.

UNIT 2

Dying and Death across the Life Cycle

Unit Selections

Key Points to Consider

- With children experiencing death situations at an average age of eight years, what societal steps can be taken to help children better cope with the death of a person or a pet? What do you recall from your own childhood experiences with death? Were these experiences positive or negative?

- Sudden infant death syndrome (SIDS) has been causing the deaths of infants for centuries around the world. In what ways might such a horrible event be prevented?

- Coping with a dying child or adult is certainly a challenging experience for anyone. What sources exist to aid with such a trauma in one's life? How can physicians help parents relieve misplaced guilt over the death of a newborn or a small child?

- How can caregivers be helped to lessen their "assignment" of dealing with a dying family member? What kinds of support are available for caregivers?

- Do the living really communicate with the dead or are they simply hallucinating? Do you believe in ghosts? Have you ever seen a ghost?

Student Web Site

www.mhcls.com

Internet References

CDC Wonder on the Web—Prevention Guidelines
  http://wonder.cdc.gov
Children with AIDS Project
  http://www.aidskids.org
Light for Life Foundation
  http://www.yellowribbon.org
National SIDS Resource Center
  http://www.sidscenter.org/
Palliative Care for Children
  http://www.aap.org/policy/re0007.html

Death is something that we must accept, though no one really understands it. We can talk about death, learn from each other, and help each other. By better understanding death conceptualization at various stages and in different relationships within the life cycle, we can help each other. It is not our intent to suggest that age should be viewed as the sole determinant of one's death concept. Many other factors such as level of intelligence, physical and mental well-being, previous emotional reactions to various life experiences, religious background, other social and cultural forces, personal identity and self-worth appraisals, and exposure to or threats of death influence this cognitive development. Indeed, a child in a hospital for seriously ill children is likely more sophisticated regarding death, as she/he may be aware of dying and death, more so than an adult who has not had such experiences. Nonetheless, we discuss dying and death perceptions at various stages from the cradle to the grave or, as some say, the womb to the tomb.

The death of a child and the death of a spouse are both among the top five in the list of 100 stresses that an individual has in life. The death of a child is so illogical, as the child has not lived through the life cycle. One can anticipate attending the funeral of a grandparent and then a parent. We do not, however, anticipate attending the funeral of a child, since the adult is "expected" to die before the child. Such is the rational sequence of the life cycle. "Rituals of Unburdening" discusses the death of a newborn and the difficulty of trying to relieve parents of misplaced guilt.

"To Live with No Regrets: Death Is a Transition for the Dying—and for Those Left Behind" discusses a husband dying from cancer, from the point of view of his wife. As individuals move into the "autumn" of their lives and are classified as "elderly," death surrounds them, and they are especially made aware that they are reaching the end of the tunnel. Though old age is often pictured as gloom and doom, it can be viewed as "the best is yet to be," as poet Robert Browning noted. The aging professional athlete, Satchel Paige, observed years ago that aging is really mind over matter; as long as you don't mind, it really doesn't matter. You are as old (or young) as you feel. Research suggests that the elderly are accepting of death, having lived a normal life span, and are grateful for the life they have had. "Cast Me Not Off in Old Age" discusses problems of living longer today and ethical issues such as euthanasia.

An often forgotten member of any caregiving team for an individual with a terminal illness is the caregiver. What provisions are made for them as they often have a 24-7 "shift" with little respite? This topic is addressed by Deborah Waldrop in "Caregiving Systems at the End of Life: How Informal Caregivers and Formal Providers Collaborate." Some caregivers relate to individuals whose personalities are changing and are soon not the same persons that they had previously

© Ryan McVay/Getty Images

known. Such is the case with Carol Levine's "Altered States: What I've Learned about Death and Disability."

As individuals move into the "autumn" of their lives and are classified as "elderly," death surrounds them, and they are especially made aware that they are reaching the end of the tunnel. Though old age is often pictured as gloom and doom, it can be viewed as "the best is yet to be," as poet Robert Browning noted. The aging professional athlete Satchel Paige observed years ago that aging is really mind over matter—as long as you don't mind, it really doesn't matter. You are as old (or young) as you feel. Research suggests that the elderly are accepting of death, having lived a normal life span, and are grateful for the life they have had. Some of these issues are addressed in the following three articles. Wijk and Grimby's "Needs of Elderly Patients in Palliative Care" discusses the end-of-life needs of elderly patients in a Swedish geriatric palliative care unit. Finally, Bill Newcott surveyed individuals over the age of 50 and asked about their beliefs on life after death.

Rituals of Unburdening

Mark R. Mercurio

Death in the newborn intensive care unit, as elsewhere, is often marked by rituals. Some, like the cadence of a code or helping parents with their grief, are included in both the formal and informal education of physicians. Among these, though perhaps not named as such, is the "unburdening" of the parents—an attempt to relieve them of misplaced guilt. A parallel ritual that is seldom taught or discussed, however, is the unburdening of the physician who has tried and failed to save a child. The unburdening of parents, typically done by the child's physician, is strikingly similar to the unburdening of the physician, done by one or more colleagues. As with so many rituals surrounding death, both may address an emotional need and provide some relief to those left behind.

A baby girl is born at 2:00 A.M. with life-threatening medical problems. The neonatology team resuscitates her and places the necessary lines and tubes. Initially her vital signs stabilize, but the honeymoon is brief. The team works for hours to reverse her downward course. The attending physician brings the parents to their daughter's bedside and tells them gently but clearly that he believes the child will probably not survive the night. They ask that everything possible be done to save her. They understand, they say, that the chance of success is low, and that even if she were to survive, she could be left with permanent disabilities. Still, they ask that everything possible be done. "How could we live with ourselves otherwise?" the father asks.

The attending watches as the neonatology fellow, almost an attending herself, expertly directs the team. He stands just behind her and off to her left, occasionally making suggestions, fine-tuning her management. He knows he is fortunate to have such an excellent group. The fellow, nurse, nurse practitioner, pediatric resident, and respiratory therapist are all experienced and skilled in their respective roles. Also, each of them has confidence in the attending's clinical judgment. As stressful as these situations can be, there is some comfort in having a veteran physician, and the clinician ultimately responsible, right there with you making sure you're doing it right—making sure you don't miss anything. This is an advantage they all share, save one.

The oxygen saturation drifts downward. Eventually the baby's heart rate begins to slow. The team initiates a code, but in truth all their efforts since the child's birth could well be described as one long code. Despite their best efforts, the situation continues to worsen. Its hopelessness seems apparent, and the fellow asks the attending how much longer they should proceed.

Acceptance seems to work its way up the ranks. The one who has the final responsibility is often the last to acknowledge that the patient will not survive. But in time the attending calls it, and efforts cease. He thanks the team and tells them they did a great job. He truthfully reassures them that they gave the baby the best chance she could have had. As the nurse gently removes the tubes and tape and machines, preparing the baby to be held, the attending sits with the parents and tells them what happened, offers condolences, answers their questions, and assures them he did everything he could.

He also unburdens them as much as possible. Parents of infants who are born sick, premature, or with congenital defects often fear they are somehow to blame. This is particularly true of mothers, who may feel they have failed in their responsibility to nurture and deliver a healthy baby. Parents often wonder what they did to cause such a catastrophe. Perhaps worse, they sometimes believe (almost always mistakenly) that they already know what they've done wrong, but are afraid to ask lest they have their theory confirmed. When their concerns are anticipated and their misplaced sense of guilt is addressed, the relief in their eyes is apparent. And then, sometimes, specific questions emerge, about having painted the apartment or missed prenatal vitamins, or something else usually unrelated to the child's death.

The attending in this case knows the ritual and understands its importance to parents. He does not need to hear the question to know it should be addressed, and so he tells the parents, "I'm so sorry this happened, but it did not happen because of anything you did or didn't do. This is absolutely not your fault. Many parents, especially moms, think it's somehow their fault when their newborn dies. It's clearly not true here. If you had done something to cause this, I'd tell you, so it wouldn't happen again. But you didn't cause this, and you couldn't have prevented it."

After more discussion, he leaves the parents and returns to the unit. There, he goes over the details of the previous night in his mind. Given the outcome, it is easy to understand why a physician would second-guess himself. There were many decision points where he might have gone another way, and of course in retrospect he may well wish he had—after all, he might think, he couldn't have done any worse. Perhaps a trial of high-frequency ventilation, which usually helps in patients like this, led in this particular case to a clinical deterioration. With the benefit of hindsight, he may wish he hadn't tried it, but it does not necessarily follow that it was a bad decision at the time he made it. He knows it is not fair to judge clinical management in retrospect, basing that judgment on information not available when the decision was made—such reasoning is not lost on him but fights with the fact that a child for whom he was responsible has died.

When a patient dies, one naturally feels sadness for the child, and for the parents. Occasionally, in cases such as this one, the physician's sadness is compounded by a fear that he might have—should have—done better. Later he may relate the story of the night to a family member or close friend, and that person may offer welcome words of comfort. But the words he most needs to hear right now are more likely to come from a respected colleague.

A more senior neonatologist, just coming in for the day, joins him at the X-ray board. She sits with him and listens as he describes the case. They go over the story, the films, and the interventions tried; left unspoken is his concern that his patient died because of something he did, or failed to do. She does not need to hear him state his insecurities to know they are there, or to know what to say. She echoes what he told the grieving parents. No, he didn't miss anything that she can see. There was nothing that he did, or failed to do, that led to the child's death. She does not see how this child could have been saved. Finally, she gets up, leaving him with one last comforting thought: "I would have handled it the same way."

He is tired. He has eight more hours to work and numerous decisions to make, some of them critical, before he goes home. Her words, in addition to alleviating his distress, may make it easier for him to focus on the patients who remain in the unit. The relief of his anxiety and the clearer focus are thus gifts not just to him, but also to those under his care. Just as his words may have left the parents more able to deal with their pain and loss, he may now be more able to deal with his ongoing responsibilities.

Had the senior neonatologist felt that he missed something truly important, their conversation would have been different, as it would not have been appropriate or helpful to lie to him. She is able to unburden him not only because he trusts her clinical judgment, but also because he trusts her to tell him the truth. But even if the conversation were different, it may still have offered some relief and could perhaps have ended with a statement like, "That could have happened to anyone," or "I've done the same thing myself." Fortunately, in this case as in most, she was able to tell him honestly that his management was sound and that he had missed nothing of consequence.

At some point in the next several weeks the case will be reviewed at a morbidity and mortality conference. There the patient's care will be discussed, likely in greater detail and with greater scrutiny. More data, such as the results of an autopsy, may be available. The committee of neonatologists, pathologists, and radiologists may well identify things that could have been done differently—things that, if they are done differently in a future case, may lead to a different outcome. This formal process, however, is distinct from the unburdening ritual that experienced physicians sometimes share in the hours immediately following an unsuccessful attempt to save a child, when the responsible physician is the most vulnerable.

The guilt some parents feel after the death of a newborn, however misplaced, can be an emotional burden to them for years to come. Most experienced neonatologists recognize the importance of unburdening parents of this guilt. In so doing, they fulfill an old teaching about pediatric death: After the physician is finished caring for the child, he must still care for the parents. The unburdening of the physician by a trusted colleague, in contrast, is less often taught. But like so much in medicine, it is transmitted through the culture and by example, though inconsistently so. It is not always performed, is not always necessary, and one could surely argue that it is less important than the unburdening of the parents. But, when performed by a skilled and empathetic physician who observes a colleague in need, it can provide reassurance, relief, and release.

From *Hastings Center Report*, March/April 2008, pp. 8–9. Copyright © 2008 by The Hastings Center. Reprinted by permission of the publisher and Mark Mercurio.

To Live with No Regrets
Death Is a Transition for the Dying— and for Those Left Behind

Nina Utne

I recently stopped by the house of our friends Jack Heckelman and Linda Bergh for an evening of singing and music. Like the others gathered there, I was part of an extended community the two had created over the years. Jack was up and sitting with the group, weaker than when we last saw him, taking oxygen but present and alert. Linda told us that her husband had reached a turning point that day. He'd moved from holding on to life to preparing himself for impending death. Jack died four days later.

When Jack was diagnosed with cancer last fall, Jack and Linda decided that they wanted to share their journey with family and friends. They looked upon his dying as a natural event in life and wanted to be open about it, rather than being in denial. So friends and family were linked by special gatherings to support Jack and Linda on the journey, and by a Web site where the process was shared with friends around the world.

Six months later, as Jack's cancer spread, he and Linda began to welcome death with intention and gratitude. Before he and Linda took their last trip together, Jack completed his ethical will—a tradition of stating the values and beliefs that the dying hope will live on among those they leave behind. As friends came to visit or to join in a night of singing, they asked Jack questions: Are you afraid? Why not? What do you see happening to you after you die? Jack gladly answered, understanding their curiosity about such a huge transition.

"Those conversations were remarkable," Linda says. "They shouldn't be unusual, but they were." They shared some of these thoughts on the Web site.

Linda also wrote about the challenges of being a caregiver. And in the weeks just before his death, she candidly shared with Jack her struggle to reconcile her roles as caregiver and spouse—telling him the truth and working things through even when he was dying.

Their openness was partly a reflection of the fact that both were well-acquainted with death. Jack had nursed his first wife of 40 years for more than a decade as a degenerative muscle disease slowly took her life. At first he turned his engineer's mind to creating an accessible mobile home in which they could travel despite her illness. By the end he was feeding her through a stomach tube and communicating with blinks and hand pressure. Throughout it all, his passion for the earth and desire to be of service to it remained strong. So did his taste for adventure. He celebrated his 75th birthday by skydiving.

After falling in love with Linda, he just as enthusiastically uprooted himself to start a new life with her in a new city. Though she was much younger than Jack, she too had endured some of life's hardest lessons. I met Linda 17 years ago when she was my son Sam's kindergarten teacher. In 1995 her husband died suddenly of cardiac arrest, a shock for her and for their only child, Kirsten, then 16. A year later, Kirsten and a close friend were killed in a car accident. Linda, a passenger in the car, was the only one to survive, albeit after a long and difficult recovery.

Some people are darkened by unbearable grief; others become incandescent. Linda is one of the latter: her presence, her humor, her honesty, her joy and sadness all pouring through a shattered heart. But how?

I found clues in *She Would Draw Flowers,* a book of Kirsten's poems and drawings that Linda published after her daughter's death. Even apart from the tragic circumstances, Kirsten's poems are truly beautiful testaments of love—for her friends, for her lost father, and, most poignantly, for her own vital young self. It's a marvel to follow her thoughts as she confronts the trauma of her father's sudden death and transforms it into a deepening joy for life and its possibilities. Kirsten was a gifted artist. In one of the final poems in the collection, she concludes, "So, I carry you in me, not as the fading memory of a father, but rather as a growing, glowing child, until we become one, and I can let you go."

The words that helped Kirsten also helped Linda endure what is often said to be the most crushing bereavement, losing a child. "As a mother, each day facing this unimaginable loss, I question how I might remain connected to my beloved daughter while leaving her free to journey on," she writes in the introduction. Kirsten's drawings and poems were among the few tangible ties left to her daughter, she adds. "But the profound path of her inner transformation shared in these poems has also served as my guide for letting her go."

After the accident, Linda says, she realized that everything in her life was now open. And so, when she and Jack married, they shared openly their process of living and relationship with those who were interested. "It became something so simple and so rare," she says, "something we are all so hungry for: conscious community and conversation. Aren't we all growing and struggling in our relationships?"

When Jack and Linda fell in love, it was cause for celebration for an extended community. Their wedding at a friend's farm included a visit from a dragonfly that flew onto Jack's back and stayed there. The couple created a ceremonial arch using branches from a tall rose bush that Linda had planted years before in the rain, at a time of great grief, on the first of Kirsten's birthdays she spent alone. Now, both the dragonfly and the roses became symbols of the new happiness Jack and Linda found together. On each anniversary they re-exchanged their vows in the garden next to Kirsten's rose bush.

As word spread among us that Jack's life was nearing its end, a niece agreed to build his casket. She felt an urgency to finish it, though others assured her there was plenty of time. As it turned out, Jack's last act before going to bed the day before he died was to receive his casket, lined with rainbow silk as he had requested, and carved with maple leaves and dragonflies.

He grew restless in his final hours, with Linda curled sleeplessly on the bed beside him. "It is enough," he finally said, answering a question he'd posed earlier to his sister, wondering aloud if he'd know when it was time to slip away. "Honey, you can just go home," Linda told him, and he grew calm. She left his side to doze for a few minutes on the couch. When she went back half an hour later, Jack had died peacefully in his sleep. Shortly after that, Linda says, she was feeling deep regret that she hadn't been with Jack at the moment of his last breath. Suddenly she heard inside herself an unfamiliar voice saying clearly and firmly, "No regrets." In a flash, she realized that to live and die without regrets had become Jack's life mission.

The community began to gather to help wash the body and prepare for a three-day, around-the-clock vigil during which people took turns sitting in the living room with Jack's body, displayed in the coffin embellished with dragonflies. There was singing and reading and meditating and playing music; there were tears and laughter, and anyone who wanted to could drop by at any time. It was strangely comforting and peaceful to be there. Those who hadn't been sure about coming didn't want to leave. It was time to be together as a community and to say good-bye to Jack.

There was a moment early in the morning the day after he died when, Linda says, "I felt so deeply at peace, as if something was breathing me. My body and the air were one thing. There was just the quiet and my presence in it. And that peace has stayed for me to tap back into when I get anxious or sad."

Though the hard realities of paying bills and planning a new life without Jack are often with her, so are these moments of grace. "I want to give a sense of that place to everyone, a sense of that inner quiet that just is," she says.

One way she anchors that place in herself is by beginning the day with a poem or passage that embodies the qualities that she wants to cultivate in herself. For the year before his death, Jack and Linda recited together a verse written by Rudolf Steiner that begins, "Quiet I bear within me . . ." Now Linda says the St. Francis prayer: "Lord, make me an instrument of thy peace." Through intention and repetition, "the words become cellular," Linda says. "It is such a simple gift, but so powerful."

A few days ago, two months after his death, on the anniversary of her marriage to Jack, Linda went out, alone, to Kirsten's roses. She was repeating her wedding vows when a dragonfly lit on the bush she'd planted. "I have never seen a dragonfly in our garden before," she says. "And I don't care what logic says about all of this. Love is not logical. I believe in whatever created that dragonfly in that moment. I believe in the rainbow that can hold the joy and the grief as one. And I believe that we can internalize all those on the other side in this life. They are always with us, and we just have to open to them."

What is a good death? When I put that question to Linda the other day, she listed three components: lack of fear, openness to spirit, and love of community. After a moment she quietly added that, whatever our circumstances, those same qualities lie at the heart of a good life.

NINA UTNE is chair and CEO of *Utne*. You can visit Jack and Linda's Web site at www.caringbridge.org/mn/jackheckelman/history.htm. Kirsten Savitri Bergh's book *She Would Draw Flowers* is available through Steiner Books (www.anthropress.com).

"Cast Me Not Off in Old Age"

ERIC COHEN & LEON R. KASS

Death and dying are once again subjects of intense public attention. During his confirmation hearings, Chief Justice John Roberts was grilled about his views on removing life-sustaining treatments from debilitated patients and warned by various liberal Senators not to interfere with the "right to die." In California and Vermont, state legislators are working to legalize assisted suicide, while the Bush administration is trying to restrict the practice by prohibiting doctors from using federally-controlled narcotics to end their patients' lives. All this comes in the aftermath of the bitter fight over Terri Schiavo, a profoundly disabled woman whose husband removed the feeding tube that kept her alive, but only after years of legal battles with Schiavo's parents and myriad political efforts to stop him.

The Schiavo case revealed deep divisions in how Americans view debility and death. Some saw pulling her feeding tube as an act of mercy, others as an act of murder. Some believed she possessed equal human dignity and deserved equal care despite her total lack of self-awareness; others believed keeping her alive year after year was itself an indignity. For many, what mattered most was discerning "what Terri would have wanted"; for many others, what mattered was loving the needy woman on the television screen, not abandoning her when the burdens of care seemed too great.

Yet the Schiavo case was also highly unusual—involving a young woman, afflicted suddenly, in the prime of her life. In our aging society, most severe disability involves instead the frail elderly, who gradually but inexorably decline into enfeeblement and dementia, often leaving grown children to preside over their extended demise. The greatest challenges involve not only deciding when to let loved ones die, but figuring out how to care every day for those who can no longer care for themselves.

Although growing old is a natural part of being human, the circumstances in which most Americans age and die are increasingly "unnatural" and surely unprecedented. Longer life expectancies and lower birth rates lead to the graying of society; smaller and less stable families weaken the ties that bind. Death comes on the doctor's watch and in high-tech surroundings, almost always following years of chronic illness, typically preceded by decisions about further medical intervention, increasingly made on behalf of patients incapable of making decisions for themselves. Caregivers often do not know how to honor those who have lost their most human qualities. Thanks to medicine's prowess in sustaining life on the edge, it is harder than ever to know when it is "time to die."

II

The miseries of aging and decline were hardly unknown to our ancestors, and are eloquently attested in the biblical plea from which we have taken our title. When asked if he would choose to live over

again, Thomas Jefferson said yes, but only between ages twenty-five and sixty. Thereafter, he wrote, "the powers of life are sensibly on the wane, sight becomes dim, hearing dull, memory constantly enlarging its frightful blank and parting with all we have ever seen or known, spirits evaporate, bodily debility creeps on palsying every limb, and so faculty after faculty quits us, and where then is life?" Yet in Jefferson's time, most people never reached this extended period of debility, because they died suddenly in the nursery of life or at the peak of their flourishing. Living to old age was the dream of the vulnerable many; living with old age was the problem of the fortunate few.

In developed societies today, by contrast, old age is the norm. Average life expectancy in the United States is now seventy-eight years and rising (up from forty-seven in 1900), and those over age eighty-five are already the fastest growing segment of the population. People are not only living longer; they are staying healthier well into their sixties, seventies, and eighties, and they expect to enjoy many years of vigorous retirement. On balance, it is a wonderful time to be old, and the democratization and expansion of old age are among modernity's greatest achievements.

Yet the coming of the mass geriatric society is also a source of tremendous anxiety. Americans worry about the soaring costs of Social Security and Medicare, the collapse of private pensions, the shortage of good nursing homes, and the potential clash between the young and the old over resources and priorities. Our deepest worries are personal: we dread spending our final years in a degraded state, resented by caregivers or abandoned by loved ones, of little use to ourselves, never mind to others.

Such worries are not unjustified. Although most Americans can expect to live healthily well past sixty-five, many will also live long enough to endure a prolonged period of frailty. According to a recent Rand study, roughly 40 percent of deaths in the United States are now preceded by a period of enfeeblement, debility, and (often) dementia lasting up to a decade. Prominent are those suffering from Alzheimer's disease, a condition that steadily destroys the mind and body, strips individuals of self-awareness and self-control, and often requires that they spend their final years in an institution, incapable of feeding or bathing themselves or of using a toilet. Today, over 4 million Americans suffer from Alzheimer's; by mid-century, that number is expected to rise to over 13 million—all of them requiring many years of extensive, expensive, and exhausting full-time care.

Yet precisely as the need is rising, the pool of available family caregivers is dwindling. Families are smaller, less stable, and more geographically spread out. Most women are now employed outside the home. The well-to-do can afford to hire professionals, but there are already shortages of geriatricians and nurses. Those jobs requiring great humanity but offering little paid reward—like feeding Alzheimer's patients or changing bedpans—are greatly undersubscribed.

All this creates a perfect social storm. As the number of retired baby-boomers expands, they will seek to augment existing social programs for the elderly, creating novel fiscal challenges for Medicare and Medicaid. Politically, long-term-care benefits might become the sequel to prescription-drug benefits—and far costlier. At the same time, the burdens of caring for needy elders will test the strength of already fragile modern families. Those in middle age may wonder about the wisdom (or duty) of sacrificing so much, for so long, on behalf of lives that seem so diminished. And they may come to believe that the death of the elderly is preferable to life in what seems like such a miserable condition.

In the face of such burdens, two "solutions" appeal today to different strains of American pragmatism. Both are seductive, and both, in instructive ways, are misguided.

III

In an age of medical triumphs, it is not surprising that our first approach to the dilemmas of old age is to think we can cure our way out of them. Commemorating the 40th anniversary of Medicare and Medicaid last July, Dr. Mark B. McClellan, the top official at the Centers for Medicare and Medicaid Services, said that "Medicare can do so much more than give you dignity in old age." It can, he continued, extend life; it can improve health; it can save money by preventing and curing debilitating diseases.

This is the medical gospel of healthy aging. In its triumphalist vision, things for older Americans are, in McClellan's words, "always getting better." Nearly everyone in public life embraces this faith in the saving powers of medical progress, although conservatives tend to emphasize drug development and free-market medicine while liberals emphasize embryonic stem-cell research and cheap drugs from Canada.

Many of McClellan's reform initiatives are quite sensible, including the promotion of preventive health measures, enhanced "customer service" for Medicare recipients, and new efforts to improve post-surgical care. And the twin goals of attacking debility and caring for the debilitated are not intrinsically or necessarily opposed to each other. But it is also foolish to act and speak as if medical progress (whether in prevention or in cure) will liberate us from the realities of decline, debility, and death or from the unavoidable duties of caregiving at the end of life.

First, medical progress often leads to *greater* debility in later years even as—and precisely because—it cures deadly diseases at earlier ages. This is the paradox of modern aging: *we are vigorous longer and we are incapacitated longer.* To be sure, no one wants to turn back the clock to a time when mothers and children died regularly in childbirth, when infectious diseases decimated helpless communities, when heart disease was largely undiagnosed and untreated, and when a diagnosis of cancer meant swift and certain death. But severing medicine's sweetest fruits from its sourest consequences may prove impossible.

Second, to see medical progress as a "cost saver" is simplistic at best. Medical care is more expensive than ever precisely because we can do so much more to diagnose and treat disease, and Medicare and Medicaid are costlier because more people are living longer. Even if curing today's diseases becomes less expensive over time, no one knows the cost of dealing with the diseases that will replace them. Only if people live free of illness to the very end and then die suddenly will medical progress really result in cheaper medicine. Otherwise, it will continue to purchase greater longevity and better health at an increased overall expense.

Finally, there is something weird about treating old age as a time of life when things should always be "getting better." While aging affords some people new possibilities for learning and "growth," it also means—eventually and inevitably—the loss of one's vital powers. Some people may ride horses or climb mountains into their seventies and eighties, just like in the commercials for anti-arthritis medication, but such idealized images offer a partial and misleading picture of the realities of senescence, that series of small dyings on the way to death. Endless chatter about "healthy aging" is at bottom a form of denial. Ultimately, the nursing home refutes the dream of limitless progress toward ageless bodies, and America will surely be building many more nursing homes in the years ahead.

None of this implies ingratitude for the blessings of medical progress—including current research aimed at curing age-related diseases like Alzheimer's. But in fueling our love of youthfulness and limitless life, and our hatred of senescence and decline, the campaign for healthy aging also subtly encourages us to devalue the need to give care and comfort to those we cannot cure. When, moreover, aging does not bring the good tidings we were promised, we may seek instead an even more absolute control over death and come to embrace the pseudo-mastery of "death-on-demand" as the cure for our unconquerable miseries.

IV

The goals of mastery and control in the face of death also lie behind the second prominent "solution" to the dilemmas of aging and debility: the legal gospel of the living will.

During the national drama over Terri Schiavo, the real problem, in the eyes of many, was that her wishes were never put clearly in writing; the moral lesson was therefore that everyone should prepare a living will, saying exactly what should be done if and when incapacity strikes. Living wills are as "vital as regular exams," editorialized the *San Antonio Express-News.* According to the *San Francisco Chronicle,* "The case of Terri Schiavo may have one important legacy: spurring more people to talk with family members and put down in writing what they would want if they become incapacitated." And so on, in virtually every major newspaper in the country.

This enthusiasm for living wills did not emerge overnight. In the 1960's and 70's, many people began to fear the prospect of living indefinitely on machines in a profoundly diminished condition. They feared the indignity of becoming a permanent burden on loved ones, a living body without a life, a helpless ward of the nursing home. To prevent this dehumanizing possibility, people began putting their treatment preferences in writing, to be followed by surrogates in the event of serious illness or injury. During the 1970's, state legislatures and courts began to extend formal recognition to these "living wills." Since then, this legal instrument has gained a passionate chorus of defenders and advocates—including lawyers, doctors, hospitals, patient-advocacy groups, and most bioethicists.

At first glance, the case for living wills seems compelling, especially in a nation that places such a high value on individual autonomy. Living wills extend our irrevocable right to speak for ourselves, even when our powers of speech and reason are gone. They honor our preferences regarding how we wish to die, by allowing us to dictate all future medical interventions. They protect debilitated patients from having other people's wishes imposed on them, whether in the form of overtreatment or undertreatment. They give family members explicit permission to fight on or let go, especially in medically ambiguous situations where they might otherwise be incapable of making morally wrenching decisions about life and death. They protect financial resources from being squandered, whether on heroic interventions made in crisis or on seemingly endless long-term care.

But after three decades, there is increasing evidence that living wills have failed to meet these practical objectives. The social-science data—compiled by Carl Schneider, Rebecca Dresser, and many others—are compelling. To begin with, most people do not have living wills, despite a very active campaign to promote them. In 2001, the completion rate nationwide remained under 25 percent, and even the chronically ill do not draft living wills in significantly higher numbers. Then, too, even those who complete living wills often do not express clear treatment preferences, or, unable to comprehend the clinical conditions they might face in the future, leave vague instructions or change their preferences depending on how a given medical situation is described. To complicate matters further, living wills often do not get transmitted to those making medical decisions; in one study, only 26 percent of medical charts contained accurate information about a living will, and only 16 percent included the actual document.

Finally, and most telling, the written instructions contained in living wills—even when they are consulted!—often have little effect on the actual decisions made. In one study, decisions made by surrogates using a pre-drafted living will were no more likely to reflect the patient's prior wishes than decisions made by family members judging on their own. What mattered most was a lifetime of familiarity: family members predict patient preferences better than physicians, and primary care doctors better than anonymous experts reading legal documents.

The shortcomings of living wills have still deeper roots. The animating ideas behind them—preserving autonomy until the end, giving precedence to prior wishes over present needs—are deeply problematic. Imagine, for example, a professor who has watched his own father die of Alzheimer's and vows never to live like that, never to burden a child with his own care, never to behave shamefully the way his father did in the throes of that terrible disease. So he drafts a living will stating clearly that, once he starts to have trouble recognizing his daughter, he is to receive no more medical interventions. When the time comes, should the daughter really leave him to die when he contracts a urinary infection, rather than give him antibiotics? Is she simply to be the executor of her father's wishes, or is she first of all a moral agent with her own moral responsibilities?

And what about the professor himself? One can admire his desire to spare his child the burdens of long-term care and the pain of witnessing his extended demise. But he is probably deluded in thinking that seizing an earlier occasion for his death will prove less painful to her. One can also admire his willingness to confront mortality rather than pretend he will live forever. But he is assuredly mistaken in believing that he can control every detail of his own future care with a voice from the past—or that he can rightly assess the worth of a diminished future life from the height of his own flourishing. No less admirable is his pride in his *self*-control. But being human also means accepting and enduring one's own vulnerabilities and dependencies.

When the time does finally come, no legal instructions written in advance—no matter how perfect—can replace the need for loving and devoted caregivers. Inasmuch as the gospel of the living will denies this truth, it perpetuates an illusion of perfect independence, isolating individuals at the very moment when they need others most of all.

As it happens, this unavoidable reliance on others is recognized by a different—and superior—form of advance directive: the "proxy directive" or "health-care power of attorney." Instead of dictating various potential courses of action, it empowers surrogates to make medical decisions on our behalf, naming them as the parties with whom doctors and nurses must deal when we cannot speak for ourselves. Reflecting the reality of human interdependence, this approach clarifies the responsibility of physicians and family members to make judgments for patients whose own judgment is gone.

All that having been said, however, trusting others makes sense only if there are others who are trustworthy—willing to care, able to care, wise enough to care well. Sad to say, this is often not the case—either in medicine or in families.

V

One of the ironies of medical progress is that we stand in greatest need of family doctors and general practitioners just as medical super-specialization has turned them into endangered species. Especially for the frail elderly, comprehensive and continuous care is virtually impossible to obtain. One doctor treats our failing heart, another our wheezy lungs, a third our sluggish bowels, a fourth our tired blood, and a fifth our fraying nerves, but often no physician is willing or able to look after *us*. In eldercare and especially in nursing homes, burnout is common and high turnover rates prevent continuity of care, not only from doctors but also from nurses and social workers. Even the wealthy are not protected. As they age, many will outlive their physicians, and replacement doctors will have no familiarity with their lives. If trustworthy and dependable long-term care is to be had, only the steadfast efforts of devoted family members can secure it—or, in many instances, provide it themselves.

Yet, in an aging society, we stand in greatest need of families just as family life has been most weakened. There are the well-known and widespread phenomena of divorce and family rupture, lower birth rates, geographical mobility, and the weakened social importance of extended family. Moreover, many of today's old people—and many aging baby boomers—never had children, and many more have little claim on their children's loyalty. When a neglectful parent needs care from the children he neglected, the sins of the absent father or rejecting mother are often repaid in kind.

Even in the best of intact families, the picture is sobering. When a husband or wife acquires Alzheimer's disease or some other progressive disability, the front line of care is generally manned by the spouse—if he or she is healthy enough for the task. Fidelity between spouses, displayed most poignantly when the marriage bed becomes a nursing station, is anticipated in the wedding vow, wherein husband and wife pledge their mutual devotion "for better, for worse." However invisible to them when they choose to marry, caregiving at the end of life is part of the marital vocation, and many a husband and wife rises to the occasion with strength and dignity.

Eventually, however, even the most blessed and long-lived marriages produce a widow or a widower, and then the prospects of faithful long-term care become truly uncertain. Studies indicate that only someone with three or more daughters or daughters-in-law can reasonably expect to escape institutionalization for long-term care. This is not the consequence of mere filial ingratitude or heartless indifference. In truth, it is passing strange for a whole society of adult children to be summoned to care on a long-term basis for those who once cared for them.

In contrast to caring for the young, the care of the elderly by their grown children is unrewarded by the joyful experience of seeing a new life unfold and flourish. Even in the best cases, when children gladly discharge their obligation to "honor thy father and mother," there is unavoidable sadness and indignity. As the Yiddish proverb has it, "When the father helps the son, both laugh. When the son helps the father, both cry." No child wants to uncover the nakedness of his father or mother. No mother or father wants to stand incompetent before the children.

More fundamentally, there is also a disruption of the naturally forward-looking thrust of intergenerational life. The burdens of caring for one's parents, and of being cared for by one's children, risk obscuring the stake that both the old and the middle-aged have in the rising third generation. For a grown child best "repays" the gifts of his parents by raising children of his own, and grandparents have a greater interest in seeing grandchildren flourish than in maximizing the comfort of their own last days.

In these circumstances, trying to discern what is required by intergenerational fidelity can give rise to anguishing dilemmas. A daughter raising young children of her own might see the pneumonia afflicting her father, who already suffers from advanced Alzheimer's, as nature's way of restoring the generational balance, to be accepted with sorrow rather than opposed with penicillin. Or, conversely, she might wish to demonstrate to her children what it signifies to love another in his gravest need, and to appreciate the blessings of health in the face of the miseries of disease.

Many people experience caring for aged parents as a vocation—a duty lovingly fulfilled, giving life its true meaning. Many others experience it as a curse—a duty grudgingly accepted (or not), robbing life of its true pleasures. In some cases, the demands of caring for the elderly reveal the family at its best, faithful to the end; in others, the very presence of the helpless elderly suffocates everything else in family life. Yet what would family become if the old were abandoned in the name of the young, or the weak left to die in the name of the flourishing?

In the years ahead, the greatest dilemmas will confront the middle-aged of the middle class—those who are wealthy enough to have choices (like hiring paid professionals), yet limited enough to make every choice a real sacrifice (like having to forgo extra income to stay at home with an aging mother, or depleting retirement savings to pay for a father's assisted living). Compelled to make such choices, even the most devoted may feel both resentment and guilt—resentment at what they must give up, guilt that they may not have done enough. Inevitably, the questions will arise: are these sacrifices "worth it"? Are we really helping Dad by extending a life that seems so diminished? Is that life still worth living?

VI

Until now, our society has been largely spared such questions. And when they have been raised, usually in private, we have had solid moral answers, backed by our religious and political traditions as well as by the venerable teachings of medical ethics. When it comes to the right to life and human care, most Americans are committed—at least in the abstract—to the view that all human beings are "created equal." And since the days of Hippocrates, physicians for their part have eschewed judging the worth of the lives they treat and have refused "to give a deadly drug if asked" or even "to make a suggestion to that effect." Never are the disabled deemed unworthy of medical or humane care; on the contrary, their need for care is precisely the reason we are obliged to provide it.

But as we saw in the Schiavo debate, this general agreement regarding equal human worth can disappear in certain cases.

Although many continue to believe that every human life, regardless of debility, possesses equal dignity, others now argue openly that equal treatment for all is best advanced by not diverting precious resources to the severely disabled. Still others believe that the indignities of old age—especially dementia—belie all sanctimonious talk of "equal worth."

Among these people are the advocates of euthanasia or mercy killing. For the time being, America seems immune to embracing this particular "solution" to the burdens of an aging society. Even in those states—like California and Vermont—that have considered joining Oregon in legalizing assisted suicide, the justification is "personal choice," not a category of human beings officially defined by hospitals or the state as "life unworthy of living" or "better off dead." At the same time, however, more and more commentators are deploring the amount of money spent on medical care for people near the end of life. As the American population ages, we can expect to hear even more talk of people with "low quality of life," unworthy of the resources "wasted" on them. What begins today as a campaign to give individuals a right to ease themselves out of life can easily turn into a campaign to get the enfeebled and demented to exercise their "right to die," or, since they are unable to do the deadly deed themselves, to "exercise it for them."

Against this danger, the assertion that "life is sacred and should always be sustained" will prove an insufficient defense. Indeed, even those who pledge their belief in the sanctity of every human being will often wonder whether intervening medically really benefits the life they hold to be so precious. Is it love or is it cruelty, for instance, to cure the pneumonia in an elderly person suffering from a painful form of terminal cancer—especially one so demented that the mitigating comforts of family and friendship cannot be appreciated? Is it love or is it cruelty to extend a life marked by incontinence of bladder and bowel, uncontrollable outbursts of rage, or psychophysical misery caused by Alzheimer's? Is it love or is it cruelty to force a patient with mild dementia to continue kidney dialysis that he vigorously resists, knowing that he cannot understand either how the dialysis can help him or that ceasing treatment will bring imminent death? Faced with these painful choices, and in moments of weakness, hastening death's arrival may seem the compassionate thing to do.

Traditional medical ethics, ever mindful of this temptation, has been very clear about the duty to resist it: never to kill, always to care. If doctors and others are faithfully to benefit the life the patient still has, they cannot sit in ultimate judgment of its worth, and cannot ever think that lethal intervention is an acceptable "therapeutic option." This holds true even for those (non-demented) patients who knowingly ask doctors or family members to help them die—whether in the present because they are suffering now, or in the future because they cannot bear the thought of living with dementia.

But traditional medical ethics has also long taught that benefiting the life a debilitated person still has does not mean taking every possible medical action to extend it. Senescence leads inevitably to death, medicine or no medicine. And so, while "active killing" may be incompatible with true caregiving, "letting die" is always part of it. In this reasoning, life-sustaining treatment may be—and often should be—forgone or terminated if the interventions themselves impose undue burdens on the patient or interfere with the comfortable death of someone irretrievably dying. Guidance in this area comes from distinguishing between the burdens of a treatment (imposed by caregivers and for which they are thus responsible) and the burdens of living with a terrible disease (imposed by nature and for which they are not responsible).

Yet as we enter the mass geriatric society, it is clear that our new technological capacities are putting pressure on these sensible distinctions. A century ago, Dr. William Osier could write: "Pneumonia may well be called the friend of the aged. Taken off by it in an acute, short, not often painful illness, the old man escapes these cold gradations of decay so distressing to himself and to his friends." Today, thanks to antibiotics, the aged have no natural friends—or few that are not more commonly regarded as enemies. Life-sustaining interventions, if effective and not especially burdensome, have come to be regarded as standard care and morally obligatory. As a result, well-meaning and morally sound decisions to treat intervening illnesses—like curing the professor's urinary infection despite his living will—can make us complicit in the continuing miseries and degradations of those we love.

Here then is the most poignant dilemma faced by caregivers: not wishing to condemn the worth of people's lives, yet not wanting to bind them to the rack of their growing misery; not wishing to say they are better off dead, yet not wanting always to oppose their going hither. Under these circumstances, with no simple formulas for finding the best course of action, individuals and families must find their way, case by case and moment to moment, often with only unattractive options to choose from and knowing that whatever path they choose, they will feel the weight of the path not chosen.

VII

Even if the burdens of aging and death are always borne most fully by individuals and families, how we age and die are not only private matters. Our communal practices and social policies shape the environments in which aging and care-giving take place—not only in moments of crisis, when life-or-death decisions need to be made, but in the long days of struggle and everyday attendance. Faith-based institutions and community groups support families in meeting those needs they cannot meet alone. Programs like Medicaid assist those who are old and impoverished, in need of nursing that they cannot themselves afford.

In the years ahead, this need for social supports will only increase, especially if we are to fight the temptation to turn caregiving entirely into a state responsibility. Affordable insurance, respite relief for caregivers, reliable and reimbursable home services, technologies to assist in giving basic bodily care—all these and more can enhance the economic and social supports of those coping with extended debility. Recruitment of volunteers to aid in eldercare is a perfect objective for the many groups, both liberal and conservative, interested in promoting civic engagement and renewing civil society.

But we cannot pretend that individual families, or society as a whole, will have unlimited resources, particularly in a populace with more elderly persons and fewer young workers. Americans will need to make hard choices among competing goods, and to confront the limits of even our own affluent society. And even then the biggest challenges before us will not be economic in nature but cultural and spiritual—how to deepen our understanding of what it means to age and die, how to combat the overly medicalized view of old age that now dominates our attitudes and our institutions, how to recover the wisdom contained in the human life cycle.

As we noted earlier, Americans increasingly regard old age as a bundle of needs and problems demanding solution, or as a time of life whose meaning is defined largely by the struggle to stay healthy and fit. This outlook has generated discontent with the life cycle itself, producing an insatiable desire for more and more medical miracles, and creating the fantasy that we can transcend our limitations—or that death itself may be pushed back indefinitely. More deeply, this same outlook has engendered the illusion that independence is the whole truth about our lives, causing us to undervalue those attachments and obligations that bind and complete us.

We live already in a world in which the life cycle has largely lost its ethical meaning. Aware as we may be that we are on a solitary journey that ends inevitably in the grave, few of us take our bearings from nature's eternal teaching that there is a time to be born and a time to die. We learn little from the rhythm of growth and decay, everything in its season, our own finitude transcended and redeemed by generation upon generation of new birth and renewal, transforming each singular finite trajectory into a permanently recurring cycle of life.

This cultural myopia is no trivial matter. Indeed, in the mass geriatric society it could have deadly consequences. For unless we learn to accept both our frailties and our finitude, we are likely to find the burdens of caregiving intolerable. And unless we learn how to let loved ones die when the time comes, we will be tempted to kill—self-righteously, of course, in the guise of a false compassion. Sooner or later, when the medical gospel of healthy aging and the legal gospel of living wills are shown to have been false teachings, we may easily fall prey to the utilitarian gospel of euthanasia, whose prophets are patiently waiting in the wings for their time upon our cultural stage. Paradoxically, a dogmatic insistence that patients must be kept alive regardless of the depth of their disabilities—that severe dementia or unmanageable suffering deserves no consideration in deciding when to "let nature take its course"—may only make mercy killing appear to be the more compassionate remedy for the miseries of extended decline.

In the end, there is no "solution" to the problems of old age, at least no solution that any civilized society could tolerate. But there are better and worse ways to see our aging condition. The better way begins in thinking of ourselves less as wholly autonomous individuals than as members of families; in relinquishing our mistaken belief that medicine can miraculously liberate our loved ones or ourselves from debility and decline, and instead taking up our role as caregivers; and in abjuring the fantasy that we can control the manner and the hour of our dying, learning instead to accept death in its proper season as mortal beings replaced and renewed by the generations that follow.

ERIC COHEN is the director of the program in biotechnology and American democracy at the Ethics and Public Policy Center, editor of the *New Atlantis,* and senior research consultant to the President's Council on Bioethics. **LEON R. KASS,** the Hertog fellow at the American Enterprise Institute and professor in the Committee on Social Thought at the University of Chicago served until recently as chairman of the President's. Council on Bioethics. Parts of this article rely on the newly released Council report, *Taking Care: Ethical Caregiving in Our Aging Society,* available online at www.bioethics.gov.

Caregiving Systems at the End of Life

How Informal Caregivers and Formal Providers Collaborate

DEBORAH P. WALDROP

End-of-life care has been moving out of hospitals and families are replacing professionals in the delivery of sometimes unfamiliar and complex care for their terminally ill relatives (Holland, 2002; McCorkle & Pasacreta, 2001; McMillan & Moody, 2003). About one-quarter of all Americans die at home (Centers for Disease Control, 2004). Hospice programs provide medical, instrumental, educational, emotional, and spiritual support for terminally ill people and their families during the final stages of life; over half of the people who receive this care die at home (National Hospice and Palliative Care Organization [NHPCO], 2004). For home care to be a positive alternative to institutionalized end-of-life care (in hospitals or long-term-care facilities), family needs, desires, and preferences must be understood and considered in care planning (Grbich, Maddocks, & Parker, 2001; Wennman-Larsen & Tishelman, 2002). Alleviating the problems of families who provide end-of-life care has begun to draw substantial professional attention (Kinsella, Cooper, Picton, & Murtagh, 1998; Lynn et al., 1997).

Family needs are central to the dying process and providing care becomes a final shared experience. Supporting the naturally occurring family caregiving network is a crucial component of good care for people who are dying (Americans for Better Care of the Dying, 2003; Early, Smith, Todd, & Beem, 2000). Because terminal illness has historically been viewed as a medical event that is to be managed by health care providers, families have not typically been seen as collaborators in the process (Stetz & Brown, 2004). Research in end-of-life care has primarily focused on the terminally ill person and has not addressed the needs of the family as a whole. Further, research on caregiving in long-term illness has most often focused on the needs of one "primary" caregiver, but has not examined them in the context of other family members and their informal support system. Learning from families who have provided end-of-life care can deepen our understanding about the interrelationship between informal and formal care during a terminal illness.

Guided by the social care model (Cantor, 1991; Cantor & Brennan, 2000), this article examines how families and friends, together with health care and human service providers, become a caregiving system at the end of life. After a brief literature review of caregiving networks, results of a study about the interrelationship between informal and formal caregiving are reported. This line of inquiry moves away from focusing only on the primary caregiver and views the family network at the core of the caregiving process. It has implications for health care and human service professionals who may encounter terminally ill persons and their family members in a variety of settings and at different stages of terminal illnesses.

Literature Review

Overall, research on caregiving has often portrayed informal and formal caregiving as separate processes, subsequently missing the essential interrelationship between them (see Lyons & Zarit, 1999, for a review). Studies have examined how one type of caregiving influences the other, for example focusing on how deterioration of the informal caregiving network predicts increased formal service use or how community care influences nursing home utilization (Bass, Noelker, & Rechlin, 1996; Jette, Tennstedt, & Crawford, 1995; Zarit & Pearlin, 1993). Other research has focused on family dynamics (Aneshensel, Pearlin, Mullan, Zarit, & Whitlatch, 1995; McGoldrick & Carter, 2003). Numerous studies have explored the issues of families who care for someone with dementia, but relatively few have investigated changes that accompany other types of terminal illnesses (Brown & Stetz, 1999; Chenetsova-Dutton et al., 2000; Rainer & McMurry, 2002; Teno, Casey, Welch, & Edgman-Levitan, 2001). The changes brought by terminal illness reverberate through families and the informal social network.

Theoretical Framework

Concepts from the social care model were employed to address some of the gaps in the caregiving literature. The term *social care* is sometimes used to describe formal services, but Cantor (1991) has demonstrated how informal and formal activities coexist. Emphasizing the reciprocal relationship between an older (or terminally ill) person, his or her family, their social support network, and professional or formal caregivers, this model envisions an individual at the center of a series of concentric circles, each representing a different kind of support. The informal system most often consists of kin (spouse and children) followed by friends and neighbors. The quasi-formal or tertiary level of care encompasses mediating support elements, such as churches and neighborhoods or senior centers. At the midrange, quasi-formal support has elements of social support (friendly conversations and expressions of care) and formal care (support is offered by individuals within formal organizations). The formal support system includes voluntary and governmental organizations as well as political and economic institutions (Cantor, 1991; Cantor & Brennan, 2000). This study advances the social care model by using the concepts to articulate the interconnections among individuals, families, sources of quasi-formal support, and formal caregivers as death approaches.

Informal Caregiving Networks

Families provide the majority of care for terminally ill patients. When family members cannot be available, others assist with care (Emanuel et al., 1999; Kissane, Bloch, McKenzie, McDowall, & Nietzan, 1998; Teno et al., 2001). Two hypotheses have been advanced for describing how informal caregiving networks (family, friends, and neighbors) are formed (Barrett & Lynch, 1999). The *substitution hypothesis* posits that when close relatives are not available, more distant relatives, friends, and formal helpers provide care. The *supplementation hypothesis* posits that primary caregivers are typically drawn from the informal support network and function as a link between the ill person and the formal care system. Formal support supplements rather than substitutes for informal care.

Ongoing membership in a social support network helps both terminally ill persons and their families maintain a sense of belonging while they manage difficult transitions, but the nature and composition of social networks can vary greatly. Five types of social networks have been identified: (a) primarily close family members, (b) family neighbors and friends, (c) small and mostly neighbor-based, (d) large and primarily friendship-centered, and (e) absent kin and minimal ties with neighbors (Litwin, 2001). Faith communities, typically overlooked as a source of quasi-formal social support, are also important components of the informal social care network; churches, temples, synagogues, and other religious organizations provide outreach through their members (Braun & Zir, 2001; McMillan & Weitzner, 2000). The care configurations of informal caregiving networks have been found to change frequently (Peek, Zsembik, & Coward, 1997). Human service practitioners have historically recognized the importance of these sources of support, often drawing upon individuals' informal relationships in planning for ongoing care (Levine & Kuerbis, 2002; Penrod, Kane, & Kane, 2000).

Formal Caregiving Networks

Support and guidance from health and social service professionals are central components of care (Hudson, Aranda, & McMurray, 2002). In general, good patient–family relationships with medical professionals have been found to be based on shared power and expertise, mutual influence and understanding, clarification and negotiation of differences, and respect for the caregiving network (Farber, Egnew, & Herman-Bertsch, 2002; Teno et al., 2001). Ongoing supportive relationships with providers can strengthen caregivers' sense of competence and help them manage illness-related changes (Greenberger & Litwin, 2003; Nijboer, Triemstra, Tempelaar, Sanderman, & ven den Bos, 1999). In addition, professionals help facilitate concrete assistance such as transportation, finances, home care, homemaking services, and personal care as needs intensify (Bern-Klug, Gessert, & Forbes, 2001; Emanuel, Fairclough, Slutsman, & Emanuel, 2000).

Many studies have examined either formal care provision or informal family caregiving, but few have explored how each of the components supplement and extend the other. The purpose of this study was to explore and describe (a) the interrelationship between informal and formal care, and (b) caregivers' perspectives about the salient features of professional help with terminal care. This study was part of a larger, longitudinal project that aimed to investigate the experiences of family caregivers before and after the death of a loved one. The long-range goal is to identify ways to improve care for people who are dying and their families.

Methods
Study Design and Procedures

This exploratory descriptive study involved interviews with one or more family members who were receiving hospice care. Hospice care is available for people with a terminal illness who have been diagnosed with a terminal illness that will end in death within 6 months (NHPCO, 2004). Family research in end-of-life care presents distinct methodological challenges. Because the responses of one person who answers questions may not completely represent those of the whole family, researchers are often encouraged to seek multiple family members' perspectives (Arstedt-Kurki, Paavilainen, & Lehti, 2001). However, gathering the perspectives of all members is difficult and particularly burdensome for a family who is actively engaged in caregiving for someone who may die soon. The perspectives of the hospice patient and multiple caregivers were sought but not required for participation in this study.

Qualitative methods were employed because they offer the means to learn from participants' in-depth descriptions of their experiences and are particularly germane to family research in end-of-life care for two reasons. First, because families are vulnerable during the end-stage of a terminal illness, these methods simultaneously allowed the interviewer to enter the home and learn from families who were in the midst of major changes. Second, because families are unique and complex systems, particularly when they are providing care at the end of life, this type of research calls for methods that are both flexible and sensitive (Astedt-Kurki et al., 2001). In addition, family research generates multiple levels of data: individual-level data (about the patient and caregiver), which is nested within dyadic-level data (patient–caregiver, spousal, and adult child–parent relationships), which is subsequently nested within family-system-level data. This study about caregiving networks also generated data about contacts with health care and social service providers. The flexibility of qualitative methods made it possible to combine these multiple units of analysis for a deeper, richer description of the caregiving network.

Care was taken to develop study procedures that allowed the interviewer to learn from participants as they were experiencing the end stage of an illness while simultaneously being respectful of family needs during this potentially difficult period. Procedures were developed by reviewing guidelines for research in end-of-life care, as well as through discussions with the administration of the participating hospice and the Institutional Review Board of the University at Buffalo (Agrawal & Danis, 2002; Task Force on Palliative Care, 1997). Two important issues were considered. First, although admission to hospice care requires signed documentation about the incurable nature of the illness, words such as "terminal" or "dying" can still cause surprise and distress for families. Thus, the illness was described as "serious" in all written and verbal communications to assure that participation did not become a catalyst for changing the participants' perceptions of the illness. Second, because discussing experiences of caregiving and loss can generate intense emotions, an emergency protocol was developed which included contact with a crisis hotline and hospice social worker if needed. Talking about experiences can also increase awareness of unmet needs. When this happened, families were linked with the hospice team for referral to appropriate community resources.

Recruitment for the study was focused on identifying families in which the hospice patient was terminally ill but not actively dying. The study was conducted collaboratively with one hospice that is the sole provider of hospice services for an entire county. An informational letter about the project was included in all hospice home care admission packets during the study period. Although the hospice provides care in nursing home, inpatient, and hospital units, only patients who were receiving in-home care were contacted. The rationale for involving only home-care patients was to focus on family experiences with community-based care.

The sampling strategy for the study was purposeful. Admissions personnel helped identify patients who were still receiving care 2 weeks after admission and who had been admitted with a midrange Palliative Performance Score (PPS). The PPS is used to assess ambulation, activity, evidence of disease, self-care, consciousness, and intake (Anderson, Downing, & Hill, 1996). It has a 100-point scale, and a midrange score (40–50) indicates that the person has extensive disease, is mainly bed-bound, unable to work, requires assistance with self care, eats and drinks little, and may fluctuate from being mentally clear to confused or drowsy, but in most situations, the final terminal decline has not begun (Anderson et al., 1996).

Families that met study criteria were contacted by telephone. The study was explained to either the patient or a caregiver and followed by an invitation to participate. Hospice patients were always invited, but because the later stages of an advanced illness can be tenuous, some were unable to do so. Multiple caregivers were invited to participate; some families were interested, but for others, conflicting demands, such as work or child care, were barriers. Ongoing sample development can be described as naturalistic and qualitative. The number of participants was not predetermined but it evolved as contacts were made with families (Drisko, 2003; Padgett, 1998). It is important to note that additional participants from each family would have provided multiple convergent perspectives, and this was encouraged but not required primarily because it was important that participation in the study not become burdensome or intrusive (Astedt-Kurki et al., 2001; Berg, 1995; Demi & Warren, 1995). Recruitment ceased when theoretical saturation was achieved. Theoretical saturation is defined as the continuation of data gathering until no new data emerges and the findings have become well established and clear (Strauss & Corbin, 1998).

Interviews

Interview appointments were scheduled at the family's convenience and confirmation calls were made on the day of the interview. Interviews were cancelled if the ill person's symptoms became uncontrolled. Interviews were conducted either by the author or one of two research assistants, all of whom had prior social work experience in health care settings. Interviewers attended a training session and observed the author conduct interviews before working independently. The author reviewed transcripts and met with interviewers regularly during the data collection phase of the project. Interviews were conducted in participants' homes and lasted between 1 and 2-1/2 hours.

Drawing upon concepts from the social care model, an interview guide was developed to gather the family's experiences with both formal (medical and social service) systems and informal care (family members, friends, and neighbors). Open-ended questions were used to explore the history of the illness and treatment, experiences with health care providers, and social service assistance, as well as family and social support. Example questions include "What was your experience with health care providers (doctors, nurses, and hospital and office staff) during the course of your (loved one's) illness?" "What was most helpful?" "How did you receive information about the illness?" "What experiences did you have with social or community agencies?" "Did you have assistance from a faith community? If so, what type and how did it help?" Probing questions were used to encourage greater depth of discussion. Participants were encouraged to proceed at a pace and in a direction that was comfortable for them.

Analysis

Individual-level data about patients and their caregivers was collected from the hospice admission records and entered into SPSS (Version 12). This deidentified information included admission diagnosis, patient's PPS score, and age. Dyadic information, including the relationships of the persons listed as "primary caregiver" and "emergency contact," was collected from hospice admission records. Frequencies and descriptive statistics were calculated.

Qualitative data from taped interviews were transcribed and entered into Non-numerical Unstructured Data Indexing, Structuring and Theorizing software (NUD*IST; Version 4). Qualitative data analysis involved multiple iterations. First, each transcript was coded independently by the author and a second coder to decrease bias and increase the rigor of the analysis (Padgett, 1998). Both open and axial coding were used. Initially, open coding, or identifying meaning units by examining the data line by line, was used to generate naturally occurring themes from within the participants' descriptions (Padgett, 1998). Next, axial coding, or the systematic use of concepts for data exploration, was accomplished by using a start list of codes from the social care model (Cantor & Brennan, 2000; Miles & Huberman, 1994; Strauss & Corbin, 1998). Sections of textual data were partitioned and copied under headings that corresponded to each concept.

The second phase of qualitative data analysis involved the development of genograms and ecomaps of each family caregiving system. Developed by Hartman (1978), the ecomap is an organizing tool that can be used to visually portray the family within a social context. The genogram presents family information and relationships so that the connections, themes, and the quality of inter-generational relationships are clear (Carter & McGoldrick, 1980). Different types of lines were used to signify tense, distant, or particularly close relationships on both diagrams. Ecomaps have previously been used in end-of-life care research as a way of guiding participants in discussion of their social network (Early, et al., 2000). Genograms and ecomaps were not constructed during interviews in this study, but were developed from the transcribed narratives as a way of organizing the voluminous data about the informal and formal care networks and to represent the interrelationship between them. The genograms and ecomaps were developed by a research assistant who had not conducted interviews. Using an outside coder is "observer triangulation" (two observers explore the same data independently) and is a strategy to enhance the rigor of the analysis and decrease bias in the results (Padgett, 1998).

Constant comparative analysis was used to analyze the 64 genograms and ecomaps. Constant comparative analysis is an iterative process that involves both induction and deduction. First, themes emerge from initial coding (induction); the coder then reviews the coded data making certain that they clearly portray the themes (deduction). New codes can emerge as the data are reviewed and compared against earlier themes (Padgett, 1998; Strauss & Corbin, 1998). The results were compiled into a visual representation of informal and formal care.

Results
Sample Demographics

Interviews with members of 64 families in which a terminally ill person was a hospice patient were included in this study. The sample included interviews with 30 hospice patients and 34 were unable to participate. At least one caregiver from each of the 64 families and more than one from 5 families participated, yielding interviews with a total of 69 caregivers. The sample includes three different units of analysis: individual-level,

Table 1 Patient Demographics (N = 64)

	Patients Interviewed[a]		Total	
	n	%	n	%
Men	16	25	31	48
Women	14	22	33	52
Admission Diagnosis				
Noncancer	3	5	9	14
Cancer	27	42	55	86
Ethnicity				
African American	1	1	5	8
Caucasian	28	44	58	91
Hispanic	1	1	1	1
Religion				
Catholic	21	33	29	45
Protestant	8	13	20	31
Other	5	8		
None	5	8		
Nonactive	3	5		
Jewish	2	3		

[a]Information was collected on 64 hospice patients and 30 of these were directly interviewed.

dyadic-level, and family-level data, each of which is important for describing the nature of caregiving systems.

Demographic information about all of the hospice patients is presented in Table 1. The mean age of the patients was 74.6 years ($N = 64$, range = 54–88). The majority of patients had either Medicare benefits alone ($n = 20$; 31%) or Medicare in combination with a supplemental policy ($n = 34$; 53%). Smaller numbers had private insurance alone ($n = 8$; 13%) or Medicaid ($n = 2$; 3%). A majority of the patients in the study had cancer ($n = 55$; 86%), and the greatest number had lung cancer ($n = 21$; 30%). The smaller group of noncancer patients ($n = 9$; 14%) had chronic obstructive pulmonary disease, congestive heart failure, and debility unspecified which is a term used to connote the coexistence of multiple conditions.

The mean age of the caregivers who were interviewed was 55.4 years ($n = 69$; range = 21–83). Caregiver interviews were conducted with 53 women and 16 men. Hospice admission protocol involves information about spouses, primary caregivers, and emergency contacts. The family relationships of the caregivers who were interviewed, as well as those who were listed on the hospice record as the primary caregiver or as emergency contacts, are presented in Table 2. The table also includes a tabulation of additional caregivers who were discussed by the participant during the interview ("Others mentioned"). These individuals were not listed in hospice records but were described by participants as being involved in the caregiving network.

The Interrelationship between Informal and Formal Caregivers

Figure 1 presents a visual adaptation of the social care model, illustrating the interrelationship between informal and formal care at the end of life. The interrelationship between the

Table 2 Caregiver Demographics

	Caregivers Interviewed[a]		PCG of Record[b]		Emergency Contact Listed[c]		Others Mentioned[d]
	n	%	n	%	n	%	n
Men							
Husbands	5	7	11	16	0		1
Sons	9	13	11	16	11	16	8
Brothers	2	3	1	1	2	3	3
Grandson	0		1	1	0		3
Nephew	0		0		1	1	0
Women							
Wife	19	28	22	32	0		0
Ex-wife	1	1	1	1	0		0
Daughter	28	41	14	20	24	35	8
Daughter-in-law	2	3	1	1	4	6	1
Sisters	1	1	1	1	3	4	5
Granddaughter	1	1	0		3	4	2
Good friend	1	1	1	1	1	1	4
Grandmother	0		0		1	1	0
Mother	0		0		0		1
None listed	—		—		19	28	—
Total	69		69		69		36

Note. Sixty-nine caregivers were interviewed; more than 1 from five families.

[a] Caregivers who responded to the invitation for participation.

[b] Person listed on the hospice admission record as the "primary caregiver."

[c] Person listed on the hospice record as the "emergency contact."

[d] Members of the informal support network that were discussed in the narratives.

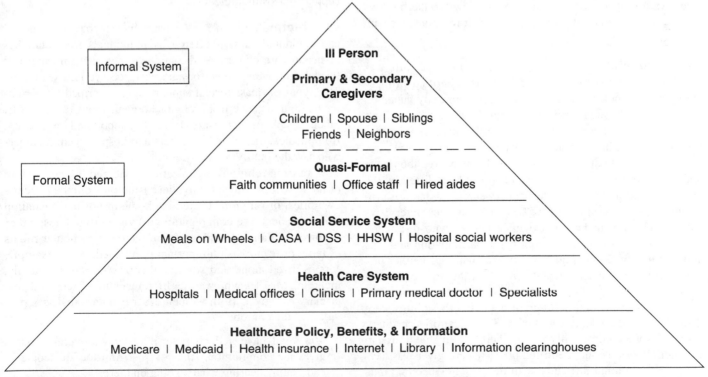

Figure 1 The interrelationship between formal and informal caregiving at the end-of-life.

Note. Guided by concepts from the social care model (Cantor, 1991). CASA = Community Alternative Systems Agency; DSS = Department of Social Services; HHSW = Home Health Social Worker.

terminally ill person and the system for care-giving in the home should be envisioned as a three-dimensional sphere: at the core of the sphere is the ill person and primary and secondary caregiving, which is successively surrounded by informal, quasi-formal, and formal networks. (Cantor, 1991; Cantor & Brennan, 2000).

Primary care. Primary relationships between the terminally ill person and those who were closest (spouses, adult children, siblings or friends) most often evolved into caregiving relationships as the disease progressed. Primary caregiving included increased numbers of hands-on tasks (assistance with toileting, bathing, and/or using a bedpan) as well as with managing medical symptoms and end-of-life decision making. In some families, caregiving was shared as shift-work where those involved in primary care split the days or nights. The words of Mr. O's daughter describe how her family developed shifts:

> We all pitch in. We know where we stand—we want to be with Dad and help him, but we all work and some of us have families. It's good because most of the five of us go on shifts in this house and it works out really well—and he can stay in his own home.

In other families, the tasks of primary care were split; one primary caregiver would manage the medications and another would handle baths, bed changes, or medical tasks such as catheter care. A private aide was hired to provide hands-on assistance when persons in primary relationships could not provide full-time care. In other situations, one person quit a job or took a leave of absence to move in with the ill person; other family members provided respite and financial support. The division of primary care tasks was related to the family's finances, the number of members, and their relationships with the dying person.

Caregiver shift. The concept of the caregiver shift was developed to reflect the finding that the identified primary caregiver was not, in fact, always involved in daily hands-on care as it would seem from the record. In 17 (25%) families, interviews were conducted with a family member who was not listed on the hospice admission record as the primary caregiver. In these situations, the person who answered the phone and was subsequently interviewed had not been listed by the hospice admissions team as the primary caregiver, but was providing significant care. In 5 (7%) of the families, interviews were conducted in the home with a person who responded positively to the telephone request for participation and was actively involved in caregiving, but was listed as neither primary caregiver nor emergency contact on the hospice admission record. In some families the identified primary caregiver was a spouse, but adult children or the patient's siblings were actually providing daily assistance. Some identified primary caregivers were chronically ill and therefore unable to assist. In other situations, the identified primary care-giver was having great emotional difficulty with the patient's decline; thus

one or more other "alternate care-givers" (e.g., adult children) assumed more of the care responsibilities. In still other instances, the identified primary caregiver was an adult child who was employed full-time or lived out of town. In these situations, the adult child was viewed as the decision maker, and others, such as siblings, friends, or neighbors, became caregiving proxies and provided hands-on care.

Secondary care. Secondary caregivers were those individuals who became "reinforcements" when primary caregivers needed respite and additional support. Siblings, grandchildren, and in some situations friends who were described as being as "close as family" provided assistance. Secondary care included instrumental tasks such as shopping, errands, meal preparation, transportation, and laundry. Emotional support for primary caregivers was also a component of secondary care.

Social support. A key component of the end-of-life caregiving network was social support (distinctly different from secondary care). Friends who offered social support were from faith communities (e.g., churches or temples), social organizations, or were neighbors who called, visited, and sent notes. Not formally considered to be caregiving per se, these acts of social support validated ongoing membership in a social network. The importance of social support is illustrated by Mrs. N. (age 81), whose son and daughter-in-law were interviewed 3 days before Christmas and 4 days before she died. Mrs. N. called for help and her daughter-in-law responded. Returning to the interview, her daughter-in-law said, "Mom was just so alert! She asked me to read all of her Christmas cards and notes to her. She smiled after each one and occasionally made a comment about the person." Many caregivers fulfilled primary, secondary, and social support roles simultaneously.

Quasi-formal. Quasi-formal support is the instrumental and emotional support offered by individuals from churches or health care clinics. At the midlevel between informal and formal caregiving, quasi-formal assistance overlaps with both. Two types of quasi-formal support were described by participants: (a) assistance from religious organizations (e.g., priests, rabbis, chaplains, lay visitors), and (b) support and information from medical office staff members and hospice team members who saw the family regularly.

Care from religious organizations emerged in one or more of the following ways: (a) regular visitation from the patient's own priest or religious leader, (b) home or hospital visitation from members of a congregation, (c) visits from a hospital or hospice chaplain, (d) and the attention to the particular rituals of faith, or (e) it was unimportant or avoided. As an example, Mrs. S. lived alone and was cared for by her church family, including Mrs. L., who was her lifelong church friend and now primary caregiver. Both women described care that was provided by the church:

> *Mrs. S.:* I have a Eucharistic minister who comes and gives me communion. I have visits from lots of people and I enjoy hearing what's going on there.

Mrs. L.: Three of us are all widows and we help her when we can. We come every day to fix meals, do her laundry and errands. Her paid aide now is the daughter of a person who goes to our church. We all belong to the same church. That church and what goes on there has always been the foundation of our friendship. It's where we met and we have belonged to it all our adult lives; we've raised our children together.

Health care professionals who demonstrated interest, kindness, and compassion provided quasi-formal support. This sometimes took the form of lighthearted teasing or discussions about a shared interest (e.g., sports). In other situations, these individuals provided information about symptom management or ways to manage care issues at home. Professionals who made strong connections with participants during visits that were otherwise medically focused provided quasi-formal support. Mrs. N. described her experience with this type of support:

I feel Hospice has helped me and they are very supportive too. I feel they care and they don't treat you in a way like, ya know, sometimes the nurses in the hospital say, "darling," "dear" and all that jazz. You don't need that because you're not their dear, you're not their darling, you're not their honey. The Hospice nurses are forthright. They speak to me like I'm their sister; they treat me like I have a brain.

Formal providers. Formal caregiving was offered by both health care and social service providers. Health care providers included physicians, physicians' assistants and nurse practitioners, nurses, aides, and technicians that families encountered in hospitals, home health, hospice, clinics, and medical offices. Primary care physicians referred patients to 1–8 specialists (e.g., oncologist, hematologist, radiation oncologist, rheumatologist, pulmonologist, and nephrologist). A majority of patients (92%) had 1–4 hospitalizations before entering hospice, a small number (2%) were seen only in outpatient settings, and 6% had more than 4 hospitalizations. Social service providers included human service professionals from all educational backgrounds who were employed in health care or community social service agencies that provided home-delivered meals, transportation, case management, and home care. Participants also interacted with social workers from hospitals, home health agencies, and hospice. Home health services were used by 31% of participants before hospice admission.

Positive Characteristics in Relationships with Health Care and Social Service Professionals

Five themes that distinguished the qualities of good relationships with professionals were distilled from participants' descriptions: (a) kindness and compassion, (b) clear and straightforward communication, (c) concrete, understandable information, (d) respect for self-determination, and (e) anticipatory

guidance. Characteristics of these themes in social service and health care domains are presented in Table 3.

Kindness and compassion. Characterized as the ability to help the ill person and family members feel cared about and understood, this quality also included sensitivity, sincerity, and concern for family well-being. Compassionate formal caregivers focused on the presenting concern and did not gloss over its importance even if it was clinically or procedurally insignificant. Providers offered emotional support and reassurance while seeing the ill person as someone who was also a parent or spouse and not just a diagnosis or disposition.

Clear, straightforward communication. Characterized as the ability to present complex information in specific, comprehensible, and simple terms without jargon, this quality was most often related to interactions about diagnosis, prognosis, benefits, or available community resources. Explanations that are straightforward, direct, frank, and brutally honest while also being sensitive are the most helpful. Direct communication (in person, not by letter), family conferences, and prompt telephone responses are highly valued modes of communication.

Concrete, understandable information. Characterized as the use of printed or easily available material (e.g., Web sites), the most salient feature of this resource is its ability to be reproduced and reviewed after being introduced. People who are in stressful situations are not able to completely comprehend complex information, thus being able to return to a concrete resource ensures greater long-term comprehension. Participants described the value of seeing x-rays, CAT scans or MRIs for illustration while a provider gave diagnostic information and the value of receiving written information or handouts about benefits, community agencies, and caregiving instructions. After being presented only with verbal explanations, families often sought additional information from the Internet, library, or information clearinghouses to meet their needs for information.

Respect for self-determination. Characterized as encouragement to consider the facts without the pressure of a hurried decision (for example, learning about treatment options or types of in-home assistance), this component of formal care becomes increasingly important as the terminally ill person loses physical or mental function or both. Having one's choices respected makes the terminal illness experience feel more controllable. Having time to consider all the options is a way of honoring the ill person's wishes. Alternatively, when forced to choose quickly or accept preselected options, participants described feelings of regret.

Anticipatory guidance. Characterized simply as preparing for what is ahead, this function of formal caregiving provides terminally ill persons and their families with education about symptom recognition and management, caregiver concerns and techniques, and end-of-life policies and decision making before the final moments. It was best articulated by a participant who said, "Especially when it's the end of your life that you're

Table 3 Helpful Components of Relationships with Health Care and Social Service Professionals

Component	Health Care	Social Service
Clear, straightforward communication	Diagnostic and prognostic information is given in understandable terms.	Benefits, programs, and community resources are explained clearly and simply; referrals are followed up.
Kind and compassionate attitude	The family impact of medical procedures is understood and considered.	The patient and family (rather than discharge plan) is the priority.
Anticipatory guidance	Families are educated about the disease progression; conversations about incurability are initiated by provider.	End-of-life decision making is described; caregivers are helped to understand and prepare for a loved one's decline.
Information	Written information is provided (checklists, brochures, suggestions).	Community resources and alternatives others have found helpful are provided.
Respect for self-determination	Options are provided and patient choice is respected; treatment is not forced; patient's end-of-life choices are understood by the care provider.	Options are provided (e.g., decisions about a temporary nursing home placement are not forced); there is time to think it over and visit; explanations of end-of-life documents and decisions are facilitated.

dealing with, it's not a good time for surprises." This feature is crucial for easing distress both during the final stage of life and in preparing families for bereavement.

Discussion

Terminally ill people face their approaching death within their own naturally occurring and distinct social network. End-of-life caregiving becomes the culmination of one's lifetime-long relationships and the incarnation of enduring family and social care. The analyses of interview transcripts, genograms, and ecomaps that were created from in-depth interviews with members of 64 families yielded rich description of how a terminal illness transforms families, friends, and formal care providers into a caregiving system. The essential interrelationship between informal and formal caregiving was illuminated by concepts from the social care model (Cantor, 1991; Cantor & Brennan, 2000).

The term *primary caregiver* is a simple, transparent concept that has previously been used to describe one person who provides a majority of hands-on care for an ill person. The primary caregiving paradigm, which has been adopted by hospitals, nursing homes, rehabilitation centers, and hospice, is reassuring and efficient; formal providers can direct questions and medical information to one person. However, in this study, the "caregiver shift" underscored how multiple caregivers work together to fulfill complementary functions by forming shifting care configurations, thus extending the work of Peek et al. (1997). Study findings bring the conceptualization of a caregiving network to life and document how social support is a core element of care at life's end. These results suggest that perhaps instead of asking "Who is the primary caregiver?" health care and social service providers should ask, "Who helps and how?"

These results extend the literature about caregiving and suggest the need for a revised paradigm of caregiving that emphasizes the link between formal and informal care networks. The social care model is a valuable conceptual framework from which to view caregiving, primarily because it emphasizes how levels of care overlap, deepening and extending the essential interrelationship between them (Cantor, 1991; Cantor & Brennan, 2000). Traditional models of caregiving have overlooked the contribution of both quasi-formal care and social support, and although these forms of social care have typically not been defined as caregiving, this study illustrates how they link informal and formal care. In addition, building on the work of Barrett and Lynch (1999), these results support the conceptualization of a caregiving system by illustrating how substitution and supplementation both become necessary when around-the-clock care is needed. As end-stage care needs intensify, families adapt by depending more frequently on others (friends and neighbors as well as formal caregivers) for help with caregiving.

Families are unique and distinct systems whose internal relationships develop from personal and dyadic characteristics. How family networks develop relationships with others in the social network is an important feature that contributes to the distinctive and individual nature of caregiving systems. It is important to note that the 5 types of social networks described by Litwin (2001) could each develop into a distinctly different but equally supportive type of caregiving system. This previous research, together with the findings of the present study, illustrate that the nature of caregiving systems is dynamic rather than static, and is seen in how people work together in caregiving as death approaches.

Implications for Practice

Attending to the family's needs can directly improve care for people who are dying. Observing a family member experience "a good death" can ease caregivers' stress and can have significant implications on their long-term health and well-being

(Christakis & Iwashyna, 2003). Family members who receive support from formal care providers in hospitals and health care organizations as they face an approaching death may have had no previous experience seeking formal emotional support and problem-solving assistance. Thus, the five themes that illustrate what care-givers found most helpful is particularly germane to health care and social service professionals who encounter family members at these important turning points; these themes both support and extend prior findings about the long-term implications of good relationships with formal providers (Farber et al., 2002).

Described as "context interpreters," social workers fulfill important functions for the families of people facing the end of life in health care settings (Bern-Klug et al., 2001; Patterson & Dorfman, 2001; Wennman-Larsen & Tishelman, 2002). The results of this study suggest the need for an extension of this role. Human service professionals can provide "social context interpretation" to help health care providers understand and utilize informal care as a resource. It is also important to emphasize that human service practitioners encounter people who are providing end-of-life care even when this is not the presenting problem and in myriad settings beyond the purview of health care organizations (e.g., family service agencies, mental health centers, and employee assistance programs). Caregiving systems, even when they are extensive, well-meaning, and supportive can be fraught with stress and conflict; these issues may precipitate the need for help (Bourgeois, Beach, Schulz, & Burgio, 1996).

Formal providers enter the caregiving system as powerful and influential strangers who represent and become extensions of "the system." Encounters with both health care and social service providers can substantiate the hard realities of an illness. New models of medical education promise to enhance family–provider communication (Farber et al., 2002; Maguire, 2000). This study emphasizes how significantly families are influenced by care that involves kindness and compassion, concrete and retrievable information, clear and straightforward communication, support for self-determination, and anticipatory guidance. These qualities are important for all professionals who encounter families when they are vulnerable and facing terminal illness and death. Health and human service providers are advised to ask family members, "What do you need?" and "How do you learn?" Enhanced attention to the needs of the patient–family unit can strengthen the caregiving system and may enhance informal care-givers' experience with grief and bereavement.

This study had several limitations. Only one interview was conducted with each family during hospice care, thus limiting the breadth of family perspective. A follow-up interview would have added depth to our understanding of the family experience. An additional limitation was that the sample was primarily Caucasian, and although hospice is utilized by White people more frequently than minorities (NHPCO, 2003), this also reflects the importance of advanced understanding about the influence of culture and race in the family end-of-life experience. A third limitation is that the sample was developed naturalistically; interviews were arranged with family members (both patients and caregivers) who were available and responsive.

Other members were not aggressively pursued to minimize the potential burden from participation, which created gaps in the family perspective. Finally, the genograms and ecomaps were completed as a form of secondary analysis. Completing them during the interview and seeking family input would have enriched the results and enhanced our understanding about key components of social support networks.

Conclusion

Previous research has created widespread awareness of the emotional, social, and physical difficulties which accompany family caregiving; the results of this study advance the literature by illuminating the essential and previously unexplored relationship between informal and formal care providers. Care provision for a person in the context of a terminal illness produces widely variant experiences for the families who become caregiving networks. Caregivers' explicit descriptions of what is helpful portray the fundamental importance of significant human connections with formal providers and illustrate the importance of family–provider communication. Influenced by the unique needs, abilities, and concerns of those in the immediate social network as well as by interactions with providers, caregiving experiences at the end of life produce memories that influence caregiver health and well-being long after the death.

Now on the national agenda, the burgeoning number of family caregivers presents important opportunities for both intervention research and innovative human service programming (Chernesky & Gutheil, 2002). Each family care-giving system has unique needs for information and education as well as "teachable moments" when their needs are greatest (Thielmann, 2000). Research that is designed to learn from families who are consumers of services can continue to enlighten providers about meaningful interventions.

References

Agrawal, M., & Danis, M. (2002). End-of-life care for terminally ill participants in clinical research. *Journal of Palliative Medicine, 5,* 729–737.

Astedt-Kurki, P., Paavilainen, E., & Lehti, K. (2001). Methodological issues in interviewing families in family nursing research. *Journal of Advanced Nursing, 35,* 288–293.

Americans for Better Care for the Dying. (2003). *The palliative care toolkit* (Chap. 4). Retrieved January 15, 2004, from: http://www.abcd-caring.org/

Anderson, F., Downing, G. M., & Hill, J. (1995). Palliative Performance Scale (PPS): A new tool. *Journal of Palliative Care, 12,* 5–11.

Aneshensel, C. S., Pearlin, L. I., Mullan, J. T., Zarit, S. H., & Whitlatch, C. J. (1995). *Profiles in caregiving.* New York: Academic.

Barrett, A. E., & Lynch, S. M. (1999). Caregiving networks of elderly persons: Variation by marital status. *The Gerontologist, 39,* 695–704.

Bass, D. M., Noelker, L. S., & Rechlin, L. R. (1996). The moderating influence of service use on negative caregiving consequences. *Journal of Gerontology, 51B,* S121–S131.

Berg, B. L. (1995). *Qualitative research methods for the social sciences.* Boston: Allyn & Bacon.

Bern-Klug, M., Gessert, C., & Forbes, S. (2001). The need to revise assumptions about the end of life: Implications for social work practice. *Health and Social Work, 26,* 38–43.

Bourgeois, M., Beach, S., Schulz, R., & Burgio, L. (1996). When primary and secondary caregivers disagree: Predictors and psychosocial consequences. *Psychology and Aging, 11,* 527–537.

Braun, K. L., & Zir, A. (2001). Roles for the church in improving end-of-life care: Perceptions of Christian clergy and laity. *Death Studies, 25,* 685–704.

Brown, M. A., & Stetz, K. (1999). The labor of caregiving: A theoretical model of caregiving during potentially fatal illness. *Qualitative Health Research, 9,* 182–197.

Cantor, M. H. (1991). Family and community: Changing roles in an aging society. *The Gerontologist, 31,* 337–346.

Cantor, M. H., & Brennan, M. (2000). *Social care of the elderly: The effects of ethnicity, class and culture.* New York: Springer.

Carter, E.A., & McGoldrick, M. (1980). *The family life cycle: A framework for family therapy.* New York: Gardner Press, Inc.

Centers for Disease Control. (2004). *Deaths from 39 selected causes by place of death.* Retrieved July 23, 2004, from http://www.cdc.gov/nchs/data/statab/VS00199_TABLE307.pdf

Chentsova-Dutton, Y., Schucther, S., Hutchin, S., Strause, L., Burns, K., & Zisook, S. (2000). The psychological and physical health of hospice caregivers. *Annals of Clinical Psychiatry, 12,* 19–27.

Chernesky, R., & Gutheil, I. A. (2002). Family caregiving as a service niche for agencies: Findings from a study of philanthropic trends. *Families in Society, 83,* 449–456.

Christakis, N. A., & Iwashyna, T. J. (2003). The health impact of health care on families: A matched cohort study of hospice use by decedents and mortality outcomes in surviving, widowed spouses. *Social Science & Medicine, 57,* 465–475.

Demi, A. S., & Warren, N. A. (1995). Issues in conducting research with vulnerable families. *Western Journal of Nursing Research, 17,* 188–202.

Drisko, J. (2003, January). Improving sampling strategies and terminology in qualitative research. Juried paper presented at the Annual Conference of the Society for Social Work and Research Annual Meeting, Washington, DC.

Early, B. P., Smith, E. D., Todd, L., & Beem, T. (2000). The needs and supportive networks of the dying: An assessment instrument and mapping procedure for hospice patients. *American Journal of Hospice and Palliative Care, 17(2),* 87–96.

Emanuel, E. J., Fairclough, D. L., Slutsman, J., Alpert, H., Baldwin, D., & Emanuel, L. L. (1999). Assistance from family members, friends, paid care givers, and volunteers in the care of terminally ill patients. *The New England Journal of Medicine, 341,* 956–963.

Emanuel, E. J., Fairclough, D. L., Slutsman, J., & Emanuel, L. L. (2000). Understanding economic and other burdens of terminal illness: The experience of patients and their caregivers. *Annals of Internal Medicine, 132,* 451–459.

Farber, S. J., Egnew, T. R., & Herman-Bertsch, J. L. (2002). Defining effective clinician roles in end-of-life care. *Journal of Family Practice, 51,* 153–158.

Grbich, C. F., Maddocks, I., & Parker, D. (2001). Family caregivers, their needs, and home-based palliative cancer services. *Journal of Family Studies, 7,* 171–188.

Greenberger, H., & Litwin, H. (2003). Can burdened caregivers be effective facilitators of elder care-recipient health care? *Journal of Advanced Nursing, 41,* 332–341.

Hartman, A. (1978). Diagrammatic assessment of family relationships. *Social Casework, 59,* 465–476.

Holland, J. C. (2002). History of psycho-oncology: Overcoming attitudinal and conceptual barriers. *Psychosomatic Medicine, 64,* 206–221.

Hudson, P., Aranda, S., & McMurray, N. (2002). Intervention development for enhanced lay palliative caregiver support: The use of focus groups. *European Journal of Cancer Care, 11,* 262–270.

Jette, A. M., Tennstedt, S., & Crawford, S. (1995). How does formal and informal community care affect nursing home use? *Journal of Gerontology, 50B,* S4–S12.

Kinsella, G., Cooper, B., Picton, C., & Murtagh, D. (1998). A review of the measurement of caregiver and family burden in palliative care. *Journal of Palliative Care, 14,* 37–45.

Kissane, D. W., Bloch, S., McKenzie, M., McDowall, A. C., & Nietzan, R. (1998). Family grief therapy: A preliminary account of a new model to promote healthy family functioning during palliative care and bereavement. *Psycho-Oncology, 7,* 14–25.

Levine, C., & Kuerbis, A. (2002). Building alliances between social workers and family caregivers. *Journal of Social Work in Long Term Care, 1,* 3–17.

Litwin, H. (2001). Social network type and morale in old age. *The Gerontologist, 41(4),* 516–524.

Lynn, J., Teno, J. M., Phillips, R. S., Wu, A. W., Desbiens, N., Harrold, J., Claessens, M. T., Wenger, N., Kreling, B., & Connors, A. F. (1997). Perceptions by family members of the dying experience of older and seriously ill patients. *Annals of Internal Medicine, 126,* 97–106.

Lyons, K. S. & Zarit, S. H. (1999). Formal and informal support: The great divide. *International Journal of Geriatric Psychiatry. 14(3);* 183–92.

Maguire, P. (2000). Communication with terminally ill patients and their relatives. In H. M. Chocninov & W. Breitbart (Eds). *Handbook of psychiatry in palliative medicine.* New York: Oxford University Press.

McCorkle R., & Pasacreta, J. V. (2001). Enhancing caregiver outcomes in palliative care. *Cancer Control, 8,* 36–45.

McGoldrick, M., & Carter, B. (2003). The family life cycle. In F. Walsh (Ed.), *Normal family processes: Growing diversity and complexity* (3rd ed.; pp. 375–398). New York: Guilford.

McMillan, S. C., & Weitzner, S. C. (2000). How problematic are various aspects of quality of life in patients with cancer at the end of life? *Oncology Nursing Forum, 27,* 817–823.

McMillan, S. C., Moody, L. E., (2003). Hospice patient and caregiver congruence in reporting patients' symptom intensity. *Cancer Nursing, 26,* 113–118.

Miles M. B., & Huberman A. M. (1994). *Qualitative data analysis* (pp. 172–206). Thousand Oaks, CA: Sage.

National Hospice and Palliative Care Organization. (2004). *Hospice statistics.* Retrieved April 7, 2004, from http://www.nhpco.org/i4a/pages/Index.cfm?pageid=3362.

Nijboer, C., Triemstra, M., Tempelaar, R., Sanderman, R., & van den Bos, G. A. M. (1999). Determinants of caregiving experiences and mental health of partners of cancer patients. *Cancer, 86,* 577–588.

Padgett, D. K. (1998). *Qualitative methods in social work research.* Thousand Oaks, CA: Sage.

Patterson, L. B., & Dorfman, L. T. (2002). Family support for hospice caregivers. *American Journal of Hospice and Palliative Care, 19*, 315–323.

Peek, C. W., Zsembik, B. A., & Coward, R. T. (1997). The changing caregiving networks of older adults. *Research on Aging, 19*, 333–361.

Penrod, J. D., Kane, R. A., & Kane, R. L. (2000). Effects of post hospital informal care on nursing home discharge. *Research on Aging, 22*, 66–82.

Rainer, J. P., & McMurry, P. E. (2002). Caregiving at the end of life. *Journal of Clinical Psychology, 58*, 1421–1431.

Stetz, K. M. & Brown, M. A. (2004). Physical and psychosocial health in family caregiving: a comparison of AIDS and cancer caregivers. *Public Health Nursing, 21*(6), 533–40.

Strauss, A., & Corbin, J. (1998). Basics *of qualitative research.* Thousand Oaks, CA: Sage.

Task Force on Palliative Care. (1997). *Precepts of palliative care.* Retrieved April 15, 2004, from http://www.lastacts.org.

Teno, J. M., Casey, V. A., Welch, L. C., & Edgman-Levitan, S. (2001). Patient-focused, family-centered end-of-life medical care: Views of the guidelines and bereaved family members. *Journal of Pain and Symptom Management, 22*, 738–750.

Thielemann, P. (2000). Educational needs of home caregivers of terminally ill patients: Literature review. *American Journal of Hospice & Palliative Care, 17*, 253–257.

Wennman-Larsen, A., & Tishelman, C. (2002). Advanced home care for cancer patients at the end of life: A qualitative study of hopes and expectations of family caregivers. *Scandinavian Journal of Caring Sciences, 16*, 240–247.

Zarit, S. H., & Pearlin, L. E. (1993). Family caregiving: Integrating informal and formal systems for care. In S. H. Zarit, L. I. Pearlin, & K. W. Schaie (Eds.), *Caregiving systems: Formal and informal helpers.* Hillsdale, NJ: Erlbaum.

DEBORAH P. WALDROP, PhD, CSW, is associate professor and Hartford Faculty Scholar, State University of New York at Buffalo School of Social Work. Correspondence regarding this article may be sent to dwaldrop@buffalo.edu or University at Buffalo School of Social Work, 633 Baldy Hall, Box 601050, Buffalo, NY 14260.

The project Caring for the Caregiver was supported by a grant from the Margaret L. Wendt Foundation, Buffalo, NY.

Needs of Elderly Patients in Palliative Care

Helle Wijk, RN, PhD and Agneta Grimby, PhD

Europe's population is aging and more people are dying from chronic diseases. Still, the range and quality of palliative care services remain rather limited and inadequate. According to the World Health Organization, many Europeans who are terminally ill die in unnecessary pain and discomfort because their health systems lack skilled staff and do not widely offer palliative care services.

Even though evidence may be lacking and the empirical studies characterized by a high degree of heterogeneity, some important areas seem to stand out considering the elderly patient's views and needs in the terminal phase of life.[1] Assessments of quality of life have shown that the lowest scores are related to the physical domain, followed by the existential, supportive, and social domains.[2] A similar trend can be observed among people wishing to hasten death.[3] Actions to avoid nutritional and pain problems are also crucial at the end-of-life stage, as are avoiding inappropriate prolongation of dying and having a sense of control.[4]

To be able to provide high-quality palliative care, it is important for the health care staff to see and understand the special needs and wishes of the patients; however, knowledge, methods, and programs for this are sparse. The patients themselves seem not to be the one to blame.[5] On the contrary, studies have demonstrated that older people are willing to talk about death and dying in a rather spontaneous way.[6]

Existing empirical evidence on elderly patients' thoughts about death and dying has so far mostly been collected after cross-sectional, quantitative, or qualitative designs, mainly using personal interviews. Open conversations are considered the optimal way of learning about needs at the end-of-life stage. The method, however, is time consuming for daily practice, where somewhat more fixed estimates of needs may be preferred.

Identifying desires and needs of the palliative patient may provide increased quality of care. This pilot study about needs at the end of life aims at describing the individual reports from 30 elderly palliative patients on their needs and their ranking of these needs by degree of concern.

Method

Participants

Thirty consecutively chosen patients, admitted for palliative care at the Geriatric Department, Sahlgrenska University Hospital in Gothenburg, Sweden, were willing to join the study. Inclusion criteria were strength enough to perform an interview and Swedish mother tongue. Exclusion criteria were aphasia, dementia, or lack of strength. The respondents (15 men and 15 women) were an average age of 79 years (75 for men, 81 for women) and had a 50:50 background of manual labor and white-collar jobs.

The primary diagnosis was different types of cancer, with a variation of length of illness of 1 month to several years. All but 1 of the patients were admitted to the palliative unit from another health care institution. All patients signed an informed consent before they participated in the study. The study was approved by the Ethics Committee of the Faculty of Medicine, University of Gothenburg, Sweden.

Procedures

The survey included demographic data and information about reason for admittance and state of health at the time of admittance, reactions to the admittance, and awareness of illness. The information was retrieved partly through patients' files and partly through patient interviews.

Individual needs were identified by semistructured interviews by a research nurse (PhD student) at the palliative unit of the Geriatric Department at Sahlgrenska University Hospital. Most of the interviews were conducted, if possible, once a week and at daytime between 9:00 AM and 2 PM. Interview length was 20 to 30 minutes in 50%; 30% lasted 30 to 60 minutes, 2 interviews lasted for more than an hour, and 2 were very short due to the patient's fatigue.

The introductory question was "How do you feel today?" This was followed by questions about (1) the patient's ranking of important needs for the moment, (2) things in particular that the patient wanted help with at the moment, and

(3) things in particular that the patient wanted to speak about at the moment. The patient was asked to try to rank the different needs by the degree of concern. The answers were categorized according to physical, psychologic, social, and spiritual needs.

Statistical Analysis

For statistical trend tests, the Fisher exact test and permutation trend tests were used.[7] All results given refer to $P < .05$ unless otherwise stated.

Results

Most patients (61%) wanted to spend their last days in their own home, whereas the rest preferred to stay at an institution where "one would receive the best help." The most common symptoms before admission were pain, lack of appetite, anxiety, sleeplessness, fatigue, vomiting, cough, and shortness of breath (Table 1). At admission, more than 50% of the patients were not quite sure of their diagnosis; of the transition from curative to palliative care, 30% were completely sure, and 20% were completely unsure. The figures were very similar among the relatives. This was mostly due to incomplete former information, not to language or communication problems.

Before admission, 11% of the patients needed practical help with most daily services, but 20% had not been in need of any help at all. The helpers were next of kin (63%), a close friend (10%), and different people (11%). Most patients considered the help to be pretty good or good, but 5 of the patients were less satisfied. More than 50% of the patients considered it pleasant to receive professional care. A few patients felt it as a relief not being a burden to their family; 4 felt resigned or depressed.

Most interviews were experienced as less strenuous. All of the patients reported some type of need. If only 1 kind of need was reported, this was rated as a primary one. More patients ranked the physical needs as primary compared with the psychologic needs, which in turn were more important than the social needs (Table 2). Spiritual needs were only mentioned by 1 person. In the first interview, 14 patients ranked their physical needs as primary, 6 as secondary, and 2 as tertiary. Ten patients ranked their psychological needs as primary, 8 ranked them as secondary, and 1 as tertiary. Social needs were ranked as primary by 6 patients; just as many patients ranked them as secondary as well as tertiary. The rankings were equal in interviews II and III.

In the continued interviews, which comprised a reduced number of patients, the ranking changed in favor of the nonphysical dimensions of need. There was no significant trend related to the kind of need; they varied extensively from 1 interview to another. Correlation analysis on primary needs and symptoms/troubles resulted in no significant outcomes apart from nausea, which was related to physical need ($P < .025$). No significant correlations were found

Table 1 Reported/Registered Symptoms and Problems at the First Interview with 30 Patients

Symptom	Patients, n	Little	Some	Much	Missing Data
Pain	12	3	7	8	0
Shortness of breath	21	1	3	5	0
Cough	23	2	1	4	0
Vomiting	9	7	4	11	0
Loss of appetite	4	5	12	8	1
Diarrhea	20	4	4	2	0
Obstipation	15	3	7	5	0
Incontinence, fecal	25	2	3	—	0
Incontinence, urinary	21	—	2	4	3
Fever	27	—	2	1	0
Bleeding	28	1	1	—	0
Pressure sores	30	—	—	—	0
Bad smells	29	1	—	—	0
Lack of energy	16	2	4	8	0
Depression	21	6	3	—	0
Nervousness	10	10	8	2	0
Sleeplessness	17	7	3	3	0
Confined to bed	12	9	6	3	0
Caring need	4	15	7	4	0
Comatose	29	1	—	—	0
Other[a]	20	3	2	5	0

[a]unsteadiness, 5 patients; infection, cramps, swollen legs, personality change, 1 patient.

between the remaining primary needs (psychologic, social, and spiritual) and symptoms or troubles.

Physical Needs

Many of the physical needs ranked as primary were related to pain. Quotes from different patients reveal a fear of pain, which for many patients seemed to be equal to the experience of pain itself. Other types of needs of a physical character ranked as primary were often related to severe nausea or feebleness. Shortness of breath and a feeling of choking resulted in agony of death. Cough, phlegm, and oral hygiene problems were a recurrent source of irritation for some patients. The lack of opportunities for taking care of personal hygiene made some of the men and women feel in physical decay. Others complained about being cold, that they didn't get any better, or that they wanted to get well and be discharged. A few of the patients had more unusual requests of a physical character.

Table 2 Reported Primary, Secondary, and Tertiary[a] Needs of Patients at the Geriatric Palliative Ward

Interview	Respondents	Physical Needs	Psychologic Needs	Social Needs	Spiritual Needs
I	30	14-6-2	10-8-1	6-6-6	0-0-0
II	20	10-6-3	6-5-1	4-3-2	0-0-0
III	10	6-0-0	3-2-1	1-2-1	0-0-0
IV	4	2-0-1	1-2-0	1-1-0	0-0-0
V	2	2-0-0	0-1-0	0-0-0	0-0-0
VI	2	1-1-0	0-0-0	0-1-0	1-0-0
VII	1	0-0-0	1-0-0	0-1-0	0-0-0
VIII	1	0-1-0	1-0-0	0-0-1	0-0-0

[a]The combinations of figures refer to the number of patients reporting primary, secondary, and tertiary types of needs, respectively.

The physical needs of a secondary nature (ie, the second most important need) were often similar to the primary ones, which may or may not have been attended to.

Tertiary physical needs mainly concerned the feeling of feebleness. A few patients emphasized the importance of appearance and getting good food.

"I suffer from such perspirations, sometimes I'm soaking wet. To remain without any pain the rest of my days! Shortness of breath and pain make me scared. Spare me this feebleness, feels awful, may as well finish the old man."

"Don't want to be so tired [falls asleep several times during the conversation], that's the only thing!"

"I want to feel cleaner, don't even have the strength to care for my personal hygiene! My only wish is that I get to lie comfortably, but now I have been given a comfortable mattress."

"There is a draft from the fan. I get cold easily, at the same time I perspire a lot. I suffer a lot from it. The nausea is troublesome, but it comes and goes. I want my hair to grow back. The scalp is itchy from the wig and it is so hot. Some people say that the hair may turn blond and curly when it grows out, we'll have to wait and see [laughs]."

Psychologic Needs

Anxiety, uncertainty, and security were explicit and frequent primary psychologic needs among many of the patients. A feeling of longing was often directed towards their home environment, belongings, and "the ordinary" and "freedom." But at the same time, staying at home was associated with anxiety and worry. The wish for taking 1 day at a time and not having to contemplate the future occurred quite frequently.

There was a need for seclusion to get some peace and quiet, maybe to have the opportunity to see relatives, and to be freer to express emotions and reactions to the situation.

A common wish was to think back on their lives, maybe to recapitulate. Some of the patients pointed to psychosocial needs, for example, to restore broken relationships and becoming reconciled before it was too late.

Physical and psychologic fatigue often went hand-in-hand, and they often seemed to have a reciprocal effect. The power of initiative sometimes fell short, but if conquered, there was a feeling of great victory. For example, a patient who had been lying in a draft found the greatest triumph (primary need) when he succeeded at closing the vent. "I knew I could make it. One should never give up!" Worries could also be directed towards variations in psychologic functions such as memory and cognitive functioning.

The psychologic needs to find a meaning in life, feel security, or have opportunities to go out were ranked as second most important (secondary). So were also worries about the future for the spouse and other relatives. Pleasurable needs could include the opportunity to have a good meal. Moreover, there were also expressed needs for contemplating, thinking over their life and to summing up things, and finally, to having their life substantiated by telling others of what their life had been like.

Quite a few psychologic needs were given a tertiary ranking, for example, a mixed anxiety and expectation when awaiting a move to a nursing home or feeling the need to keep their private room.

"What is it going to be like? Where will I end up? What if I didn't have to worry about what the future is going to look like. Want to avoid the anxiety of feeling nauseous and vomiting all the time, don't dare to go anywhere, not even to the hairdresser."

"Want to avoid thinking ahead, just want to relax, take it easy, one day at a time."

"There is no point in wishing to see what the future holds; how my grandchildren will do in life or what is going to happen to the world. No use in worrying; better to live in the present and to take one day at a time."

"I only want to be left in peace."

"I lack the strength to both think and do things now. It's a shame."

"If only I didn't have to wait for answers about everything and being worried about people at home!"

Social Needs

The primary needs of a social nature were often associated with visits from family and close friends, reunions, and practical and economical tasks when moving back home or to a nursing home.

Social needs of a secondary nature often included, as did the primary ones, contact with or care for the family. For a few of the patients, that meant reunion or reconciliation. Practical tasks related to finances or accounting also came up as well as being given some privacy.

Social needs, which had been ranked as tertiary, were also similar to primary and secondary wishes; that is, they comprised troubles about family and finances, the longing for their relatives and privacy, but also retrieving parts of their former way of life.

> "Mostly I wish to come home to friends and family. I do have to think about my wife, to help each other and to be together!"

> ". . . to see my brother, never told you that I have a brother, did I? I regret not staying in contact with him during all these years. But I do hear from my son now. It made me happy and moved me. But is it too late now?"

> "I need to have someone to talk to about anything but illness all the time!"

> "I want the caravan to be ready, cleaned and connected to the car. I need to sort my finances. I don't have a will, do I?"

> "Mostly, I'm worried about the boy; what's going to happen when I'm gone. How will he do in school?"

> "Want to be able to handle my bills and finances."

Spirituality

One person had a primary need of a spiritual nature. However, spiritual needs of secondary and tertiary rank did not occur.

> "I've started to ponder. Ask myself if I'm religious. I've never thought about those things before, but I do now."

Discussion

During the 4 months of observation, the initial (at admission) general state seemed to be dominated by a rather extensive need for care, bad physical condition with nausea, emaciation, pain, anxiety, and feebleness. The palliative care, however, appeared to have had a rapid and intended effect on the physical troubles. Because the observations were made only at the ward, the state and needs of the patients were recorded most thoroughly during the first period after admission. A small portion of the patients could be interviewed for a longer period, a few of them until their deaths.

To have the opportunity to speak about one's fear of being in pain and to have it confirmed that pain relief could be guaranteed seemed to dominate the physical picture of need and was just as prominent as the need of pain relief itself. These findings may suggest that adequate pain relief was accomplished but that the memory of the pain itself was very dominating and strong. Perhaps it points to a need for assurance of relief of recurrent pain. However, the frequent wishes of reduced nausea and increased energy were more difficult to fulfil because of type and course of illness.

Successful pain relief and other types of palliative care may be behind the fact that a great number of psychologic needs were reported. The relief of physical needs may have facilitated the expression of needs of security when being cared for in the hospital. One patient did even admit of pleasurable aspects of life, for example, to allow oneself to long for something or somebody, or maybe to have that feeling of longing fulfilled. It could mean having satisfied the need to come back home to well-known things or being offered a good meal. Many of those who had been uneasy at the time of admission later seemed to have improved their abilities to better specify needs and wishes of psychologic nature, particularly if symptoms of the disease did not stand in the way.

Social needs bore a clear socioeconomic touch. Many patients wished to be with their life partner or children, as well as to look over and secure their future lives. To make sure there were enough pension benefits and savings for continuous care also seemed be important. Moreover, patients expressed a longing for having things taken care of. Issues that had been ignored for a lifetime were now of highest priority, maybe because the patient suspected that not much time was left.

Very few of the patients were interviewed when they were in the very final stage of their lives. Maybe that was one of the reasons why only 1 patient expressed a wish to talk about existential issues and their relation to divine powers (spiritual-existential needs). Great psychologic torment, remorse over the past, and a wish for forgiveness or understanding from significant individuals was also expressed.

Interpreting and describing a strict mapping or preference of needs in the terminal stage of life is risky, however. Depending on the state of illness, identifying and reporting needs can be difficult. Boundaries between categories of needs can become blurry, and the intensity of wishes can be hard to perceive. There may be rapid and wide variations in needs, and individual and unstable preference on wishes can vary under different circumstances.

Conclusion

Despite the limitations of the study, considering the small number of patients, certain tendencies could be noticed in the outcome. Physical pain overshadows everything, at least in the very last stage of life. Furthermore, pain seems to hinder the recognition of other psychologic, social, and spiritual needs. Merely the fear of physical pain, originating from prior experiences of pain, may be the most common feeling to be relieved from. Other important needs appear when pain and other health problems, for example, vomiting and shortness of breath, no longer generate fear of death. The feeling of security mediated by the presence of loved ones, as well as worries about their future, seems to occupy a severely ill person's mind even during the last days of his or her life.

The study was small, and the results may not be accurate for all types of palliative units; however, it did seem to confirm former, unrecorded observations of the priorities of needs among our patients. We intend to repeat the study including a larger number of patients to further investigate end-of life needs.

Notes

1. Hallberg, RI. Death and dying from old people's point of view. A literature review. *Aging Clin Exp Res.* 2004;16:87–103.
2. Lo RS, Woo J, Zhoc KC, et al. Quality of life of palliative care patients in the last two weeks of life. *J Pain Symp Man.* 2002;24:388–397.
3. Kelly B, Burnett P, Pelusi D, Badger S, Varghese F, Robertson M. Terminally ill patients' wish to hasten death. *Palliat Med.* 2002;16:339–345.
4. Singer PA, Martin DK, Kelner M. Quality end-of-life care: patients' perspectives. *JAMA.* 1999;281:163–168.
5. Ottosson JO. *The Patient-Doctor Relationship* [Swedish]. Stockholm, Sweden: *Natur och Kultur*; 1999:282–308.
6. Thomé B. *Living with Cancer in Old Age: Quality of Life and Meaning.* Thesis. Lund University, Faculty of Medicine; 2003.
7. Cox DR, Hinkley DV. *Theoretical Statistics.* London: Chapman & Hall; 1974.

From the Institute of Health and Care Sciences, Sahlgrenska Academy, University of Gothenburg and Sahlgrenska University Hospital (HW) and Department of Geriatric Medicine (AG), Sahlgrenska University Hospital, Gothenburg, Sweden.

Address correspondence to: Helle Wijk, Sahlgrenska University Hospital, Röda stråket 8, 413 45 Göteborg, Sweden; e-mail: helle .wijk@vgregion.se.

Acknowledgments—This study was facilitated by grants from the Coordinating Board of Swedish Research Councils, the Swedish Medical Research Council, Medical and Social Services Administrations, the Helge Axson Johnson Foundation, and the Hjalmar Svensson Foundation. Thanks are due to Valter Sundh, BSc, for statistical discussions and invaluable help with the data processing.

Altered States
What I've Learned about Death & Disability

CAROL LEVINE

More than a year after the death of Terri Schiavo, discussions about her case remain highly polarized. What principles should guide decisions about people who can no longer speak for themselves? Who should make those decisions, and what do various religious traditions say about such cases? The debates may be provocative, frustrating, or both, but they usually take place on the level of theory, principle, and ideology. As a result, they often neglect the lived experience of persons with disabilities and their caregivers. As someone who has cared for a severely disabled person for nearly seventeen years, I can testify that the reality is unromantic, unpleasant, and often unrewarding. Yet I am unwilling to give it up.

In June I marked my fiftieth wedding anniversary. It was not a celebration. For the past several years I have been living with a man who is not my husband. No disapproving frowns, please. This man and I don't share the same bedroom. He has his own room, complete with hospital bed and all the trappings of a mini-clinic. This man-who-is-not-my-husband and I do share many things: children, grandchildren, a past—although not much of a future. He is my husband, although I see only glimpses of the man I married a half-century ago. It is not by chance, I think, that marriage vows place "in sickness" before "in health," because illness can undermine even longstanding, happy relationships. I do not live with this man-who-is-and-is-not-my husband because of some words I said when I was twenty-one, or because the law says I am responsible for his care, or because my religion says it is my duty. I live *with* him because after all these years I do not know how to live *without* him.

What happened to him happened to me as well. We were both in a terrible automobile accident. I was not injured, but he suffered a near-fatal brain-stem injury. He was in a coma for four months, and had to undergo painful therapy for years. As a result of medical error, his right forearm had to be amputated. He is essentially quadriplegic. Without medication he is in a state of perpetual rage, and even with it, he sometimes becomes disoriented and unreachable. With each medical crisis, we adjust to the "new normal," which is invariably a decline.

In previous generations, people with disabilities were stigmatized, and often hidden away from the outside world. Thanks to advocates for the disabled, that has changed. Inclusion rather than exclusion is the goal. This is a good and just approach, but sometimes in our enthusiasm for accommodating people with disabilities, we can overlook the real challenges these conditions impose. The mantra among advocates for the disabled is "we are all dependent and only temporarily able-bodied." True enough, but how helpful is this notion if you are, say, dependent on a mechanical respirator, not just on the ties that bind a family or a neighborhood? Or, more prosaically, if you are kept waiting on a rainy street corner for a wheelchair-accessible van while the "temporarily able-bodied" jump in cabs?

Accommodations notwithstanding, major disabilities are inherently limiting, in different ways for different people. This is particularly true for people who suffer from cognitive disorders. In *Rescuing Jeffrey,* the story of his seventeen-year-old son's devastating spinal-cord injury, Richard Galli writes: "Jeffrey,' I said, 'you are not your legs. Jeffrey is up here.' I tapped his head. 'Jeffrey is up here, and that means you are still here, all of you." Would he have been able to say that if Jeffrey had suffered a traumatic brain injury? If Jeffrey were in a coma? Or, like Terri Schiavo, in a persistent vegetative state?

Ethicists have suggested that victims of brain injuries must deal with a "drastically altered" sense of self. I cannot say with certainty how my husband perceives himself. As long as he is comfortable, pain-free, and taken care of, he seems to accept his limited life. He even enjoys some of it, like visits from his grandchildren, football on television, and frozen yogurt. But at some level he hates it. He screams and howls in his sleep, and sometimes when he is awake as well. This once sociable, outgoing man now has only a few people in his life—me, our children and grandchildren, the kind and patient home-care aides who take care of him while I work, and underemployed actors I pay to read to him every afternoon.

Yet my husband definitely has a "self," as drastically altered as it is. As I understand it, to have a "self," an "identity," one must be able to perceive one's existence as separate from other people, from sources of pleasure and pain, from the wind and the rain, from the universe. One must be conscious of one's body and mind, however impaired. When my husband was in a coma, he had no "self" in this sense, and afterwards, no memory of the accident, or any of its consequences. I helped him construct a new "self," gave him a narrative of the events that he could integrate into his new identity. But it was a selected narrative—my version of his story—that he now accepts as his own.

I can speak more confidently of my own "drastically altered self." Novelist and essayist Joan Didion calls the year after her husband John Gregory Dunne's sudden death "the year of magical thinking." While rationally she understood that Dunne was dead, at some level this was so unacceptable that she could not bring herself to get rid of his shoes because when he came back he would need them. If magical thinking is common after a loved one's death, how much more powerful it is when the person is not dead but in a coma or persistent vegetative state. How comforting it is to believe that the magic of a kiss, a favorite song, a new drug, a new procedure will restore this precious person to us.

For many years I believed that I could bring back the person I loved by sheer persistence and will. I tried various medical, psychological, and spiritual remedies. My husband was one of the first people in New York to be injected with Botox when it was an experimental drug, not to smooth his wrinkles but to try to release some of the tightness in his legs that was inhibiting physical therapy. A nurse performed "therapeutic touch"—a kind of waving of hands over his body that was supposed to release negative energy. Prayers—many prayers of different religions—were said for him.

Yet all that magical thinking failed, and now I live with the man-who-is-and-is-not-my-husband. The person-who-was-me rarely spoke in meetings, avoided confrontation, and trusted doctors. This person-who-is-now-me rages—politely of course—at a health-care system that saved her husband's life but then abandoned him, at politicians who give bouquets to caregivers and then cut services, and at people who express surprise that "she is still working" (don't they know that insurance doesn't cover "custodial" care?). To all these people I say: Come, be my drastically altered self for a week, including being the night nurse (who never has a full night's sleep), and then we'll talk.

But this person-who-is-now-me is also a better writer, a less fearful speaker, a more determined advocate for her husband, if not for herself. She knows how to reattach a motor under a hospital bed. She knows that the "charge nurse" is the go to person in the ER. She is not afraid to die. She is sometimes, however, afraid to keep on living.

Kristi Kirschner, a rehabilitation physician, recently wrote an article about the dilemmas facing people who suffer debilitating injuries. She notes that while some people initially want to die, most patients ultimately adjust to their condition. She writes about Jeffrey Galli, the young man with a spinal-cord injury, and then allows Jeffrey to respond to her analysis. Now in his early twenties, Jeffrey has a pragmatic view of life. Kirschner writes: "There are other experiences that will be available to Jeffrey because of his injury. He will live life at a slower pace." To this Jeffrey replies: "This was forced on me, it did not become 'available.' I am unable to refuse it." Another benefit of his new condition, Kirschner says, is that "he will learn about interdependency." Jeffrey: "Not learn about, but again, forced to be dependent. And it's not very 'inter.'" Says Kirschner: "Jeffrey feels a strong sense of self-determination—when it comes to his life, he is the 'final authority.'" This Jeffrey does not dispute.

My husband also wants to be the final authority on his life, which includes his death. As confused as he is about some things, he has been very clear and consistent about his wishes about death. He has even planned his own funeral. Advance directives and health-care proxies may be flawed, but they are all we have to turn to in the face of the medical-care system that always seems to have one more test, one more procedure, all designed to delay the inevitable.

As for me, appropriately enough in his centenary year, I turn to Samuel Beckett who wrote in *The Unnameable:* "I can't go on. I'll go on."

CAROL LEVINE, former editor of the Hastings Center Report, directs the Families and Health Care Project at the United Hospital Fund in New York City. This article is based on a presentation at "Reflections on the End of Life: Schiavo Plus One," sponsored by the Fordham Center on Religion and Culture last April.

Life after Death

If life is a journey, what is the destination? We asked people 50 and over to share their most deeply held beliefs. The result is an illuminating glimpse into America's spiritual core.

BILL NEWCOTT

For all the nudging and pushing and jockeying for position among the sweaty tourists who surround me on the floor of the Sistine Chapel this summer morning, it's nothing compared with the cyclone of activity going on up there on the front wall.

In Michelangelo's painting *The Last Judgment* there's little doubt about who's going where. On the left, a swirl of saints and martyrs ascend Heavenward, their faces a mix of rapture and shock. They soar triumphantly, flanking the figure of a Risen Christ. On the right, it's a decidedly downward trend, a slightly more populated mix of eternal unfortunates being dragged, pushed, and hurled into the abyss. I step around behind the altar—a vantage virtually no one else seems interested in—and marvel at the nearly hidden figures of three apelike creatures, seemingly the gatekeepers of a fiery furnace that is glimpsed just beyond.

In appearance and execution *The Last Judgment* is archetypical Mannerist art. But the fact is, the nuts and bolts of Michelangelo's vision are shared by the vast majority of 50-plus Americans.

In an exclusive survey of 1,011 people 50 and over, AARP THE MAGAZINE sought to learn just what Americans in the second half of life think about life after death. Over the years we've seen countless surveys examining Americans' attitudes and beliefs about the afterlife, but we wanted to hear specifically from the AARP generation—those who are more than halfway to the point of finding out, once and for all, precisely how right or wrong they were about life after death.

To begin, we found that people 50 and over tend to be downright conventional in their basic beliefs: nearly three quarters (73 percent) agree with the statement "I believe in life after death." Women are a lot more likely to believe in an afterlife (80 percent) than men (64 percent).

A copyeditor I once knew insisted that you should always capitalize the word *Heaven*. "Heaven," he explained, "is a place. Like Poughkeepsie."

Two thirds of those who believe also told us that their confidence in a life after death has increased as they've gotten older. Among

them is 90-year-old Leona Mabrand. Born in North Dakota, she moved to Oregon in her 20s, married—and watched, one by one, as every member of her family passed on before her. "I'm the only one left of my family tree," she says, her voice a mix of pride and sadness.

Turning down her radio to chat one recent afternoon—Paul Harvey is one of her favorite companions these days—she tells me that the longer she lives, the more miracles she sees, and the more that convinces her that what her Christian faith tells her about the hereafter is true.

77% are not frightened by thoughts of what happens after death.

"The Lord has shown me a lot of good miracles happen," she says. "I'm looking forward to seeing my husband and my family and all those who have gone to their rest before me."

Of course, Christians like Leona aren't the only ones with their eye on an afterlife.

"It reflects our multicultural environment," says Barnard College professor of religion Alan F. Segal, author of *Life After Death: A History of the Afterlife in Western Religion* (Doubleday, 2004). "Most Americans believe they will be saved no matter what they are. In the '60s and '70s there was this thought that the boomers were not particularly religious; they were busy finding jobs and setting up house. But as they entered their fourth decade, they returned. I'm not sure it was a religious revival—it may have been they were just returning."

It may also reflect a repudiation of the long-held notion that science is the source of all of life's answers, adds Huston Smith, Syracuse University professor emeritus of religion and author of the 2.5 million-copy-selling *The World's Religions: Our Great Wisdom Traditions* (HarperSanFrancisco, 1991).

"Belief in an afterlife has risen in the last 50 years," he says. "Serious thinkers are beginning to see through the mistake modernity made in thinking that science is the oracle of truth."

Believers show general agreement over the choice of destinations in the afterlife, as well: 86 percent say there's a Heaven, while somewhat fewer (70 percent) believe in Hell.

After that, the groups break down into subsets. While most people 50 and over believe there's life beyond the grave, there's a spectrum of visions regarding just what's ahead.

Location, Location, Location

A copyeditor I once knew insisted that you should always capitalize the word *Heaven*. "Heaven," he explained, "is a place. Like Poughkeepsie." He'd be in the minority among those 50 and over who believe in Heaven. Just 40 percent believe Heaven is "a place," while 47 percent say it's a "state of being." As for the alternate destination, of those who think Hell exists, 43 percent say it's a "state of being"; 42 percent say it's "a place" (although not, presumably, like Poughkeepsie). "Heaven's a place, all right," says Ed Parlin, 56, of Salem, New Hampshire, about Heaven. And he's got some ideas of what to expect. "It's a better place than this is—that's for sure," he says. "And I guess everybody gets along. It's always a beautifully clear day, and sunny, with great landscaping."

86% believe in Heaven.

"Americans see life after death as a very dynamic thing," says Barnard College's Segal. "You don't really hear about angels and wings, sitting on clouds playing melodies. A lot believe there will be sex in the afterlife, that it'll be more pleasurable, less dangerous, and it won't be physical, but spiritual. They talk about humor in the afterlife, continuing education, unifying families—like a retirement with no financial needs."

There's a line in Matthew's Gospel that states: "It is easier for a camel to go through the eye of a needle than for a rich man to enter the kingdom of God." And perhaps not so coincidentally, our survey shows the richer people are, the less likely they are to believe there's a Heaven. Among those with a household income of $75,000 or more per year, 78 percent believe in Heaven—compared with 90 percent of those earning $25,000 or less. Similarly, 77 percent of college-educated people think there's a Heaven, compared with 89 percent of those who have a high school diploma or less.

The Price of Admission

While the overwhelming majority of Americans 50 and over believe in Heaven, there's a lot of splintering when it comes to just what it takes to arrive there. The largest group, 29 percent of those who believe in Heaven, responded that the prerequisite is to "believe in Jesus Christ." Twenty-five percent said people who "are good" get in. Another 10 percent said that people who "believe in one God" are welcomed into Heaven. Likewise, 10 percent took a come-one, come-all philosophy, saying everyone gets into Heaven.

94% believe in God.

And while 88 percent of people believe they'll be in Heaven after they die, they're not so sure about the rest of us. Those responding said 64 percent of all people get to Heaven. And many think the percentage will be a lot smaller than that.

"Fifteen percent," says Ira Merce of Lakeland, Florida. He admitted it's just a guess on his part, but he's still not happy about it. "I'd like to see the percentages turned exactly around, but I can't see it happening. If you read Scripture, it says, 'Broad is the way that leads to destruction, and narrow is the way that leads to eternal life.'"

Among those who told us they believe in Hell, their attitudes about who goes there generally mirrored the poll's results about Heaven. Forty percent of those who believe in Hell said "people who are bad" or "people who have sinned" go there; 17 percent said, "People who do not believe in Jesus Christ" are condemned to spend their afterlife in Hell. And in what has to be the understatement of all eternity, Ed suggests, "It's probably a place where you're gonna do things that you don't like to do."

70% believe in Hell.

Second Time Around?

Twenty-three percent of those responding said they believe in reincarnation—meaning there are a fair number who have an overlapping belief in Heaven and a return trip to Earth. The percentage was highest in the Northeast (31 percent), and boomers were most likely to believe in reincarnation.

"It's controversial here [in the United States], but reincarnation is a mainstay of the Eastern religions—Hinduism, Jainism, and Sikhism," says Ishani Chowdhury, executive director of the Hindu American Foundation. "You see more and more people of the younger generation weighing it at the same level as Western religions and not dismissing it."

Adds Jeffrey Burton Russell, professor emeritus of history at the University of California, Santa Barbara, and author of *A History of Heaven* (Princeton University Press, 1998): "If you took this study 50 years ago, the belief in reincarnation would be down at about one percent. Generally, the traditionally clear Christian vision of Heaven has declined, while the vaguer visions of the continuation of life have taken its place."

One true believer is Linda Abbott of St. Louis. "We have to come back," she tells me. "We come back over and over until we get it right!"

More than half of those responding reported a belief in spirits or ghosts—with more women (60 percent) than men (44 percent) agreeing. Boomers are a lot more likely to believe in ghosts (64 percent) compared with those in their 60s (51 percent) or 70s or older (38 percent). Their belief is not entirely based on hearsay evidence, either. Thirty-eight percent of all those responding to our poll say they have felt a presence, or seen something, that they thought might have been a spirit or a ghost.

"We've had some strange experiences," says Ed, who once lived in a house he suspected might be haunted. "Doors closing that shouldn't close, things falling down when you know they're stable. Kind of like someone on the other side was trying to get our attention."

Still, despite all those great stories about old haunted houses in the Northeast and Deep South, it was respondents from the West (50 percent) who were especially likely to say they'd felt the presence of a spirit or a ghost.

What's with That White Light?

Can you die and live to tell the tale? Some people come awfully close, and a few return with a remarkable story: of euphoria, a bright light (sometimes at the end of a tunnel), encounters with dead relatives, or an out-of-body experience, in which they feel as if they're hovering over their physical body. Scientists call these near-death experiences, or NDEs; polls show 4 to 5 percent of Americans say they've had one.

Some experts dismiss NDEs as nothing more than an altered state of consciousness. "It's very likely that REM [rapid eye movement] sleep and the arousal system of the brain are contributing to NDEs," says Kevin Nelson, M.D., a University of Kentucky neurophysiologist. His research suggests that people with NDEs have a "different brain switch" that blends sleep with wakefulness—which reduces the ordeal of dying to a dreamlike state.

But lots of people believe NDEs are glimpses of the afterlife—and there's some data to indicate there's something happening beyond the realm of physiology.

Some of the most intriguing findings come from Pim van Lommel, a retired cardiologist from the Rijnstate Hospital in Arnhem, Netherlands, who followed 344 survivors of cardiac arrest; 18 percent reported having had NDEs while their brains showed no wave activity. This perplexes van Lommel because, he says, "according to our current medical concepts it's impossible to experience consciousness during a period of clinical death."

"The out-of-body component of the NDE is actually verifiable," says Sam Parnia, M.D., PH.D., a critical-care physician at New York City's Weill Cornell Medical Center. He says patients who report watching their own resuscitation from above may have had visions—or they may be recollecting false memories. He plans to place markers, visible only from the ceiling, in emergency rooms across the United Kingdom, then quiz patients who report having had NDEs.

"If they correctly identify these targets," says Parnia, "that suggests the experience was real."

—Anne Casselman

No Place to Go

Nearly one quarter of those responding agreed with the statement "I believe that when I die, that's the end." It's not the sort of statement that invites a lot of questions for clarification, but Tom, a friendly, outspoken fellow I chatted with from the Lake Champlain region of upstate New York, took a shot at it.

To the question "Is there life after death?" Tom responds, "Nope. I've always felt that way. Life's short enough without having to worry about something you can't do anything about anyway. It's just reality, you know? I mean, I'm a Catholic."

Tom waits while I lift my jaw from the table. A *Catholic?*

"Sure. They preach life after death, you know? I just say, hey, people preach a lot of stuff. You just gotta make up your own mind about things. I go to Mass. I live my life like there's life after death, but I don't believe there is. If it's true, well, hey, it's a plus. But if it ain't, I didn't lose nothing."

He laughs, and I laugh with him. (He does ask that I not divulge his last name, and I wonder if that's to cover his tracks just in case God picks up this issue of AARP THE MAGAZINE.) Nonetheless, it's interesting that Tom tries to live as if there were an afterlife, even though he doesn't believe in one. It seems to echo what others tell me about how their beliefs in the hereafter—or lack thereof—impact the way they live their lives. Surprisingly, few confess their beliefs have any effect at all. And everyone I talk to agrees we should be living our lives according to a moral code—which many would define as God's code—whether there's a God at all, or a reward awaits.

As 90-year-old Leona puts it, "I just want to be faithful to Jesus every day and do what's right."

The sentiment, I discovered, is echoed across a wide spectrum of belief—and disbelief. "Atheists celebrate life, but we know death is a reality," says Margaret Downey, president of Atheist Alliance International. "We believe the only afterlife that a person can hope to have is the legacy they leave behind—the memory of the people who have been touched by their lives."

No matter what your belief, adds Omid Safi, former cochair for the study of Islam at the American Academy of Religion, "even though we use words like *afterlife,* or the *next life,* the *life beyond,* it is actually a great mirror about how people like to see themselves now, and the way they see God, and the way they see themselves interacting with other people."

For my money, there have been two great books written about the afterlife: Dante's *The Divine Comedy* and C.S. Lewis's *The Great Divorce.* Of course, Lewis's book is funny, and shorter, so it's better: a guy gets on a commuter bus and finds himself on a tour of Heaven and Hell. Still, both writers seem to reach similar conclusions: whether we choose to take any side in the afterlife conversation, the reality is heading relentlessly toward us. We can straddle the line between belief and unbelief all we want, but in a world where we love to split the difference when it comes to spiritual matters, where inclusiveness often means reaching consensus on conceptual matters, the answer to the ultimate question of life after death leaves no room for quibbling. The position you took during your earthly life is either spot on or dead wrong.

The figures on Michelangelo's monumental fresco seem ready to tumble over me, and I figure it's time to make room for some new tourists. At the back of the Sistine Chapel, I notice two doors: a large one to the left and a smaller one to the right. I ask an English-speaking tour guide which way I should go.

"That way"—he points to the right—"is a lovely long staircase. And if you keep going, there's a shortcut to St. Peter's Basilica. That way"—he jerks his head to the left—"you snake through a dozen more galleries and stand on a two-hour line to get into the basilica."

He pauses, then adds, "It's Hell."

Additional reporting by Emily Chau.

UNIT 3
The Dying Process

Unit Selections

Key Points to Consider

- What is palliative care? Palliative care is often thought to apply to end-of-life issues only, but why not practice palliative care with all patients, whether terminally ill or not? Pain is pain, whether dying or otherwise. Palliative care addresses not only an individual's physical needs but also the spiritual, social, and psychological needs.

- The homeless and prisoners are biologically alive, yet sometimes it seems that they are socially dead. They unfortunately are viewed by some individuals as outcasts, as they are not integrated into society as a whole. They are "imprisoned," literally and/or figuratively. What are their attitudes and concerns toward end-of-life issues?

- Do the living really talk to the dead? Do they "see" deceased family members and friends? Have you ever had such an experience? Were you hallucinating or were you actually observing such things?

Student Web Site

www.mhcls.com

Internet References

American Academy of Hospice and Palliative Medicine
http://www.aahpm.org

Hospice Foundation of America
http://www.hospicefoundation.org

Hospice Hands
http://hospice-cares.com

National Prison Hospice Association
http://www.npha.org

The Zen Hospice Project
http://www.zenhospice.org

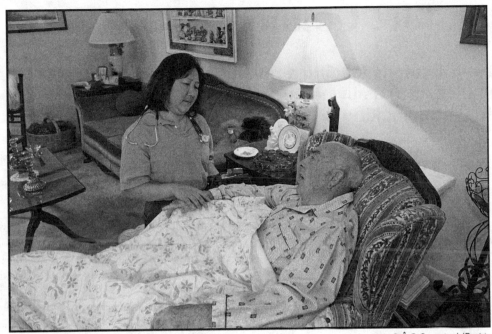

Although death comes at varied ages and in differing circumstances, for most of us there will be time to reflect on our lives, our relationships, our work, and what our expectations are for the ending of life. This is called the dying process. In recent decades, a broad range of concerns has arisen about that process and how aging, dying, and death can be confronted in ways that are enlightening, enriching, and supportive. Efforts have been made to delineate and define various stages in the process of dying so that comfort and acceptance of our inevitable death will be eased. The fear of dying may heighten significantly when actually given the prognosis of a terminal illness by one's physician.

Awareness of approaching death allows us to come to grips with the profound emotional upheaval that will be experienced. Fears of the experience of dying are often more in the imagination than in reality. Yet, when the time comes and death is forecast for the very near future, it is reality, a situation that may be more fearful for some than others. Perhaps you know someone who has communicated with and even "seen" a deceased family member or friend. What is really happening here? Is such an experience a hallucination or is it real? Stafford Betty looks into this "twilight zone" to determine if this is real or a mere hallucination.

In "The Comfort Connection," Joanne Kenen addresses the importance of comfort for the dying via palliative care.

On the "fringe" of society are prisoners and homeless individuals. What does a homeless person with no health insurance, and perhaps no known family members, do when illness strikes? What happens when he/she becomes seriously ill and is facing death? What are the concerns and desires of inmates and the homeless? These questions are addressed in "Dying on the Streets" and "Aging Prisoners' Concerns Toward Dying in Prison."

The Comfort Connection

Dr. Diane Meier is quietly leading a revolution to treat patients (and their families, too) as living, breathing, feeling individuals. And why is that so shocking?

JOANNE KENEN

When a loved one dies, the first thing you usually receive from a doctor is a bill. When a patient of Diane Meier, M.D., dies, the family receives a call or a note.

"She was with me when my wife died at home," says Bert Gold, of New York City, still missing Sylvia, his wife of 57 years. "She took me into the living room and put her arms around me and started to cry. She thanked me for letting her take care of Sylvia. Imagine."

Meier, 55, of the Mount Sinai School of Medicine in New York City, is one of the leading exponents of a new and growing discipline known as palliative care. Palliative care means soothing the symptoms of a disease, regardless of whether a patient is seeking a cure. It's a concept that's totally transforming the way doctors and hospitals treat seriously ill patients. The idea of easing pain and improving the quality of a patient's life may not seem radical, but classic medical training focuses on attacking the disease. Most doctors simply don't have time to be supersensitive Marcus Welbys checking up on patients to see how they feel. Even if they *do* have the time, they lack the advanced training of palliative-care doctors and nurses to ease symptoms such as anxiety, pain, or severe nausea. Most are better equipped to deal with microorganisms than matters of comfort.

When people first hear about palliative care, they often confuse it with hospice care. It's not. Hospice focuses on terminally ill patients: people who no longer seek treatments to cure them and expect to live about six months or less. Palliative-care teams—consisting of everyone from social workers to physical therapists—can follow patients for days, months, or years.

Thanks in large part to the training and outreach programs Meier runs as the head of the Center to Advance Palliative Care (CAPC) in New York City, the number of hospitals with palliative-care programs has nearly doubled, from 632 in 2000 to 1,240 in 2005. Palliative care has the potential to change the way doctors and nurses address pain and emotional distress—not to mention how they help patients and families sort through their choices as life nears its end.

Bert Gold is doing pretty well for a man who recently turned 91. A retired professor of social work, he lives at home. But he is frail. He takes a lot of medicines. He falls sometimes. He lost a big toe five years ago and still deals with pain and an awkward gait.

Bert visits Meier in her office today before going back to the foot surgeon, and Meier spends more than an hour with him—yes, an hour—reviewing his symptoms, his diet, his medications, his mood. Open or stubborn wounds can be dangerous for elderly patients, but Meier, who has worked with Bert for 12 years, also worries that the pain has isolated him, kept him home watching television instead of going to the Y for his regular bridge game.

"Are you having fun?" she asks.

"No," he says, frowning.

"You're not?"

"No. I'm not depressed, but I'm not having fun."

Meier keeps listening. She offers some advice, more in the spirit of a friend than a doctor. She gently reminds him that even if he doesn't like his wheelchair, it can get him out to a movie now and then. They talk about his diet, good-naturedly negotiating over . . . prunes. Though he flat out refuses to eat them for breakfast, he agrees to have them at lunch. Bert smiles. He has been listened to by a doctor who took the time to treat him not as a collection of symptoms, but as a person who deserves to get the best he can out of life, even at 91.

Meier believes strongly that palliative care should not be the "death team," and she sees patients early in the course of a disease. On one recent day, two palliative-care nurses at Mount Sinai were treating a French-speaking African woman in her 30s dying of AIDS, and a man in his 80s with cancers of the skin, prostate, bladder, and pancreas, who now had relentless hiccups from the march of his tumors through his belly.

"Sometimes something like that—hiccups—will get us in the door, to then say, 'What else is going on? How's life when you're at home and not in the hospital,' " says Sue McHugh-Salera, a palliative-care nurse at Mount Sinai.

Which brings us to another of palliative care's radical-but-shouldn't-be concepts: family meetings. That's right—actually sitting down with patients and their families to discuss the good, the bad, and the scary. Ira Byock, M.D., a longtime leader in hospice care who now heads palliative care at Dartmouth, recalls a man who had been languishing in the ICU for months. The patient was "stable," but no one had helped his family see the chasm between the clinical realities and their hopes for a miracle. So the man's doctor called in the palliative-care team, and Byock set up family meetings to discuss the patient's condition and the family's expectations.

"We couldn't change the fact that he was not going to survive," says Byock. "But when he did die, his family's sadness—as deep as it was—was free of the doubts, the 'could haves' and 'should haves,' that often complicate grief."

Although most of the programs, such as Meier's, are consultant teams, moving through the hospitals and clinics, a few have dedicated inpatient units, such as the 11-bed section at the Massey Cancer Center at Virginia Commonwealth University in Richmond. It's peaceful, without the jarring bustle of a typical hospital floor. Families have their own lounge, with a TV, a computer, games for the kids, and cookie dough in the fridge. Some patients will go home when their symptoms are under control. Some will shift to home hospice. Others will die on the unit, with a lot of hands-on care and fine-tuning of medications. All will have received more focus on their comfort than they would get in a traditional hospital environment.

Traditional doctors focus only on the disease; Meier shifts the balance to quality of life.

Meier's goal is to improve the treatment of seriously ill patients, but she sells hospitals on the idea that palliative care can cut costs. CAPC estimates that hospitals can save up to $3,000 per patient, in part by moving people out of the ICU sooner, avoiding a flurry of tests when it's too late, and slowing the revolving door between nursing homes and emergency rooms.

But not everyone is sold on the benefits. Some health-policy experts are skeptical of the savings (they want more detailed data); others wonder if palliative care should even be its own entity, or whether all physicians should provide the caring, coordination, and communication that Meier gives to her patients. Meier agrees—to a point:

"It's like saying, 'Shouldn't cardiology not have to be there; shouldn't every doctor know how to handle hypertension, congestive heart failure, angina?' Of course every doctor should. But nobody would argue that we don't need specialists to handle the more complex aspects of cardiology."

Palliative-care specialists are needed, she says, to step in and manage the challenging cases that other doctors don't have the skills, or perhaps the time, to manage themselves. "It's the rare primary care practitioner who can do repeated 90-minute family meetings, because they've got 50 patients in the waiting room," she says.

So Meier keeps pushing for more programs. Thirty percent of U.S. hospitals and 70 percent of teaching hospitals now offer palliative care. The more hospitals buy into the philosophy, she says, the better it will be for patients. Too many are stuck in a medical nowhere-land, forced to choose between comfort care and emotional support in a hospice—or a chance to keep fighting their illness. "It's not human nature to accept death and agree to give up on life," says Meier. With palliative care, we don't have to.

JOANNE KENEN is a health writer in Washington, D.C. Learn more about palliative care at www.getpalliativecare.org.

Are They Hallucinations or Are They Real? The Spirituality of Deathbed and Near-Death Visions

L. Stafford Betty, PhD

W hen I try to unpack the many meanings of the word "spirituality," I try not to forget that the word comes from "spirit," and that one of the main meanings of "spirit" is, as my dictionary puts it, "a supernatural being or essence." Thanatologists have long been aware that people very near death, especially if they have *not* been heavily sedated, frequently "see spirits." French historian Philippe Ariès reports that a thousand years ago throughout Western Europe, most slowly dying people saw such spirits—presumably because sedation was unknown (M. Morse, 1990, p. 60). Even today, with heavy sedation the rule rather than the exception, some hospice nurses report that seeing and communicating with spirits is a "prevalent theme" of the dying patients they provide care for (Callanan & Kelley, 1992, p. 83). Usually these spirits bring comfort and a sense of wonder, not only for the dying, but also for the family of the dying. To put it another way, they "spiritualize" death. They suggest to all concerned that this world is not the only one, but that a "spiritual" world awaits the deceased. What is the nature of these spirits and the world they apparently live in? Is the "romance of death" generated by them a false comfort, a useful fiction, or is there something real and sturdy about them? In this article we will look at the evidence on both sides of the question, then come to a tentative conclusion.

Typical Deathbed or Near-Death Visions

According to Callanan and Kelley, visions of the dying come in two types. The first, and more common, are sightings of spirits who come, for the most part, to greet and encourage those who are dying. Most spirits are recognized by the one dying as a dead relative or friend. These spirits may visit for minutes or even hours; they are not seen by those at the bedside of the dying person, but it is often obvious that the dying person is communicating with an unseen presence or presences. Dozens of such communications are recorded by Callanan and Kelley, of which the following is typical: "Martha described several visitors unseen by others. She knew most of them—her parents and sister, all of whom were dead—but couldn't identify a child who appeared with them" (Callanan & Kelley, pp. 87–88). Martha goes on to explain to her nurse, "They left a little while ago. They don't stay all the time; they just come and go. . . . sometimes we talk, but usually I just know that they're here. . . . I know that they love me, and that they'll be here with me when it's time" (p. 88).

The other type of vision is a transcendental glimpse of the place where the dying think they're going. "Their descriptions are brief—rarely exceeding a sentence or two—and not very specific, but usually glowing" (p. 99). At the end of Tolstoy's famous novella "The Death of Ivan Ilych," Ivan exclaims on his deathbed, "So that's what it is! What joy!" (1993, p. 63)—the last words he ever spoke. His words are typical of visions of this second kind. But since there is no way to ascertain whether this type of vision is veridical or hallucinatory, I won't give much attention to it. Suffice it to say that those who have such visions invariably report them as glimpses of a real world, not as chimeras.

So we will be concentrating on the visions that people close to death have of beings, not of places. Are these visions more than likely veridical? Are they sightings of real beings that any of us, properly equipped, could see, and who exist in their own right whether we see them or not? Or are they hallucinations? Are they as the word is commonly used, sensory perceptions that are unrelated to outside events—in other words, seeing or hearing things that aren't there?

I should add here that two types of people close to death have visions of deceased spirits: (1) those dying slowly, often of cancer, who see spirits at their bedside, and (2) those not necessarily dying who have a potentially fatal experience that culminates in a near-death experience (NDE). Those dying slowly are usually aware of their surroundings and can communicate simultaneously with both the living and the dead—as if they have one foot in this world and one in the next. Those who meet dead relatives or friends during NDEs are completely cut off from our world as they communicate with the deceased. Yet the descriptions of these spirits given by NDErs after their return from the "Other World" are the same as the descriptions given by the slowly dying. The spirits are usually recognizable, loving, and supportive. Sometimes they are described as "takeaway spirits" or "greeters."

The Argument for the Spirit Hypothesis

Social scientists usually have little patience with any theory that takes seriously the reality of beings on the "Other Side." Words used to describe them like "transcendental" or "spiritual" are often looked at with suspicion if not dismissed as nonsense. But there are excellent reasons for taking them seriously. I will list them under four headings.

1. First, persons near death usually insist that the phantasms they see are not hallucinations, but living spirits existing in their own right. This insistence is especially impressive when the dying person is an atheist or materialist who does not believe in life after death. "I'm an atheist. I don't believe in God or Heaven," a 25-year-old woman named Angela, and dying of melanoma, declared to her nurse (Callanan & Kelley, p. 89). Blind and partially paralyzed, she nevertheless had a vision, and it changed her outlook on death. "I don't believe in angels or God," she told her nurse, "but someone was here with me. Whoever it was loves me and is waiting for me. So it means I won't die alone" (p. 90).

Angela's claim is of course easy to dismiss. One can claim, not without reason, that Angela hallucinated a takeaway spirit to ease her despair in the face of eternal extinction. NDErs are typically just as adamant about the reality of the spirits they encounter while out of their body, and social scientists usually react to these claims in the same skeptical fashion. But the sheer volume of such claims by persons near death is impressive. And it is all the more impressive when put alongside similar claims made by other visionaries *not* near death. Conant's study of bereaved but otherwise healthy widows (1996), to take but one example, reveals the same insistence by some of the widows that the spirits who visited them were real. Conant reports that the "vividness of the experience amazed them. The comparison to hallucinations was voiced simultaneously five times and was always rejected. These were *not* hallucinations" (p. 186). Some of the widows "seemed to be amazed by the emotional power of the experience more than by its vividness because of the conviction they had been in contact with the spirit of the deceased [husband]" (p. 187). Not all the widows in the study were confident that the spirits of their

husband actually paid them a visit; most felt that their culture discouraged a "spiritual interpretation" of their visions, and several worried about "the connotation of craziness" (p. 188) that such an interpretation carried. But all agreed that the vision "feels real" (p. 194). And all, even the most skeptical, derived "reassurance that life after death was possible for the deceased . . . as well as for themselves when they would eventually die" (p. 192). I myself am impressed enough by all these visions, especially their feeling of "realness," to keep an open mind about their ontological status. Not so Conant herself. While acknowledging that such visions "served as a safe haven to help mend the trauma of loss, as an inner voice to lessen current social isolation, as an internal reworking of self to meet new realities, and as reassurance of the possibility of immortality" (p. 195), she describes them as "vivid hallucinations." The ontological status of the visions is never discussed. She appreciates that the visions are useful fictions and therefore salutary, but the possibility that they might be real apparently never occurred to her.

Conant's study is especially relevant to our study for two reasons. First, even though she is not studying visions of the dying or potentially dying, the visions of her collection of widows seem to be of the same quality. Though invisible to everyone else, they are convincingly real to the one having the vision, they are recognizable, and they usually convey a message of reassurance. Second, Conant is a cautious, thoroughgoing social scientist with, if anything, a bias against drawing transcendental conclusions based on her research. What she wanted to show was that visions of the deceased should be regarded as successful coping mechanisms, not as delusions that should be discouraged. Her interests run in a completely different direction from mine, yet I find her useful. When two minds so differently attuned find a common ground, there is often something important going on.

2. The second prong of the argument for the reality of spirits comes from a careful analysis of them. The spirits of persons who are identified by NDErs or by the slowly dying have one thing in common: They are almost always spirits of the deceased. You might ask yourself why all these hallucinations are so tidy. Everywhere else hallucinations are higgledy-piggledy. Aunt Adelaide alive on earth is just as likely to be hallucinated as Aunt Jill who died five years before. But these hallucinations, if that's what they are, have sorted themselves out. With uncanny regularity only the dead show up. Why should that be?

The materialist might answer that it would be *illogical* to hallucinate someone you thought was still alive. After all, a person can't be living on earth and living on the Other Side at the same time. If you had a vision of someone alive on this side of the veil, that would be *proof* you were hallucinating and would undercut the benefit you might derive from the hallucination. So the subconscious mind sorts out who's died and who hasn't. It keeps track. And when your time is up, it decks out a nice dead relative for you to hallucinate, a nice dead relative to take care of you when you finally die. Your fear of death vanishes. So the argument goes. But this argument is not as convincing as it might first appear. After all, how logical *are* hallucinations? Hallucinations are made of memory fragments, and those fragments are no more orderly as they come and go in the theater of the mind than the stuff of our daydreams. Zen masters compare the behavior of this mental detritus to a pack of drunken monkeys. And Aldous Huxley refers to them as "the bobbing scum of miscellaneous memories" and as "imbecilities—mere casual waste products of psycho-physiological activity" (1945, pp. 126–127). The materialist's line of reasoning is plausible up to a point, but it overlooks the almost random nature of hallucinations.

But let us grant for the sake of argument that it does have force. I think I can show that whatever force we grant it for the moment is not good enough in the face of the facts. Here is why.

Let us say I am very sick in my hospital bed and have a near-death experience. I see in my vision my grandpa, long dead, and my cousin Manny, whom I think to be very much alive. They present themselves as spirits, and I recognize them as such, but I am confused. For how can Manny be a spirit since he's alive in the flesh? I come out of my NDE, and I express this confusion to the loved ones gathered around me. But they know something I don't know. They know that Manny was killed in an automobile accident two days before. They didn't tell me because they thought it would upset me. There are quite a few cases like this in the literature, and one whole book, a classic, devoted to them (Barrett, 1926). More recently, Callanan and Kelley presented three cases like this in their book on the slowly dying (Chapter Seven), and the Guggenheims (1995) devote a whole chapter to them in their study of after-death communications (ADCs). Here is why I think these cases are so important. If I believe my dear Aunt Mary and Uncle Charlie and my five siblings and my wife and dozens of other relatives and friends, *including my cousin Manny,* are all alive, why should I hallucinate only my cousin Manny from among all these possibilities? Why should my hallucination be so well informed and so selective? It could be a coincidence, but there are too many cases like this for them all to be coincidences. There is always the possibility that I could have known telepathically that Manny, and only Manny from among those I just named, was dead. But if I had never had any powerful telepathic experiences before, isn't this explanation *ad hoc*? I think the best explanation for Manny's appearance alongside my grandpa in my vision is that the newly dead Manny *actually came* (in spirit), along with grandpa, to greet me during my NDE. He was not a hallucination after all. He was not a delusion. He should be taken at face value.

3. The third prong of the argument derives from the physiology of near-death experiences. Recent research by a team of Dutch doctors, led by van Lommel (van Lommel, van Wees, Meyers, & Elfferich, 2001), makes it clear that the typical features of the NDE, including

meetings with deceased relatives, occur while the electro-encephalogram (EEG) is flat-lined—in other words, when the brain is inactive and the whole body is "clinically dead." Van Lommel summarizes the findings:

From these studies [involving 344 cardiac patients studied over an 8-year period] we know that . . . no electric activity of the cortex of the brain (flat EEG) must have been possible, but also the abolition of brain stem activity like the loss of the cornea reflex, fixed dilated pupils and the loss of the gag reflex is a clinical finding in those patients. However, patients with an NDE [18% of the total] can report a clear consciousness, in which cognitive functioning, emotion, sense of identity, and memory from early childhood was possible, as well as perception from a position out of and above their "dead" body. (van Lommel, no date)

Van Lommel elaborates further: Even though the EEG is flat, people

experience their consciousness outside their body, with the possibility of perception out of and above their body, with identity, and with heightened awareness, attention, well-structured thought processes, memories and emotions. And they also can experience their consciousness in a dimension where past, present and future exist at the same moment, without time and space, and can be experienced as soon as attention has been directed to it (life review and preview), and even sometimes they come in contact with the "fields of consciousness" of deceased relatives. And later they can experience their conscious return into their body. (van Lommel, no date)

Van Lommel then asks the obvious question: "How could a clear consciousness outside one's body be experienced at the moment that the brain no longer functions during a period of clinical death with flat EEG?" (van Lommel et al., 2001).

What does all this mean for our thesis? It means that the typical elements of the NDE, including meetings with deceased relatives, are not hallucinations. Hallucinations are produced by an *active* brain, one whose wave pattern would be anything but flat. What, then, could account for the visions of deceased loved ones? It appears that the dying person or nearly dead person, free from her physical body for a few moments, enters a world, an ethereal world, close by but undetectable by the physical senses. She looks like a corpse to an outside observer, but she is having the experience of a lifetime—in another dimension. An experience of what? She says an experience of real beings, embodied beings, dead people she recognizes. Is there any good reason to keep our minds closed to this possibility, given the unintelligibility of the alternative?

4. The fourth and last prong of the argument is, like the one we've just looked at, exclusively concerned with the near-death experience, and not the visionary experiences of the slowly dying who do not have an

NDE. Glimpsing spirits of deceased relatives is a standard feature of the NDE, so anything that argues for the veridicality of the NDE *as a whole* gives support for our thesis.

There is quite a bit that does. I will organize it under three headings.

First, many reports of things seen by NDErs having an out-of-body experience (OBE) turn out to be veridical. There are hundreds of examples in the serious literature on NDEs. One woman saw a shoe sitting on an upper-story ledge of her hospital—a shoe invisible from the street or from her room—as she drifted out of the building during her NDE; the shoe, upon inspection, turned out to be exactly where she said it was. Another woman took a trip to see her sister and later reported what her sister was doing and wearing at the time—a report later verified by the surprised sister who wondered how she knew. A five-year-old child described in detail, and with impressive accuracy, what happened when her body was being resuscitated while she, out of her body, watched from near the ceiling of her hospital room. In fact it is common for NDErs to describe their resuscitations while they are clinically dead. Michael Sabom, an Atlanta cardiologist, conducted an experiment involving resuscitation accounts to see how accurate they were:

Sabom asked twenty-five medically savvy patients to make educated guesses about what happens when a doctor tries to get the heart started again. He wanted to compare the knowledge of "medically smart" patients with the out-of-body experiences of medically unsophisticated patients.

He found that twenty-three of the twenty-five in the control group made major mistakes in describing the resuscitation procedure. On the other hand, none of the near-death patients made mistakes in describing what went on in their own resuscitations. (M. Morse, 1990, p. 120)

It is difficult to account for the accuracy of NDE accounts if NDErs are hallucinating. Why should hallucinations be so accurate? Why should they yield far more accuracy than the accounts of imagined resuscitations provided by "medically savvy" patients relying on their memory?

Second, NDEs are often profoundly life-changing. Melvin Morse did an extensive "Transformations study" to quantify what every NDE researcher already knew: that people who have a deep, well-developed—or "core"—NDE are dramatically transformed by their experience. He reported "amazing results": "After we finished analyzing the data from the more than four hundred people who participated in the research project, we discovered that the near-death experience causes many long-term changes" (M. Morse, 1992, p. 60). He grouped them under four headings: decreased death anxiety, increase in psychic abilities, higher zest for living, and higher intelligence. In the exhaustive study referred to above, van Lommel and his cohorts reported that the "transformational processes after

an NDE were very similar" and encompassed "life-changing insight, heightened intuition, and disappearance of fear of death" (van Lommel et al., 2001, p. 3).

The question that is natural to ask at this point is, Can hallucinations transform the people who have them? D. Morse, a clinical psychologist and hard-nosed materialist until he had his own NDE, has this to say about hallucinations:

Descriptions given of hallucinations are often hazy and contain distortions of reality, while NDE descriptions are usually normally ordered and lifelike. Hallucinations are often accompanied by anxiety feelings, while NDEs are generally calm and peaceful. Hallucinations afterwards rarely cause life-changing occurrences as do NDEs. (D. Morse, 2000, pp. 48–49)

NDErs, like the widows we surveyed above, typically insist on the "realness" of their experience and that it is this realness that gives them hope of seeing their loved ones again. This quality of "realness," and the transformative quality that derives from it, is verified by van Lommel. He found in follow-up studies that most of his patients who did not have an NDE (the control group) did not believe in an afterlife, whereas those who had one "strongly believed in an afterlife" (no date, p. 8) and showed "positive changes." Furthermore, these changes were more apparent at the eight-year follow-up than the two-year (p. 8). Something deeply and lastingly transformed this second group of people. Which is more likely: That a hallucination did this, or that an overwhelming slap in the face by something very real did it?

Third, near-death researchers, beginning with Moody (1975), have consistently identified the "core features" of the NDE, and claim that these features recur in individuals having very little in common other than their NDE. It appears that NDEs from cultures as different as Japan, India, sub-Saharan Africa, and the West all exhibit these core features. Now, it is known that hallucinations vary radically from person to person—so much so that it would be surprising if one person's hallucination was at all similar to his next-door neighbor's, not to mention someone's from a different culture. How can the similarity in this core experience be explained? If by hallucination, then obviously not by any ordinary hallucination.

Rather than go out on a limb and posit a universal hallucination that all humans carry seed-fashion deep in their brains, most NDE researchers suspect the commonality is explainable by a common environment, or world, that opens up to the NDEr. In other words, they all see much the same thing because the world that opens up to them is not infinitely variable, like hallucinations, but is simply the way it is. It is real, in other words; and reality, while it admits of considerable variation and can be interpreted in a variety of ways, is malleable only up to a point. Beyond that point, all NDErs experience very much the same thing—just as an Inuit and a Zulu, in spite of radically different cultures and geographies, would experience the one world that belongs to us all and be able to talk about it meaningfully to each other. The Zulu and the Inuit might have different feelings about the spirits they met in their respective NDEs, but they would at least be able to say they encountered beings, many whom they recognized, that did not belong to the world of the living.

So again we must choose: Is it more reasonable to explain away the core experience as hallucinatory, or as a reflection of something that is real and is encountered? The only skeptical theory that makes sense is the "seed theory" I mentioned above. It is not a preposterous explanation, but is it the more likely? We must each decide for ourselves. Given the other prongs of the argument presented here, however, it seems much more likely, at least up to this point, that the spirits we see during our NDEs or as we near death after a long illness are what they seem to be: real beings from the world we might be about to enter.

The Weakness in the Spirit Hypothesis

It would be dishonest of me to fail to point out the weak link in the spirit hypothesis I've been defending up to this point. Melvin Morse appreciates it fully and asks the question:

> But we shouldn't forget about the woman who saw Elvis in the light, should we? As one skeptic pointed out, "If these experiences are real and not just dreams, how can you explain Elvis?" Or Buddha? How can NDEs of children be explained where they see pet dogs, or elementary school teachers who are still alive? They show up in some NDEs too. How can they be explained? (M. Morse, 1992, p. 128)

The skeptic asks a good question, and the skeptic in me worries more than a little about the idiosyncratic features of some NDEs, especially as found in children. Morse presents a cornucopia of cases involving children, and quite a few play into the skeptic's hands as he dredges the literature for signs of hallucination. For example, take the NDE of a five-year-old who nearly drowned in a swimming pool. Now a scientist in his forties of distinguished reputation, "Tom" recalls passing down a long tunnel toward the Light. All seems quite normal for an NDE until he sees "God on a throne. People—maybe angels—were below looking up at the throne." He goes on: "I sat on the lap of God, and he told me that I had to go back. 'It's not your time,' he said. I wanted to stay but I came back" (M. Morse, 1990, p. 167). Suffice it to say that very few NDErs report seeing God sitting on a throne. In another case, eight-year-old Michelle had an NDE during a diabetic coma. In typical NDE fashion she felt herself float out of her body and watched the resuscitation effort, later describing it in accurate detail. Eventually she was allowed to make a decision to return or not to return to her body, a typical feature of the NDE. But Michelle expressed her will to return in a novel manner: "In front of me were two buttons, a red one and a green one. The people in white kept telling me to push the red button. But I knew I should push the green one because the red one would mean I wouldn't come back. I pushed the green one instead and woke up from the coma" (M. Morse, 1990, p. 39).

Is there really a red and a green button in a world beyond ours? Does God really sit on a throne and talk to little children in that world? Not a chance, I would say. "Then the NDErs must have been hallucinating these bizarre features of the NDE," says the skeptic, "and if these are hallucinations, then doesn't it stand to reason that the entire experience is a hallucination?"

I raised this question to Greyson, editor of the *Journal of Near-Death Studies,* and this was his reply:

> As for Melvin Morse's 8-year-old patient who pushed the green button to return from her coma, I also find it hard to believe that the button was "real." But then I also have difficulty taking as concretely "real" a lot of things described by NDErs, including, in SOME cases, encounters with deceased loved ones and religious figures. I do not think that these are hallucinations, however, or that the experiencers are lying or fabricating memories. What I think is happening is that they are interpreting ambiguous or hard-to-understand phenomena in terms that are familiar to them.
>
> Many NDErs tell us that what they experienced was ineffable—and THAT I believe wholeheartedly. I think that what happens after death is so far beyond our feeble understanding that there is no way for us to describe it accurately in words. Although experiencers may understand fully while they are "on the other side," once they return to the limitations of their physical brains, they have to unconsciously force-fit their memories of incomprehensible events into images they CAN understand. That's why we hear Christians talk about seeing Jesus or Mary, and we hear Hindus talking about yamatoots (messengers of Yama, the god of the dead), and we hear NDErs from "advanced" Western societies—but not NDErs from "primitive" societies—talk about tunnels. (One NDEr who was a truck driver told me about traveling through a chrome tailpipe, an image he could relate to.)
>
> Many NDErs talk about not wanting to return, and yet here they are, so they have to construct some reason to explain their return. Westerners often say that a deceased relative or religious figure told them it was not yet their time, or their work was not finished. That's an acceptable and believable reason for a time-conscious and achievement-oriented Westerner to return. On the other hand, it is common for Indians to say that they were told a mistake had been made, and that the yamatoots were supposed to have taken Ravi Singh the incense-maker, not Ravi Singh the baker. That kind of "bureaucratic bungling," I am told, is more believable in India, as it is typical of the way things often happen in their society. I suspect that an 8-year-old girl with limited understanding had to come up with a concrete image like pushing a green button to return. She did not hallucinate the button, but after the fact her mind came up with that interpretation of what really happened to her to effect her return. It was a misinterpretation rather than a hallucination.

Am I splitting hairs? I don't think so. A hallucination is a perception that occurs in the ABSENCE of any sensory stimulation. I think NDErs DO "see" SOMETHING that is "really" there—but it is so far beyond our understanding that they have to interpret it subsequently in terms of familiar images. It is more like an illusion than a hallucination. If at night you imagine out of thin air that there is a person in your room, that is a hallucination. But if, in the darkness, you misinterpret a hat-rack for a person in your room, that is an illusion, an imprecise interpretation of something that is really there rather than something that sprang up solely from your imagination. That's what I think a lot of NDE imagery is: imprecise interpretations of things that are comprehensible in the bright light of the NDE, but incomprehensible in the dim light of our physical brains. (Personal communication, January 10, 2005)

Greyson has given us a rich, plausible account of the idiosyncratic features of NDEs. But the skeptic might remain dubious. After all, if there really is a world beyond ours, it is hard to imagine what in it would be confused with a green and a red button. To deal with this challenge, I veer slightly away from Greyson's analysis. It seems more plausible to me that the subconscious imagination of the NDEr is *actively supplying material* for the experience; or, alternatively, that someone else over there is actively supplying it for the benefit of the NDEr. In other words, the mysterious world entered into by the NDEr is made more approachable and intelligible—more *friendly* is perhaps a better word—by his own imagination or someone else's (a spirit guide's?) interpretive or artistic power. Whatever be the case, on balance there are, in my judgment, far too many indicators that the NDE is an experience of another world that exists *in the main* independently of the experiencer, even though certain reported features of it might be explainable by a coloring of the experience or by faulty memory of exactly what happened. The claim that the *entire experience* is a hallucinated fictive world strikes me as incredible. Nevertheless, there is room, based on all the evidence at our disposal, for such a claim. It is not a claim with no basis.

A final clarification of my position is in order. I believe that visions of the dying or nearly-dying are a combination of real transcendental material and imaginative projection. For example, Julian of Norwich, very near death when she had her famous visions of the dying Christ, could not have seen Krishna or Vairocana Buddha: They would have had no meaning for her, and the Mind who assisted her in coloring the vision, or alternatively her own imagination, would not have allowed such a thing. Nor could a South American Indian shaman have glimpsed Christ while entranced. But their visions are not purely the stuff of imagination either: were there no transcendental "canvas" to project them onto, there would not have been any vision. As for glimpses of the dying, especially deceased relatives, these visions are much closer to the realities they seem to be. I don't believe they are so much projections outward from dying persons, as projections "toward" them from deceased relatives

who come to greet them. If the skeptic insists on reducing all transcendental phenomena to hallucination, we will not be able to agree on much. We *would* agree, however, that all these visions are, to some extent, cultural, personal, and historical. And we also would agree that most hallucinations in normal subjects (as when a moose charges a sleep-deprived sledder in the Arctic) are not grounded in a transcendental world. In contrast to the visions we have been studying, they exist only in the mind of the subject. They are truly hallucinations.

The Relevance of This Study to the Spirituality of Death

I agree with Lucy Bregman, in her article in this issue, that the word "spirituality" is a wonderful word in search of a meaning. As I tried to show in my opening paragraph, I think the word must be anchored in a transcendent world if it is to retain its distinctive meaning. Otherwise it can become a synonym for *mystique* or *romance*—as when we speak of the spirituality of motherhood or of a sunset or of golf. Each of these can provide wonderful experiences, but they are not what we have in mind when we speak of the *spirituality of death*. As Sherwin Nuland (1995) showed us in his award-winning book *How We Die,* death is not usually a time of wonderful experiences. It is frequently, however, a time of healing experiences, as when long estranged relatives or friends are coerced by death's finality into an act of mutual forgiveness. Perhaps it is not stretching too far the meaning of the word *spirituality* to apply it to such meaningful moments. But there is a time when the word is ideally applicable. That is when a person close to death glimpses a world he or she is about to enter—what we will call the spiritual world, a world where spirits reside, and where the dying will reside when he or she becomes a spirit.

My grandmother transmitted to her family something of the excitement of that world shortly before she died. A devout Christian, she became comatose, or apparently comatose, hours before her death at 94. None of us could reach her, even when whispering our love into her ear. But then my mother happened to whisper that she would soon be with Jesus. So suddenly that we were startled, her eyes opened and her face lit up in great excitement. Like Ivan Ilych, she died joyously. She had a foretaste of the eternal world, the world where spirits reside, and her spirit practically jumped out of her body. Hers was a spiritual experience in the truest sense of the word. The *spirituality of death* may mean many things, but Granny epitomized its meaning for all of us.

But I am not concerned with linguistics or etymology. What I have tried to show here is that books are available to get us ready for death. So are the dying. Callanan and Kelley tell the following story:

> Bobby [who was dying] had spoken clearly for the first time in three days.
>
> "He told us, 'I can see the light down the road and it's beautiful,'" Bill said.

This glimpse of the other place gives immeasurable comfort to many, and often is perceived as a final gift from the one who died.

"I've never been a religious person, but being there when Bobby died was a real spiritual experience," his sister said later. "I'll never be the same again."

Bill echoed her sentiments at the funeral. "Because Bobby's death was so peaceful, I'll never be as scared of death," he said. "He gave me a little preview of what lay beyond it for him, and, I hope, for me." (p. 102)

Whether dying persons are telling us of their glimpse of the next world or conversing with people we can't see, we should consider ourselves immensely blessed when it happens. If we don't make the mistake of assuming they are "confused," we are likely to feel some of the excitement they convey. For we are witnessing the momentary merging of two worlds that at all other times remain tightly compaftmentalized and mutually inaccessible. That merging is what I mean by the spirituality of death

References

Barrett, W. (1926). *Death-bed visions*. London: Methuen.

Callanan, M., & Kelley, P. (1992). *Final gifts*. New York: Bantam.

Conant, R. (1996). Memories of the death and life of a spouse: The role of images and *sense of presence* in grief. In D. Klass, P. Silverman, & S. Nickman (Eds.), *Continuing bonds: New understandings of grief*. Washington, DC: Taylor & Francis.

Guggenheim, B., & Guggenheim, J. (1995). *Hello from heaven!* New York: Bantam.

Huxley, A. (1945). Distractions—I. In C. Isherwood (Ed.), *Vedanta for the western world*. Hollywood: Vedanta Press.

Moody, R. (1975). *Life after life*. New York: Bantam.

Morse, D. (2000). *Searching for eternity*. Memphis: Eagle Wing.

Morse, M. (1990). *Closer to the light*. New York: Ivy.

Morse, M. (1992). *Transformed by the light*. New York: Ivy.

Nuland, S. (1995). *How we die*. New York: Vintage.

Tolstoy, L. (1993). *The Kreutzer Sonata and other short stories*. New York: Dover.

van Lommel, P., van Wees, R., Meyers V., & Elfferich, I. (2001). Near-death experience in survivors of cardiac arrest: A prospective study in the Netherlands. *Lancet, 358*(9298). Retrieved from World Wide Web: . . ./get_xml.asp?booleanTerm=SO=The+Lancet+AND+SU+Near+Death+Experiences&fuzzy Term

van Lommel, P. (no date). A reply to Shermer: Medical evidence for NDEs. Retrieved June 26, 2005 from the World Wide Web: http://www.skepticalinvestigations.org/whoswho/vanLommel.htm.

Dying on the Streets

Homeless Persons' Concerns and Desires about End-of-Life Care

Background: There is little understanding about the experiences and preferences at the end of life (EOL) for people from unique cultural and socioeconomic backgrounds. Homeless individuals are extreme examples of these overlooked populations; they have the greatest risk of death, encounter barriers to health care, and lack the resources and relationships assumed necessary for appropriate EOL care. Exploring their desires and concerns will provide insight for the care of this vulnerable and disenfranchised population, as well as others who are underserved.

Objective: Explore the concerns and desires for EOL care among homeless persons.

Design: Qualitative study utilizing focus groups.

Participants: Fifty-three homeless persons recruited from agencies providing homeless services.

Measurements: In-depth interviews, which were audiotaped and transcribed.

Results: We present 3 domains encompassing 11 themes arising from our investigation, some of which are previously unreported. Homeless persons worried about dying and EOL care; had frequent encounters with death; voiced many unique fears, such as dying anonymously and undiscovered; favored EOL documentation, such as advance directives; and demonstrated ambivalence towards contacting family. They also spoke of barriers to EOL care and shared interventions to improve dying among the very poor and estranged.

Conclusions: Homeless persons have significant personal experience and feelings about death, dying, and EOL care, much of which is different from those previously described in the EOL literature about other populations. These findings have implications not only for homeless persons, but for others who are poor and disenfranchised.

JOHN SONG, MD, MPH, MAT[1,2], DIANNE M. BARTELS, RN, MA, PHD[1,2], EDWARD R. RATNER, MD[1,2], LUCY ALDERTON, MPH[4], BRENDA HUDSON, MS[3], AND JASJIT S. AHLUWALIA, MD, MPH, MS[2,3]

[1]Center for Bioethics, University of Minnesota, N504 Boynton, 410 Church Street S.E., Minneapolis, MN 55455, USA;
[2]Medical School, University of Minnesota, Minneapolis, MN, USA;
[3]Academic Health Center, University of Minnesota, Minneapolis, MN, USA;
[4]Worldwide Epidemiology, GlaxoSmithKline, Mail Stop UP4305, Collegeville, PA 19426-0989, USA.

Background

There remain many deficiencies in how society addresses the needs of dying individuals.[1] One shortcoming is the fundamental assumptions behind end-of-life (EOL) care: it focuses on individuals with loved ones, health care, and a home. Society has not considered homeless persons, who often die without these resources. It is necessary to address EOL care in this population for several reasons. First, the high prevalence of homelessness in the United States, with estimates ranging up to several million,[2] and the disproportionate amount and severity of illness in this population[3,4] is a public health crisis. Homeless persons also suffer high mortality rates—several times the rate of domiciled populations[5-7]—and premature mortality (average ages of death in Atlanta, San Francisco, and Seattle are 44, 41, and 47).[8,9] In addition, homeless persons encounter many barriers to health care[10-12] and, it may be hypothesized, to EOL care. Homeless persons, for example, die with little medical care immediately prior to their deaths.[13] Finally, additional concerns are raised by the unique personal, cultural, and medical characteristics of homelessness. Given the immediacy of basic human needs while living without shelter, homeless persons' concerns beyond daily survival may be different from those of persons who do not worry about food or shelter.

Few studies have addressed EOL care for underserved or disenfranchised persons,[1] and existing work is limited as it reflects the concerns of people with health care and personal resources and relationships. Three studies have previously examined homeless persons and EOL care. One demonstrated that homeless persons are eager to address EOL issues,[14] and a second explored EOL scenarios among homeless persons.[15] A third study addressed ICU care preferences.[16] The first 2 studies, however, are limited by their small and homogeneous samples, and the third focused on one specific aspect of EOL care.

This work represents the first in-depth exploration of a homeless population and their attitudes towards EOL care. We hypothesized that they would have concerns different from those of other previously studied populations. We previously reported how life on the streets influences attitudes towards death and dying (Song et al. submitted for publication) The present paper's objective was to examine how homelessness influences concerns and desires about care at the time of death.

Design

We conducted a qualitative investigation utilizing focus groups of homeless individuals. The study was funded by the NIH/National Institute of Nursing Research and approved by the University of Minnesota Institutional Review Board.

Participants

Participants were recruited from 6 social service agencies that serve homeless persons in Minneapolis and St. Paul, MN. These agencies provide a variety of services, including food, shelter, and health care. Participants were required to be at least 18 years old, speak English, and able to give informed consent. Participants were required to have been homeless at least once in the last 6 months, ascertained by a demographic questionnaire consistent with the federal guidelines.[17]

Participants were recruited through a mixture of random and purposive sampling, utilizing key informants[18]; details of this procedure are detailed elsewhere (Song et al. submitted for publication). Six focus groups were held, with an average of 9 participants per group. Participants were compensated $20. Interim analyses were conducted, and interviews were held until theme saturation was achieved.

Table 1 Interview Guide for Focus Groups

Questions

General questions

Do you have any experience with a serious illness or injury or a close friend or relative who had a serious illness or injury or who has died?

Are you concerned about dying?

Do you think about dying, care while dying, or death? Is this an issue that concerns you?

Is this an issue that you would like to talk about more?

Specific questions

Do you have any one that you can talk to about these issues?

Probes: Do you have family that you are in contact with? Do you have friends that you trust? Do you know any social workers, service providers, or health care providers whom you trust?

What concerns do you have regarding dying, care at the end of life, and death?

Probes: Are you concerned about what happens to your body? Your health care? Pain, symptom management, discomfort? Are you concerned about being stuck on life support? Are you concerned about dying alone?

If you were sick or dying, are there people you trust or love that you can get support from? Who can make decisions for you?

Probes: Do you have family that you are in contact with? Do you have friends that you trust? Do you know any social workers, service providers, or health care providers whom you trust? Have you ever heard of a living will or durable power of health attorney?

Describe a "good death."

Probes: Where would you like to die? Who would you like to have by your side? Who do you need to make peace with? What would you like to have happen to your body? What are you afraid of when dying?

What stands in the way of you having a good death?

Probes: What stands in the way of good health care? What would you need to die in comfort and dignity? What are some problems with services that you have encountered?

What kind of services would you say would be needed so that homeless people might die in comfort and with dignity?

Measurement

Interviews were conducted between July 2003 and January 2004. A semistructured interview guide consisting of open-ended questions was developed through a pilot study,[14] community consultants, and the EOL and homelessness literature (Table 1).

The sessions were audio-taped and investigators took field notes on the group process and nonverbal communication, which served to contextualize the interviews and verify congruence of verbal and nonverbal communication.[18] Audiotapes were transcribed, and Atlas ti software was used to facilitate analysis.

Analysis

Investigators utilized a modified consensual qualitative research (CQR) approach to analyze data, which has proven effective in evaluating complex psychosocial phenomena.[19] This method involves an inductive analytic process to identify themes, which the team derives by consensus and verifies by systematically checking against the raw data.[19] This CQR approach incorporates a 3-step process to identify salient themes; details of CQR utilized by this team are provided elsewhere (Song et al. submitted for publication).

Results

Fifty-three people participated in the 6 focus groups. The mean age of participants was 47, and 35% were female. Thirty-six percent were identified as Native American, 8% reported an advanced degree, and 40% responded that they experienced more than one living situation during the last 6 months (Table 2).

Main outcomes were participants' concerns about and wishes for EOL care. We found 11 themes grouped into 3 domains, by locus of concern: personal themes, relational concerns, and environmental influences (Table 3).

Personal Themes

This domain involves participants' experiences with and attitudes towards EOL care. These results represent internal dynamics and considerations—the experiences that have influenced participants' conceptions about EOL care, including their wishes and concerns about their own care. Within the "personal theme" domain, we found 6 themes: experience with EOL care, fears and uncertainties, advance care planning, preferences/wishes/hopes, spirituality/religion, and veteran status (Table 3).

Experience with End of Life Care

Participants consistently had experiences with serious illnesses and deaths of loved ones or acquaintances, or their own encounters with serious illness. These experiences influenced their beliefs and attitudes towards EOL care. Past experiences with death and EOL care were frequently poor and frightening:

> When she (my mom) got sick, they put her in a nursing home, and they denied me access . . . she deteriorated, she lost her hair, she was almost comatose . . . I never got to see her. What they did to her I'll never know. One thing I knew—when she saw me she said, 'Call a taxi; get me out of here.' . . . So everything right now is in a nightmare. I'm trying to find out how she

Table 2 Participant Demographics

Characteristics	%
Age, years	
<35	15
36–45	25
46–55	45
56–65	9
>65	6
Gender	
Female	35
Race	
Hispanic or Latino	2
Not Hispanic or Latino	2
American Indian or Alaskan Native	36
Asian	2
Black or African American	27
Native African	2
Hawaiian/other Pacific Islander	0
White	22
Not reported	7
Years of education	
5–8	8
9–11	39
12–15	32
16+	8
Not reported	13

died . . . nobody told me . . . In my mind I'm thinking she's still alive . . . I never thought I'd lose my mom, or not in this way, not this hideous mess that happened that I can't understand.

This perception of EOL care as being out of the control of patients and family was common: "My mother lacked two weeks being 94 years old when she passed away. She was forced into a nursing home . . . She lost her freedom . . ." So, too, was the feeling that EOL care was unresponsive to the suffering party: "It was a situation where he didn't want to come out of there, living off the machine. When the time came for him to start to die, they wanted us to resuscitate him . . . That kind of weighed heavy on me because I thought I was letting him down. The last of his hours, he was kind of in pain. I just kept asking the doctor to give him something for his pain. They never did."

Because experiences contributed to an attitude that care is imposed, most interventions are seen as an unwanted and invasive: "After I saw my mom die, I'm almost thinking alone would be better. I don't want to be hooked up to tubes and all that crap when it comes time for me to go." Loss of control was a common concern, "Once I got real sick and got [put] in a nursing home. I don't care how old I was, I can't deal with not

Table 3 Domains and Themes of EOL Care Expressed by Homeless People

Domain	Definitions	Representative quote(s)
Personal themes		
Experience with EOL care	Experience with deaths of loved ones, friends, and acquaintances on the streets or personal experiences with illness or injury, and the care received	I've had a lot of tragedy. My girlfriend died in my arms with my baby. She was four months pregnant at the time . . . and she comes back in my dreams. He had a stroke and was on dialysis. Me and him, being about the same age, it made me fear for my life.
Fears and uncertainties	Concerns and fears about dying and EOL care	Me? I'd just like to be remembered by somebody. The only thing I'm worried about is that I don't want to die on the streets. After I've passed, my biggest fear would be not making it back home to Canada and my reservation. . . . they'll throw you in a pauper's grave someplace and nobody's going to mourn you.
Preferences/ wishes/hopes	Possibilities related to what would be a "good death"	If that was to happen, I would want it to happen some place where it was noticeable. Yeah, you may be dead there for three, four years . . . I'll be somewhere where nobody could find me. But also, once you see the doctor, the doctor should spend a little more time and get to know you a little bit better and show a little more compassion.
Advance care planning/ documentation	Strategies to influence outcomes in the event of death or serious illness	You gotta have it wrote down, or else they'll do just what they want. I'm going to have one of those made out, a living will, because if I end up in the hospital, I don't think I'd want no life support keeping me alive. My will says that if I go into a diabetic coma or if I get hit by a car, they can start life-saving techniques, and then my brother Bob's name is on that. They are to call him and say John's in the hospital, doesn't look good; do you want to come down and sign the papers to pull the plug; we will try to keep him going for some time to see if he improves. If he doesn't improve, then come down. That is exactly how it's worded.
Spirituality/religion	Influence and role that an individual's spirituality or religious convictions has on dying and EOL care	Personally, death comes like peace, but like John said, we look forward to it if we're Christian because I can go and get my reincarnate body and dance without this one.
Veteran status	Thoughts about death and EOL care related to having served in the armed forces	Even though I'm a serviceman, if I was buried in a national cemetery, I feel that my soul would be lost. I went to get medical care, something that they guaranteed me for life. They looked at me and said, 'OK, you have an honorable discharge.' As a matter of fact, I have two. 'Do you have insurance on your job?' and I'm like, whoa. The insurance on my job, OK, when I signed these contracts you didn't say that my insurance would be primary. You said that you would take care of it. So the VA does nothing.
Relational themes		
Relationships with known people	How current relationships with family, friends, and peers affect desires and fears about dying and EOL care	Most of these guys, they don't want their family to know. They ask you what happened. Why are you homeless? What's the problem? But I notice that homeless people, or street punks, whatever you call them, whatever is right for them, prostitutes or whatever, sometimes these type of people, another street person they have known for years and seems more like a family member than their own family. For me that is considered a family member. They'd be there for me, but I wouldn't want them to make all them changes. It takes a lot of money to travel and I don't want them wasting money. Not because I ain't worth the money, but I don't want them.

Table 3 Domains and Themes of EOL Care Expressed by Homeless People (*continued*)

Domain	Definitions	Representative quote(s
Relationships with strangers	How individuals' relationship with institutions and its representatives influence their views dying and EOL care	Have a doctor, an intern, or even have a medical student for a doctor, come and work at a shelter for a week to two weeks, just to see how it is, to get woke up at 6:00 in the morning and booted out, and getting a cold bowl of cereal from the branch for breakfast, and just shadowing somebody that has been homeless or is homeless, just to feel what it's like to, if just to say 'I know this guy; he's homeless and this needs to be taken care of right away' and not making him wait. Then they will have an ideal of what it's like being homeless. The doctor called me a goddamn drug addict and told me to get the hell out of his office.
Communication tools/ strategies	The communication between the subjects and their loved or valued ones, and strategies homeless persons have to communicate with loved ones during a health care crisis or if unable to communicate directly	My sister, I put her name on everything that I have. There can be contact with her and she will communicate with my daughter. My living will says my family will have no say or discussion of what is done. Basically, they don't know me, so why should they have a say in whether I live or not. I made sure to talk to him (nephew) on the telephone. It just came into my mind. I said, 'I'm going to leave this in your hands. I'm going down hill now.
Environmental		
Environmental Barriers/facilitators to good EOL care	Barriers or facilitators identified by subjects to good EOL care	They don't give you proper medical care because they know you are homeless. They think because we live in the streets, we're all junkies that don't feel no pain. Even if your family is not around at the hospital, there are these great hospice people. If you could spend your last time talking with them . . . that would be a good death. Living without life insurance, who's going to put me away—stuff like that? I had cancer just last year. My fear was being alone because my children ain't here. But I had support from the people at Listening House, friends.
Participant-suggested interventions	Interventions suggested by participants to improve dying and EOL care for homeless persons	What we do need is a shelter somewhere between Minneapolis and St. Paul that would be fully staffed 24/7 . . . and if you came out and just had surgery, you could go there . . .

EOL end of life.

having my freedom. There's no way. I need to be free . . . once you're in a nursing home or hospital you lose control."

Fears and Uncertainties

Participants expressed many fears and uncertainties similar to those of domiciled people: "Don't prolong my life. I don't want to carry on laying there as a vegetable . . ." However, the derivation of these fears may be different in this population—a combination of experience and the impotence and indignity of homelessness: "I was thinking of my friend Jeff wound up under the bridge. They look at it like another junkie guy, but he was trying really, really hard to work every day. And just to see him treated with little dignity was [not] right . . ."

Another common fear was dying anonymously, which may be unique to this population: "It makes a difference when you're homeless and you're dying by yourself. You're

here by yourself, no one to care"; and, "Me? I just want to be remembered by somebody." A dreaded consequence expressed by many was that their passing, and life, would go unnoticed and without memorialization. Similar fears include not being found and dying in a public place: "I wouldn't want to be under a bridge. If you die somewhere and not be found."

Participants also expressed many misconceptions and uncertainties about surrogate decision-making, persistent vegetative states and heroic treatments, and advance care planning: "A good buddy of mine that used to be a street person . . . fell out and ended up in a coma . . . There [were] doctors and nurses . . . calling, asking anybody to come down and say you were his family, just so you could sign a waiver to pull the plug." This was one of many urban EOL myths expressed by participants.

Another common concern was the final disposal of their body, a fear that appears unique to this population; they believed a homeless, disenfranchised person's body would be anonymously cremated, buried in a common grave, or used in medical experimentation: "I don't know if the city will just take me to the furnace down there and burn me." Participants were not aware of Minnesota state law that forbids cremation without consent of patient or family.

Preferences, Wishes, and Hopes

Participants expressed preferences and hopes, many echoing those articulated in the mainstream EOL literature, such as a wish for reconciliation with loved ones or avoiding heroic interventions. However, the wish for companionship had a unique twist in this disenfranchised population. While some desired reunion with their families, many more simply wanted anyone compassionate at the time of death, whether homeless friends or even anonymous care providers: "I would wish someone to be there, especially since I know my folks won't be."

Given the misconceptions and fears about body disposal, there were explicit and detailed desires that participants' bodies be laid to rest in a personally and culturally acceptable manner. Native Americans, for example, often stated a preference that their body be taken to native lands for proper burial.

Another common desire expressed was that EOL care focus on symptom management, particularly pain control. At the end of a long dialogue on pain control, one participant summed up the prevailing mood: "I'm kind of on the same page as him . . . if I'm dying, just give me my drugs. Make sure I'm loaded; then I'm cool. I'm not going to sell it to anybody; I just want to . . . Let me go in peace."

Finally, participants desired simply to be treated with respect: "deal with us not as some sleaze bag out for trouble, but we are just homeless." A lack of respect fostered fear of dying among subjects: "Right now I'm afraid of dying mostly because I don't have nothing. It's like a disgrace or shame to me to die that way . . . Even though I can't hear it and I won't know it, talking about, 'He was a tramp. He was a no-good tramp."

Advance Care Planning

A major finding is the importance of advance care planning and documentation for this isolated population: "My fear is being found on the street, but no one knowing how to help me or who I am." It appears that this desire for advance care planning arises from several concerns. One is, as reflected above, anonymity and estrangement. Given the belief that EOL care is paternalistic and unresponsive, advance care planning was also seen as a way to maintain control: "In '73, I was actually declared brain dead . . . I regained consciousness . . . my only real fear about death is that the doctor tried too aggressively to keep me alive, and because of this, I created a living will."

For some participants advance care planning meant discussion with significant others and/or appointment of a proxy; however, the most cited forms of advance care planning included written documentation of wishes or contact information, personal identification, or written directive or other advance care planning document. One participant voiced a typical strategy to dictate circumstances of his death: "In my wallet, I have a card with my sister's name and a phone number. Do I want to be buried in Minnesota? Hell no!"

When speaking of surrogate decision-makers, nearly all who had thought of this issue or who had appointed one chose surrogates who were not related; they were most often service providers; friends; and, occasionally, romantic partners.

Sprituality/Religion

Spirituality and religion were means of finding comfort and solace when confronting death while homeless: "Can you die alone? I remember when Bill Cosby's son died on the street . . . nobody came to touch him and hold him, but if he's a child of God, then God was holding him and taking him home." Despite the physical reality of dying alone, religion made it possible to believe that, spiritually, one was not alone.

Veteran Status

Many opinions about EOL care related to prior military experience. Participants identified veteran status as either a positive or negative factor. Some, for example, felt reassured they would have care or even a grave provided by the U.S. government: "If I drop dead or die or get my head blown off, if my parents don't do it or my family, put me in the national cemetery, too, with other veterans, my brothers." Others feared poor VA care or did not want burial in a veteran's cemetery.

Relational Themes

A second major domain was "relational themes," which we organized into 3 categories: relationships with known people, relationships with strangers, and communication tools/strategies. This domain captures how current personal and institutional relationships affect attitudes towards EOL care.

Relationships with Known People/Burden to Others

Relationships were described as complex, fractured, or nonexistent. Many were estranged from their family of origin. Some homeless persons viewed dying as an opportunity for reconciliation, though they were uncertain whether this would happen: "Truthfully, I couldn't honestly say who would and who wouldn't [be there]. I'll just have to see when I get there . . . Sometimes when they say they'll be there, they're never there."

A majority of participants did not want contact with their families while dying or after their deaths. There were several reasons for this preference, including the assertion that their families, "abandoning" them in life, had no right to claim a relationship or authority in death: "I got 6 sisters and five brothers . . . but, dead is dead. So don't cry; help me while I breathe, not when I'm stiff and frozen." This rejection extended into surrogate decision-making: "My living will says my family will have no say or discussion of what is done. Basically, they don't know me, so why should they have a say in whether I live or not." Others feared that their families would not be compassionate: "They'd be saying, 'bury him like he lived,' or 'we don't want nothing to do with him.'" Some did not want to be a burden on their families, either emotionally or financially, or feared revealing their circumstances and homelessness: "When I die, don't tell them. I don't want them to know that I'm homeless." Finally, many others did not want their families contacted because they had found, while living on the streets, trusted friends and service providers to serve as surrogates.

Relationships with Strangers

Most respondents commented that society, including police, medical professionals, and social service agency staff, does not treat them with respect or compassion. When discussing physicians, one respondent insisted: "We are homeless. They say, 'well this guy's homeless . . . You ain't got to worry about it.'" They cited slow and poor service at health care facilities, and felt betrayed by the social services system. Based on these experiences, they expected poor care at the EOL: "He'd a died more dignified if they [the counselors] actually sat down and listened to him, instead of saying, 'we're too busy; get out of here . . .'"

However, not all comments were negative. Compassionate providers were described gratefully. Several respondents claimed a particular social service provider as their most trusted confidant and indicated that this individual should be contacted as a surrogate decision-maker. "John," said one respondent, referring to a street case manager, "knows what I want. I trust him."

Communication Tools/Strategies
Those who did wish communication or reconciliation at the EOL had different strategies to insure that this occurred. These strategies were often inventive and adapted to the disenfranchised lives many led. Many, for example, carried phone numbers of loved ones or left them with various social service providers. Although in jest, this comment demonstrates how difficult communication may be: "If I was going to die in three months, I'd probably rob a bank . . . I figure if I robbed a bank, I would get caught. [My family] heard about it in the newspaper and call me up . . . "

Environmental Factors

Our final domain's common thread is the environment in which dying occurs and the structural boundaries of EOL care. We organized it into 2 categories: barriers/facilitators to good EOL care and participant-suggested interventions.

Barriers/Facilitators to Good EOL Care

Health care professionals' attitudes were most often cited as a barrier to good EOL care, while others found care inaccessible or inadequate because of financial or insurance insufficiencies. Because of poverty, even the simplest aspects of EOL care cause worry in this population: "My goal is to get me some type of burial plan. $300 won't bury nobody at this table. Then I wouldn't mind it so much, but right now I'm afraid of dying mostly because I don't have nothing." Inappropriate care also resulted because of preconceptions about homeless persons, such as the denial of pain medication for fear of abuse. Respondents also complained about the lack of respite or hospice facilities and programs; once discharged from the hospital, they only have shelters to go to.

Participant-Suggested Interventions

Finally, participants suggested many interventions to improve care for dying homeless people. Some were educational, directed towards both health care providers and homeless people. Another frequently suggested intervention was some form of advance care planning or document to preserve autonomy: "It's a legal document. Let's say that's your wish, but it's not written anywhere, and someone says, 'keep him on the respirator.' They [would] . . . unless you written it down." Indeed, any kind of identification was considered essential and encouraged for a disconnected population. Finally, homeless participants demanded special accommodations to facilitate dying among this population.

Discussion

In our study, homeless participants demonstrated more differences than similarities in their attitudes and beliefs towards EOL care compared to other populations studied.[20–25] First, many participants have had personal experiences with death, dying, and EOL care. These experiences led them to view EOL care as paternalistic, unresponsive, and poor. Other unique concerns expressed include fear of dying anonymously, without memorialization or remembrance; fear of not being found or identifiable in death; and worry about the final resting place of their bodies. These concerns are all new to the EOL literature.

Another unexpected finding is participants' advocating advance care planning, especially the appointment of surrogate decision-makers and the preparation of advance care documents, such as living wills. These findings are interesting, given the current disfavor toward advance care documents[1] and the intuition that homeless individuals would not value or utilize documentation. According to participants, documents serve different functions among a population that is anonymous, voiceless, or lacks obvious surrogate decision-makers.

Important relational findings were also expressed. Though some participants wished reconcilement and contact, a greater number did not want their families contacted when seriously ill, when dying, or after death. These desires derived from several different reasons, including avoiding emotional and financial burdens on their families, shame, and anger over abandonment. Many had made surrogate decision-making plans that did not include family.

Relationships with institutions also figured prominently in the EOL experiences and desires of homeless persons—which is expected given the role institutions play in the daily lives of homeless persons, providing food, shelter, and other necessities. These relationships were occasionally positive. Participants spoke of trusted service providers, such as shelter personnel, some of whom were even designated as surrogate decision-makers. Most often, though, relationships with systems of care were described as poor, and contributed to give views of dying.

Participants spoke of "environmental" contexts or contributors to EOL care, noting multiple barriers to EOL care, including poor relationships, lack of insurance or finances, poor health care, lack of respect, and lack of knowledge of available resources or rights. Some participants, though, cited factors that led to satisfactory health care experiences or positive expectations of EOL care, such as advance care planning, facilitation of health care by social service workers, and physician advocacy.

Finally, subjects suggested interventions for improving EOL care for homeless or underserved persons. These included patient and provider education, advance care planning, living wills and other documentation, and special programs and facilities for dying or seriously ill homeless persons. A Medline and web search yields no reports of specific efforts focused on dying homeless individuals. Clearly, interventions are needed to serve this population.

The recent NIH state-of-science statement on improving EOL care reported that insufficient research has focused on individuals from different cultural and socioeconomic backgrounds.[1] While there is a growing body of evidence that these individuals may experience disparities in EOL care,[23-29] relatively little attention has been paid to the desires of these populations or interventions to improve their care.[1] Our study provides new and important information on EOL issues among homeless persons, among the most unfortunate of overlooked populations.

Our study's limitations include the selection of subjects from one urban area, a high number of Native Americans represented, and potential selection bias, as our participants are those who accessed service providers. The findings of our study are not necessarily generalizable. Rather, our data are exploratory, examining a previously unknown health-related phenomena: we are among the first to characterize in-depth the EOL concerns and desires of a vulnerable and disenfranchised population from their perspective.

Conclusions

Our study demonstrates that homeless persons have extensive, and often unique, concerns about dying and EOL care. The experiences and circumstances of homelessness inform and influence a view of death and EOL care unlike previously reported findings in the study of EOL care. Our work has implications for further study of this population, as well as study of other underrepresented and underserved populations. This work also suggests examining interventions to improve care for this and other vulnerable populations.

Notes

1. National Institutes of Health State-of-the-Science Conference Statement on Improving End-of-Life Care December 6–8, 2004. Available at: http://www.consensus.nih.gov/2004/2004EndOfLifeCareSOS024html.htm. Accessed March 16, 2006.

2. Burt MR. Homelessness: definitions and counts. In: Baumohl J, ed. Homelessness in America. Phoenix, AZ: Oryx Press, 1996:15–23.

3. Breakey WR, Fischer PJ, Kramer M. Health and mental problems of homeless men and women in Baltimore. *JAMA* 1989; 262:1352–7.

4. Gelberg L, Linn LS. Assessing the physical health of homeless adults. *JAMA* 1989; 262:1973–9.

5. Barrow SM, Herman DB, Cordova PBA. Mortality among shelter residents in New York City. *Am J Public Health* 1999; 89:529–34.

6. Hibbs JR, Benner L. Mortality in a cohort of homeless adults in Philadelphia. *N Engl J Med* 1994; 331:304–9

7. Cheung AM, Hwang SW. Risk of death among homeless women: a cohort study and review of the literature. *CMAJ* 2004; 170(8):1243–7.

8. Hwang SW, Orav EJ, O'Connell JJ, Lebow JM, Brennan TA. Causes of death in homeless adults in Boston. *Ann Intern Med* 1996; 126:625–8.

9. King County Public Health 2004. Available at: http://www.metrokc.gov/HEALTH/hchn/2004-annual-report-HD.pdf. Accessed January 20, 2006.

10. Gallagher TC, Andersen RM, Koegel P, Gelberg L. Determinants of regular source of care among homeless adults in Los Angeles. *Med Care* 1997; 35(8):814–30.

11. Gelberg L, Andersen RM, Leake BD. Healthcare access and utilization. *Health Serv Res.* 2000;34(6):1273–1314.

12. Gelberg L, Thompson L. Competing priorities as a barrier to medical care among homeless adults in Los Angeles. *Am J Public Health* 1997; 87:217–20.

13. Hwang SW, O'Connell JJ, Lebow JM, Bierer MF, Orav EJ, Brennan TA. Health care utilization among homeless adults prior to death. *J Health Care Poor Underserved* 2001 Feb; 12(1):50–8.

14. Song J, Ratner E, Bartels D. Dying while homeless: Is it a concern when life itself is such a struggle? *J Clin Ethics.* Fall 2005;16(3):251–61.

15. Tarzian A, Neal M, O'Neil J. Attitudes, experiences, and beliefs affecting end-of-life decision-making among homeless individuals. *J Palliat Med.* Feb 2005, Vol. 8, No. 1: 36–48.

16. Norris W, Nielson E, Engelberg R, Curtis JR. Treatment preferences for resuscitation and critical care among homeless persons. *Chest* 2005; 127(6):2180–7.

17. Stewart B. McKinney Homeless Assistance Act (42 U.S.C. 11431 et seq.)

18. Bernard HR. Reseach Methods in Cultural Anthropology. Beverly Hills, CA: Sage Publications 1988.

19. Hill CE, Thompson BJ, Williams EN. A guide to conducting consensual qualitative research. *Couns Psychol* 1997; 25:517–72.

20. Singer PA, Martin DK, Kelner M. Quality end of life care: patients' perspectives. *JAMA* 1999; 281:163–8.

21. Steinhauser KE, Clipp CC. In search of a good death: observations of patients, families, and providers. *Ann Intern Med.* 2000; 132:825–31.

22. Vig EK, Pearlman RA. Quality of life while dying: a qualitative study of terminally ill older men. *J Am Geriatr Soc* 2003 Nov; 51(11):1595–601

23. Born W, Greiner KA, Sylvia E, Butler J. Ahluwalia JS. Knowledge, attitudes, and beliefs about end-of-life care among inner-city African Americans and Latinos. *J Palliat Med.* 2004 7(2): 247–56.

24. Blackhall LJ, Murphy ST, Frank G. Ethnicity and attitudes toward patient autonomy. *JAMA* 1995;274:820–5

25. Caralis PV, Davis B, Wright K, Marcial E. The influence of ethnicity and race on attitudes toward advance directives, life-prolonging treatments, and euthanasia. *J Clin Ethics* 1993;4(2):155–65.

26. Carrese JA, Rhodes LA. Western bioethics on the Navajo reservation. *JAMA* 1995;274:826–9.

27. Daneault S, Labadie J. Terminal HIV disease and extreme poverty: a review of 307 home care files. *J Palliat Care* 1999; 15:6–12.

28. Degenholtz HB, Thomas SB, Miller MJ. Race and the intensive care unit: disparities and preferences for end-of-life care. *Crit Care Med.* 31(5 Suppl):S373–8, 2003 May.

29. Cleeland CS, Gonin R, Baez L et al. Pain and treatment of pain in minority patients with cancer. *Ann Intern Med* 1997;127:813–6.

Corresponding Author: **JOHN SONG,** MD, MPH, MAT; Center for Bioethics, University of Minnesota, N504 Boynton, 410 Church Street S.E., Minneapolis, MN 55455, USA (e-mail: songx006@umn .edu).

Acknowledgements—The authors would like to thank the clients and staff of St. Stephen's shelter; Holy Rosary Church; Listening House; Hennepin County Outreach Services; Health Care for the Homeless, Minneapolis; and Our Saviors Church who were so generous with their time, thoughts, and dedication to serving others. We would also like to thank LeeAnne Hoekstra for administrative support, Tybee Types for transcription, and Karen Howard for manuscript preparation. This study was funded by the National Institute of Nursing Research, National Institutes of Health, grant RO3 NR008586-02.

Aging Prisoners' Concerns toward Dying in Prison

Prison populations are experiencing rapid increases and many more offenders are dying in prison. This study investigated key variables associated with death anxiety among a group of aging prisoners. For this research, 102 respondents residing in a maximum security prison with a mean age of 59 completed Templer's Death Anxiety Scale. A regression analysis showed that age, inmate social supports, and a number of health related variables were important predictors of death fear. The findings revealed that fear of death is slightly higher among older prisoners than for similar age groups in the community. Qualitative information based on personal narratives found that some inmates see death as an escape, while others expressed fears of dying in prison or the stigma associated with imprisonment.

RONALD H. ADAY, PhD

Introduction

Prison populations have increased dramatically over the past two decades. Of the more than 1.3 million inmates currently held in state and federal prisons over 125,000 are 50 years or older (*Corrections Yearbook,* 2003). More than tripling since the early 1990s, this increase in the aging prison population represents one of the most dramatic changes in the American correctional system (Aday, 2003). As a result, the aging prison population has created an increasing number of end-of-life issues as more offenders are dying in prison (Granse, 2003). Over a 10-year period inmate deaths in state and federal prisons have doubled increasing from 1630 in 1991 to 3,203 in 2001 (*Corrections Yearbook,* 2002). While the data on deaths in prisons are not-age specific, correctional systems with a significant percentage of older inmates do report a greater number of natural deaths (*Corrections Yearbook,* 2003). The percentage of inmate deaths due to natural causes has steadily increased from 58.8% in 1996 to 80.0% in 2001. The mortality rate is expected to continue to increase due primarily to the graying of the U.S. prison population and as a result of the increasing number of offenders receiving sentences that will keep them imprisoned for the remainder of their lives.

Death is becoming an almost everyday occurrence in many correctional systems, and little is known about inmates' attitudes toward death and how they react to the notion of their imminent mortality. While previous research has explored home versus institutional death (Gallo, Baker, & Bradley, 2001; Meier & Morrison, 1999), little attention has been given to the rapidly growing number of older adults aging and dying in state and federal prisons (Mezey, Dubler, Mitty, & Brody, 2002). To address this void, this exploratory research examines the potential role the threat of death can have on the lives of a group of aging male prisoners. Age, race, physical and mental health factors, and the influence of a social support network are introduced as possible correlates of death anxiety for this sub-population of prison inmates. The consequences for identity of dying in a total institution and how aging inmates cope with this possibility are also explored.

Attitudes toward Death

Previous research on attitudes toward death has explored a remarkable range of topics (Neimeyer, Wittkowski, & Moser, 2004) including a handful of studies focusing on death anxiety in male felons. Incorporating a sample of 56 male prisoners between the ages of 20 to 58 years, researchers explored the length of incarceration and death anxiety (Schumaker, Groth-Marnat, Dougherty, & Barwick, 1986). Using 60 nonoffenders matched by age, race, and socioeconomic background as controls, these authors found no significant difference in death anxiety between the two groups. Templer et al. (1979) utilized his own death anxiety scale to assess the degree and correlates of death anxiety in 101 male inmates. Although death anxiety among the inmates was only slightly higher than in most normal male populations, the inmate's score correlated positively with age. Other studies have concentrated on end-of-life issues such as hospice care and the coping mechanisms of terminally ill, incarcerated inmates (Granse, 2003; Maull, 1998) or HIV/AIDS (Freudenberg, 2001). I will briefly examine the literature reviewing death attitudes in the elderly and the relationship of death concerns to age, physical illness, ego integrity, race, and social support.

Place of Death

The critical issue for many older people is not so much death, but how and where the death will take place (Leming & Dickinson, 1998). Marshall (1976) found the major difference in the living environment was the degree to which residents had control over the course of their dying. In an institution such as a prison, which controls living as well as dying, a sense of helplessness is almost unavoidable. Prisons are punitive institutions in which the primary goal of care is confinement and punishment. The care provided is typically not inmate-centered, but prison-centered, and the inmate's wishes are usually not taken into account (Mezey et al., 2002). Inmates, according to Goffman (1961), undergo a process of mortification in which the institution strips away their sense of self by means of isolation. If the institution takes away an inmate's identity, the journey into the unknown becomes even more ominous.

When sick inmates are removed from the general prison population, they are frequently placed into even more restrictive medical units with their every movement highly monitored (Haney & Zimbardo, 2001). Higher levels of fear of death have been associated with living in restrictive settings such as nursing homes and other institutional settings (Neimeyer & Fortner, 1997). Dying in prison brings unique challenges for both the prison and the inmate (Granse, 2003). The prospect of dying in a foreign place in a dependent and undignified state is a very distressing thought for older adults. Inmates fear spending their last hours in agony and separated from family on the outside. Frequently having suffered lifelong alienation from society, dying in prison is what inmates dread most (Byock, 2002).

Ego Integrity

Most studies relevant to this correlate of death anxiety have used a variety of measures in conjunction with ego integrity. For example, concepts such as self-esteem (Davis, Bremer, Anderson, & Tramill, 1983), meaning and purpose in life (Amenta & Weiner, 1981; Bolt, 1978; Tomer, 1992), and life satisfaction (Lockart et al., 2001; Nehrke, Bellucci, & Gabriel, 1977–1978) have been found to be negatively correlated with death anxiety. Gesser, Wong, and Reker (1987) found fear of death/dying to be negatively related to happiness and positively related to hopelessness. Thus, those individuals who exhibit a low level of death anxiety are more than likely to experience a greater satisfaction with life and have a more positive mental outlook. For example, it appears that variables which tend to reduce or threaten quality of life in the elderly, such as poor physical and mental health, being widowed, or being institutionalized, are likely to be inversely associated with higher levels of fear of death (Lockhart et al., 2001).

Age

Age is another equally important variable that has frequently been associated with attitudes toward death. Previous studies suggest that the fear of death tends to be higher among middle-aged groups and relatively low for their elderly counterparts (Fortner & Neimeyer, 1999; Neimeyer & Van Brunt, 1995; Straub & Roberts, 2001; Thorson & Powell, 2000). Leming and Dickinson (1998) note that a complete change in the time perspective occurs during the middle years. During the middle years, time is perceived as time-left-to-live rather than time-since-birth. Katz (1979) supports this view by reporting his middle-aged sample to be more frightened of death than either their pre-mid-life or post-mid-life cohorts. Other data suggest that elderly members of all ethnic groups think and talk more about death, but were less anxious about it than were the respondents at earlier stages in the life cycle (Kalish, 1985; Thorson & Powell, 1998). These findings are similar to that of Gesser, Wong, and Reker (1987–1988) who found that death anxiety was highest in middle adulthood, then stabilized during the final stage of life.

Health Status

It seems sensible to suggest that one's own health status, in particular in the later stages of life, may influence one's view of death. Overall, the literature has supported a significant association between one's health condition and death anxiety (Cicirelli, 1997; Fortner, Neimeyer, & Rybarczyk, 2000; Lockhart et al., 2001). As health declines and greater physical problems emerge, higher levels of death anxiety are reported in elderly people (Fortner & Neimeyer, 1999). Mullins and Lopez (1982) found that nursing home patients who reported worse health and diminished functional ability scored higher on the Death Anxiety Scale regardless of their age. Viney's (1984) research similarly found that ill persons displayed higher death concern than well persons and surgical patients were more anxious about death than were other patients. Research has also indicated that death anxiety increased among elderly individuals when they thought about being sick or dependent upon someone to take care of them for an extended period of time (Lockhart et al., 2001).

Race

While several studies across diverse populations and using global measures of fear of death have reported that African Americans report higher levels of anxiety than Caucasians (Dodd & Mills, 1985; Myers, Wass, & Murphey, 1980), other research findings have been mixed. For example, Thorson and Powell (1998) found Euro-Americans were more concerned with the uncertainty associated with death and the loss of being. African Americans, on the other hand, expressed more anxiety over the pain associated with the process of dying. However, there was no significant difference in total scores for the two groups. When investigating an older sample, Depaola, Griffin, Young, and Neimeyer (2003) discovered that Caucasian participants displayed higher fear of the dying process than did older African American participants. Cicirelli's (2002) research examined ethnic differences using Hoelter's (1979) Multidimensional Fear of Death Scale. Consisting of eight subscales, he found that older African Americans reported higher levels of death anxiety on the Fear of Conscious Death Scale while older Caucasians were found to have a higher fear of death on the Fear of Dying Scale. No differences were found on the other subscales: Fear of the Dead, Fear of Being Destroyed, Fear for Significant Others, Fear for the Body after Death, Fear of the Unknown, and Fear of Premature Death.

Social Support

Research has documented the importance of social support among people with life-threatening illnesses and related problems and concerns frequently experienced at the end of life (Arnold, 2004). Previous research has found an inverse relationship between supportive relationships and death anxiety (Fry, 2003). Considerable research has specifically shown that the greater degree to which older people are embedded in supportive social networks, the more likely they will enjoy better physical (Berkman, Glass, Brissette, & Seeman, 2000) and mental health (Krause, 1997; Litwin, 2001) compared to senior adults who do not maintain close ties with others. Activities including telephone contact, participation in religious and other social groups, and informal visits with friends are equally important. The provision of emotional or instrumental support by family and friends helps to reduce the distress involved in the major life transitions such as declining health and pending death.

Study Measures
Procedures

This project used the normal protocol of submitting a research proposal to the Director of Policy, Planning, and Research at the Mississippi State Department of Corrections. Upon approval, a contact person was identified and arrangements were made to visit the prison to conduct individual interviews. Using the designated staff person, all older male inmates age 50 or older were contacted prior to the initial visit to inform them about the research objectives as well as length and nature of the interview process. The prison provided a private space for each interview and at the initial meeting inmates were given an informed consent form and notified they could withdraw from the project at any time. While the majority of participants remained in the research pool, approximately 20 inmates were unable to participate due to health issues or conflicts in their work schedules.

Sample

This study reports on a convenience sample of 102 older male inmates' 50 years of age or older housed at the maximum prison at Parchmam, Mississippi. Sixty-one percent of the sample was African American with the remainder being Caucasian. The average age of the participants was 59 years with 80% falling between the age of 50–64; the other 20% between 65 and 84 years of age. Only 27% were married in this sample with the majority being either divorced (26%) or widowed (20%). Seventy percent of respondents' parents were deceased. Seventy-two percent had living children and 53% had living grandchildren. This sample was under educated when compared to the elderly older adult population with only 18% having completed high school and over half (54%) having achieved no more than an eighth grade education. Of the remaining sample 20% had completed some high school, 4% some college, and 4% were college graduates. About 75% of the geriatric prisoners in this sample are incarcerated for three categories of crimes: homicide and manslaughter; criminal sexual conduct; and drugs. Eleven years was the average span of time to parole consideration for all respondents.

Demographic Variables

Age was measured as a continuous variable. Race consisted of African American and Caucasian respondents. Offender status was measured in terms of whether the older prisoners were late offenders, chronic, or long-termers housed for 10 years or more.

Health Status

Using a Likert scale, participants were asked to rate their physical and mental health using the responses of excellent = 1, good = 2, fair = 3, and poor = 4. Respondents were also asked to "agree" or "disagree" with the question, "Does your health prevent you from doing things you would like to do?" Relying on a non-Likert technique, self-report of the number of chronic illnesses, medications, and the frequency of participation in sick call were summed by actual scores.

Ego Integrity

The life satisfaction variable was measured by a series of 12 statements about general life issues. Respondents were asked a variety of questions including if they sometimes feel "unsafe," "bored with life," "depressed," or "on top of the world." A 3-point Likert scale of never = 0, sometimes = 1, and often = 2 was used. This particular set of life satisfaction variables produced an Alpha reliability of .71.

Social Support

This variable was measured by a group of questions pertaining to inmate's contact with family members. Family contact was measured by the frequency of inmate visitors, telephone conversations, and letter exchanges (mean = 17.2; SD = 4.9). Institutional support was measured by a checklist (often, sometimes, rarely, and never) of shared activities and conversation topics producing an Alpha reliability of .88. These combined measures represented social support for this study.

Fear of Death

Subjects in this sample were administered Templer's (1970) Death Anxiety Scale. The DAS is a 15-item simple assessment instrument utilizing short statements aimed at determining the extent to which the respondent is preoccupied with issues surrounding death (e.g., "I am very much afraid to die" and "I am often distressed by the way time flies so very rapidly"), which the respondent rates as true or false. The number of negative responses is taken as a measure of death anxiety. Reliability estimates on the DAS have been moderately high and the alpha reported in this study was .83.

Quantitative Results

Aging inmates in this sample reported a mean score of 5.02 when using Templer's Death Anxiety Scale. Although the variable of race was not significantly related to fear of death, age was found to be inversely correlated with death anxiety ($r = -.24$; $p < .01$). This findings supports previous research conducted on fear of death in the general population. Offender status (chronic vs. long-termers), occupation (unskilled vs. professional), education, and length of time left to serve failed to significantly influence respondent's attitudes toward death.

Physical Health

Prisoners typically tend to be physiologically older than their actual age and from a health perspective a prisoner who is 50 years of age may already have significant health issues usually associated with a more elderly person on the outside. This sample supports this view as only 27% considered themselves in good health with 28% saying fair and 45% self-rated themselves as in poor health. Inmates reported on average 3.2 chronic illnesses and used 2.6 medications daily resulting in frequent visits to sick call with 41% going on a regular basis (weekly or bi-weekly).

Table 1 presents bivariate associations among the major variables used in this study. Immediately noteworthy is the link between fear of death and a number of health related measures. In fact, the number of chronic illnesses, frequency of sickcall, number of medications, and self-reported physical health appear to be important indicators of death anxiety. Lower ratings of self-reported mental health and life satisfaction were negatively correlated with higher levels of death anxiety. Finally, the less social support available, the higher the fear of death ($r = -.25$; $p < .01$).

To explore the concept of death anxiety and self-reported health more fully, the median score for death anxiety was

Table 1   Bivariate Correlations among Major Study Variables

Variables	(1)	(2)	(3)	(4)	(5)	(6)	(7)	(8)	(9)
1. Death anxiety	—	−.26	−.33	.37	.22	.26	.31	−.20	−.24
2. Mental health rating		—	.22	.09	.06	.14	.09	−.06	.05
3. Physical health rating			—	.32	.35	−.39	−.40	.05	.22
4. Ego-integrity				—	.24	.22	.29	−.10	−.33
5. Number of medications					—	.24	.67	.07	.04
6. Frequency of sickcall						—	.32	.14	−.09
7. Number of illnesses							—	.01	.16
8. Age								—	−.22
9. Social support									—

Note. Correlations greater than .21 are significant at the .01 level.

used to divide the variable into high and low categories. Using Chi-Square as an exploratory measure, a number of significant associations were found. Older inmates in poor health were more likely to report a significantly higher fear of death (Chi-Square = 7.65; $df = 2$; $p < .01$) and over 50% of older offenders in this sample whose health was defined as poor indicated they were more likely to think about death on a regular basis. The presence of poor health tends to create a feeling of increased vulnerability among older inmates. Analyzing specific questions from the DAS, older inmates who stated their health as poor expressed a greater fear of getting deathly sick, getting cancer, having a heart attack, and a marked fear of dying a painful death in prison.

Ego Integrity

Using a self-report measure, 59% of this sample indicated their mental health was good compared to only 14% who considered their mental health to be poor. Inmates reporting a lower perception of their mental health were more likely to experience feelings of death anxiety ($r = .26$; $p < .004$) and those with a poor mental outlook also reported a greater fear of death ($r = .37$; $p < .001$). Statistical findings from a series of Chi Square's also produced numerous positive associations between indicators of life satisfaction and fear of death. Using the categories of low and high levels of death anxiety, two-thirds of the inmates who indicated they frequently felt unsafe in their current living environment exhibited significantly higher levels of death anxiety (Chi Square = 7.49; $df = 2$; $p < .05$). This finding illustrates the importance of social supports as an important link to reducing death anxiety. Also, over 70% of those who reported they felt lonely or unloved were more likely to fall into the higher death anxiety group. Indicators of depression such as feeling bored, helpless, and upset were also significantly associated with higher levels of death anxiety in this sample.

Social Support

This variable also proved to be an important indicator of fear of death. Supporting Fry's (2003) earlier findings, the less social support available, the higher the fear of death ($r = -.25$; $p < .01$). An analysis of descriptive statistics found that while one-quarter of inmates received visitors on a regular basis (often or fairly often), the others relied more on letter exchanges and phone calls. Forty-one percent claimed they were "never" visited by family and a lesser 26% responded "never" to other forms of communication.

Institutional support measured by a list of conversation topics and activities was inversely correlated with family support ($r = -.41$, $p < .001$) indicating inmates having less support from the outside turned to other prisoners for intimacy and support. Inmates were more likely than not to discuss: prison conditions (76%), feelings about being

in prison (63%), religious ideas (62%), their health or illnesses (76%), and life outside of prison. Inmates were just as or nearly as likely to discuss feelings about being lonely (50%), things they were sad about (35%), feelings about death or about loved ones who have died (58%), things they are happy about (47%), relationships with family or children (45%), and their feelings about being bored (41%). Inmates who exhibited a higher level of death anxiety were more motivated to discuss their fears associated with imprisonment ($r = .22$; $p < .01$). Because of the isolation from the outside world, friendships in prison may be even more highly valued than kin relationships. Close personal relationships with friends can help cushion the shock of physical deterioration, the loss of loved ones, and other sources of stress in the prison environment.

Regression Analysis

A standard multiple regression was conducted to determine which of the health, demographic, social, and psychological variables were more likely to be predictors of death anxiety. A summary of the multiple regression analysis is shown in Table 2. The number of medications provided the greatest prediction of death anxiety (Beta, .41). Younger inmates with a negative mental outlook were also important predictor variables. The lack of an adequate support group was also a significant variable. Overall, the multiple regression coefficient R was .82, with the adjusted R Square of .55 indicating that the five variables accounted for 55% of the variance for fear of death. Aging prisoner's notions about perceptions of receipt of adequate health care, perceived self-reported health, and number of chronic illnesses were not significantly related, but appear to be approaching significance.

Qualitative Results

Understanding the social world experienced by aging inmates requires a fundamental knowledge of Goffman's (1961) notion of "total institutions" and the extent to which prisons, as total institutions, strip inmates of their former identities while placing them in settings with "undesirable" populations. Within this social context, death anxiety may be reduced through the incorporation of a variety of coping mechanisms such as "life review, life planning, identification with one's culture, and religiosity." Coping strategies are especially helpful to individuals who are struggling to reconcile the final stage of life in an incarcerated state. To more fully understand the attitudes and coping strategies of aging inmates who are confronted with the possibility of dying in prison, several open-ended questions were included for respondent reactions: "Do you ever think about dying in prison? If your answer is yes, how do you cope with these thoughts? What are your fears and concerns about dying here?" Two-thirds of this sample indicated they frequently think about dying in prison. Reactions to this possibility

Table 2 Results of Hierarchical Ordinary Least Squares Regression Analysis Predicting Death Anxiety

Variables	R	Adj. R Square	B	Std. Error	Beta
Self-reported health			−0.52	0.71	−.13
Age			−0.27	0.08	−.39**
Receive adequate health care			−1.72	1.05	−.23
Mental outlook			−1.63	0.63	−.37**
No. of medications			0.50	0.28	.41**
No. of illnesses			−0.26	0.27	−.22
Social support			−0.19	0.10	−.30*
Self-reported mental health			−1.63	0.63	−.37**
	.82	.55			

$*p < .05. **p < .01.$

varied ranging from fearful attitudes to the view that death might serve as a relief to the life they now lead. Regardless, the following themes seem to capture the range of emotions and coping strategies found among those who live in an environment where every move is monitored and where few norms and rituals are available to help sustain and guide inmates toward end-of-life consequences.

Stigma of Dying in Prison

Dying in an institution such as prison is widely considered the ultimate defeat, the ultimate punishment. As a result many fear that dying in prison will have a negative impact on their children, grandchildren, and other family members. As a 57-year-old child sex offender said, "I don't want to think about the impact on my children and grandchildren." Another stated, "Dying here is a disgrace to my family." Thus, in addition to dying alone, inmates also feel the shame from dying as a prisoner, and regret at dying without atonement or forgiveness (Granse, 2003). These views support Williams (1989) findings that for many aging prisoners, there seems to be a stigma associated with dying in prison. Byock (2002) has stressed that dying prisoners are in a special category he referred to as "the last among us," and are similar to other disenfranchised groups such as those with dementia. Individuals with such irreversible conditions are devalued by society, considered highly unuseful and marginal.

As a result, a substantial number (one-third) of older inmates indicated they never think about death or at least they deliberately avoid thinking about the topic. For example, as one inmate mentioned, "When I think about death, I just have to turn it off. . . . The last thing I want to think about in here is death." Another stated, "I just try and stay busy with activities so I won't think about it." It appears some inmate's are plunged deep beneath the surface of everyday prison activities, often remaining highly concealed. For some inmates, thinking or talking about the topic, especially in prison, may be considered beyond their realm of imagination. As Moller (2000) has suggested, when death becomes meaningless in an environment such as the prison culture, there is a tendency toward widespread avoidance and denial.

Fear of Death

Older adults have been found to react differently to perceptions of one's limited time remaining. A large number of cultures, including our own, attach fearful meaning to death and death-related situations. Most people fear being abandoned, humiliated, and lonely at the end of their lives. Numerous inmates openly expressed a fear of dying linked with the severance of personal relationships or, at least, not dying in their presence. As one inmate expressed, "The worst fear is not dying with family members present. My main fear of growing old in prison is dying here." Another stated, "I'm afraid I'm going to die in here and never see my wife again." These fears are in keeping with Kalish's (1985) view that when people consider the prospect of death they need the assurance that their close friends and family will not abandon them to die alone. Weisman (1972) has also suggested that close friends and family are those most likely to be able to relate to the dying person in terms of identity and achievements. For some inmates, dying in prison is the final and egregious indignity. "It diminishes your existence. You're not with the people who truly love you. . . . You feel you are only half the human you should be."

Fearful meanings can also be ascribed to death because of a traumatic death-related experience. Being a witness to a death can increase death anxiety for certain individuals (Leming & Dickinson, 1998). For example, numerous inmates mentioned they had watched other inmates die and several expressed fears relating to how correctional staff treat a dead person. As one immate related, "I've seen a few people die in here and I wouldn't want to. This idea of handcuffing the corpse when they take you out of here is my main fear."

Religious Activities

Although inmate's religious beliefs were not officially measured in this study, a significant number reported using religious beliefs and activities as a key coping strategy in dealing with thoughts or, in some cases, the likelihood of dying in prison. About 20% of the inmates mentioned prayer as a common activity in coping with the thought of dying behind bars. Some inmates reported attending church services as a way of buffering their fears. Most, inmates, however, indicated they were more likely to engage in informal religious activities such as reading their bible or praying. A few inmates mentioned talking to the prison chaplain to gain some peace of mind regarding the possibility of dying in prison. The importance of one's faith is illustrated by one 75-year-old inmate who stated, "I really trust in the Lord and I know he is not going to let me die here." Another expressed, "I try to make the best of each day. I let God handle tomorrow." Yet another inmate who frequently thought about the possibility of dying in prison turned to the thought of afterlife as a way of coping when he mentioned, "To be absent from the body is to be present with the Lord."

This theme supports the commonly held view that religion serves as an important buffer against the fear of death (Wink & Scott, 2005). It has been noted that religious groups and activities attract more inmate participation than any of the other prison programs (Aday, 2003). Imprisonment is considered a lonely, soul-searching experience and religious activities can make prison life more bearable. Finding solace in religion provides many offenders with the internal stability that enables them to make a successful adjustment to the prison subculture. Prior research indicates that religion can function to give hope, meaning, optimism, and a sense of security to those spending the remainder of their life behind bars (Williams, 1989).

Death as an Escape

Dying in an environment where death is a frequent occurrence can help socialize inmates toward the inevitable. Long-term inmates find prison to be a mind-numbing experience especially for those who know they will never leave. Having internalized society's views, prisoners may see their lives as having ever-decreasing social value, thereby reducing any positive view of the future. As a convicted murderer expressed "It seems to me there's no outside world. . . . It's dead. Everything is dead. Although you're living, you feel like you're dead." As a result, death may seem to represent a better alternative to isolation, illness, and other pains of imprisonment. Inmates may welcome a prospective end to physical fatigue and pain and suffering. The recognition that the future is limited by life in prison, declining health and social status, and a longing for relief from pain and loneliness may serve to influence older prisoner's view of death as a welcomed escape. As one of the oldest inmates stated: "You're just a number, that's all." He says of prison life, "I really don't worry about dying. I think it would be a great relief." The necessity of coming to terms with death may be what has been termed "neutral acceptance" (Gesser et al., 1987). In other words, older adults have received their "fair share" of life, and now there is no point in worrying about something they cannot control. Support for this notion is illustrated by the following comments:

> I would rather die a free man, but you have to resign yourself to the fact you must die like everyone else.

> I accept the fact that I will probably die in prison and I've donated my body to a university hospital for research purposes and the possible use of my organs.

Another illustration of incorporating this acceptance philosophy is reflected in the statement of a 63-year-old incarcerated for sexual battery and suffering from depression and suicidal thoughts who claimed, "Death might be a blessing." Vernon has observed that "for most people the fear of living under certain conditions is stronger than the fear of dying" (Vernon, 1972, p. 134). This view illustrates the fact that as inmates move toward accepting the inevitable, a decline in death fear may very well be the result.

Discussion

The results of the current study uncovered significant concerns about dying in a prison setting. In comparison to other research findings, TDAS scores for the aging prisoners in this study (mean = 5.02) were lower than that found for a younger overall prison population (mean = 6.17; Schumaker et al., 1986) using the TDAS. A study using an older retired population and nursing home residents (Nehrke et al., 1977–1978) reported mean scores of 4.25 and 4.08 respectively on the TDAS. White and Handal (1990–1991) reported from an extensive TDAS meta analysis a general population norm of 6.16. Using this limited assessment, it appears the older prisoners' fear of death is somewhat higher than that of the older populations in the community, but still lower than that of the general population.

Supporting previous research, middle-aged inmates (50–59) reported a significantly higher level of death anxiety than older inmates ranging in age from 60–84. A number of factors may explain this lessoned fear of death of the oldest-old. Perhaps long-term inmates who have spent years dealing with their friends' deaths have found this helped provide the necessary socialization toward acceptance of their own deaths. It can be suggested that by more frequent exposure to death, the oldest inmates are more likely to think and talk about death than are younger inmates and to develop effective means of coping (Lester & Templer, 1993; Lund, 1993). Marshall (1980) also suggested that disengaging from outside activities can facilitate self-focusing and life review and allows more time for reflecting and coming to terms with an impending death.

Similarly to the elderly in the free world, older inmates in poor health are more likely to think more frequently about death. Supporting previous studies (Cicirelli, 2002; Fortner et al., 2000), the presence of poor health tends to create a feeling of increased vulnerability among older inmates leading to a substantial fear of death for some. Perhaps contributing to this fear was the fact that 36% of the 102 respondents alleged the correctional facility did not provide them with adequate health care and over one-third saw their health as getting worse over time. Slightly over one-third (35%) wanted medical services to be more responsive at the time services were needed. Housed in a remote rural area, inmates voiced concerns over the amount of time needed for emergency personnel to reach them if a health crisis should occur.

Additionally, perceptions of better mental health significantly predicted less fear of death. Other studies have also explored the general mental outlook of older inmates (Ditton, 1999; Douglass, 1991; McCarthy, 1983) with similar results. Bachand (1984) reported the health status of elderly inmates as compounded by excessive mental worry. This view is supported by McCarthy (1983) who described about half of 248 elderly offenders as "worriers," concerned about their health or for their safety. Depression and anxiety symptoms are common in the older prison population and can serve to trigger higher negative thoughts about death (Aday, 2003). This also seems to be the case in this study as inmates conveyed their fears of indifferent health providers, inadequate medications and delays, as well as general worry about their frail physical condition in a harsh prison environment.

Finally, this exploratory study supported Aiken's (1995) notion that friends function as a source of emotional support, information, and entertainment, and hence can contribute to the older person's sense of belonging and meaningfulness. Close personal relationships with friends can help cushion the shock of physical deterioration, the loss of loved ones, and other sources of stress in the prison environment. The prison social structure can provide an antidote to loneliness and loss of status in old age. Older inmates frequently seek out each other's company in preference to that of younger inmates. Gallagher (1990) found, in her comparison of older and younger inmates, older inmates, ranging in age from 45 to 87, had significantly more friends in prison and were more likely to have a confidant inside the prison.

Conclusions and Implications

This study has highlighted some of the death concerns facing inmates who are finding themselves incarcerated in old age. As the number of aging inmates continues to increase, prison systems are beginning to respond to the tragedy of dying in prison. Long-termers, whose family and friends have grown old and died or faded away, die and are buried where they have spent the greater part of their lives. While most correctional systems have some mechanism for releasing medically qualified inmates, few are actually released before dying. States housing a large number of lifers have witnessed significant increases in prison funerals. Some prisons have introduced more dignified ways of handling the growing number of inmate deaths on prison grounds. A number of states are now operating formal prison hospice programs while others are offering some type of palliative care. Other correctional systems are becoming more sensitive to the dying in prison issue by introducing special funeral services providing greater dignity (Carr, 2001). However, prison is still a harsh environment and one not conducive for dying with dignity. Inmates condemned to a permanent separation from their families and the outside world will increasingly find their way into prison cemeteries.

References

Aday, R. H. (2003). *Aging prisoners: Crisis in American corrections.* Westport, CT: Praeger Publishers.

Aiken, L. R. (1995). *Aging: An introduction to gerontology.* Thousand Oaks, CA: Sage.

Amenta, M. M., & Weiner, A. W. (1981). Death anxiety and purpose in life in hospice workers. *Psychological Reports, 49,* 920–921.

Amenta, M. M. (1984). Death anxiety, purpose in life and duration of service in hospice volunteers. *Psychological Reports, 54,* 979–984.

Arnold, E. M. (2004). Factors that influence consideration of hastening death among people with life-threatening illnesses. *Health and Social Work, 29,* 17–27.

Belkman, L. F., Glass, T., Brissette, I., & Seeman, T. (2000). From social integration to health: Durkheim in the new millennium. *Social Science & Medicine, 51,* 843–857.

Bachand, D. J. (1984). The elderly offender: An exploratory study with implications for continuing education of law enforcement personnel. Unpublished dissertation, University of Michigan.

Bolt, M. (1978). Purpose in life and death concerns. *Journal of Geriatric Psychology, 132,* 159–160.

Byock, I. R. (2002). Dying well in corrections: Why should we care? *Journal of Correctional Health Care, 12,* 27–35.

Carr, M. (2001). Lawmakers push medical parole for older prisoners. *New Orleans Times-Picayune,* 3A.

Cicirelli, V. G. (2002). *Older adults' view on death.* New York: Springer Publishing Company.

Cicirelli, V. G. (2001). Personal meanings of death in older adults and young adults in relation to their fears of death. *Death Studies, 25,* 663–683.

Cicirelli, V. G. (1997). Relationship of psychosocial and background variables to elders' end-of-life decisions. *Psychology and Aging, 12,* 77–83.

Corrections Yearbook. (2002). South Salem, NY: Criminal Justice Institute.

Corrections Yearbook. (2003). South Salem, NY: Criminal Justice Institute.

Davis, S. F., Bremer, S. A., Anderson, B. J., & Tramill, J. L. (1983). The interrelationships of ego strength, self-esteem, death anxiety and gender in undergraduate college students. *Journal of General Psychology, 108,* 55–59.

DePaola, S. J., Griffin, M., Young, J. R., & Neimeyer, R. A. (2003). Death anxiety and attitudes toward the elderly among older adults: The role of gender and ethnicity. *Death Studies, 27,* 335–354.

Ditton, P. M. (1999). Mental health and treatment of inmates and probationers. Washington, DC: Bureau of Justice Statistics.

Dodd, D. K., & Mills, L. L. (1985). A measure of the fear of accidental death and injury. *Psychological Record, 35,* 269–275.

Douglass, R. L. (1991). *Oldtimers: Michigan's elderly prisoners.* Unpublished report. Michigan Department of Corrections.

Fortner, B. V., & Neimeyer, R A. (1999). Death anxiety in older adults: A quantitative review. *Death Studies, 23,* 387–411.

Fortner, B. V., Neimeyer, R. A., & Rybarczyk, B. (2000). Correlates of death anxiety in older adults: A comprehensive review. In A. Tomer (Ed.), *Death attitudes and the older adult: Theories, concepts, and applications* (pp. 95–198). Philadelphia, PA: Taylor & Francis.

Freudenberg, N. (2001). Jails, prisons, and the health of urban populations: A review of the impact of the correctional system on community health. *Journal of Urban Health, 78,* 214–235.

Fry, P. S. (2003). Perceived self-efficacy domains as predictors of fear of the unknown and fear of dying among older adults. *Psychology & Aging, 18,* 474–486.

Gallagher, E. M. (1990). Emotional, social, and physical health characteristics of older men in prison. *International Journal of Aging and Human Development, 31,* 251–266.

Gallo, W. T., Baker, M. J., & Bradley, E. H. (2001). Factors associated with home versus institutional death among career patients in Connecticut. *Journal of the American Geriatrics Society, 49,* 771–778.

Gesser, G., Wong, P. T. P., & Reker, G. T. (1987–1988). Death attitudes across the life span: The development and validation of the death attitude profile. *Omega, 18,* 113–128.

Goffman, E. (1961). *Asylums: Essays on the social situation of mental patients and other inmates.* Garden City, NY: Doubleday.

Granse, B. L. (2003). Why should we even care? Hospice social work practice in a prison setting. *Smith College of Social Work, 74*(3), 359–375.

Haney, C., & Zimbardo, P. (2001). Twenty-five years after the Stanford prison experiment. In P. G. Herman (Ed.), *The American prison system* (pp. 25–34). New York: H. W. Wilson Company.

Hoelter, J. W. (1979). Multidimensional treatment of fear of death. *Journal of Consulting and Clinical Psychology, 47,* 996–999.

Kalish, R. A. (1985). The social context of death and dying. In R. H. Binstock & E. Shamas (Eds.), *Handbook of aging and the social sciences* (2nd ed.; pp. 149–170). New York: Van Nostrand Reinhold.

Katz, S. (1979). The relation of the mid-life transition to death anxiety and self-actualization. *Dissertation Abstracts International, 39,* 4039.

Krause, N. (1997). Received support, anticipated support, and mortality. *Research on Aging, 19,* 387–422.

Leming, M. R., & Dickinson, G. E. (1998). *Understanding dying, death, & bereavement* (4th ed.). New York: Harcourt Brace.

Lester, D., & Templer, D. (1993). Death anxiety scales: A dialogue. *Omega, 26,* 239–253.

Litwin, H. (2001). Social network type and morale in old age. *The Gerontologist, 41,* 516–521.

Lockhart, L. K., Bookwala, J., Fagerlin, A., Coppola, K. M., Ditto, P. H., Danks, J. H., & Smucker, W. D. (2001). Older adults' attitudes toward death: Links to perceptions of health and concerns about end-of-life issues. *Omega: The Journal of Death and Dying, 43,* 331–348.

Lund, D. A. (1993). Widowhood: The coping response. In R. Kastenbaum (Ed.), *Encyclopedia of adult development.* Phoenix, AZ: Onyx Press.

Marshall, V. W. (1976). Organizational features of terminal status passage in residential facilities for the aged. In L. H. Loffland (Ed.), *Toward a sociology of death and dying* (pp. 115–134). Beverly Hills, CA: Sage.

Marshall, V. W. (1980). *Last chapters.* Monterey, CA.: Brooks/Cole Publishing Company.

Maull, F. W. (1998). Issues in prison hospice: Toward a model for the delivery of hospice care in a correctional setting. *The Hospice Journal, 13*(4), 57–82.

McCarthy, M. (1983). The health status of elderly inmates. *Corrections Today,* February: 64–65, 74.

Meier, D. E., & Morrison, R. S. (1999). Old age and care near the end of life. *Generations, 23,* 6–11.

Mezey, M., Dubler, N. N., Mitty, E., & Brody, A. A. (2002). What impact do setting and transitions have on the quality of life at the end of life and quality of the dying process? *The Gerontologist, 42,* Special Issue III, 54–67.

Moller, D. W. (2000). *Life's end: Technocratic dying in an age of spiritual yearning.* Amityville, NY: Baywood.

Mullins, L. C., & Lopez, M. A. (1982). Death anxiety among nursing home residents: A comparison of young-old and the old-old. *Death Education, 6,* 75–86.

Myers, J. E. Wass, H., & Murphey, M. (1980). Ethic differences in death anxiety among the elderly. *Death Education, 4,* 237–244.

Nehrke, M., Bellucci, G., & Gabriel, S. J. (1977–1978). Death anxiety, locus of control and life satisfaction in the elderly: Toward a definition of ego-integrity. *Omega: The Journal of Death and Dying, 3,* 359–368.

Neimeyer, R. A., & Van Brunt, D. (1995). Death anxiety. In H. Wass, F. Berado, & R. Neimeyer (Eds.), *Dying: Facing the facts* (pp. 49–58). New York: Taylor & Francis.

Neimeyer, R. A., & Fortner, B. V. (1997). Death attitudes in contemporary perspective. In S. Strack (Ed.), *Death and the quest for meaning* (pp. 3–29). New Jersey: Jason Aronson.

Neimeyer, R. A., Wittkowski, J., & Moser, R. P. (2004). Psychological research on death attitudes: An overview and evaluation. *Death Studies, 28,* 309–340.

Schumaker, J. F., Groth-Marnat, G., Dougherty, F. I., & Barwick, K. C. (1986). Death anxiety, mental health and length of incarceration in male felons. *Social Behavior and Personality, 14,* 177–181.

Straub, S. H., & Roberts, J. M. (2001). Fear of death in widows: Effects of age at widowhood and suddenness of death. *Omega, 43,* 25–42.

Templer, D. I. (1970). The construction and validation of a death anxiety scale. *Journal of General Psychology, 82,* 165–177.

Templer, D. I. (1971). Death anxiety as related to depression and health of retired persons. *Journal of Gerontology, 25,* 521–523.

Templer, D. I., Barlow, V. L., Halcomb, P. H., Ruff, C. F., & Ayers, J. L. (1979). The death anxiety of convicted felons. *Journal of Corrective and Social Psychiatry, 25,* 18–20.

Templer, D. I., & Ruff, C. (1971). Death anxiety scale means, standard deviation means, and embedding. *Psychological Reports, 29,* 173–174.

Thorson, J. A., & Powell, F. C. (1998). African- and Euro-American samples differ little in scores on death anxiety. *Psychological Reports, 83,* 623–627.

Thorson, J. A., & Powell, F. C. (2000). Death anxiety in younger and older adults. In A. Tomer (Ed.), *Death attitudes and the older adult: Theories, concepts, and applications* (pp. 123–136). Philadelphia, PA: Taylor Francis.

Tomer, A. (1992). Attitudes toward death in adult life—Theoretical perspectives. *Death Studies, 16,* 475–506.

Viney, L. (1984). Concerns about death among severely ill people. In F. R. Epting & R. A. Neimeyer (Eds.), *Personal meanings of death* (pp. 143–158). Washington, DC: Hemisphere.

Vernon, G. (1972). Death control. *Omega, 3,* 131–138.

Weisman, A. (1972). *On dying and denying.* New York: Behavioral Publications.

White, W., & Handal, P. J. (1990–1991). The relationship between death anxiety and mental health/distress. *Omega, 22,* 13–24.

Williams, G. C. (1989). *Elderly offenders: A comparison of the chronic and new elderly offenders.* Unpublished thesis. Murfreesboro, TN: Middle Tennessee State University.

Wink, P., & Scott, J. (2005). Does religiousness buffer against the fear of death and dying in late adulthood? Findings from a longitudinal study. *The Journals of Gerontology, Series B: Psychological Sciences and Social Sciences, 60,* 207–214.

RONALD H. ADAY, PhD, Department of Sociology, Middle Tennessee State University, Murfreesboro.

From *Omega,* Vol. 52, no. 3, 2005/2006, pp. 199–216. Copyright © 2006 by Baywood Publishing Co., Inc. Reprinted by permission via the Copyright Clearance Center.

UNIT 4

Ethical Issues of Dying, Death, and Suicide

Unit Selections

Key Points to Consider

- The question, "What is a good death?" has been asked for centuries. What would constitute a good death in this time of high-tech medical care? Does the concept of a good death include the taking of a life? Defend your answer.

- Does the role of the health-care provider include taking life or providing the means for others to do so? Why or why not?

- Are constraints required to prevent the killing of persons we do not consider worthwhile contributors to our society? Explain.

- Should limits be placed on the length of life as we consider the expenses involved in the care of the elderly and the infirm?

- For some individuals, suicide may seem to be the best solution to their situation. How might our society help such individuals "solve" their problems?

- Is the concept of "rational suicide" rational? Why or why not?

- Do you believe that high-risk-taking persons—such as heavy smokers, race-car drivers, overeating or undereating individuals, or persons mixing alcohol and drugs—are suicidal? Explain.

- Should colleges and universities be held accountable or responsible when their students commit suicide?

Student Web Site

www.mhcls.com

Internet References

Articles on Euthanasia: Ethics
http://ethics.acusd.edu/Applied/Euthanasia/

Euthanasia and Physician-Assisted Suicide
http://www.religioustolerance.org/euthanas.htm

Kearl's Guide to the Sociology of Death: Moral Debates
http://WWW.Trinity.Edu/~mkearl/death-5.html#eu

The Kevorkian Verdict
http://www.pbs.org/wgbh/pages/frontline/kevorkian/

Living Wills (Advance Directive)
http://www.mindspring.com/~scottr/will.html

Not Dead Yet
http://www.notdeadyet.org/

Suicide Awareness: Voices of Education
http://www.save.org

UNOS: United Network for Organ Sharing
http://www.unos.org/

Youth Suicide League
http://www.unicef.org/pon96/insuicid.htm

One of the concerns about dying and death that is pressing hard upon our consciences is the question of helping the dying to die sooner with the assistance of the physician. Public awareness of the horrors that can visit upon us by artificial means of ventilation and other support measures in a high-tech hospital setting has produced a literature that debates the issue of euthanasia—a "good death." As individuals think through their plans for care when dying, there is a steady increase in the demand for control of that care. The recent case of Terri Schiavo had brought national attention to the need for more clarity in end-of-life directives and the legitimacy of passive euthanasia.

Another controversial issue is physician-assisted suicide. Is it the function of the doctor to assist patients in their dying—to actually kill them at their request? The highly publicized suicides in Michigan, along with the jury decisions that found Dr. Kevorkian innocent of murder, as well as the popularity of the book *Final Exit,* make these issues prominent national and international concerns. Legislative action has been taken in some states to permit this, and the issue is pending in a number of others. We are in a time of intense consideration by the courts, by the legislatures, and by the medical and nursing professions of the legality and the morality of providing the means by which a person can be given the means to die. Is this the role of health-care providers? The pro and contra positions are presented in several of the unit's articles. Although the issue is difficult and personally challenging, as a nation we are in the position of being required to make difficult choices. There are no "right" answers; the questions pose dilemmas that require choice based upon moral, spiritual, and legal foundations.

The word *suicide,* meaning "self" and "to kill," was first used in English in 1651. Early societies sometimes forced certain members into committing suicide for ritual purposes and occasionally expected such of widows and slaves. There is also a strong inheritance from Hellenic and Roman times of rational suicide when disease, dishonor, or failures were considered unbearable. Attitudes toward suicide changed when St. Augustine laid down rules against it that became basic Christian doctrine for centuries.

In recent years, suicide has attracted increasing interest and scrutiny by sociologists, psychologists, and others in efforts to reduce its incidence. Suicide is a major concern in the United States today, and understanding suicide is important so that warning signs in others can be recognized. To what extent are nonfamily members responsible for the suicides of young adults when they do not intervene?

© Stockbyte/Getty Images

Just what constitutes suicide is not clear today. Risky behavior that leads to death may or may not be classified as suicide. We have differing attitudes toward suicide. Suicide rates are high in adolescents, the elderly, and males. A person with high vulnerability is an alcoholic, depressed male between the ages of 75 and 84. Suicidal persons often talk about the attempt before the act and display observable signs of potential suicide. Males are more likely to complete suicide than females because they use more lethal weapons. For suicidal persons, the act is an easy solution to their problems—a permanent answer to an often temporary set of problems. The public push for suicide prevention can also be a method of resolving the grief caused by a child taking his own life.

Death and the Law

LAWRENCE RUDDEN

Evelyn was diagnosed with breast cancer in 1997. She spent the next four years dying.

At first she waged war on the cancer, attacking her own body with radiation and pills until she was left inhabiting something limp and unresponsive. Still, the cancer continued to grow inside her, replicating through her spine, shoulders, hips, pelvis, and liver.

She watched as her body began to fail her. There were awful waves of pain, violent coughing, constipation, abdominal cramps, convulsions, and humiliation. She had trouble breathing and walking. The sickness was overwhelming her. Evelyn was moved to an assisted living facility, where she was told she had less than six months to live. Plastic tubes were strung up, around and through her body. She lay on her hospital bed like a wax figure. There was nothing heroic about barely persisting.

Evelyn had seen her mother die a horrible, cringing death. She did not want that for herself. She wanted to die with dignity. On September 24, 2001, Evelyn asked the hospice nurse to help end her life. The nurse provided her with a number for Compassion in Dying, a nonprofit organization that supports the right of terminally ill patients to hasten their deaths. It agreed to help.

Richard Holmes, who suffered from terminal colon cancer, appeared in Portland, on November 7, 2001, to announce that he was upset with Attorney General Ashcroft's blocking of Oregon's assisted suicide law.

Evelyn thought about having her family and medical personnel with her as she ended her life. This made her happy. On November 27, 2001, she swallowed a glass of liquid medication, slipped immediately into a coma, and died fifteen minutes later, at the age of seventy-two. Two days earlier, she had written a letter: "On Thanksgiving, I hope everyone in my family will take time to feel thankful that I live in Oregon and have the means to escape this cancer before it gets any worse. I love you all."

Ashcroft declared that any doctor who prescribed lethal doses of painkilling medication with the specific intent of ending his patient's life would lose his license to prescribe medications and would serve a mandatory twenty-year sentence.

Oregon's Law

In 1997, Oregon passed the Death with Dignity Act, making it the only state to permit physician-assisted suicide. Since then, the act has survived an attempt by Congress to overturn it, court hearings on its constitutional validity, and two voter initiatives, in which Oregon residents approved the measure first by a slim margin in 1994, then overwhelmingly in 1997. To qualify for assistance, patients must make two oral requests and one written request at least two weeks apart, be terminally ill with less than six months to live, and be judged mentally competent to make the decision by two separate physicians. Patients are also required to administer the medication themselves. Court records indicate that ninety-one people—mostly cancer patients—have used the provision to end their lives.

"Oregon's law is written with safeguards that prevent patients from using the law prematurely or impulsively," says George Eighmey, executive director of the Oregon branch of the Compassion in Dying Federation. According to Eighmey, patients have sought to end their lives primarily to avoid the profound loss of bodily control and dignity that often accompanies the late stages of a terminal illness.

Can the federal government deny this opportunity to spend one's final months or days in a manner that one does not consider repulsive? According to Attorney General John Ashcroft, it not only can but should. The nation's highest lawyer has declared that assisted suicide is not a "legitimate medical purpose"; in between leading the war on terror, he has been hard at work attempting to punish Oregon doctors for prescribing medications intended to help terminally ill patients end their lives.

"For an oncologist to be unable to prescribe pain medication is incomprehensible." explains Oregon's Dr. Peter Rasmussen. "I would have to retire. . . . I want to continue to be a practicing physician.

In November 2001, Ashcroft declared that any doctor who prescribed lethal doses of painkilling medication with the specific intent of ending his patient's life would lose his license to prescribe medications and would serve a mandatory twenty-year sentence. He defended this ultimatum on the vague grounds that doctors prescribing lethal doses of painkilling medication were in violation of the federal Controlled Substances Act (CSA), a statute intended to punish illicit trafficking of pharmaceuticals.

Many of Oregon's dying and their family members are less enthusiastic about forcing terminal patients to die slowly, in pain and without dignity.

Supporters of the Ashcroft directive are fond of observing that it does not actually forbid doctors from helping patients end their lives. "Oregon's physicians could still practice assisted suicide, but they could not prescribe federally controlled substances for that purpose," explains Rita Marker, executive director of the International Task Force on Euthanasia and Assisted Suicide. In other words, doctors would still be free to prescribe, say, lethal doses of rat poison to Oregon's dying citizens. For obvious reasons—medical ethics, fear of lawsuits, the semblance of something resembling empathy and compassion—this will not happen. Nor, for that matter, would a doctor who had his license to prescribe drugs stripped under the Ashcroft directive be likely to remain a doctor for long. "For an oncologist to be unable to prescribe pain medication is incomprehensible," explains Oregon's Dr. Peter Rasmussen. "I would have to retire. . . . I want to continue to be a practicing physician. I would not be able to help my patients." So, despite some semantic zigzagging, the effect of the directive is really quite straightforward: to prevent states from experimenting with the practice of physician-assisted suicide.

Psychiatrist Greg Hamilton, of Portland's Physicians for Compassionate Care group, thinks this is plainly a good thing. "Helping a patient to die is to spend time with the patient and to treat his symptoms. It's not to overdose the patient. That's not helping a patient during his dying process. That's murdering the patient."

Many of Oregon's dying and their family members are less enthusiastic about forcing terminal patients to die slowly, in pain and without dignity. Linda Kilcrease watched as cancerous tumors wrapped around the blood vessels in her mother's neck, slowly constricting the flow of blood to and from the brain. "Her death was a race between her brain slowly exploding in one stroke after another when blood could not drain from her head, or her heart exploding trying to pump more blood into her head. . . . We watched as her head blew up like a balloon, forcing her eyes closed. When the blood first began to back up and could not drain, we watched as her heart began to beat so hard and fast, nearly ripping through her chest, trying to get blood into her head. The hospital staff gave us heartbeat and blood pressure monitors and we watched the wild fluctuations in vital statistics. We learned how to position Mom's head so her heart would calm down. We watched her change from a robust woman to a shriveled skeleton. . . . It was torture for everyone, but especially Mom. . . . Those who say pain medication and psychiatric help are all that is needed to help someone facing death have it all wrong. Neither would be of any use to my mother."

Denied the opportunity for physician-assisted suicide, some patients chose a more violent way of ending their lives. During the late stages of Emanuel McGeorge's cancer, he often found himself in a stupor from the morphine that was being pumped into his veins. A fiercely independent man, McGeorge worried that he was losing control over his life. "Mac did not want to be a sedated vegetable," recalls his wife, Patsy. And so one day he handed her a note, kissed her weathered cheek, then stumbled into the front yard, where he carefully lodged a shotgun in his mouth and pulled the trigger.

Personal ideology is an admittedly imprecise thing, and attempts by the government to dictate what is good for the character of the nation raise a more difficult question: to whose ideology should the law adhere?

By providing terminal patients with the opportunity to die peacefully, under medical care and with loved ones present, the Death with Dignity Act "has prevented more than fifty-seven people from committing violent suicides during the past five years," says Eighmey.

Ashcroft Digs in His Heels

Theoretically, the matter of physician-assisted suicide should be left to the states, as indicated by a 1997 Supreme Court ruling. "Throughout the nation," observed Chief Justice William Rehnquist in his majority opinion, "Americans are engaged in an earnest and profound debate about the morality, legality, and practicality of physician-assisted suicide. Our holding permits this debate to continue, as it should in a democratic society."

Having seemingly arrived at the principle that physician-assisted suicide is wrong, Ashcroft will be damned if he's going to allow the terminal patients of Oregon to exercise their legal right to end their unbearable suffering. Without so much as providing notice to Oregon officials or the general public, he has declared the practice "not medically legitimate," raising concerns that the country's top lawyer is being guided not by the nuances of law but rather by the moral certainties of personal ideology.

Of course, personal ideology is an admittedly imprecise thing, and attempts by the government to dictate what is good for the character of the nation raise a more difficult question: to whose ideology should the law adhere? Lacking a national religion or a single cultural custom, many legal issues take on a gray shade in America. Plainly, this is a good thing. History indicates that when the law and personal ideology get too close, the law often becomes a straightjacket to individual liberties. The Nazis maintained their power in part by using vague moral codes to destroy any threat to their power base. More recently, the Taliban used the law to punish all variety of sinners, from the heretics to the merely thoughtful. Early on, America's Puritan founders were also hard at work persecuting their neighbors for real and imagined shortcomings—a fact that continues to find expression in the numerous state codes regulating sexual conduct.

Though in general practice our society now tends to keep a proper distance between the law and personal ideology, this Puritan zeal for punishing what our leaders call sin may still rear its head from time to time. Exhibit A: Ashcroft's attempt to invalidate Oregon's Death with Dignity Act. Ashcroft carried the same tune while in Congress, where he twice supported legislation that would subject doctors to twenty years in prison if they prescribed federally regulated drugs to cause a patient's death. Both times the legislation failed.

Now, as attorney general, he is again insisting that physician-assisted suicide is "not a legitimate medical practice," an assessment he defends by observing that doctors are charged with helping patients live, not making them dead. Very good. Nevertheless, the Court has already allowed the administration of "risky pain relief," that is, doses of pain relief that are likely to hasten the death of a terminally ill patient. Is this procedure somehow more "legitimate" than assisted suicide? Is it medically legitimate to deny someone a right to die with dignity? Is such a right "fundamental" to patients whose condition is so severe that pain-relief medication is not sufficient to relieve their suffering? Is it somehow more medically legitimate to have politicians second-guessing doctors? And might strict federal oversight of doctors who prescribe pain medication actually have the broader effect of scaring them into undermedicating dying patients? These are all terribly complicated questions, though Ashcroft doesn't seem to mind ducking his head and smashing right through them.

Along the way, Ashcroft has set the stage for a classic battle of states' versus federal rights. Since Oregon doctors are prescribing federally controlled medications to help Oregon residents kill themselves, the Justice Department claims jurisdiction over the process. It argues that the CSA authorizes the attorney general to revoke a practitioner's license to prescribe medications, if he determines that the practitioner is acting in a manner that "threatens public health," regardless of state laws.

Advocates of states' rights maintain that Ashcroft is expanding the scope of the CSA beyond its original intent—regulating the illegal sale of pharmaceuticals. They also dispute that he has the authority to determine whether physician-assisted suicide constitutes "a legitimate medical practice" and quiver at the idea of an unelected, unaccountable government official dictating some of the most personal decisions of their lives. This intrusion, they maintain, is a violation of the spirit of the Constitution.

Round 1 went to the states' advocates. In his harshly critical rebuke of the Ashcroft directive, Oregon federal judge Robert Jones wrote that it would be "unprecedented and extraordinary" for Congress to assign the attorney general the authority to interpret what constitutes a legitimate medical practice. While Jones acknowledged that Ashcroft may be "fully justified, morally, ethically, religiously," in opposing assisted suicide, he emphasized that the attorney general's strong feelings alone do "not permit a federal statute to be manipulated from its true meaning, even to satisfy a worthy goal."

The Supreme Court emphasized that the right to physician-assisted suicide is a matter that should be decided by the states.

Intrepidly, the Justice Department carries on. On September 25, 2001, it filed an appeal with the Ninth U.S. Circuit Court of Appeals—the same court that previously ruled that the due process clause of the Fourteenth Amendment prevents the government from flatly banning physician-assisted suicide. The case will be heard in spring 2003, after which an appeal to the U.S. Supreme Court is expected.

Supreme Court Precedence and Individual Rights

In their 1997 ruling, the Supreme Court justices voted 9–0 that terminal patients do not have a generalized constitutional right to physician-assisted suicide. The ruling applied only to the cases before the Court and did not take into account the Oregon law. At the same time, the justices littered their opinions with enough qualifiers about specific constitutional rights and principles to effectively make a tangled mess of things. Justice Souter, for example, noted that a total ban on physician-assisted suicide could in fact be deemed unconstitutional if it violated certain basic and historically protected principles of personal autonomy. He added that there exist arguments of "increasing forcefulness for recognizing some right to a doctor's help in suicide."

Justice Breyer emphasized that forcing dying patients to live out their final days in great pain might violate a general right "to die with dignity." Justice Stevens wrote a separate opinion in which he plainly stated that if presented with an appropriate case, he would overrule a ban on physician-assisted suicide. In effect, Stevens recalled that our country does not have a national religion or culture. As our multicultural mélange of citizens may have very different moral, religious, or personal ideas about how they ought to spend their final days, terminal

Why the Government Has an Interest in Preserving Life

Gerard V. Bradley

Attorney General Ashcroft wants to stop doctors who kill. He has good reason: doctors have a special responsibility to show by word and deed, in season and out, that intentionally killing another person is simply wrong. Yes, even if that person is, like Evelyn, terminally ill.

A doctor's calling is always to heal, never to harm. A doctor's calling is special, though not unique. None of us possesses a license, privilege, or permission to kill, but the healer who purposely kills puts into question, in a unique way, our culture's commitment to the sanctity of life. The scandal created by doctors who kill is great, much like that caused by lawyers who flout the law, or bishops—shepherds—who do not care about their flocks. Whenever someone whose profession centers upon a single good—healing or respect for law or caring for souls—tramples that good, the rest of us cannot help but wonder: is it a good after all? Maybe it is for some, but not for others? Who decides? Is all the talk of that good as supremely worthwhile idle chatter or, worse, cynical propaganda?

Do not intentionally kill. This is what it means—principally and essentially—to revere life. Making intentional killing of humans a serious crime is the earmark of society's respect for life. All our criminal laws against homicide (save for Oregon) make no exception—none whatsoever—for victims who say they want to die. Our law contains no case or category of "public service homicides," of people who should be dead. People hunting season is never open. Our laws against killing (except Oregon's) make no exception for those who suffer, even for those near death. None.

When someone commits the crime of murder, all we can say is that the victim's life was shortened. We know not by how much; the law does not ask, or care. After all, no one knows how much longer any of us shall live. Many persons who are the picture of health, in the bloom of youth, will die today in accidents, by another's hand, or of natural causes. Yes, we can say with confidence that someone's death, maybe Evelyn's, is near at hand. But so long as she draws breath, she has the same legal and moral right that you and I have not to be intentionally killed.

It is not that life is the only good thing which we, and our laws, strive to protect. Life is not always an overriding good; we accept certain risks to life. What is the alternative? Do nothing at all that creates some (even a small) chance of death? Would we get up in the morning? Drive our cars? Take medicine? Go swimming? Fly in airplanes? Some risk to life is acceptable where the risk is modest and the activities that engender it are worthwhile.

Sometimes the risk can be great and still worth accepting. We might instinctively step in front of a car, or jump into a freezing lake to save a loved one, or a stranger's wandering toddler. We might do the same upon reflection, but we do not want to die. We do not commit suicide.

Religious martyrs may face certain death, but they do not want to die. They submit to death as the side effect of their acts, whether these be described as witnessing to the truth, or, in the case of Saint Thomas More, avoiding false witness. The axman, the lion tamer, the firing squad—they kill. They intend death.

This distinction between intending and accepting death is not scholarly hairsplitting. This distinction is real, as real as space shuttles. The *Columbia* crew knew all along that they risked death by flying into space. That which they risked came to be, but they were not suicides.

Of course doctors may—even must—prescribe analgesics. Doctors should try to relieve the suffering of their terminal patients, up to and even including toxic doses. Not because they want to kill, any more than they want to kill patients in exploratory surgery. Doctors who prescribe strong painkillers want to help, even to heal. Given how ill some patients are, the risk of death is worth running, just as some very risky surgeries are a risk worth taking.

Evelyn wants to let go, and she needs help to do so. Yet, none of us walks into a doctor's office and demands a certain treatment. Doctors do not fetch medicines upon demand. They are not workmen at our services. Yes, doctors work toward our health in cooperation with us. They have no right to impose treatment we do not want. But we have no right to drugs, surgery, or anesthesia.

Or to lights out—even for Evelyn.

Why? Because autonomy, or self-rule, is not an all-consuming value. It is not a trump card. Evelyn honestly wishes to bring down the curtain. We may find her condition hideous, as she evidently does, but our feelings (of repulsion, sympathy, or whatever) are unreliable guides to sound choosing. Feelings certainly do not always, or even usually, mislead us. Often, though, they do.

Pause a moment and you will, if you try, think of something attractive and pleasing you did not choose today, because it would have been wrong, and something unappealing, even repulsive, you chose to do because it was right. For me, some days, it has to do with my mother, who suffers from advanced Alzheimer's. Enough said.

On what basis does a society and its governing authorities decide that life is a great common good? Because it is true: life is good. The law is a powerful teacher of right and wrong. Like it or not, what our laws permit is thought by many to be good, or at least unobjectionable. What the law forbids is believed to be, well, forbidden.

Why should our government take such an unyielding stand in favor of life? Because we are all safer where everyone's life is prized, not despised.

—Gerard V. Bradley is professor of law at the University of Notre Dame patients should have the freedom to pursue these convictions so long as their actions affect only their own morality. In other words, an individual should not be forced to spend his final days in excruciating pain simply because this is what his neighbor feels is right.

During a recent speech on Oregon's physician-assisted suicide law, Justice Scalia was even more straightforward: "You want the right to die," snorted Justice Scalia to his audience at the Northwestern School of Law of Lewis and Clark College. "That's right and that's fine. You don't hear me complaining about Oregon's law."

So, what to do? The Supreme Court emphasized that the right to physician-assisted suicide is a matter that should be decided by the states. Indeed, the democratization of this issue would have the beneficial effect of making real-world experience relevant to the law. Rather than freezing the law in accordance with the speculation of political or religious groups, we could learn from experience in a systematic fashion and thus make law adaptive to the individual needs of terminal patients.

Diagnosed with terminal ovarian cancer, Penny Schlueter of Pleasent Hill, Oregon, could no longer sit without pain and had to lie on her side. She planned to take advantage of the state's assisted suicide law when the time came.

For critics, experimentation with physician-assisted suicide would come at the unacceptable cost of making terminally ill patients vulnerable to increased pressure to end their lives—either by profit-oriented HMOs or out of implicit guilt for the financial and emotional burden they are exacting on relatives. "In an era of cost control and managed care, patients with lingering illnesses may be branded an economic liability, and decisions to encourage death can be driven by cost," says Cathy Cleaver of the U.S. Conference of Catholic Bishops. Cleaver points to the Netherlands, where physician-assisted suicide is legal and occurring at an alarming rate: "For years Dutch courts have allowed physicians to practice euthanasia and assisted suicide with impunity, supposedly only in cases where desperately ill patients have unbearable suffering. In a few years, however, Dutch policy and practice have expanded to allow the killing of people with disabilities or even physically healthy people

with psychological distress; thousands of patients have been killed by their doctors without their request. The Dutch example teaches us that the 'slippery slope' is very real."

Even at this late date, some of our highest government officials remain dedicated to the idea of regulating the most intimate decisions of this country's citizens, even when the outcome affects only the morality of the actor.

In short, Cleaver worries that if we let doctors end the pointless suffering of terminal patients, the practice would quickly become the norm. Soon depressed people would be demanding a right to die, our palliative-care options would begin to lag behind the rest of the civilized world, and our doctors would be transformed into stalking butlers. An alarming thought, but just one thing: For years the Dutch had almost no formalized procedure in place to regulate the process. Physicians were expected to report themselves to a governing board, which would determine after the fact whether they had broken the law.

By contrast, Oregon's law requires extensive reporting requirements, and, after five years, "evidence points to 100 percent reporting compliance and no deviation from the rules in Oregon," says Barbara Coombs Lee, president of the Compassion in Dying Federation. In fact, a survey of Oregon physicians who have had experience with the Death with Dignity Act reports that some candidates are being screened out of the program. According to the study, only 29 (18 percent) of the 165 people who had requested medication under the act actually received a prescription.

For those who did receive one, control over their final few days, not access to healing options, was the point. It is unlikely that critics will pause long enough to acknowledge this rousing fact. Even at this late date, some of our highest government officials remain dedicated to the idea of regulating the most intimate decisions of this country's citizens, even when the outcome affects only the morality of the actor.

Truly, that is alarming.

LAWRENCE RUDDEN is director of research for the Graham Williams Group in Washington, D.C. He writes on *politics and culture.*

What Living Wills Won't Do
The Limits of Autonomy

ERIC COHEN

In the aftermath of the Terri Schiavo case, it seems clear that most Americans are uncomfortable at the prospect of politicians' intervening in family decisions about life and death. This is not only understandable, but usually wise. Americans understand that eventually they will have to make medical decisions for loved ones, and that such decisions are wrenching. Most people have little faith that the state—or the courts—can make better judgments than they can. And they are usually right.

But it is precisely the complexity of these life-and-death decisions that sometimes makes state involvement inevitable. The state was involved in the Schiavo case long before Congress intervened, from the time Terri's parents went to court in Florida to challenge her husband's fitness as a guardian back in 1993. State judiciaries must decide when family members clash, or when doctors and families disagree, or when surrogates wish to override a loved one's living will. And state legislatures have a responsibility to set the parameters for judicial decisions in particular cases. They must decide the admissibility of casual conversations in determining a person's prior wishes, or the appropriate weight to give a person's desires (such as requests for assisted suicide) even when they are clearly expressed.

For decades, we have deluded ourselves into believing that living wills would solve our caregiving problems; that healthy individuals could provide advance instructions for what to do if they became incompetent; that such a system would ensure that no one is mistreated and that everyone defines the meaning of life for himself until the very end. But it is now clear that living wills have failed, both practically and morally.

In the March–April 2004 issue of the *Hastings Center Report*, Angela Fagerlin and Carl E. Schneider survey the social science data, and their conclusions are damning: Most people do not have living wills, despite a very active campaign to promote them; those who do usually provide vague and conflicting instructions; people's opinions often change from experience to experience; and people's instructions are easily influenced by how a given scenario is described. These are not problems that any reform can fix. A person simply can't grasp in the present every medical and moral nuance of his own future case.

Most people do not have living wills, despite a very active campaign to promote them; those who do usually provide vague and conflicting instructions.

The dream of perfect autonomy—everyone speaking for himself, never deciding for another—should fade each time we change a parent's diaper, or visit a grandparent who does not recognize us, or sell an uncle's property to pay for the nursing home. After all, the only fully autonomous death—with every detail governed by individual will—is suicide. And suicide is hardly a basis for dealing more responsibly with the burdens of caregiving.

As the baby boomers age, we are entering a period when long-term dementia will often be the prelude to death, and when caregivers will regularly have to make decisions about how or whether to treat intervening illnesses like infections, heart trouble, or cancer. When should we accept that death has arrived, and when does stopping treatment entail a judgment that Alzheimer's patients are "better off dead"? What do we owe those who are cognitively disabled and totally dependent?

On these hard questions, the most vocal critics of Congress and "the religious right" in the Schiavo case have revealed the shallowness of their own thinking. Defending the "right to privacy" ignores the moral challenge of deciding how we should act in private, as both patients and caregivers. Asserting that "the state should stay out" of these decisions ignores the fact that some hard cases will always end up in court; that legislatures have a civic responsibility to pass the laws that courts apply; and that a decent society should set some minimum moral boundaries, such as laws against euthanasia and assisted suicide. And claiming that we should "defer to medical experts" ignores the potential conflict between the ideology of living wills and the ethic of medicine, since some people will leave instructions that no principled physician could execute.

In the end, the retreat to moral libertarianism and liberal proceduralism is inadequate. We need, instead, a moral philosophy, a political philosophy, and a medical philosophy that clarify our roles as caregivers, citizens, and doctors attending to those who cannot speak for themselves.

Any moral philosophy of care should begin with the premise that disability—even profound disability—is not grounds for seeking someone's death. But seeking death and accepting death when it arrives are very different matters. And while we should not seek death, neither should we see extending life at all costs as the supreme goal of care.

Imagine, for example, that a person with advanced Alzheimer's is diagnosed with cancer, and there is a burdensome treatment (like radiation) that might extend the person's remaining life from three months to six months. In this case, family members seem morally justified in rejecting the treatment, even knowing that an earlier death is the likely result. But they don't reject treatment *so that* the patient will die; they reject it so that the patient will not suffer excessively as death arrives. They choose minimum discomfort, not death. By contrast, if the same Alzheimer's patient gets an infection that is easily treated by antibiotics, it is hard to see any moral ground for withholding treatment. Holding back ordinary care is not the same as euthanasia, but it is still a choice that hastens death as its aim.

In reality, many dementia cases involve multiple illnesses, with uncertain prognoses, and a menu of treatment options. Often, there are various morally justifiable choices. Personal values do matter. But what is always needed is a moral framework that governs such private decisions, based on the belief that every life is equal, and no life should be treated as a burden to be relinquished, including one's own.

Given the infinite complexity of these clinical situations, the scope of the law should always be limited. What is legally permissible is not always morally right, but what is morally wrong should not always be outlawed. Nevertheless, it is foolish to ignore the extent to which the current legal framework shapes how people make private decisions, or to ignore the proper role of the state in setting certain minimum boundaries. Legally, no competent person should ever be forced to accept medical treatment in the present that he does not want. Legally, no one should have the right to commit suicide or procure assistance in doing so, and no one should be killed or forced to die against his will or that of his guardians. And legally, guardians should not be forced to implement living wills that aim at death as their goal.

As for the courts that are called upon to settle certain cases, they will need some political guidance or governing principles to do so. For example, what if a tenured professor of bioethics, unable to bear the loss of his cognitive powers, leaves written instructions not to treat any infections if he ever suffers dementia? Decades later, now suffering from Alzheimer's, the former professor is mentally impaired but seemingly happy. He can't recognize his children, but he seems to enjoy the sunset. He's been physically healthy for years, but then gets a urinary tract infection. All his family members believe he should be treated.

Should the state intervene to prohibit antibiotics—to protect the incompetent person's "right to die"? Or should the state leave the family members alone, so they can do what they believe is in the best interests of the person the professor now is? If Andrew Sullivan and other critics are worried about "theocons" using the power of the state to undermine the right to self-determination, are they willing to use the power of the state to impose death when families choose life? Is this what their idea of "autonomy" really requires?

And this leads us, finally, to the ethics of medicine. We have already gone very far in turning medicine into a service industry and doctors into technicians who simply use their skills to do our bidding. The physicians who perform abortions when the life and health of the mother are not in danger, or the cosmetic surgeons who give breast implants to healthy women, or the doctors who prescribe growth hormone for kids of average height are not really practicing medicine; they are serving desires. Most doctors take their medical oath seriously, struggling daily and often heroically to provide for those entrusted to their care. But some have succumbed to various forms of utilitarianism, or simply believe that people with cognitive disabilities are already humanly dead. In cases like Terri Schiavo's—a disabled woman, not dead or dying, whose feeding was keeping her alive without imposing additional burdens—it is hard to see how any doctor could ethically remove a feeding tube. And if we are to respect medicine as a moral profession, no court should compel doctors of conscience to do so.

As America ages and dementia becomes a common phenomenon, the dilemmas that the Schiavo case thrust onto the nightly news will only become more urgent and more profound. As a society, we will need to navigate between two dangers: The first is the euthanasia solution, and the prospect of treating the old and vulnerable as burdens to be ignored, abandoned, or put to sleep at our convenience. The second is that the costs of long-term care will suffocate every other civic and cultural good—like educating the young, promoting the arts and sciences, and preserving a strong defense.

We will face imperfect options, as societies always do. In navigating the dangers, we will need to rely on more than the gospel of autonomy, and we will need to confront the failure of living wills and the ideology they rest upon: that deciding for others is always to be avoided. In reality, deciding for others is what many of us will be required to do as parents age or spouses decline, and we will do well to accept this burden with moral sobriety rather than pretending it does not exist.

ERIC COHEN is editor of the *New Atlantis* and resident scholar at the Ethics and Public Policy Center.

From *The Weekly Standard,* by Eric Cohen, April 18, 2005, pp. 18–19. Copyright © 2005 by Weekly Standard. Reprinted by permission.

Ethics and Life's Ending
An Exchange

Robert D. Orr and Gilbert Meilaender

Feeding tubes make the news periodically, and controversies over their use or non-use seem unusually contentious. But feeding tubes are not high technology treatment; they are simple, small-bore catheters made of soft synthetic material. Nor are they new technology; feeding tubes were first used in 1793 by John Hunter to introduce jellies, eggs, sugar, milk, and wine into the stomachs of patients unable to swallow. Why does this old, low-tech treatment generate such controversy today? The important question is not whether a feeding tube *can* be used, but whether it *should* be used in a particular situation.

Too often in medicine we use a diagnostic or therapeutic intervention just because it is available. This thoughtless approach is sometimes called the technological imperative, i.e., the impulse to do everything we are trained to do, regardless of the burden or benefit. Kidney failure? Let's do dialysis. Respiratory failure? Let's use a ventilator. Unable to eat? Let's put in a feeding tube. By responding in this way, the physician ignores the maxim "the ability to act does not justify the action." Just because we know how to artificially breathe for a patient in respiratory failure doesn't mean that everyone who cannot breathe adequately must be put on a ventilator. Such a response also represents a failure to do the moral work of assessing whether the treatment is appropriate in a particular situation.

The moral debate about the use or non-use of feeding tubes hinges on three important considerations: the distinction between what in the past was called "ordinary" and "extraordinary" treatments; the important social symbolism of feeding; and a distinction between withholding and withdrawing treatments.

It was recognized many years ago that respirators, dialysis machines, and other high-tech modes of treatment are optional. They could be used or not used depending on the circumstances. However, it was commonly accepted in the past that feeding tubes are generally not optional. Part of the reasoning was that feeding tubes are readily available, simple to use, not very burdensome to the patient, and not very expensive. They were "ordinary treatment" and thus morally obligatory.

Ordinary [versus] Extraordinary

For over four hundred years, traditional moral theology distinguished between ordinary and extraordinary means of saving life. Ordinary means were those that were not too painful or burdensome for the patient, were not too expensive, and had a reasonable chance of working. These ordinary treatments were deemed morally obligatory. Those treatments that did involve undue burden were extraordinary and thus optional. This distinction was common knowledge in religious and secular circles, and this language and reasoning was commonly applied in Western society.

As medical treatments became more complicated, it was recognized that this distinction was sometimes not helpful. The problem was that the designation appeared to belong to the treatment itself, rather than to the situation. The respirator and dialysis machine were categorized as extraordinary while antibiotics and feeding tubes were classed as ordinary. But real-life situations were not that simple. Thus began a change in moral terminology first officially noted in the *Declaration on Euthanasia* published in 1980 by the Catholic Church's Sacred Congregation for the Doctrine of the Faith in 1980: "In the past, moralists replied that one is never obligated to use 'extraordinary' means. This reply, which as a principle still holds good, is perhaps less clear today, by reason of the imprecision of the term and the rapid progress made in the treatment of sickness. Thus some people prefer to speak of 'proportionate' and 'disproportionate' means."

This newer and clearer moral terminology of proportionality was used in secular ethical analysis as early as the 1983 President's Commission report, *Deciding to Forgo Life-Sustaining Technologies.* The "ordinary/extraordinary" language, however, continues to be seen in the medical literature and heard in the intensive care unit. Reasoning on the basis of proportionality requires us to weigh the burdens and the benefits of a particular treatment for a particular patient. Thus a respirator may be proportionate (and obligatory) for a young person with a severe but survivable chest injury, but it may be disproportionate (and thus optional) for another person who is dying of lung cancer. The same is true for (almost) all medical treatments, including feeding tubes. There are two treatments that always remain obligatory, as I shall explain below.

A second aspect of the discussion about the obligation to provide nutritional support, especially in secular discussions but also in religious debate, was the symbolism of food and water—feeding is caring; nutrition is nurture; food and water are not treatment, and therefore they are never optional. The reasoning commonly went as follows: we provide nutritional support for vulnerable infants because this is an important part of "tender loving care." Shouldn't we provide the same for vulnerable adults as well?

Certainly when a patient is temporarily unable to swallow and has the potential to recover, artificially administered fluids and nutrition are obligatory. Does that obligation change if the prognosis is poor?

This aspect of the debate continued through the 1970s and '80s. It appeared to be resolved by the U.S. Supreme Court in its 1990 decision in *Cruzan v. Director, Missouri Department of Health* when five of the nine Justices agreed that artificially administered fluids and nutrition are medical treatments and are thus optional. Since *Cruzan* medical and legal professions have developed a consensus that feeding tubes are not always obligatory. This debate is ongoing, however, and in some minds the symbolism of feeding remains a dominant feature.

Starvation

A parallel concern to the symbolism entailed in the use of fluids and nutrition is the commonly heard accusation, "But you will be starving him to death!" when discontinuation of a feeding tube is discussed. This is incorrect. Starvation is a slow process that results from lack of calories and takes several weeks or months. When artificially administered fluids and nutrition are not used in a person who is unable to swallow, that person dies from dehydration, not starvation, and death occurs in five to twelve days. Dehydration is very commonly the last physiologic stage of dying, no matter what the cause.

"But that is no comfort! Being dehydrated and thirsty is miserable." Yes and no. Being thirsty is miserable, but becoming dehydrated need not be. The only place in the body where thirst is perceived is the mouth. There is good empirical evidence that as long as a person's mouth is kept moist, that person is not uncomfortable, even if it is clear that his or her body is becoming progressively dehydrated.

I said earlier that there are two treatments that are never optional: these are good symptom control and human presence. Therefore, when a person is becoming dehydrated as he or she approaches death, it is obligatory to provide good mouth care, along with other means of demonstrating human caring and presence, such as touching, caressing, gentle massage, hair-brushing, talking, reading, and holding.

Withholding [versus] Withdrawing

A third feature of the debate over feeding tubes is the issue of withholding versus withdrawing therapy. Thirty years ago, it was common teaching in medicine that "it is better to withhold a treatment than to withdraw it." The thinking was that if you stop a ventilator or dialysis or a feeding tube, and the patient then dies from this lack of life support, you were the agent of death. Therefore, it would be ethically better not to start the treatment in the first place. Then, if the patient dies, death is attributable to the underlying disease and not to your withdrawal of life support.

Slowly, with help from philosophers, theologians, attorneys, and jurists, the medical profession came to accept that there is no moral or legal difference between withholding and withdrawing a treatment. In fact, it may be ethically better to withdraw life-sustaining treatment than it is to withhold it. If there is a treatment with a very small chance of helping the patient, it is better to give it a try. If it becomes clear after a few days or weeks that it is not helping, then you can withdraw the treatment without the original uncertainty that you might be quitting too soon, and now with the comfort that comes from knowing you are not the agent of death.

However, even if there is no professional, moral, or legal difference, it still may be psychologically more difficult to withdraw a treatment that you know is postponing a patient's death than it would have been not to start it in the first place. Turning down the dials on a ventilator with the expectation that the patient will not survive is more personally unsettling than is merely being present with a patient who is actively dying. Withdrawal of a feeding tube can be even more unsettling, especially if the professional involved has any moral reservations about the distinction between ordinary and extraordinary means, or about the symbolism of artificially administered fluids and nutrition.

Some develop this part of the debate with moral concern about intentionality. They contend that your intention in withdrawing the feeding tube is that the patient will die, and it is morally impermissible to cause death intentionally. In actuality, the intention in withdrawing any therapy that has been proven not to work is to stop postponing death artificially.

With these aspects of the debate more or less settled, where does that leave us in making decisions about the use or non-use of feeding tubes? The short-term use of a feeding tube for a patient who is unable to swallow adequate fluids and nutrition for a few days, because of severe illness or after surgery or trauma, may be lifesaving and is almost always uncontroversial. Such usage may even be morally obligatory when the goal of treatment is patient survival and a feeding tube is the best way to provide needed fluids and nutrition.

A feeding tube is sometimes requested by a loved one as a last-gasp effort to postpone death in a patient who is imminently dying and unable to swallow. This is almost always inappropriate. Good mouth care to maintain patient comfort and hygiene is obligatory, but in such cases maintenance of nutrition is no longer a reasonable goal of treatment. In fact, introduction of fluids may even lead to fluid overload that can cause patient discomfort as the body's systems are shutting down.

Long Term Use

The situation that can generate ethical quandaries, front-page news, and conflicts in court is the long-term use of feeding tubes. And these situations are not as neatly segregated into proportionate or disproportionate usage.

Long-term use of a feeding tube remains ethically obligatory for a patient who is cognitively intact, can and wants to survive, but is permanently unable to swallow, an example being a patient who has been treated for malignancy of the throat or esophagus. Protracted use of a feeding tube is also morally required in most instances when it is uncertain whether a patient will regain awareness or recover the ability to swallow—for instance, immediately after a serious head injury or a disabling stroke.

Long-term use of a feeding tube becomes controversial in patients suffering from progressive deterioration of brain function (e.g., Alzheimer's dementia), or in patients with little or no likelihood of regaining awareness after illness or injury (e.g., the permanent vegetative state). Thus, the most perplexing feeding-tube questions involve patients who are unable to take in adequate fluids and nutrition by themselves but who have a condition that by itself will not soon lead to death. The reasoning is, the patient has no fatal condition; he or she can be kept alive with the simple use of tube feedings; therefore we are obligated to use a feeding tube to keep this person alive.

Alzheimer's dementia is the most common type of brain deterioration, afflicting five percent of individuals over sixty-five and perhaps as many as 50 percent of those over eighty-five. It is manifested by progressive cognitive impairment, followed by physical deterioration. This process generally takes several years, often a decade, and is ultimately fatal. In its final stages it almost always interferes with the patient's ability to swallow. Eventually the individual chokes on even pureed foods or liquids. Continued attempts at feeding by mouth very commonly result in aspiration of food or fluid into the airway, frequently leading to pneumonia. Aspiration pneumonia will sometimes respond to antibiotics, but other times it leads to death. Such respiratory infections are the most common final event in this progressive disease.

Feeding tubes have been commonly used in the later stages of Alzheimer's. The reasoning has been that this patient is not able to take in adequate fluids and nutrition and he is not imminently dying. Several assumptions then follow: a feeding tube will improve his comfort, will prevent aspiration pneumonia, and will ensure adequate nutrition which will in turn prevent skin breakdown and thus postpone his death. However, empirical evidence, published in the *Journal of the American Medical Association* in 1999, has shown each of these assumptions to be incorrect: using a feeding tube in a patient with dementia does not prevent these complications, nor does it prolong life.

In addition, there are several negative aspects to using a feeding tube in a person with advanced cognitive impairment. There are rare complications during insertion, some merely uncomfortable, some quite serious. Having a tube in one's nose is generally uncomfortable; even having one coiled up under a dressing on the abdominal wall can be annoying. Because the demented patient doesn't understand the intended purpose of the feeding tube, he or she may react by trying to remove it, requiring either repeated re-insertions or the use of hand restraints. In addition, using a feeding tube may deprive the patient of human presence and interaction: hanging a bag of nutritional fluid takes only a few seconds, as opposed to the extended time of human contact involved in feeding a cognitively impaired person.

End Stage Alzheimer's

There is a slowly developing consensus in medicine that feeding tubes are generally not appropriate for use in most patients nearing the end stage of Alzheimer's disease. This belief can be supported from a moral standpoint in terms of proportionality. And yet feeding tubes are still rather commonly used. A recently published review of all U.S. nursing home patients with cognitive impairment found that an average of 34 percent were being fed with feeding tubes (though there were large state-to-state variations, from nine percent in Maine, New Hampshire, and Vermont to 64 percent in Washington, D.C.).

The cases we read about in the newspaper—in which families are divided and court battles fought—most often involve patients in a permanent vegetative state (PVS). This is a condition of permanent unawareness most often caused by severe head injury or by the brain being deprived of oxygen for several minutes. Such deprivation may be the result of successful cardiopulmonary resuscitation of a patient whose breathing or circulation had stopped from a cardiac arrest, near-drowning, strangulation, etc. In a PVS patient, the heart, lungs, kidneys, and other organs continue to function; given good nursing care and artificially administered fluids and nutrition, a person can live in this permanent vegetative state for many years.

A person in a PVS may still have reflexes from the spinal cord (grasping, withdrawal from pain) or the brain stem (breathing, regulation of blood pressure), including the demonstration of sleep-wake cycles. He may "sleep" for several hours, then "awaken" for a while; the eyes are open and wander about, but do not fix on or follow objects. The person in a PVS is "awake, but unaware" because the areas of the upper brain that allow a person to perceive his or her environment and to act voluntarily are no longer functioning.

Uncertainty

Some of the clinical controversy about nutritional support for persons in a PVS is due to uncertainty. After a head injury or resuscitation from a cardiac arrest, it may be several weeks or months before a patient can rightly be declared to be in a PVS—months during which the provision of nutritional support via feeding tubes is often very appropriate. Loved ones usually remain optimistic, hoping for improvement, praying for full recovery. The length of time from brain damage to declaration of a PVS can extend, depending on the cause of the brain injury, from one month to twelve months. And just to muddy the waters even further, there are rare instances of delayed improvement after many months or even a few years, so that the previously unaware patient regains some ability to perceive his or her environment, and may even be able to say a few words. These individuals are now in a "minimally conscious state." More than minimal delayed improvement is exceedingly rare. (Treatment decisions for persons in a minimally conscious state are perhaps even more controversial than are those for PVS patients, but that discussion must wait for another time.)

The greatest ethical dilemma surrounding the use or non-use of nutritional support for persons in a PVS arises from the fact that they are not clearly dying. With good nursing care and nutrition, individuals in this condition have survived for up to thirty-five years. Those who advocate continued nutritional support argue thus: this person is alive and not actively or imminently dying; it is possible to keep him alive with minimal effort; this human life is sacred; therefore we are obligated to continue to give artificially administered fluids and nutrition.

It is hard to disagree with the various steps in this line of reasoning. (Some utilitarians do disagree, however, claiming that a patient in a PVS is "already dead" or is a "non-person." Those who believe in the sanctity of life must continue to denounce this line of thought.) Let us stipulate the following: the person in a PVS is alive; he can be kept alive for a long time; his life is sacred. But does the obligation to maintain that severely compromised human life necessarily follow from these premises?

Let's first address the issue of whether he is dying. One could maintain that his physical condition is such that he will die soon but for the artificial provision of fluids and nutrition. Thus the permanent vegetative state could be construed to be lethal in and of itself. However, that fatal outcome is not inevitable since the saving treatment is simple. How does this differ from the imperative to provide nourishment for a newborn who would die without the provision of fluids and nutrition? There are two differences. Most newborns are able to take in nutrition if it is placed in or near their mouths. PVS patients can't swallow, so the nutrition must be delivered further down the gastrointestinal tract. As for sick or premature infants, they have a great potential for improvement, growth, and development. The PVS patient has no such potential.

Kidney Failure

Rather than a newborn, a better analogy for this aspect of the discussion would be a person with kidney failure. The kidney failure itself is life-threatening, but it is fairly easily corrected by dialysis three times a week. If the person has another condition that renders him unaware of his surroundings, or a condition that makes life a continuous difficult struggle, most would agree that the person is ethically permitted to stop the dialysis even if that means he will not survive. The ultimate cause of death was treatable, so that death could have been postponed, possibly for years. However, other mitigating circumstances may make the dialysis disproportionate, and so one should be allowed to discontinue this death-postponing treatment in a person who is not imminently dying.

Someone coming from a mechanistic perspective can easily and comfortably decide that a person in a PVS with no potential for recovery has no inherent value and is even an emotional drain on loved ones and a financial drain on society. But what about a person of faith? Does the sanctity of life, a basic tenet of Christianity, Judaism, and Islam, dictate that life must always be preserved if it is humanly possible to do so? Our moral intuitions tell us the answer is no.

It might be possible to postpone the death of a patient from end-stage heart failure by doing one more resuscitation. It might be possible to postpone the death of someone with end-stage liver disease by doing a liver transplant. It might be possible to postpone the death of someone with painful cancer with a few more blood transfusions or another round of chemotherapy. But these therapies are often not used—because the burden is disproportionate to the benefit. Thus the timing of death is often a matter of choice. In fact, it is commonly accepted that the timing of 80 percent of deaths that occur in a hospital is chosen.

Believers do not like to use the words "choice" and "death" in the same sentence. Doing so recalls acrimonious contests about the "right to life" versus the "right to choose" that are the pivotal point in debates about abortion, assisted suicide, and euthanasia. And certainly belief in the sanctity of human life obligates believers to forgo some choices. But does this belief preclude all choices? No: life is full of difficult choices. This is true for believers and nonbelievers alike. Believers may have more guidance about what choices to make and perhaps some limits on options, but we still are faced with many choices—such as choices about the use or non-use of feeding tubes.

When engaging in moral debate on matters of faith, it is important not to focus exclusively on one tenet of faith to the exclusion of others. In debating the use of feeding tubes—or of any mode of treatment for that matter—one must not ignore the concepts of finitude and stewardship by focusing only on the sanctity of life.

If belief in the sanctity of human life translated automatically into an obligation to preserve each human life at all costs, we would not have to debate proportionate and disproportionate treatments. We would simply be obligated to use all treatments available until they failed to work. However, because of the Fall, human life is finite. All of us will die. Since that is inevitable, God expects us to care wisely for our own bodies and for those of our loved ones, and also for our resources. Healthcare professionals similarly must be wise stewards of their skills and services.

Taking into consideration the scriptural principle of stewardship and the tradition of proportionate treatment, I conclude that there must be some degree of discretion in the use or non-use of feeding tubes. There are clearly situations where a feeding tube must be used. There are other situations where a feeding tube would be morally wrong. But there are many situations where the use of a feeding tube should be optional. And this means that one individual of faith might choose to use a tube when another might choose not to use it.

Personal Values

Because of the patient's personal values, someone might choose to continue artificially administered fluids and nutrition for a loved one in a permanent vegetative state for many years. Another might choose to continue for one year and then to withdraw it if there was no sign of awareness. Still another might choose to stop after three months or one month.

What might those discretionary personal values include? Such things, among others, as an assessment of how to deal with uncertainty, concern about emotional burden on loved ones, and cost of care. Though beliefs in the sanctity of human life and in the obligation to care for vulnerable individuals are not optional for persons of faith, an assessment of whether or not to use a given technology requires human wisdom and thus entails some discretion.

Gilbert Meilaender

There is much to agree with in Robert D. Orr's measured discussion of the moral issues surrounding the use of feeding tubes, there are a few things that seem to me doubtful or in need of clarification, and then there is one major issue that requires greater precision.

Accepted Claims

It may be useful to note first some claims of Dr. Orr that few would dispute.

- Feeding tubes are a rather low-tech form of care.
- Our ability to do something does not mean that we should do it.
- Any distinction between "ordinary" and "extraordinary" care (if we wish to use that language) cannot simply be a feature of treatments but must be understood as patient-relative. What is ordinary treatment for one patient

may be extraordinary for another, and what is ordinary treatment for a patient at one point in his life may become extraordinary at another point when his illness has progressed to a new stage.

- There is no crucial moral difference between withholding or withdrawing a treatment. (Dr. Orr actually writes that there is "no moral or legal difference" between these. The issue of legality is, I suspect, sometimes more complicated, but I take him to be correct insofar as a strictly moral judgment is involved.)

- There are circumstances, some noted by Dr. Orr, in which the use of feeding tubes seems clearly required and is relatively uncontroversial.

- Patients in a persistent vegetative state are not dying patients. (I don't quite know how to combine this with Dr. Orr's statement a few paragraphs later that the permanent vegetative state "could be construed to be lethal in and of itself." In general, I don't think his article ever really achieves clarity and precision on this question, and it will turn out to be a crucial question below.)

- A commitment to the sanctity of human life does not require that we always do everything possible to keep a person alive.

There are also places where Dr. Orr's discussion seems to me to be doubtful or, at least, underdeveloped. Among these are the following:

- The idea that the terms "proportionate" and "disproportionate" are more precise than the (admittedly unsatisfactory) language of "ordinary" and "extraordinary" is, at best, doubtful. On what scale one "weighs" benefits and burdens is a question almost impossible to answer. Even more doubtful is whether we can "weigh" them for someone else. My own view is that when we make these decisions for ourselves, we are not in fact "weighing" anything. We are deciding what sort of person we will be and what sort of life will be ours. We are making not a *discovery* but a *decision*. And if that is true, then it is obvious that we have not discovered anything that could necessarily be transferred and applied to the life of a different patient. In general, the language of "weighing" sounds good, but it is almost impossible to give it any precise meaning.

- No *moral* question was resolved by the Supreme Court's *Cruzan* decision. It established certain legal boundaries, but it did no more than that.

- I suspect that—despite the growing consensus, which Dr. Orr correctly describes—he is too quick to assume that the "symbolism" issue can be dispensed with, and too quick to assume that feeding tubes are "treatment" rather than standard nursing care. A consensus may be mistaken, after all. It is hard to see why such services as turning a patient regularly and giving alcohol rubs are standard nursing care while feeding is not. To take an example from a different realm of life, soldiers are combatants, but the people who grow the food which soldiers eat are not combatants (even though the soldiers could not continue to fight without nourishment). The reason is simple: they make not what soldiers need to fight but what they need, as we all do, in order merely to live. Likewise, we might want to think twice before endorsing the view that relatively low-tech means of providing nourishment are treatment rather than standard nursing care.

Intention

- Dr. Orr's discussion of the role of "intention" in moral analysis is, putting it charitably, imprecise. Obviously, if a treatment has been shown not to work, in withdrawing it we do not intend or aim at the patient's death. We aim at caring for that person as best we can, which hardly includes providing treatment that is useless. But the crucial questions will turn on instances in which the treatment is not pointless. If we stop treatment in such cases, it is harder to deny that our aim is that the patient should die.

- Dr. Orr's seeming willingness to allow the state of a patient's cognitive capacities to carry weight—or even be determinative—in treatment decisions is troubling. Obviously, certain kinds of higher brain capacities are characteristics that distinguish human beings from other species; however, one need not have or be exercising those capacities in order to be a living human being. Allowing the cognitive ability of a patient to determine whether he or she is treated will inevitably lead to judgments about the comparative worth of human lives.

If Dr. Orr is correct in arguing that the use of feeding tubes in end-stage Alzheimer's patients is of no help to those patients and may sometimes be burdensome to them, we would have no moral reason to provide them with tube feeding. This judgment, however, has nothing at all to do with "proportionality." It has to do, simply, with the two criteria we ought to use in making treatment decisions—usefulness and burdensomeness. If a treatment is useless or excessively burdensome, it may rightly be refused.

This brings us to the most difficult issue, which clearly troubles Dr. Orr himself, and which is surely puzzling for all of us; the patient in a persistent vegetative state. We cannot usefully discuss this difficult case, however, without first getting clear more generally on the morality of withholding or withdrawing treatment. As I noted above, on this issue the language of proportionality is unlikely to be of much use for serious moral reflection.

Morality of Treatment

At least for Christians—though, in truth, also much more generally for our civilization's received medical tradition—we begin with what is forbidden. We should never aim at the death of a sick or dying person. (Hence, euthanasia, however good the motive, is forbidden.) Still, there are times when treatment may rightly be withheld or withdrawn, *even though* the patient may then die more quickly than would otherwise have been the case. How can that be? How can it be that, as a result of our decision, the patient dies more quickly, yet we do not aim at his death? This is quite possible—and permissible—so long as we aim to dispense with the treatment, not the life. No one need live in a way that seeks to ensure the longest possible life. (Were that a moral requirement, think of all the careers that would have to be prohibited.) There may be many circumstances in which we foresee that decisions we make may shorten our life, but we do not suppose that in so deciding we are aiming at death or formulating a plan of action that deliberately embraces death as a good. So in medical treatment decisions the question we need to answer is this: Under what circumstances may we rightly refuse a life-prolonging treatment without supposing that, in making this decision, we are doing the forbidden deed of choosing or aiming at death?

The answer of our medical-moral tradition has been the following: we may refuse treatments that are either *useless* or *excessively burdensome.* In doing so, we choose not death, but one among several possible lives open to us. We do not choose to die, but, rather, how to live, even if while dying, even if a shorter life than some other lives that are still available for our choosing. What we take aim at then, what we refuse, is not life but treatment—treatment that is either useless for a particular patient or excessively burdensome for that patient. Especially for patients who are irretrievably into the dying process, almost all treatments will have become useless. In refusing them, one is not choosing death but choosing life without a now useless form of treatment. But even for patients who are not near death, who might live for a considerably longer time, excessively burdensome treatments may also be refused. Here again, one takes aim at the burdensome treatment, not at life. One person may choose a life that is longer but carries with it considerable burden of treatment. Another may choose a life that is shorter but carries with it less burden of treatment. Each, however, chooses life. Neither aims at death.

Rejecting Treatments

It is essential to emphasize that these criteria refer to treatments, not to lives. We may rightly reject a treatment that is useless. But if I decide not to treat because I think a person's life is useless, then I am taking aim not at the treatment but at the life. Rather than asking, "What if anything can I do that will benefit the life this patient has?" I am asking, "Is it a benefit to have such a life?" If the latter is my question, and if I decide not to treat, it should be clear that it is the life at which I take aim. Likewise, we may reject a treatment on grounds of excessive burden. But if I decide not to treat because it seems a burden just to have the life this person has, then I am taking aim not at the burdensome treatment but at the life. Hence, in deciding whether it is appropriate and permissible to withhold or withdraw treatment—whether, even if life is thereby shortened, we are aiming only at the treatment and not at the life—we have to ask ourselves whether the treatment under consideration is, for this patient, either useless or excessively burdensome.

Against that background, we can consider the use of feeding tubes for patients in a persistent vegetative state. (I set aside here the point I noted above—that we might want to regard feeding simply as standard nursing care rather than as medical treatment. Now we are asking whether, even on the grounds that govern treatment decisions, we have good moral reason not to feed patients in a persistent vegetative state.)

Is the treatment useless? Not, let us be clear, is the life a useless one to have, but is the treatment useless? As Dr. Orr notes—quite rightly, I think—patients "can live in this permanent vegetative state for many years." So feeding may preserve for years the life of this living human being. Are we certain we want to call that useless? We are, of course, tempted to say that, in deciding not to feed, we are simply withdrawing treatment and letting these patients die. Yes, as Dr. Orr also notes, these patients "are not clearly dying." And, despite the sloppy way we sometimes talk about these matters, you cannot "let die" a person who is not dying. It is hard, therefore, to make the case for treatment withdrawal in these cases on the ground of uselessness. We may use those words, but it is more likely that our target is a (supposed) useless life and not a useless treatment. And if that is our aim, we had better rethink it promptly.

Is the treatment excessively burdensome? Alas, if these patients could experience the feeding as a burden, they would not be diagnosed as being in a persistent vegetative state. We may wonder, of course, whether having such a life is itself a burden, but, again, if that is our reasoning, it will be clear that we take aim not at a burdensome treatment but at a (presumed) burdensome life. And, once more, if that is our aim, we had better rethink it promptly.

Choosing Life

Hence, although these are troubling cases, Dr. Orr has not given us good or sufficient arguments to make the case for withdrawing feeding tubes from patients in a persistent vegetative state. I have not suggested that we have an obligation always and at any cost to preserve life. I have simply avoided all comparative judgments of the worth of human lives and have turned aside from any decisions which, when analyzed carefully, look as if they take aim not at a dispensable treatment but at a life. "Choosing life" does not mean doing whatever is needed to stay alive as long as possible. But choosing life clearly means never aiming at another's death—even if only by withholding treatment. I am not persuaded that Dr. Orr has fully grasped or delineated what it means to choose life in the difficult circumstances he discusses.

MR. ORR is the Director of Ethics and a professor of family medicine at the University of Vermont College of Medicine. **MR. MEILAENDER** is a member of the President's Council on Bioethics. From "Ethics & Life's Ending: An Exchange," by Robert D. Orr and Gilbert Meilaender, *First Things*, August/September 2004, pages 31–38.

Suicidal Thoughts among College Students More Common than Expected

Interventions need to be offered at multiple points, not just during crisis, researchers say.

More than half of 26,000 students across 70 colleges and universities who completed a survey on suicidal experiences reported having at least one episode of suicidal thinking at some point in their lives. Furthermore, 15 percent of students surveyed reported having seriously considered attempting suicide and more than 5 percent reported making a suicide attempt at least once in their lifetime.

Presenting Sunday at the 116th Annual Convention of the American Psychological Association, psychologist David J. Drum, PhD, and co-authors at the University of Texas at Austin reported their findings from a Web-based survey conducted by the National Research Consortium of Counseling Centers in Higher Education. The survey was administered in the spring of 2006 and gathered information about a range of suicidal thoughts and behaviors among college students. The survey was reviewed by the participating campus counseling directors as well as two experts in suicidology.

Six percent of undergraduates and 4 percent of graduate students reported seriously considering suicide within the 12 months prior to answering the survey. Therefore, the researchers posit, at an average college with 18,000 undergraduate students, some 1,080 undergraduates will seriously contemplate taking their lives at least once within a single year. Approximately two-thirds of those who contemplate suicide will do so more than once in a 12-month period.

The majority of students described their typical episode of suicidal thinking as intense and brief, with more than half the episodes lasting one day or less. The researchers found that, for a variety of reasons, more than half of students who experienced a recent suicidal crisis did not seek professional help or tell anyone about their suicidal thoughts.

The researchers used separate samples of undergraduate and graduate students. College sizes ranged from 820 to 58,156 students, with 17,752 being the average. For the 15,010 undergraduates, 62 percent were female and 38 percent were percent male. Seventy-nine percent were white and 21 percent were minorities. Ninety-five percent identified themselves as heterosexual and 5 percent identified as bisexual, gay or undecided. The average age was 22. For the 11,441 graduates, 60 percent were female and 40 percent were male. Seventy-two percent were white and 28 percent were minorities. Ninety-four percent identified themselves as heterosexual and 6 percent identified as bisexual, gay or undecided. The average age was 30.

Both undergraduate and graduate students gave these reasons for their suicidal thinking, in the following order: (1) wanting relief from emotional or physical pain; (2) problems with romantic relationships; (3) the desire to end their life; and (4) problems with school or academics. Fourteen percent of undergraduates and 8 percent of graduate students who seriously considered attempting suicide in the previous 12 months made a suicide attempt. Nineteen percent of undergraduate attempters and 28 percent of graduate student attempters required medical attention. Half of attempters reported overdosing on drugs as their method, said the authors.

From the survey, the authors found that suicidal thoughts are a frequently recurring experience akin to substance abuse, depression and eating disorders. They also found that relying solely upon the current treatment model, which identifies and helps students who are in crisis, is insufficient for addressing reducing all forms of suicide behavior on college campuses.

The authors suggest a new model for dealing with the problem of student suicidal tendencies in order to address the entire continuum of suicidal thoughts and behaviors. By focusing on suicidal thoughts and behaviors as the problem, rather than looking only at students in crisis, interventions can be delivered at multiple points, they said. Furthermore, information from the survey can help match students who are at risk or who have already experienced suicidal thoughts and behaviors with the appropriate treatment. This will reduce the numbers of students entering the suicide continuum in the first place as well as reduce the progression from thoughts to attempts, they said.

With growing levels of distress among college students and diminishing resources to handle the consequences, suicide prevention needs to involve a cross section of campus personnel—administrators, student leaders, advisers, faculty, parents, counselors—and not just involve the suicidal student and the few mental health professionals available. "This would reduce the percentage of students who engage in suicidal thinking, who contemplate how to make an attempt and who continue to make attempts" said Drum.

From *APA Office of Public Affairs*, August 17, 2008. Copyright © 2008 by American Psychological Association. Reprinted by permission.

When Students Kill Themselves, Colleges May Get the Blame

ANN H. FRANKE

Experts estimate that more than a thousand students at American colleges and universities will commit suicide this year. After a death, the grieving family will pack up the victim's belongings and, within a matter of months, lose touch with the institution. A few families, however, will return with their lawyers to charge that the institution bears legal responsibility.

While the number of such lawsuits remains very small, they are growing in frequency. Five years ago college lawyers discussed among themselves perhaps one or two pending suicide cases at any given moment. Today the cases total about 10 nationwide, with the prospect that many more suicides could, over time, move into the courts. Although a study of student suicides committed between 1980 and 1990 at 12 large Midwestern universities, published in 1997, found that college students killed themselves at a lower rate than others of their same age in the general population, whenever a death does occur, the potential for institutional liability looms larger today than ever before.

Whose responsibility is it to put the pieces together? When and how should well-meaning people intervene?

These are awful lawsuits. They can exacerbate grief, guilt, and blame on all sides. The cases can drag on for years. The courts have, so far, provided little guidance on the legal tests for institutional responsibility. We have only a fairly small number of reported decisions (many court decisions are unpublished), and the outcomes of each of those cases have turned less on general legal principles than on close analyses of the facts.

The current wave of litigation will likely lead to some clarification. In the meantime, we might usefully look at the types of claims that the families typically assert. Evaluating previous allegations can help us re-examine campus policies and procedures with two goals in mind: preventing deaths and, should a suicide occur, preventing institutional liability.

The most common claims have been:

The institution put the student in harm's way. Take the example of when a college holds a student in custody for some reason. In 1992 a Michigan court held that a state university might bear some responsibility for the 1982 suicide of a student who hanged himself with his socks and belt while detained for about 35 minutes in a campus-security, short-term holding cell. The institution had in effect at the time a policy that no prisoner should be left unattended unless he (in the vocabulary of the era) was first searched and relieved of objects that might be used to harm himself or others. The message for today is that all institutions owe a heightened duty of suicide prevention to those who may be in their custody.

Custodial suicides are, fortunately, rare. More common is the allegation that the institution negligently created unreasonable access to the means of suicide. To understand that allegation, it is helpful to review the most common methods of student suicide. According to the study of Midwestern universities, those methods are hanging or asphyxiation, jumping, gas inhalation, chemical poisoning (including drugs and cyanide), firearms, and, to a lesser degree, vehicles, knives, and drowning. If cyanide from the chemistry lab or a gun from an unlocked cabinet in the public-safety office were used in the suicide death of a student, the family could seek to blame the institution.

For example, in the 1990s the mother of a college football player who committed suicide argued that the athletics department's carelessness in casually dispensing large quantities of prescription medications, including Darvocet and Tylenol #3, contributed to her son's death. The young man had died from a self-inflicted gunshot wound, yet the family argued that the drugs were a phase in his general deterioration, and the Arkansas Supreme Court found that argument plausible enough to send the case back to the trial court for further proceedings.

Take note. From a public-health perspective, as well as a legal one, it is prudent to keep under lock and key dangerous substances and objects that might appeal to students as a means of suicide. Colleges should lock their roofs, towers, and other high perches from which depressed students can jump.

Sometimes differentiating suicide from an accidental death can be tricky. A student's fatal alcohol or drug overdose, for

Some Suicide Warning Signs among Young Adults

Behaviors Requiring Immediate Response

- Indicating intent to harm themselves (talking, threatening)
- Seeking availability of or obtaining ropes, weapons, pills, or other ways to kill themselves
- Talking or writing about death, dying, or suicide

Associated Behaviors Requiring Evaluation

- Feeling hopeless
- Expressing rage or anger; seeking revenge
- Acting recklessly or impulsively or engaging in risky activities, seemingly without thinking
- Feeling trapped, like there's no way out, or nothing else will help
- Increasing alcohol or drug use or abuse
- Withdrawing from friends, school activities, community, and family
- Expressing anxiety, agitation, an inability to sleep, or sleeping all the time
- Exhibiting dramatic mood changes
- Expressing loss of interest or reason for living; no sense of purpose or meaning in life
- Acting "immaturely" and/or displaying disregard for others' safety, feelings, or property

Source: M. Silverman, "College Student Suicide Prevention," *College Health Spectrum* (March 2004).

themes of despair in a student's poetry. Whose responsibility is it to put these pieces together? When and how should well-meaning people intervene?

Many institutions conduct educational programs to raise campus awareness about suicide and increase the possibility that fellow students, residence-hall workers, and faculty members will help the student into treatment. Good online screening programs—available through organizations like the Jed Foundation and Screening for Mental Health—reach students directly, providing a rough evaluation of their own suicide risk and encouraging them to seek treatment. Although such programs are not legal necessities, they certainly can advance student well-being.

Some colleges have also created committees that meet weekly to evaluate the behavior of students who pose potential risks to themselves or others. A leading program at the University of Illinois at Urbana-Champaign enlists many people across the campus, including public-safety officers, residence-hall administrators, and faculty members, to report any signs that a student might be considering self-harm to a suicide-prevention task force. The task force has the authority to require students to attend four mandatory assessment sessions at the counseling center, sessions that have proved very effective in reducing students' suicidal thoughts and intentions.

Administrators sometimes worry that any program to increase student safety may also increase the institution's liability, should a problem fall through the cracks. College lawyers can help structure programs to minimize that possibility. For example, should an institution conduct a screening program and retain in its records, without following up, information that a specific student is at high risk of suicide, then the prospect of its liability for that student's suicide is greatly increased. To protect against that, a screening program could clearly state that it is voluntary and anonymous, and that the institution will not keep a record of the results or follow up with the student.

The institution failed to respond appropriately to warning signs. Family members could argue that the institution knew, or at least should have known, that the student was at high risk of suicide. With the clarity of hindsight, they will point to steps that the institution should have taken, including, most pointedly, notifying them about the problem.

Issues of how to notify parents about a student's potential for self-harm have confounded many administrators. Some campus mental-health providers argue strenuously that they enjoy a legally privileged and confidential relationship with their patients. (The specifics vary by state and by type of profession.) A dean of students may feel that the Family Educational Rights and Privacy Act, which restricts the information that colleges can release about students, inhibits her from picking up the phone. The student's consent can, of course, avert the impasse. Experienced student-affairs staff members and counselors can usually build sufficient trust with a disturbed student to persuade him to contact his family. But sometimes the student adamantly refuses.

Administrators should then begin a collaborative analysis of the situation. The element of collaboration spreads the burden of

example, might have arisen from ignorance or miscalculation, or it might have been an intentional act of self-harm. After such deaths, the families may point to lax enforcement of institutional policies against drug and alcohol abuse. Do the trash cans in the first-year dorms overflow with beer bottles every Monday morning? If so, whether they view the death as accidental or intentional, the grieving parents may allege that the institution recklessly contributed to the student's alcohol poisoning. An institution that fails to enforce its existing policies faces an uphill battle in court.

The institution failed to recognize suicide warning signs. Depression can impair an individual's ability to seek help, and fewer than 20 percent of students who seriously consider suicide have received either therapy or antidepressant medication. Campus mental-health professionals are often not on the front lines of these problems, as suicidal students frequently don't come to see them, leaving to others the task of catching the cues and enlisting assistance for such students. A residence-hall adviser may notice signs of a student's emotional deterioration. An English professor may become concerned by the dark the decision whether to notify the family beyond the shoulders of just one individual. As a substantive matter, both the therapist–patient privilege and FERPA contain exceptions for emergencies, and a risk of self-harm counts as an emergency. In fact, some prudent student-health and counseling centers disclose on their Web sites, in their brochures, and on their patient paperwork that in emergency situations they may contact others.

From a legal standpoint, the safest course is to notify the family of a genuinely suicidal student unless previously known indicators, like a history of child abuse, suggest that parental notification would be harmful. Sometimes it just comes down to picking your lawsuit. A student's suit for invasion of privacy is, by most any reckoning, preferable to a suit over a suicide. Be ready, however, for the unexpected. One college, after making the decision to contact the family of an international student, ran into the unanticipated difficulty that the overseas parents did not speak English.

Hospitalization can be another appropriate response to a suicidal student. One large private university had 18 student psychiatric hospitalizations during a five-week period at the beginning of a recent fall semester. A national provider of student health insurance reported a rate of psychiatric hospitalizations in 2002 of 3.4 per 1,000 students.

Such numbers reflect the important role that community resources play in responding to student mental-health needs. The counseling center at Northwestern University, for example, devotes considerable attention to coordinating care with the hospitals and community mental-health practitioners who may be treating a student. Hospitalization may be easier if a suitable facility is nearby and the student has health insurance, or if the state has a flexible involuntary-commitment law.

Whether or not a college plays an active part in hospitalizing the student, it may be that a suicidal student's mental health is too fragile for him or her to function on the campus. Involuntary medical withdrawal is a good option in such situations, and it is prudent to have rules in place establishing the standards and procedures for that withdrawal, as well as for the return of such students to the campus. Washington and Lee University, Cornell University, and the University of North Carolina at Greensboro are among the institutions with involuntary-medical-withdrawal protocols available on their Web sites.

Perhaps the most important message about a college's liability for student suicide is to know your personal and institutional limits as a helper. An institution can work to resolve some problems internally, but others are beyond its scope and call for the intervention of families and external resources. A counseling center struggling even to meet its nonemergency appointment load should not lead students and parents to think that it provides full emergency care. A faculty member can do more harm than good by providing, over an extended period, a shoulder for a depressed student to cry on rather than aiding the student in getting treatment. If the student is relying on the professor for general comfort, then that student may be disinclined to get the medical help that he or she really needs.

The institution mishandled the emergency response to a suicide attempt. If a young man reports that his girlfriend is locked in her dorm room sending instant messages saying farewell and announcing plans to end it all, will the institution respond swiftly and effectively? The best approach is to contact local emergency services or to respond immediately with trained campus public-safety officers or medical personnel. College personnel should not, in any event, leave the student alone.

Institutions should plan for such emergencies in advance and develop operating procedures, conducting drills of imaginary student-suicide scenarios and working through the communications and response issues that might involve student-affairs and counseling staff members, residence-hall personnel, and public-safety officers. During what may be the last moments of a student's life, the institution's emergency response needs to be credible and to follow established protocols.

Fewer than 20 percent of students who seriously consider suicide have received either therapy or antidepressant medication.

After a suicide, sensitive outreach to the family is crucial. Senior campus officials should attend the funeral and express condolences in writing. The college should involve the family in planning college-sponsored memorial services and other activities in the name of the student, as well as maintain contact over an extended period. Most families welcome the occasional phone call just to say "We're thinking of you." The student's birthday and the anniversary of the death will be especially hard for them, so a note or call on those occasions would be particularly appropriate. Caring outreach will not increase the risk of institutional liability, and demonstrations of genuine concern can help keep the family's grief from turning to rage at the institution.

ANN H. FRANKE is vice president for education and risk management at United Educators Insurance and a former counsel to the American Association of University Professors.

UNIT 5
Funerals

Unit Selections

Key Points to Consider

- Describe how the funeralization process can assist in coping with grief and facilitate the bereavement process. Distinguish between grief, bereavement, and funeralization.

- Discuss the psychological, sociological, and theological/philosophical aspects of the funeralization process. How does each of these aspects facilitate the resolution of grief?

- Describe and compare each of the following processes: burial, cremation, environmentally friendly alternatives, cryonics, and body donation for medical research. What would be your choice for final disposition of your body? Why would you choose this method, and what effects might this choice have upon your survivors (if any) and the stewardship for the earth's resources? Would you have the same or different preferences for a close loved one such as a spouse, child, or parent? Why or why not?

Student Web Site
www.mhcls.com

Internet References

Cryonics, Cryogenics, and the Alcor Foundation
http://www.alcor.org
Funeral Consumers Alliance
http://www.funerals.org/
Funerals and Ripoffs
http://www.funerals-ripoffs.org/-5dProf1.html/
The Internet Cremation Society
http://www.cremation.org

© Kent Knudson/PhotoLink/Getty Images

Decisions relating to the disposition of the body after death often involve feelings of ambivalence—on one hand, attachments to the deceased might cause one to be reluctant to dispose of the body, while on the other hand, practical considerations make the disposal of the body necessary. Funerals or memorial services provide methods for disposing of a dead body, remembering the deceased, and helping survivors accept the reality of death. They are also public rites of passage that assist the bereaved in returning to routine patterns of social interaction. In contemporary America, 79 percent of deaths involve earth burial and 21 percent involve cremation. These public behaviors, along with the private process of grieving, comprise the two components of the bereavement process.

This unit on the contemporary American funeral begins with a general article on the nature and functions of public bereavement behavior by Michael Leming and George Dickinson. Leming and Dickinson provide an overview of the present practice of funeralization in American society, including traditional and alternative funeral arrangements. They also discuss the functions of funerals relative to the sociological, psychological, and theological needs of adults and children.

The remaining articles in this section reflect upon the many alternative ways in which funerals, rituals, and final dispositions for the deceased may be constructed.

The Tuneful Funeral

TONY GONZALEZ

He practices scales and etudes on organ and piano every day, but when it comes to playing what families choose for funeral music, it's often studied improvisation—in finding sheet music, then playing—that saves organist Kraig Windschitl.

It could be a hymn or a hum over the phone, some secular tune, a heritage folk song or music written by the deceased, and Windschitl, the 30-year-old organist at Mount Olivet Lutheran Church in south Minneapolis, makes it his duty and his joy to ready the request before the service.

"In this business, you have to be a jack-of-all-trades and be able to deliver what the grieving family wants, whether that be Marlene Dietrich, the Beatles, Judy Garland, J.S. Bach, Scott Joplin or even Stevie Wonder," Windschitl said. "Bottom line: We just want to make sure the family is consoled through music. It's our job to use music as a sense of soothing the pain and the grief. Whether I like (the selection) or not, that's immaterial."

Like all aspects of funeral services, song selection continues to move away from tradition and toward personalization. Funerals are becoming more individual, more celebratory and more often planned well in advance, say funeral directors, many of whom suggest the same theory for the change: baby boomers.

"When I started as a funeral director 32 years ago, everybody who came in the door pretty much expected things to be done the same way," said Dan Delmore of Gearty Delmore Funeral Chapels. "Now, across the gamut it's how the baby boomers do it and they want to put their own stamp on how they do it."

For Windschitl, who was "raised in the balcony at the cathedral" alongside his organist mother, diverse music selections mean his playing skills and song library never stagnate. He has trained on pipe organ since age 14 and has degrees in church music and organ performance.

A single funeral service can take Windschitl from playing Bach to simple jazz, the blues or "anything secular or sacred." In fact, secular selections continue to rise in popularity. At some funeral homes, half of services no longer include hymns.

John Pose, funeral director with Morris Nilsen Funeral Chapel, listed "Somewhere Over the Rainbow," Frank Sinatra tunes and even polkas as common selections. He would call about 20 percent of selections at the chapel non-traditional.

"It used to be they would let the clergy dictate the course of the service, but now people like to have a say," Pose said.

At traditional funeral homes, families still follow liturgical styles. Nick Radulovich, owner of Kozlak Radulovich Funeral Homes, said personalization continues to grow, but in terms of secular music, it appears in only about 5 percent of services.

Daniel McGraw, president of Gill Brothers Funeral Chapels, said music remains traditional, except that Protestant and Catholic hymns are crossing over more often.

Families, too, don't always agree on music.

"As a funeral director you survey the situation and you realize not everybody in the family is on the same page," Delmore said. "You have to become a compromiser, and tell them, 'This part is fine here, but this part won't go over big at the Basilica.' Some days, a funeral director's suggestions are much needed and other times they walk in the door and they're pretty self-sufficient."

Windschitl enjoys the hunt for obscure sheet music but sometimes gets tall orders. When asked to play Swedish, Russian, Irish or Somalian folk songs, he must consult colleagues.

"My library's only so big," said Windschitl, who never throws out a piece of music, even if it's a melody line jotted on a paper towel. "I thrive on the challenge, and yes, it's my job."

He'll play with accompaniment (sometimes performed by friends and relatives of the deceased) and has performed original music submissions. For his efforts, Windschitl often hears little feedback. That's OK, he said, because his service is to keep music constantly playing, right through to the time when attendees leave.

"Silence, especially at that point in someone's life, isn't always well-taken," he said.

Although organizing and playing services is often somber, Windschitl said a single smile can be rewarding.

Once, Windschitl agreed to a grieving woman's request to play "The Entertainer" by Scott Joplin.

"The biggest joy for me," Windschitl said, "was to see her break into this huge smile at the opening notes."

How Different Religions Pay Their Final Respects

From mummies to cremation to drive-up wakes, funeral rituals reflect religious traditions going back thousands of years as well as up-to-the-minute fads.

WILLIAM J. WHALEN

Most people in the United States identify themselves as Protestants; thus, most funerals follow a similar form. Family and friends gather at the funeral home to console one another and pay their last respects. The next day a minister conducts the funeral service at the church or mortuary; typically the service includes hymns, prayers, a eulogy, and readings from the Bible. In 85 percent of the cases today, the body is buried after a short grave-side ceremony. Otherwise the body is cremated or donated to a medical school.

But what could be called the standard U.S. funeral turns out to be the funeral of choice for only a minority of the rest of the human race. Other people, even other Christians, bury their dead with more elaborate and, to outsiders, even exotic rites.

How your survivors will dispose of your body will in all likelihood be determined by the religious faith you practiced during your life because funeral customs reflect the theological beliefs of a particular faith community.

For example, the Parsi people of India neither bury nor cremate their dead. Parsis, most of whom live in or near Bombay, follow the ancient religion of Zoroastrianism. Outside Bombay, Parsis erected seven Towers of Silence in which they perform their burial rites. When someone dies, six bearers dressed in white bring the corpse to one of the towers. The Towers of Silence have no roofs; within an hour, waiting vultures pick the body clean. A few days later the bearers return and cast the remaining bones into a pit. Parsis believe that their method of disposal avoids contaminating the soil, the water, and the air.

Out of the Ashes

The Parsis' millions of Hindu neighbors choose cremation as their usual burial practice. Hindus believe that as long as the physical body exists, the essence of the person will remain nearby; cremation allows the essence, or soul, of the person to continue its journey into another incarnation.

Hindus wash the body of the deceased and clothe it in a shroud decorated with flowers. They carry the body to a funeral pyre, where the nearest male relative lights the fire and walks around the burning body three times while reciting verses from Hindu sacred writings. Three days later someone collects and temporarily buries the ashes.

On the tenth day after the cremation, relatives deposit the ashes in the Ganges or some other sacred river. The funeral ceremony, called the *Shraddha,* is then held within 31 days of the cremation. Usually the deceased's son recites the prayers and the invocation of ancestors; that is one reason why every Hindu wants at least one son.

Prior to British rule in India, the practice of suttee was also common. Suttee is the act of a Hindu widow willingly being cremated on her husband's funeral pyre. Suttee was outlawed by the British in 1829, but occasionally widows still throw themselves into the flames.

Like the Hindus, the world's Buddhists, who live primarily in China, Japan, Sri Lanka, Myanmar, Vietnam, and Cambodia, usually choose cremation for disposing of a corpse. They believe cremation was favored by Buddha. A religious teacher may pray or recite mantras at the bedside of the dying person. These actions are believed to exert a wholesome effect on the next rebirth. Buddhists generally believe that the essence of a person remains in an intermediate state for no more than 49 days between death and rebirth.

While Hindus and Buddhists prescribe cremation, the world's 900 million Muslims forbid cremation. According to the Qu'ran, Muhammad taught that only Allah will use fire to punish the wicked.

If a Muslim is near death, someone is called in to read verses from the Qu'ran. After death, the body is ceremonially washed, clothed in three pieces of white cloth, and placed in a simple wooden coffin. Unless required by law, Muslims will not allow embalming. The body must be buried as soon as possible after death—usually within 24 hours. After a funeral service at a mosque or at the grave side, the body is removed from the coffin and buried with the head of the deceased turned toward Mecca. In some Muslim countries the women engage in loud wailing and lamentations during the burial.

Some Islamic grave sites are quite elaborate. The Mogul emperor Shah Jahan built the world-famous Taj Mahal as a mausoleum for his wife and himself. The Taj Mahal, which is one of the finest examples of Islamic architecture, was finished in 1654. It took 20,000 workers about 22 years to complete the project.

The Baha'i faith, which originated in Persia in the nineteenth century as an outgrowth of the Shi'ite branch of Islam, also forbids cremation and embalming and requires that the body not be transported more than an hour's journey from the place of death. Because Bahaism has no ordained clergy, the funeral may be conducted by any member of the family or the local assembly. All present at the funeral must stand during the recitation of the Prayer for the Dead composed by Baha'u'llah. Several million Baha'is live in Iran, India, the Middle East, and Africa; and an estimated 100,000 Baha'is live in the United States.

In Judaism, the faith of some 18 million people, the Old Testament only hints at belief in an afterlife; but later Jewish thought embraced beliefs in heaven, hell, resurrection, and final judgment. In general, Orthodox Jews accept the concept of a resurrection of the soul and the body while Conservative and Reform Jews prefer to speak only of the immortality of the soul.

Orthodox Judaism prescribes some of the most detailed funeral rites of any religion. As death approaches, family and friends must attend the dying person at all times. When death finally arrives, a son or the nearest relative closes the eyes and mouth of the deceased and binds the lower jaw before rigor mortis sets in. Relatives place the body on the floor and cover it with a sheet; they place a lighted candle near the head.

Judaism in its traditional form forbids embalming except where required by law. After a ritual washing, the body is covered with a white shroud and placed in a wooden coffin. At the funeral, mourners symbolize their grief by tearing a portion of an outer garment or wearing a torn black ribbon. The Orthodox discourage flowers and ostentation at the funeral.

The Jewish funeral service includes a reading of prayers and psalms, a eulogy, and the recitation of the Kaddish prayer for the dead in an Aramaic dialect. Like other Semitic people, Jews forbid cremation. Orthodox Jews observe a primary mourning period of seven days; Reform Jews reduce this period to three days. During the secondary yearlong mourning period, the Kaddish prayer is recited at every service in the synagogue.

Dearly Beloved

Christianity, the world's largest religion, carries over Judaism's respect for the body and firmly acknowledges resurrection, judgment, and eternal reward or punishment.

These Christian beliefs permeate the liturgy of a Catholic funeral. Older Catholics remember the typical funeral of the 1940s and '50s: the recitation of the rosary at the wake, the black vestments, the Latin prayers. They probably recall the *"Dies Irae,"* a thirteenth-century dirge and standard musical piece at Catholic funerals prior to the liturgical changes of the Second Vatican Council in the 1960s.

Nowadays, those attending a Catholic wake may still say the rosary, but often there is a scripture service instead. The priest's vestments are likely to be white or violet rather than black. Prayers tend to emphasize the hope of resurrection rather than the terrors of the final judgment.

As death approaches, the dying person or the family may request the sacrament of the Anointing of the Sick. Once called Last Rites or Extreme Unction, this sacrament is no longer restricted to those in imminent danger of death; it is regularly administered to the sick and the elderly as an instrument of healing as well as a preparation for death.

Sacred Remains

The Catholic Church raises no objections to embalming, flowers, or an open casket at a wake. At one time Catholics who wished to have a church funeral could not request cremation. In 1886 the Holy Office in Rome declared that "to introduce the practice (of cremation) into Christian society was un-Christian and Masonic in motivation." Today Catholics may choose the option of cremation over burial "unless," according to canon law, "it has been chosen for reasons that are contrary to Christian teaching."

The church used to deny an ecclesiastical burial to suicides, those killed in duels, Freemasons, and members of the ladies' auxiliaries of Masonic lodges. Today the church refuses burial only to "notorious apostates, heretics, and schismatics" and to "sinners whose funerals in church would scandalize the faithful." Catholics who join Masonic lodges no longer incur excommunication, although they still may not receive Communion.

The church has also softened its position on denying funeral rites to suicides. Modern pastoral practice is based on the understanding that anyone finding life so unbearable as to end it voluntarily probably was acting with a greatly diminished free will.

For Roman Catholics, the Mass is the principal celebration of the Christian funeral; and mourners are invited to receive the Eucharist. Most Protestant denominations, except for some Lutherans and Episcopalians, do not incorporate a communion service into their funeral liturgies. The Catholic ritual employs candles, holy water, and incense but does not allow non-Christian symbols, such as national flags or lodge emblems, to rest on or near the coffin during the funeral. In many parishes the pastor encourages the family members to participate where appropriate as eucharistic ministers, lectors, and singers. In the absence of a priest, a deacon can conduct the funeral service but cannot preside at a Mass of Christian burial.

The revised funeral liturgy of the Catholic Church is meant to stress God's faithfulness to people rather than God's wrath toward sinners. The Catholic Church declares that certain men and women who have lived lives of such heroic virtue that they are indeed in heaven are to be known as saints. The church also teaches that hell is a reality but has never declared that anyone, even Judas, has actually been condemned to eternal punishment.

Unlike Protestant churches, Catholicism also teaches the existence of a temporary state of purification, known as purgatory, for those destined for heaven but not yet totally free from the effects of sin and selfishness. At one time some theologians suggested that unbaptized babies spent eternity in a place of natural happiness known as limbo, but this was never church doctrine and is taught by few theologians today.

At the committal service at the grave site, the priest blesses the grave and leads the mourners in the Our Father and other prayers for the repose of the soul of the departed and the comfort of the survivors. Catholics are usually buried in Catholic cemeteries or in separate sections of other cemeteries.

Dressed for the Occasion

The funeral rite in the Church of Jesus Christ of Latter-day Saints, which is the fastest growing church in the United States, resembles the standard Protestant funeral in some ways; but one significant difference is in the attire of the deceased. Devout Mormons receive the garments of the holy priesthood during their endowment ceremonies when they are teens. These sacred undergarments are to be worn day and night throughout a Mormon's life. When a Mormon dies, his or her body is then attired in these garments in the casket. At one time Mormon sacred garments resembled long johns, but they now have short sleeves and are cut off at the knees. The garments are embroidered with symbols on the right and left breasts, the navel, and the right knee, which remind the wearer of the oaths taken in the secret temple rites.

Mormons who reached their endowments are also clothed in their temple garb at death. For the men, this includes white pants, white shirt, tie, belt, socks, slippers, and an apron. Just before the casket is closed for the last time, a fellow Mormon puts a white temple cap on the corpse. If the deceased is a woman, a high priest puts a temple veil over her face; Mormons believe the veil will remain there until her husband calls her from the grave to resurrection. Mormons forbid cremation.

Freemasons conduct their own funeral rites for a deceased brother, and they insist that their ceremony be the last one before burial or cremation. Thus, a separate religious ceremony often precedes the Masonic rites. Lodge members will bury a fellow Mason only if he is a member in good standing and he or his family has requested the service.

All the pallbearers at the Masonic services must be Masons, and each wears a white apron, white gloves, a black band around his left arm, and a sprig of evergreen or acacia in his left lapel. The corpse is clothed in a white apron and other lodge regalia.

Masonry accepts the idea of the immortality of the soul but makes no reference to the Christian understanding of the resurrection of the soul and the body. The Masonic service speaks of the soul's translation from this life to that "perfect, glorious, and celestial lodge above" presided over by the Grand Architect of the Universe.

In Memoriam

Other small religious groups have much less elaborate and formalized funeral services. Christian Scientists, for example, have no set funeral rite because their founder, Mary Baker Eddy, denied the reality of death. The family of a deceased Christian Scientist often invites a Christian Science reader to present a brief service at the funeral home.

Unitarian-Universalists enroll many members who would identify themselves as agnostics or atheists. Therefore, in a typical Unitarian Universalist funeral service, the minister and loved ones say little about any afterlife but extol the virtues and good works of the deceased.

Salvation Army officers are buried in their military uniforms, and a Salvationist blows taps at the grave side. In contrast, the Church of Christ, which allows no instrumental music during Sunday worship, allows no organs, pianos, or other musical instruments at its funerals.

The great variety of funeral customs through the ages and around the world would be hard to catalog. The Egyptians mummified the bodies of royalty and erected pyramids as colossal monuments. Viking kings were set adrift on blazing boats. The Soviets mummified the body of Lenin, and his tomb and corpse have become major icons in the U.S.S.R.

In a funeral home in California, a drive-up window is provided for mourners so that they can view the remains and sign the book without leaving their cars. In Japan, where land is scarce, one enterprising cemetery owner offers a time-share plan whereby corpses are displaced after brief burial to make room for the next occupant. Complying with the wishes of the deceased, one U.S. undertaker once dressed a corpse in pajamas and positioned it under the blankets in a bedroom for viewing.

The reverence and rituals surrounding the disposal of the body reflect religious traditions going back thousands of years as well as up-to-the-minute fads. All of the elements of the burial—the preparation of the body, the garments or shroud, the prayers, the method of disposal, the place and time of burial—become sacred acts by which a particular community of believers bids at least a temporary farewell to one of its own.

From *U.S. Catholic*, September 1990, pp. 29–35. Copyright © 1990 by Claretian Publications. Reprinted by permission.

The Arlington Ladies

American volunteerism at its most moving.

SHAWN MACOMBER

One afternoon towards the end of March, 200 mourners slowly trekked under a bright blue sky to the plot where 20-year-old Army Pfc. Michael Anthony Arciola was about to become the 123rd soldier killed during Operation Iraqi Freedom laid to rest at Arlington National Cemetery. Arciola, a recipient of both the Purple Heart and the Bronze Star, was shot and killed on patrol in Al Ramadi on February 15. The larger than usual crowd was no surprise. The young man had been so well loved in his hometown of Elmsford, New York, that more than a thousand people came to his memorial service there. Dying young carries with it an implicit sense of tragedy that draws people—emotionally and physically—to it.

Nevertheless, Pfc. Arciola was not the only one laid to rest that Friday at Arlington. Sixteen other servicemen, most of them veterans many years older than Arciola, were likewise buried. An average week at Arlington will see between 80 and 100 burials on its 612 acres, and the final week of March was within that margin. Arciola's funeral was the largest the cemetery had held in a few weeks. Others attracted dozens or fewer mourners. A smattering had no friends or loved ones in attendance at all.

As in most matters, however, the military prefers to focus on cohesion rather than dissension; on the ties that bind rather than the walls that separate. This is as true of funerals as it is of boot camp. Most people are aware of one aspect of this, the Honor Guard. But there is another unifying element, much less publicized than the 21-gun salute, but just as important in both a practical and symbolic sense. It comes in the form of a conservatively dressed woman who—whether amongst a throng of mourners, seated alongside the family, or standing as the sole attendee—is there to help shepherd the fallen soldier during his final mile.

These volunteer women are known as "The Arlington Ladies." They attend every funeral at Arlington to ensure, first and foremost, that no soldier is ever buried with no one in attendance, and second, to serve the needs of family members, whether they are present at the funeral or not.

Normally it isn't difficult to get someone to go on record about a noble pursuit. The first reaction to the prospect of a laudatory article is rarely reticence. But this group of no-nonsense women did not jump at the chance to talk about themselves.

In fact, they were surprisingly difficult to track down at all. This is probably at least partially because the vast majority of Arlington Ladies are either retired servicewomen themselves or from military families, a culture not given to bragging.

"They don't seek publicity," Army Major Kevin Stroop, a regimental chaplain who performs funerals at Arlington, said. "What they do here is absolutely vital to our mission, but those moments they share with the families and our servicemen and women are intensely personal. The Arlington Ladies, as a group, really are committed to keeping those moments and their work sacred."

When I finally get Linda Willey, wife of a retired Air Force Colonel and a 13-year veteran of the Arlington Ladies, on the phone, she is effusive and cordial, but makes it plain she is not looking for any outside affirmation of what she does.

"We're here to pay our respects and support the families of those lost," Willey said. "We don't want a pat on the back or any gold stars. This is about something bigger than flaunting what we do for brownie points."

Interviews with other Arlington Ladies quickly make it clear that Willey's claims are not frivolous false modesty, but truth. There is, it seems, still such a thing as selfless service.

The story of the Arlington Ladies stretches back to a day in 1948 when Air Force Chief of Staff General Hoyt Vandenberg happened upon the funeral of an airman at Arlington. What he saw disturbed him: There wasn't a soul at the service, save the chaplain and the Honor Guard members conducting it. Vandenberg, the nephew of the legendary Republican Senator Arthur Vandenberg, was about as dedicated an airman as they come. After winning the Distinguished Service Medal and Silver Star for his service during and tactical planning of the Normandy invasion, Vandenberg began a dizzying series of promotions that landed him in the Air Force's top spot at the sprightly age of 49. He took pride in defending his men from the enemy and Washington bureaucrats alike. It did not sit well with him to watch a fellow airman make this final journey alone.

When he brought this black cloud of concern home, his wife Gladys worked to soothe her husband's worries by personally

The Old Guard

AMY K. MITCHELL

Beginning in the early morning of Memorial Day, some 1,000 soldiers from "The Old Guard" will spend nearly five hours placing an American flag in front of each of the more than 260,000 tombstones at Arlington National Cemetery. Each flag will be inserted exactly one boot length from the center of each tombstone, creating lines as perfectly straight as those of the white tombstones.

Silent precision is the hallmark of the Old Guard—the Army's 3rd US Infantry. In addition to serving as the official Army Honor Guard, it is responsible for protecting Washington, D.C., a duty of greater consequence since September 11. Night and day, it stands watch over those we have lost and the nation's capital.

This May more than 70 veterans of World War II will be buried and honored by the Old Guard at Arlington National Cemetery. "The pride of that unit is enduring," reflects Major Kevin Stroop, one of the two Old Guard chaplains based at Fort Myer, headquartered next door to the cemetery. Recently Stroop met a WWII first sergeant at the burial of a colonel who fought in the China-India-Burma theater. The first sergeant had met the colonel at a reunion of vets last year. "After the service," says Stroop, "he commented that this year it would just be himself. Many of the vets have little family left."

By contrast, the services for those killed in Iraq are not sparsely attended. "The soldiers are much younger, there is more grief," says Stroop. Staff Sergeant Otto Maiorana of Echo Company adds, "One of the most gripping moments is when the families let their emotions out."

Many Americans became familiar with the Old Guard last June during President Ronald Reagan's state funeral. For nearly 13 years, two times a week, the Old Guard prepared for that moment, perfecting every detail, from escorting the presidential caisson to leading the riderless horse with the reversed boot. It practiced one last time through the dead of night before the farewell parade down Pennsylvania Avenue to the U.S. Capitol.

The Old Guard accompanied the body of President Reagan to California for the sunset burial with full military honors in Simi Valley.

At Reagan's funeral, the Old Guard appeared on center stage, but every day, out of public eye, these "quiet professionals," as Sergeant Jason Cauley describes them, silently pay respect to our nation's fallen heroes. They stand guard over the Tomb of the Unknowns 365 days, serve at 35 U.S. Army burials a week, and perform at more than 1,600 military ceremonies each year.

The Old Guard's protocol at funerals, says Stroop, is "always the same. Whether it is a veteran of World War II or an active duty death, this is one of the enduring gifts that is given to the family from the Army—the same amount of honor and tradition." Maiorana says each "ceremony is as perfect as it can be for the family's benefit and the fallen soldier. To give him the proper representation he deserves."

Practice for each and every burial is ongoing, which makes the Old Guard's movement so imperceptible and unobtrusive. They act "as one unit," says Cauley, bringing an atmosphere of comforting order to the shroud of Arlington National Cemetery for families whose special requests are always accommodated.

Out of respect for these families, says Maiorana, the Old Guard is "as silent as possible." Only a few sounds break their silence: the clip of a soldier's shoes, the clop of the horses' hooves, the creak of the caisson wheels. In the distance, the rifle team stands as rigid as sentinels, ready to fire in homage to the fallen soldier.

AMY K. MITCHELL is managing editor of *The American Spectator*.

---

attending Air Force personnel burials and founding the Arlington Committee. Thus, an Arlington institution—eventually to become known as the Arlington Ladies—was born. The complimentary Army Arlington Ladies was founded in 1972, with the Navy following suit in 1985. The Marine Corps, true to its separate nature, does not have a contingent of Arlington Ladies, but a representative of the Commandant is at every funeral. There are now more than 160 active Arlington Ladies.

The Arlington Ladies' mission has evolved since those early days. If there are family members present, an Arlington Lady will deliver a personal note of condolence from the chief of staff's office. They also write their own note of condolence, based upon an information sheet provided by the government with dates of service, awards given, and name of next of kin, as well as any other information the chaplain can provide.

"You get pretty good at reading between lines," Willey said. "When you see what period they served in, you have a good idea of what that person may have gone through."

If family is unable to attend a funeral, an Arlington Lady will send a letter describing the service and the day, right down to the sounds and smells in the air.

"What we do is always important and meaningful, but when you are alone at a funeral there is an added relevance," Willey said. "You feel an even greater need to be there, like you're helping to close the circle. For those grieving far away, a personal letter letting them know that someone was there can help soothe their sorrow. It shows them that their loved one's service was not forgotten and also that their loss has not been ignored."

The connection between the bereaved and an Arlington Lady does not end when the funeral is over, either.

"One of the first things I tell all my families is, "'I am your Arlington lady, not just now but forever, and you can always contact me," said Paula McKinley, the chair of the Navy Arlington Ladies. "It's a bond that is built to last."

This may sound like hyperbole, but consider the following: McKinley has placed roses on a grave for years at the request of a Navy widow and last summer on what would have been the couple's 50th anniversary she sent along 50 roses because it's what she imagined the husband would have done.

"We write everyone a follow-up letter six to eight weeks later, as well" McKinley said. "In most families, there's a great support group that hovers for a month or so. Then, it's not that their family abandons them, it's just that they go back to their own lives. But the grieving is not over. We just want to remind them they are still in our hearts and we are still available if they need us."

"Usually by the end of a service, families have a glazed look," Willey added. "They're gone emotionally. But hopefully they'll have a memory of somebody being there, being kind and touching to them in some way. The feedback we get suggests that's true. Oftentimes I'll get a letter a few months after a funeral from someone saying, 'I didn't comprehend what you were doing at the time, but thank you for being there.'"

For those who have not served in an official capacity, it might be difficult to understand what draws this group of women to events most of us spend our lives trying to avoid.

"It's not emotionally grueling in the least," McKinley said. "It can be emotional, but that's a different thing. We are not mourners. We are there to pay tribute."

"There is some distance you can get from the situation just by recognizing you are part of the ceremony," Willey agreed, but added that when death comes suddenly or orphaned children are involved it can be tougher. "There have been times, I'll admit, when I've had to fight back a big lump and stare at the sky or do whatever I have to do to keep myself from falling apart. And you do it, because part of my job is to protect the integrity of the ceremony, to make sure everything goes smoothly."

It's clear in speaking with these women that performing the duties of an Arlington Lady calls for something above and beyond being able to dress well. So, just as not everyone is made for the Honor Guard, the Arlington Ladies are a select group. There is no sign-up form on the Internet or any open call: One must be asked to join their ranks by another Arlington Lady.

Once invited, the motivations for becoming an Arlington Lady vary, but only slightly. Mostly it comes down to the same reasoning that draws a lot of people to regular military service: Honor, duty, country.

Willey, for example, became an Arlington Lady after much cajoling from a close friend and fellow military wife.

"I agreed to try it out just to shut her up," she laughed. "It was sort of a fluke. But I quickly realized what a unique opportunity this was to serve the Air Force. It's a feeling I can't even describe, sharing these moments with people. As members of military families, we have a special insight into what their life was like. So these funerals we attend really feel like the funeral of somebody from our extended family."

"There are few things in my life that have given me as much satisfaction as serving as an Arlington Lady volunteer," Margaret Mensch of the Army's Arlington Ladies contingent added. "It's an honor to be asked to be a part of these ceremonies that pay tribute to the everyday heroes that make up the armed forces. We're just giving back a little to those who have given us so much."

For McKinley, serving as an Arlington Lady helps make up for some of the indifference to military sacrifice in modern society.

"A lot of people these days seem to believe the military is terrible," she said. "It's not easy, and it's not for everybody, that's for sure. But these people are giving of themselves every single day. There's no draft. Everyone in the military has chosen to make the military their life, and whether it's for four years or forty, they deserve to be thanked and honored. And I mean honored. That's why I'm here and I've never lost sight of that."

But there is also something larger, in the very best sense of the "one for all, and all for one" sentiment, at work here.

"One day, hopefully a long time away yet, I could be the one burying my husband," she said. "If that day comes I know there will be an Arlington Lady standing there with me. We all have our times of joy and sorrow and that's what unifies us as human beings. I'm willing to be there on both ends because I know someone will do the same for me."

SHAWN MACOMBER is a reporter and staff writer for *The American Spectator.*

Green Graveyards—A Natural Way to Go

Back-to-nature burials in biodegradable caskets conserve land.

BARBARA BASLER

In lovely woods just outside the tiny town of Westminster, S.C., discreetly scattered among the tall pines and poplars, are 20 graves, many hand-dug by Billy Campbell.

The graves, mounds of earth dotted with wildflowers and bathed in dappled sunlight, are marked with flat stones engraved with the names of the dead—from a rock-ribbed Southern Baptist to a gentle New Age hippie.

Campbell, the town's only doctor, is an ardent environmentalist. He buries patients, friends and strangers—without embalming them—in biodegradable caskets, or in no caskets at all, in the nature preserve he created along Ramsey Creek.

The burials are legal and meet all state regulations and health requirements. But in the beginning, many in this conservative town of 2,700 people were skeptical, even angry, about the Ramsey Creek Preserve, where the dead protect the land of the living.

"We weren't doing anything weird or outlandish," Campbell says, "but people accused us of throwing bodies in the creek or laying them out for buzzards to eat." He recalls one irate woman, apparently convinced of the bodies-in-the-creek rumor, who "told me I was a rich doctor who could buy bottled water, but she would have to drink my dead men's soup."

In the six years since the burial ground opened, Westminster has come, slowly but surely, to accept it. And now, Campbell's idea—nurtured in the backwoods of South Carolina—is spreading to rich, trendy Marin County, Calif.

Campbell, 49, and his new partner Tyler Cassity—a 34-year old entrepreneur who owns cemeteries in three states—are scheduled to open the new burial preserve this summer on a hillside in the shadow of the Golden Gate Bridge.

Campbell says he and Cassity hope to work with conservation groups to open similar natural burial grounds across the country, each crisscrossed—like Ramsey Creek—with hiking trails. "What we are doing is basically land conservation," Campbell says. "By setting aside a woods for natural burials, we preserve it from development. At the same time, I think we put death in its rightful place, as part of the cycle of life. Our burials honor the idea of dust to dust."

At Ramsey Creek, burial in a simple casket costs about $2,300. The National Funeral Directors Association says the average conventional funeral costs about $6,500. That includes mortuary services, embalming, a casket and a cement vault or box for the casket, which is often required for a cemetery burial. A cemetery plot adds even more to the cost.

"The mortuary-cemetery business is a $20-billion-a-year industry, and if we could get just 10 percent of that," Campbell says, "we'd have $2 billion a year going toward land conservation on memorial preserves where people could picnic, hike or take nature classes."

> **"We put death in its rightful place, as part of the cycle of life. Our burials honor the idea of dust to dust."**
>
> —Billy Campbell

A native of Westminster—his family's roots here go back to the Revolutionary War—Campbell studied to be an ecologist, then switched to medicine. Soft-spoken and wry, Campbell concedes he's a bit of an eccentric, but then "small Southern towns are good places for eccentrics," he says. Westminster, after all, was home to the Guns, Cabinets and Nightcrawlers store, "and I think that's a whole lot stranger than Ramsey Creek," he laughs.

The folksy, erudite doctor and the hip young businessman who owns Hollywood Forever, a celebrity cemetery where Rudolph Valentino and Cecil B. DeMille are buried, believe they have the potential to revolutionize the funeral industry and conserve a million acres of land over the next 30 years.

Campbell and Cassity, who has been a consultant to HBO's television series *Six Feet Under,* think the idea of burials that protect, rather than consume, green space will appeal to boomers, including those who want their cremated ashes scattered or buried. In Marin County, they plan to designate three of the site's 32 acres for interments and conserve the rest.

In place of the perpetual care fund of the conventional cemetery, "where money is set aside to mow the grass and battle back any natural growth," Campbell says, funds in memorial preserves will be used to restore the land.

Campbell's Ramsey Creek—the first "green" burial site in America—has inspired another in Florida, and a third has recently opened in Texas.

Campbell remembers that when his father died, he wanted to bury him in a simple, dignified biodegradable wood box. But his father was buried in the only wood box the funeral home offered—an eye-popping, ornate oak casket the funeral director assured him was the same model that held actor Dan Blocker, who played Hoss Cartwright on the TV hit *Bonanza*.

"You know, I didn't take any real comfort in that," Campbell says.

Over the years Campbell has spoken to environmental groups, birdwatchers and native-plant associations and found that "the idea of the preserve resonates with a lot of very different people" who aren't all young, liberal environmentalists.

"Ramsey Creek is unusual. It's different. And people will talk," says Jerry Smith, the owner of Moon's Drug Store & Gift Shop on Main Street. "But I think it's fantastic, myself."

Indeed, what is New Age and cutting edge to some is simply old-fashioned common sense to others. Sherrill Hughes, who lives in Westminster, buried her husband Rowland in Ramsey Creek Preserve with his favorite country music playing.

"Nobody would call him an environmental person," Hughes says. "Rowland grew up hard in West Virginia, and he liked plain and simple. He was a good provider, but he didn't like to waste money." When Rowland said he wanted to be buried in a plain pine box, Hughes says she told him she didn't think they did that anymore. "Then," she says, "my daughter heard about Ramsey Creek."

Campbell and his wife, Kimberly, can tell the story of everyone buried in Ramsey Creek—from the stillborn baby Hope, the first burial on the site, to the interior decorator who left instructions for an elaborate funeral with black-plumed horses to be led by Kimberly. "His relatives nixed that, though," Campbell says. "They said, 'Those horses bite, and we can't take any chances.'"

Kimberly operates the Ramsey Creek business from a room in Billy Campbell's Foothills Family Medicine office on Main Street. He treats the patients, she sells the gravesites. "Billy doesn't discuss Ramsey Creek during medical appointments," Kimberly says.

Twenty people are already buried at Ramsey Creek, and 50 other families, some from as far away as California and New York, have bought plots there.

Campbell says when he first announced the opening of his green cemetery in 1998, the local newspaper referred to it as "tree-hugger heaven," and the local funeral director—a man he grew up with—tried to get the state authorities to shut it down. "Now, several funeral homes work with us to help store or transport bodies to Ramsey Creek," Campbell says.

Bob Fells, a spokesman for the International Cemetery and Funeral Association, says the industry is always open to new ideas. "Many cemeteries," he says, "have undeveloped acreage. So it would be easy to leave the trees and rocks and dedicate that area as a green cemetery that follows the rules for green burials. We're all about consumer choice."

Campbell's company, Memorial Ecosystems, sets aside 25 percent of the Ramsey Creek burial price for conservation and for development projects like nature classes and plant surveys. It's a for-profit company, and "so far, we're about breaking even," he says. "But as word spreads, people come, and we are growing."

Jim Nichols, a computer software salesman from Greenville, S.C., buried his younger brother Chris in Ramsey Creek after the 28-year-old died of cancer in May. "Chris was what you might call a hippie, and he was very conscious of the environment," Nichols says. "When he was dying, he said he wanted to be buried here."

Standing in front of the grave, listening to the sounds of the birds and the rushing creek, Nichols recalls, "My father and I were leery, but the first time we came out here, we knew it was right for Chris. It's beautiful and peaceful. It's full of life, not death."

When he died they buried Chris in a coffin his father had made, wrapped in quilts sewn by his great-grandmothers. His dog Briar was at the graveside, along with 70 friends and family members.

"Now, my wife and I, my parents and my two uncles all plan to be buried here," Nichols says. "Ramsey Creek changed our minds about burials and death."

Social Workers' Final Act of Service: Respectful Burial Arrangements for Indigent, Unclaimed, and Unidentified People

GRACIELA M. CASTEX

Although little discussed in the professional literature, social workers have long been involved in identifying resources and making final arrangements for clients who die without an estate or heirs to assume economic responsibility; who may have been institutionalized; who are unknown to the community; or whose body may be unclaimed for burial. This task can be demanding, if only because social workers must often locate resources quickly if they are to prevent a client from being buried with no ceremony of interment and frequently in an unmarked grave or in a grave marked only by a number in ground set aside for the burial of indigents—a "potter's field."

A person's respectful final disposition is important for the living, for the deceased, and, it may be argued, for the health of the larger society. Knowledge that respectful final arrangements have been made may offer psychological comfort to a client at the end of life, help a grieving family and friends during a time of sorrow and remembrance, and also mark the community's recognition of and respect for our common humanity. This article highlights the challenges faced by many social workers as they attempt to prevent undignified burials when requested to make final arrangements for terminally ill or deceased people, especially those who are indigent, unclaimed, or unknown. ("Burial" here refers to any form of final disposition: interment burial at sea, cremation, and so forth; "indigent" is a legal term often used in reference to people whose estates lack the resources to pay for final arrangements independently.)

Death is destiny for all of us; for most of humanity, there seems to be an almost universal impulse to attend the final mystery, the final journey, of death with ceremonies of respect and remembrance, implementing local traditions and commonly seeking religious or spiritual guidance and solace (Ariès, 1974; Kastenbaum, 2004). Remembrances of the dead connect us to the past and honor the influence of those who have departed in helping us become what we are today. Observances of respect for the departed touch our common humanity; common sentiments such as "there but for the grace of God go I" and "as I am, so you will be" reinforce humility and empathy. In sum, as important as they are for emotional reasons, respectful death rites and burial practices are threads in the fabric of community that holds a society together.

Absent substantial policy reform at state and national levels, the need for "preventive" services to ensure respectful burials for all people may increase dramatically in the future. In part, an increase in indigent burials is a result of population increase, especially among the older-age cohorts. But the primary cause of an indigent burial is poverty at death.

Therefore, demography is only part of the story. Various social and political factors contribute to indigence at death; examples include the current financing of the U.S. medical system, which leaves 46 million people without insurance coverage (DeNavas-Walt, Proctor, & Lee, 2005); the political climate, which supports the diminishment of social safety nets; increasing numbers of incarcerated individuals with very long sentences, resulting in prison deaths; changes in family structure resulting in fewer offspring or other relatives available to make final arrangements; increasing numbers of immigrant residents who may have few social supports and no extended family in the United States; homelessness and all that it implies regarding lack of social attachments and unmet basic needs; and a system of payment for long-term care (assisted living, nursing, hospice, and so forth) that virtually guarantees the impoverishment of many people at death.

Private Pain, Public Bodies

Every place where groups of human beings live will be faced with burying people who have no resources or friends or relatives to attend to their final arrangements or who may be entirely unknown to the community. The number of individuals who currently die in such circumstances in the United States is not well documented; no national data on indigent burials or unclaimed bodies are collected, and data collected at the state level are often erratic and incomplete (personal communication with M. Jones, public affairs specialist, National Center for Health Statistics, June 26, 2006). In 2004, about 2.4 million people died in the United States; in addition, there are approximately 26,000 stillbirths annually. The precise number of indigent burials in the United States, however, or of those who are unclaimed or unknown, is undetermined because the data are not collected (Centers for Disease Control and Prevention [CDC], 2003; Miniño, Heron, & Smith, 2006; National Institutes of Health [NIH], 2003).

A hint of the number of indigent burials for the nation as a whole is, however, offered by extrapolation from the experience of New York City, which with 8 million residents makes up almost 3 percent of the U.S. population. About 3,000 (5 percent) of New York City's 60,000 annual deaths require some form of city burial assistance, of which about 1,500 adults and 1,000 or more infant and stillborn children are buried annually on Hart Island, the local potter's field (Corn, 2000; New York City Department of Health and Mental Hygiene, 2005). Extending New York City's experience to the nation, one might crudely estimate more than 100,000 potter's field burials annually (5 percent of the 2.4 million U.S. deaths)—perhaps too high a number, but there are at least tens of thousands of publicly assisted burials annually.

The limited state data available, and projections from a survey conducted by the Department of Veterans Affairs in 2003 (Schulman, Ronca, & Bucuvalas, Inc., 2003), suggest that even the 100,000-plus estimate may be reasonable: Michigan, for example, subsidizes 6,000 to 7,000 indigent burials each year, one-third of which occur in Wayne County (Detroit); Ohio paid for 2,000 in the year 2000 (Brickey, 2005); and Maricopa County (Phoenix), Arizona, pays for about 300 burials per year (Maricopa County Office of Management and Budget, 2000). Some regions face special challenges; for example, more than 200 immigrants died crossing the Arizona desert from Mexico in the fiscal year ending September 30, 2005, a third of whom will never be identified (Carroll, 2005; "Deaths on Border," 2005).

Although such examples illustrate the experience of a few jurisdictions for which data are available, it would be a mistake to view indigent burials as primarily a product of the anonymity or localization of poverty in urban environments. The need for social workers to provide burial assistance may arise in a rural county in North Carolina or Minnesota, perhaps for a migrant farm worker or nursing home resident.

Lack of assets at death is likely to become more common as members of the rapidly growing elderly population exhaust their retirement savings, as income distribution becomes increasingly skewed in favor of those who are wealthy, and as support for such a basic concept as social insurance faces increasing challenge. Thus, a social context that, perhaps unintentionally, promotes financial depletion at death increases the challenge facing a social worker seeking out resources to avoid a client's anonymous burial in a local potter's field, the lowest common denominator of indigent burial options funded out of the public purse.

Response of Governments to a Societal Need

Funeral and burial expenses in the United States are customarily the responsibility of the estate of the deceased or of the deceased's family. However, there may be no estate or family or the family may be unable or unwilling to pay the final expenses. Yet, the remains must be disposed of, and some government entity must ultimately assume the responsibility of ensuring a proper disposal.

In other words, whatever the time and place, what of those whose families could not and cannot afford what they regard as an appropriate disposition? What of unknown or unclaimed bodies? Who takes responsibility for their burial? Any city and most villages, whether modern or ancient, had, have, and will have people die who are poor or unknown, and recognition of the undeniable need for communities to provide for their burial is ancient (Parkes, Laungani, & Young, 1997). In the United States, state governments have generally assumed this responsibility or assigned the task to local governments. In New York State, for example, Section 4200 of the Public Health Law mandates that "every body of a deceased person, within this state, shall be decently buried or incinerated within a reasonable time after death" (New York State Cemetery Board, 2001, p. 38).

Legal scholar Virginia Murray underlined the principle that in U.S. jurisprudence, most states have legislation guaranteeing that "all persons, including paupers and prisoners, are entitled to a decent burial. Sanctity of the dead is so basic a principle that it is referred to as a "right of the dead and a charge on the quick" (Trope & Echo-Hawk, as cited in Murray, 2000, para. 2). Even so, although the law recognizes that the living must pay to ensure the rights of the dead, no governing entity at the local, state, or national level has consistently been enthusiastic about assuming the financial burden of this responsibility.

Some jurisdictions go to lengths to discourage situations in which government burials might subsidize what many people would consider standard elements of a funeral. In 2001, for example, York County, Nebraska, clarified existing guidelines regarding county burials and explicitly banned independent arrangements by family members with mortuaries or cemeteries to provide additional services such as flowers, headstones, or clergy fees (Wilkinson, 2001).

Furthermore, state policies and regulations are usually implemented in piecemeal fashion by a patchwork of town, city, county, and state agencies. In many cases, state governments dictate what local authorities are required to do, creating what is all too often a partially funded or completely unfunded mandate to bury the dead. Confusion resulting from ad hoc local responses to a state mandate can be extreme: In New Jersey, for example, in 2003 the legislature had to step in and require that county governments, not municipalities, pick up the charges for indigent burials. Furthermore, the responsible county would be that in which the deceased person resided, not that in which he or she had died; certain counties with large, regional hospitals were in effect subsidizing the indigent burial expenses of other counties (Dressel, 2003).

State reimbursement to localities for indigent burials, when it exists, has rarely kept up with inflation. In 2001, the state of Ohio eliminated a $750 reimbursement to localities. The state of Washington did the same in 1993, although it requires that "[the county] shall provide for the final disposition of any indigent person including a recipient of public assistance who dies within the county and whose body is unclaimed by relatives or church organizations" (Brickey, 2005; Crumley, 2002; Revised Code of Washington, 1993, c 4, § 36.39.030). In other states, funeral homes must accept indigent burials at a loss.

Potter's Field: A Pauper's Grave

In the United States, people planning a funeral seem to have many choices when selecting a respectful final disposition. For example, one may be interred in the earth, buried at sea, cremated, or entombed; have a green (ecologically respectful) burial; be donated for scientific research; or be cryogenically preserved. One may or may not be embalmed; one's organs may be donated to others. Eventually, the final remains may be kept in a plot, crypt, niche, urn, or tomb. Objects commonly merchandized for funerary use include caskets, clothing, grave liners, guest books, flowers, memorial jewelry, balloons, grave markers, and so forth, depending on the customs and belief systems of the deceased and his or her family. The hallmark of the indigent burial is lack of choice and, all too often, the lack of respect and dignity.

Interment and the Classic Potter's Field

The term "potter's field" derives from a New Testament Bible story (Matthew 27:3–10) in which a plot of land owned by a potter outside the walls of the city of Jerusalem is purchased "as a burial place for foreigners" with the tainted 30 pieces of silver that Judas received (and returned) for betraying Jesus (New York City Department of Corrections, 1967). In time, however, the term took on other connotations: "Potter's field: A public burial place (as in a city) for paupers, unknown persons, and criminals" (Gove, 1976).

One of the most visually dramatic examples of the dehumanization of anonymous burials at a U.S. potter's field may be observed at City Cemetery on New York City's Hart Island, which was opened in 1869 and brings the efficiency and scale of the Industrial Revolution to the medieval pauper's grave. Every weekday will find teams of men who are incarcerated stacking unpainted plywood coffins, often of tiny children, eight or 10 deep in trenches. These mass graves are then backfilled with earthmoving equipment until the ground is leveled, and backhoes move on to create the next trench (Hunt & Sternfeld, 1998; Risen, 2002). Even when faced with such images, however, the dehumanization of indigent, unknown, or unclaimed deceased individuals was not the intent of the architects of the original potter's field, or of any subsequent version.

Of course, most potter's fields in the United States do not operate on such an industrial scale. In Bradenton, Florida, for example, the 150 or so indigent funerals annually are handled by local funeral homes for a county fee of $400, with burial in a county cemetery and numbers on a concrete strip for a headstone. The newspaper reports on one such recent burial, of a 37-year-old woman who died of a heart attack after working a 14-hour shift as a short-order cook. Family and friends were unable to raise the $5,000 an average Manatee County, Florida, private funeral cost in 2005. The woman was buried at county expense in a particleboard casket sealed with duct tape. The funeral home did, however, generously donate a service complete with flowers, for which it received no reimbursement, before burial in the county potter's field (Cullinan, 2005).

Obviously, the Florida funeral and disposition was more respectful, and appears to have been more emotionally fulfilling for family, than burial in an anonymous trench on Hart Island. This difference illustrates the challenges facing the social worker advocating for an indigent client. There are no clearcut paths to a desired solution when values, norms, rules, regulations, reimbursements, and services offered can vary from state to state, town to town, and even funeral home to funeral home.

Burial Options, Costs, and Indigence: The Example of Cremation

One might assume that a key element in addressing the problem of indigence at death and respectful final dispositions would be a reduction in the cost of final dispositions. Although funeral costs have sometimes been criticized as excessive, this issue is separate from provision for the burials of indigent people. Respectful and inexpensive options exist, although options may be limited by the preferences of the deceased and prevailing customs or religious practices. Costs for modest burials are commonly trivial compared with the medical costs of a final illness. What constitutes a respectful final disposition, however, not only varies by community, but also may change over time for a community.

The key word is "respectful." Ensuring a final disposition will inevitably be assigned to an agency of the community, be that a parish in the Middle Ages or colonial America or a county government in the 21st century. Requirements or perceptions of common decency, health, and public order ultimately transcend the costs of particular burial practices. There will always be a need for intervention to ensure any final disposition, much less a respectful burial, for some clients.

Consider the option of cremation. The practice is certainly less expensive than interment, and cremations are increasingly regarded as respectful. In 2004, for example, about 30 percent of the final dispositions in the United States were cremations; interments constituted virtually all of the remaining burials, and there are predictions that the proportion of cremations will increase in the future (Cremation Association of North America [CANA], 2006). A change in burial practices favoring cremation will not in most cases, however, divert the road away from potter's field. Cremations cost less than interments, but most indigent burials involve people with, at most, a few hundred dollars in assets. The need for assistance will continue.

Although more inexpensive burial practices only marginally affect the volume of indigent burials, a social worker may be called on to intervene in a more subtle manner; a crematory may itself become a sort of potter's field. A survey conducted a decade ago by CANA found that 5.7 percent of cremated remains in 1996 to 1997 were never picked up, and 2.4 percent of cremated remains delivered to a cemetery were placed in a common grave. Of the remains that were never picked up, 46 percent were "placed in storage on the premises"; 32 percent were "disposed of in a proper and legal way"; and the remaining 22 percent were "placed in a permanent vault." Vague language leaves room for much interpretation in what, for crematory operators, are ad hoc solutions to a problem imposed on them (CANA, 1998).

Changes in burial practices are unlikely to substantially affect the larger policy issues regarding the final disposition of human remains. In addition, there may be an issue respecting religious diversity; some religious communities do not customarily practice cremation.

The Road to Potter's Field: The Growing Need for Social Work Intervention

Although a lack of data obscures the absolute number of people who spend eternity in some form of pauper's grave in the United States, in looking at the total number of people who die, their ages, and their economic circumstances, one can quickly begin to piece together a grim reality. Social workers often provide services to those who are most vulnerable in society and most at risk of not having the resources to afford a burial, much less a funeral.

The social work community has always worked with members of groups such as elderly people, those who are incarcerated, newly arrived immigrants, homeless people, and so forth. However, a number of changes in the size of certain component groups of U.S. society appear likely to greatly affect both the number and the distribution of indigent burials. For example, the tripling of the population of those incarcerated for the long term—that is, over a 20-year period—merits special attention. Those 1.5 million prisoners will make substantial although often yet undetermined, demands on the social services delivery system in many areas, not the least of which will likely be provisions for final arrangements.

Poverty and age at death tend to be reinforcing. The group that will grow the most in numbers, elderly people, constitute the age cohorts most likely to die and those second most likely to live in circumstances of economic deprivation. Members of the cohorts with the second highest mortality, the infant children of (by definition) young families, have the highest rates of poverty, particularly if the family is headed by a single mother (DeNavas-Walt et al., 2005).

The dynamic interrelationship of demographic changes and family structure that reinforce poverty are, of course, exacerbated by a number of unrelated trends that also tend to impoverish these same clients. Especially significant are the reduction in the number of people covered by defined-benefit (fixed amount per month) corporate pension systems; rising medical costs combined with declining health and life insurance coverage for the most at-risk populations; the declining supports provided by family systems at all ages; and an increase in the poverty rate for children, whose parents may not be able to pay for burials or health insurance for all family members. Many social workers would add still more. All reinforce the likelihood that the financial resources of decedents will be exhausted at the time of death.

Age at Death

One's life may end on its first day, at age 25 in an auto accident, or during one's 100th year. The CDC reported that 2,443,908 people died in 2003 in the United States, and NIH reported that there are at least an additional 26,000 stillbirths annually (to be counted as a death by the collectors of vital statistics, one must be born alive; although as of 2007, NIH calls stillbirths "fetal mortalities," they still do not contribute to the total count of deaths) (MacDorman, Hoyert, Matin, Munson, & Hamilton, 2007). As is typical of people living in industrialized societies, most mortalities occur as stillbirths (26,000), as infant mortalities in the first year of life (1.2 percent, or 28,458 in 2003), or after 65 years of age (74 percent, or 1,803,827 in 2003). As a cohort group, the death rate in the first year of life, even excluding stillbirths, is not equaled until about age 60 (Hoyert, Heron, Murphy, & Kung, 2006; NIH, 2003).

Poverty and Age

In the United States, a large number of people are born into poverty, live in poverty, and die in poverty; many millions never have the opportunity to accumulate significant assets during their lives. Others are poor only at some point in their lives. In 2004, 12.7 percent of the national population, 37 million people, lived in poverty, officially defined as an annual household income of $15,219 for a family of three. The poverty rate rose to 17.8 percent of households with children that year, encompassing 13 million children plus their parents and caretakers. The poverty rate jumped to 28.4 percent if the family was headed by a single woman. A single mother is unlikely to be able to save much for emergencies, retirement, or the final arrangements for a child (DeNavas-Walt et al., 2005).

For those age 65 and older, more than 6 million of 35 million people (17 percent) lived in households with incomes of less than $14,000 (about $1,200 per month)—about 25 percent above the official poverty threshold for this age group (DeNavas-Walt et al., 2005). The numbers of poor people with children and the numbers of elderly people who live in financially stringent circumstances are both quite large—these are households in which, by definition, some members cannot work and are therefore likely to be financially challenged.

Some regional, racial, and ethnic groups also have poverty rates, and death rates, much higher than national averages. These are among the groups most at risk of indigence at death.

Incarcerated People

On July 1, 2004, there were 2,131,180 people—one in 143 residents—incarcerated in the United States. Of those, 1,410,405 were incarcerated in state and federal prisons, up from 487,593 in 1985 as prison terms have increased dramatically as a result of draconian drug laws, three-strikes laws, and the like (Harrison & Beck, 2005). Comparing 2003 with 1995, the greatest percentage increases in the inmate population were for people 55 years of age or older (85 percent), followed by those ages 45 to 54 (77 percent), with the two groups totaling about 251,000 prisoners (Harrison & Beck, 2004).

The release of death statistics lags incarceration statistics, but there were 3,311 deaths in state and federal prisons in 2001: 57 were killed by another person and 60 were executed. With an aging population of inmates, prison "nursing homes" are a current reality (*Sourcebook of Criminal Justice Statistics*, 2004, Table 6.76.2004). Inmates have long faced the prospect of having their unclaimed remains buried in prison potter's fields, often with no marker or ceremony.

Social Work Intervention
Before and after the Death of a Client

The role of social workers reaches beyond the significant contributions made to clients and loved ones in the process of assisting with the complex issues surrounding death and dying. In many cases, social workers may prevent an individual potter's field burial by implementing a range of interventions designed to secure a dignified and respectful final disposition.

Legal requirements. Learn the legal requirements and local regulations and practices regarding indigent, unknown, or unclaimed bodies in the state and local community in which you practice.

Although each state develops its own policies, responsibility has usually been passed on to some local entity, usually a county or city government. Knowledge of local practice helps establish the parameters of interventions. It is important to establish a time frame for action—how long do you have to locate family or resources before the deceased is removed for a potter's field burial?

Government agencies. Contact the Social Security Administration, state or local human resources departments, federal and state Departments of Veterans Affairs, and other public assistance programs available in your area as soon as possible. At a minimum, almost every U.S. resident is entitled to receive a $255 social security death benefit.

VA burial benefits. A *veteran* is "a person who served in the active military, naval, or air service and who was discharged or released under conditions other than dishonorable" (U.S. Department of Veterans Affairs, 2003, para. 2). No veteran need be buried in a potter's field. The VA itself asks to be contacted to check whether any unclaimed person, male or female, qualifies for veteran's burial benefits; the VA checks identities against a database. All veterans are entitled to a variety of burial-related benefits, as in some cases are their spouses and even some dependents. So when contacting the VA, spousal information may also be helpful. Note that a man's spouse may be a veteran, even if he is not.

Collect and revise client Information. Collection and periodic revision of personal, financial, medical, and end-of-life information for a client might avoid later difficulties. Many agencies are using electronic documentation to facilitate this process, and gathering key information is already a standard part of the intake process for most assisted-living facilities, nursing homes, and so forth. Examples of pertinent information include death notification contact information; the location of wills; prearranged funeral and burial plans; segregated funds earmarked for burial expenses; wishes of the deceased regarding his or her care after death; information regarding cash, wages due or anticipated, income, savings, securities, bonds, insurance policies (including travel, auto, and credit cards), and retirement funds and accounts; client's real estate assets; vehicles owned; livestock; collections of potential monetary or emotional value; labor union membership (which may include death benefits); armed forces information (including spousal service for both genders); membership in professional, civic, or fraternal organizations; and legal residence status in the United States or other nations (U.S. citizens and residents may have accrued benefits on social insurance programs of other countries by living or working there; this is most common for refugees from Europe). Request and record all other names the client may have used—maiden name, married names other than the current name, nickname, birth name used before adoption, or name change as a result of an abusive relationship may be among the key information to be obtained.

Accessing local resources. Depending on where one practices, many organizations offer burial assistance for their members or for members of the public. Many religious organizations, such as the Jewish Federation and the St. Vincent DePaul Society, for example, have special programs for assisting coreligionists in need; professional and labor organizations, such as Actor's Equity, and fraternal and sororal groups such as the Masons, Eastern Star, and

the Knights of Columbus may all have burial benefits for members and families. Local groups may also bury individuals with dignity, such as the Garden of Angels in Desert Lawn Memorial Park outside Los Angeles, which provides burial and funeral services for abandoned babies (Roche, 2000). In many communities, organizations that advocate for the most vulnerable residents compile and distribute publications with titles such as "A Guide to Burial Assistance"; these often serve as a helpful introduction to local resources and contacts at key government agencies.

Bureau of indian affairs. For those deceased clients who are, or might be, members of a legally recognized Native American tribe or Alaska Native community, social workers should contact a representative of the group's governing body, from which burial assistance might be available. For example, the Cherokee Nation may provide substantial burial assistance in a means-tested program; information is available from http://www.cherokee.org.

Foreign nationals. If the client needing a place of eternal rest is an immigrant, it might be helpful to contact the consulate of his or her native country (if known). A consulate may be able to offer suggestions and concrete resources to assist in a burial or in contacting family members living abroad. For example, Mexican consulates have brochures available in English and Spanish offering detailed advice and suggestions to people assisting in the provision of final arrangements for Mexican nationals.

Scientific identification resources. Before an unidentified client is interred or cremated, try to ensure that key data necessary for identification—typically, photographs, fingerprints, DNA samples, dental records, and visual records—have been collected and preserved.

Posting and seeking information on web sites to identify unknown people. Many states, communities, and private organizations, through police departments or other government agencies, have a Web page with photos, drawings, or other unique markers or possessions, including dental information, of deceased individuals to aid in identification. The Mexican government is testing such a system for filing missing-persons reports in Mexico or in consulates located in the United States (Carroll, 2005). For example, one such well-established site is the Doe Network: International Center for Unidentified and Missing Persons (http://www.doenetwork.org), which also links to the North American Missing Persons Network. A social worker can assist by posting information about a missing person or in searching for loved ones or friends of an unknown person. These sites may also be very useful after natural disasters. In time, these types of registries may grow in sophistication, completeness, and importance in the search for missing people and in the identification of relatives or friends of unclaimed people or of unclaimed bodies.

Encouraging community generosity. Actively encourage the generosity of individuals, community groups, or other private, religious, or governmental groups who might donate goods and services or participate in fundraising for a particular burial. For example, on May 21, 2005, more than 200 people attended a funeral mass in Rockaway, New York, for an unidentified three-year-old child who had been found on a nearby beach with broken ribs and vertebrae. The child was named John Valentine Hope by the officiating pastor, who commented that the tragedy of a violent death was worsened by a "violence of silence" by the boy's parents, who never claimed him. "It's the violence of silence that makes this mystery continue," he said. The ceremony did offer comfort to the community, however (Kilgannon, 2005, p. 38).

Final Thoughts
Implications for Policy

Although advocacy for broad-based policy reformulation transcends the primary aims of this article, policy changes could alleviate future distress for clients and workers. Success in the profession's continuing efforts to address some issues—such as poverty, income inequality, and benefit levels—will help avoid some indigent burials. In addition, social workers could educate and influence clients, the general public, and policymakers by advocating on the following issues.

Acknowledgement and discussion. Public discussion of indigent burials; the risks of an indigent burial for the individual; local, state, and national issues relating to indigent burials; and the scope of the numbers of people potentially affected may raise public awareness of the issue. Death and burial should not be veiled, entering public discussion only in times of crisis.

Increase the social security death benefit. Beginning in September 1960, the Social Security Administration allowed the one-time, lump-sum death payment of $255 to be assigned to funeral homes. The estates of all people who have met the qualifications for social security protection qualify for this payment, which has not been increased for more than 40 years (Social Security Administration, 2004). If the final payment had been indexed for inflation, the value of this lump-sum death payment would have risen to at least $1,000. Such a final payment would go a long way toward avoiding indigent burials (DeNavas-Walt et al., 2005, p. 30). Social workers could include death benefit entitlement among social security policy debates.

Veterans benefit enhancement. Although veterans are guaranteed a respectful burial somewhere, if they wish to be buried in a particular location, perhaps on a family plot in a private cemetery, the VA may subsidize the burial with a small amount of money (up to $600) and a marker or headstone. This subsidy, too, has not been raised in decades (U.S. Department of Veterans Affairs, 2003). Enhancement would facilitate burial in cemeteries close to family and friends.

Clarification of state and local responsibilities. Many laws and implementing regulations regarding indigent burials are obsolete and based on outdated assumptions. If proposals to clarify responsibility for final dispositions come before legislative bodies, input from social workers might support protection for future clients. At the least, unfunded mandates might be opposed.

Social workers have a unique opportunity to ensure a respectful funeral and burial for clients. Securing a dignified and respectful disposition of a person's body will in many cases allow family and loved ones the opportunity to grieve and mourn by having an identifiable permanent resting place to honor their loved one. Most of us "would want to feel that our loved one is 'all right' even though

dead" (Kastenbaum, 2005, p. 6). Death marks both an ending and a beginning for family, friends, and community; our treatment of the dead also serves as a marker for our respect for the living. In earlier times, this observation would have been almost a truism. As William E. Gladstone so famously remarked more than 125 years ago, "Show me the manner in which a nation cares for its dead, and I will measure with mathematical exactness the tender mercies of its people, their respect for the laws of the land and their loyalty to high ideals" (Murray, 2000).

References

Ariès, P. (1974). *Western attitudes towards death from the Middle Ages to the present.* Baltimore: Johns Hopkins University Press.

Brickey, H. (2005, February 20). Grave consequences. *The Blade.* Retrieved July 5, 2007, from http://www.toledoblade.com/apps/pbcs.dll/section?Category=ARCHIVES

Carroll, S. (2005, May 21). Mexico database to ID border-crosser bodies. *Arizona Republic.* Retrieved August 10, 2005, from http://www.wkconline.org/resources/word/Carroll-Bodies.doc

Centers for Disease Control and Prevention. (2003). *U.S. standard certificate of death* (Rev. 11/2003). Retrieved June 25, 2006, from cdc.gov/nchs/data/dus/DEATH11-03final.pdf

Corn, L. (2000). New York City's potter's field: A visit to Hart Island's City Cemetery in Bronx County: *New York Genealogical and Biographical Society Newsletter,* Summer. Retrieved January 24, 2005, from http://www.newyorkfamilyhistory.org/modules.php?name=Sections&op=printpage&artid=60

Cremation Association of North America. (1998). *1996/1997 cremation container, disposition and service survey.* Chicago: Author. Retrieved June 26, 2006, from http://cremationassociation.org/docs/dreport.pdf

Cremation Association of North America. (2006). *Confirmed 2003 statistics.* Chicago: Author. Retrieved June 26, 2006, from http://cremationassociation.org/docs/WebConfirmed.pdf

Crumley, A. (2002, May 10). Coroner's office making the best of a difficult situation. *The Courthouse Journal, 18,* 17–18. (Reprinted from "Coroner's office making the best of a difficult situation," by A. Crumley, April 27, 2002, *Port Orchard Independent*)

Cullinan, K. (2005, July 20). Indigent burials on the increase. *Sarasota Herald-Tribune.* Retrieved August 15, 2005, from http://www.heraldtribune.com/apps/pbcs.dll/section?CATEGORY=HELP05&template=ovr2

Deaths on border of Arizona strain morgue's capacity. (2005, September 4). *New York Times,* p. A21.

DeNavas-Walt, C., Proctor, B. D., & Lee, C. H. (2005). *Income, poverty, and health insurance coverage in the United States: 2004* (Current Population Reports P60-229). Washington, DC: U.S. Census Bureau.

Dressel, W. G. (2003, January 29). *Indigent burial costs.* Trenton: New Jersey State League of Municipalities. Retrieved September 9, 2003, from http://www.njslom.org/m1012903b.html

Gove, P. B. (Ed.). (1976). *Webster's third new international dictionary of the English language, Unabridged.* Springfield, MA: G. & C. Merriam.

Harrison, P. M., & Beck, A. J. (2004, November). Prisoners in 2003 (NCJ205335). *Bureau of Justice Statistics Bulletin.* Retrieved May 5, 2005, from http://www.ojp.usdoj.gov/bjs/abstract/p03.htm

Harrison, P. M., & Beck, A. J. (2005, April). Prison and jail inmates at midyear 2004 (NCJ208801). *Bureau of Justice Statistics Bulletin.* Retrieved May 5, 2005, from http://www.ojp.usdoj .gov/bjs/pub/pdf/pjim04.pdf

Hoyert, D. L., Heron, M. P., Murphy, S. L., & Kung, H. (2006). Deaths: Final data for 2003. *National Vital Statistics Reports, 54*(13). Hyattsville, MD: National Center for Health Statistics.

Hunt, M., & Sternfeld, J. (1998). *Hart Island.* Zurich: Scalo Editions.

Kastenbaum, R. (2004). Why funerals. *Generations: Journal of the American Society on Aging, 28(2),* 5–10.

Kilgannon, C. (2005, May 22). Honoring an unknown child found on a beach, and a long-lost Vietnam War pilot. *New York Times,* p. 38.

MacDorman, M. F., Hoyert, D. L., Matin, J. A., Munson, M. L., & Hamilton, B. E. (2007). Fetal and perinatal mortality, United States, 2003. *National Vital Statistics Reports, 55(6).* Retrieved February 23, 2007, from http://www.cdc.gov/nchs/data/nvsr/ nvsr55/nvsr55_06.pdf

Maricopa County Office of Management and Budget. (2000, February 17). *Indigent burial rates in Maricopa County* [Research Report] (Catalog No. 00-006). Phoenix, AZ: Author.

Miniño, A. M., Heron, M. P., & Smith, B. L. (2006). Deaths: Preliminary data for 2004. *National Vital Statistics Reports, 54*(19). Retrieved June 25, 2006, from www. cdc.gov/nchs/data/ nvsr/nvsr54/nvsr54_19.pdf

Murray, V. H. (2000). A "right" of the dead and a charge on the quick: Criminal laws relating to cemeteries, burial grounds and human remains. *Journal of the Missouri Bar, 56*(2). Retrieved September 1, 2005, from http://www.mobar.org/journal/2000/ marapr/murray.htm

National Institutes of Health. (2003, November 19). NICHD funds major effort to determine extent and causes of stillbirth. *NIH News.* Retrieved August 24, 2005, from http://www.nichd.nih .gov/news/releases/stillbirth.cfm

New York City Department of Corrections. (1967). *Potter's Field historical resume: 1869–1967.* New York: Author. Retrieved January 15, 2005, from http://www.correctionhistory.org/html/ chronicl/hart/html/hartbook2.html

New York City Department of Health and Mental Hygiene, Bureau of Vital Statistics. (2005). *Summary of vital statistics 2004, The City of New York.* New York: Author.

New York State Cemetery Board. (2001). *Cemetery and crematory operations: Relevant laws, administrative rules & regulations of the New York State Cemetery Board.* Albany, NY: Author.

Parkes, C., Laungani, P., & Young, B. (1997). *Death and bereavement across cultures.* London: Routledge.

Revised Code of Washington. Disposal of remains of indigent persons, c 4, § 36.39.030 (1993).

Risen, C. (2002). Hart Island. *The Morning News.* Retrieved August 27, 2005, from http://www.themorningnews.org/archives/new_york_ new_york/hart_island.php

Roche, T. (2000). A refuge for throwaways. *Time, 155*(7). Retrieved July 5, 2007, from http://www.time.com/time/magazine/ article/0,9171,996127,00.html

Schulman, Ronca, & Bucuvalas, Inc. (2003). *2003 VBA survey of medical examiners' and coroners' process in identification of unclaimed remains for veteran status.* Silver Spring, MD: Author.

Social Security Administration. (2004). *Social Security handbook: Your basic guide to social security programs.* Baltimore: Author. Retrieved June 26, 2006, from http://www.ssa.gov/OP_Home/ handbook/ssa-hbk.htm

Sourcebook of Criminal Justice Statistics. (2004). *Table 6.76.2004: Number and rate (per 100,000 prisoners) of deaths among state and federal prisoners: By cause of death, 2001.* Albany, NY: Author. Retrieved August 13, 2005, from http://www.albany .edu/sourcebook/pdf/t6762004.pdf

U.S. Department of Veterans Affairs. (2003). *Burial of unclaimed, indigent veterans.* Retrieved May 5, 2004, from http://www.vba .va.gov/bln/21/topics/indigent/index.htm

Wilkinson, M. (2001, November 14). Requirements for county burials clarified. *York News-Times.* Retrieved July 18, 2005, from http://www.yorknewstimes.com/stories/111401/1oc_ 1114010019.shtml

GRACIELA M. CASTEX, EdD, ACSW, LMSW, is associate professor, Social Work Program, Lehman College, City University of New York, 250 Bedford Park Boulevard, West Bronx, NY 10468-1589; e-mail: graciela.castex@lehman.cuny.edu.

From *Social Work,* Volume 52, Number 4, October 2007. Copyright © 2007 by NASW Press. Reprinted by permission.

UNIT 6
Bereavement

Unit Selections

Key Points to Consider

• Discuss how the seven stages of grieving over death can also be applied to losses through divorce, moving from one place to another, or the amputation of a limb (arm or leg). What is the relationship between time and the feelings of grief experienced within the bereavement process?

• Describe the four necessary tasks of mourning. What are some of the practical steps one can take in accomplishing each of these tasks? How can one assist friends in bereavement?

• What are the special problems encountered in the death of a child and in a perinatal death? How can one assist friends in this special type of bereavement?

• How can one know if one is experiencing "normal" bereavement or "abnormal" bereavement? What are some of the signs of aberrant bereavement? What could you do to assist people experiencing abnormal grief symptoms?

• Provide a list of "dos" and "don'ts" for dealing with children who have experienced a death.

• How are bereavement needs of children and young adults different than those of adults?

Student Web Site
www.mhcls.com

Internet References

Bereaved Families of Ontario Support Center
http://www.bereavedfamilies.net/
The Compassionate Friends
http://www.compassionatefriends.org
Practical Grief Resources
http://www.indiana.edu/~famlygrf/sitemap.html
Widow Net
http://www.widownet.org/

In American society many act as if the process of bereavement is completed with the culmination of public mourning related to the funeral or memorial service and the final disposition of the dead. For those in the process of grieving, the end of public mourning only serves to make the bereavement process a more individualized, subjective, and private experience. Private mourning of loss for most people, while more intense at its beginning, continues throughout their lifetime. The nature and intensity of this experience is influenced by the relationship of the mourner to the deceased, the age of the mourner, and the social context in which bereavement takes place.

This unit on bereavement begins with two general articles on the bereavement process. The first article, by Michael Leming and George Dickinson, describes and discusses the active coping strategies related to the bereavement process and the four tasks of bereavement. The second article, by Kenneth Doka, provides an alternative perspective on the understanding of the bereavement process. The third article, by Charles Corr, enhances and broadens the concept of disenfranchised grief in significant ways and explains that there are aspects of most losses that are indeed disenfranchised.

The article by Therese Rando ("The Increasing Prevalence of Complicated Mourning") illustrates the principles described by Leming, Dickinson, and Doka by providing a critique of America's health-care industry for its lack of involvement in the post-death grieving experience. The final articles are focused upon bereavement and coping strategies employed by a special population of grievers.

The Grieving Process

MICHAEL R. LEMING AND GEORGE E. DICKINSON

Grief is a very powerful emotion that is often triggered or stimulated by death. Thomas Attig makes an important distinction between grief and the grieving process. Although grief is an emotion that engenders feelings of helplessness and passivity, the process of grieving is a more complex coping process that presents challenges and opportunities for the griever and requires energy to be invested, tasks to be undertaken, and choices to be made (Attig, 1991).

Most people believe that grieving is a diseaselike and debilitating process that renders the individual passive and helpless. According to Attig (1991, p. 389):

It is misleading and dangerous to mistake grief for the whole of the experience of the bereaved. It is misleading because the experience is far more complex, entailing diverse emotional, physical, intellectual, spiritual, and social impacts. It is dangerous because it is precisely this aspect of the experience of the bereaved that is potentially the most frustrating and debilitating.

Death ascribes to the griever a passive social position in the bereavement role. Grief is an emotion over which the individual has no control. However, understanding that grieving is an active coping process can restore to the griever a sense of autonomy in which the process is permeated with choice and there are many areas over which the griever does have some control.

Coping with Grief

The grieving process, like the dying process, is essentially a series of behaviors and attitudes related to coping with the stressful situation of a change in the status of a relationship. Many individuals have attempted to understand coping with dying as a series of universal, mutually exclusive, and linear stages. Not all people, however, will progress through the stages in the same manner.

Seven behaviors and feelings that are part of the coping process are identified by Robert Kavanaugh (1972): shock and denial, disorganization, volatile emotions, guilt, loss and loneliness, relief, and reestablishment. It is not difficult to see similarities between these behaviors and Kübler-Ross's five stages (denial, anger, bargaining, depression, and acceptance) of the dying process. According to Kavanaugh (1972, p. 23), "these seven stages do not subscribe to the logic of the head as

much as to the irrational tugs of the heart—the logic of need and permission."

Shock and Denial

Even when a significant other is expected to die, at the time of death there is often a sense in which the death is not real. For most of us our first response is, "No, this can't be true." With time, our experience of shock diminishes, but we find new ways to deny the reality of death.

Some believe that denial is dysfunctional behavior for those in bereavement. However, denial not only is a common experience among the newly bereaved but also serves positive functions in the process of adaptation. The main function of denial is to provide the bereaved with a "temporary safe place" from the ugly realities of a social world that offers only loneliness and pain.

With time, the meaning of loss tends to expand, and it may be impossible for one to deal with all of the social meanings of death at once. For example, if a man's wife dies, not only does he lose his spouse, but also his best friend, his sexual partner, the mother of his children, a source of income, and so on. Denial can protect an individual from some of the magnitude of this social loss, which may be unbearable at times. With denial, one can work through different aspects of loss over time.

Disorganization

Disorganization is the stage in the bereavement process in which one may feel totally out of touch with the reality of everyday life. Some go through the 2- to 3-day time period just before the funeral as if on "automatic pilot" or "in a daze." Nothing normal "makes sense," and they may feel that life has no inherent meaning. For some, death is perceived as preferable to life, which appears to be devoid of meaning.

This emotional response is also a normal experience for the newly bereaved. Confusion is normal for those whose social world has been disorganized through death. When Michael Leming's father died, his mother lost not only all of those things that one loses with a death of a spouse, but also her caregiving role—a social role and master status that had defined her identity in the 5 years that her husband lived with cancer. It is only natural to experience confusion and social disorganization when one's social identity has been destroyed.

Volatile Reactions

Whenever one's identity and social order face the possibility of destruction, there is a natural tendency to feel angry, frustrated, helpless, and/or hurt. The volatile reactions of terror, hatred, resentment, and jealousy are often experienced as emotional manifestations of these feelings. Grieving humans are sometimes more successful at masking their feelings in socially acceptable behaviors than other animals, whose instincts cause them to go into a fit of rage when their order is threatened by external forces. However apparently dissimilar, the internal emotional experience is similar.

In working with bereaved persons over the past 20 years, Michael Lemming has observed that the following become objects of volatile grief reactions: God, medical personnel, funeral directors, other family members, in-laws, friends who have not experienced death in their families, and/or even the person who has died. Mild-mannered individuals may become raging and resentful persons when grieving. Some of these people have experienced physical symptoms such as migraine headaches, ulcers, neuropathy, and colitis as a result of living with these intense emotions.

The expression of anger seems more natural for men than expressing other feelings (Golden, 2000). Expressing anger requires taking a stand. This is quite different from the mechanics of sadness, where an open and vulnerable stance is more common. Men may find their grief through anger. Rage may suddenly become tears, as deep feelings trigger other deep feelings. This process is reversed with women, notes Golden. Many times a woman will be in tears, crying and crying, and state that she is angry.

As noted earlier, a person's anger during grief can range from being angry with the person who died to being angry with God, and all points in between. Golden's mentor, Father William Wendt, shared the story of his visits with a widow and his working with her on her grief. He noticed that many times when he arrived she was driving her car up and down the driveway. One day he asked her what she was doing. She proceeded to tell him that she had a ritual she used in dealing with her grief. She would come home, go to the living room, and get her recently deceased husband's ashes out of the urn on the mantle. She would take a very small amount and place them on the driveway. She then said, "It helps me to run over the son of a bitch every day." He concluded the story by saying, "Now that is good grief." It was "good" grief because it was this woman's way of connecting to and expressing the anger component of her grief.

Guilt

Guilt is similar to the emotional reactions discussed earlier. Guilt is anger and resentment turned in on oneself and often results in self-deprecation and depression. It typically manifests itself in statements like "If only I had . . . ," "I should have . . . ," "I could have done it differently . . . ," and "Maybe I did the wrong thing." Guilt is a normal part of the bereavement process.

From a sociological perspective, guilt can become a social mechanism to resolve the **dissonance** that people feel when unable to explain why someone else's loved one has died.

Rather than view death as something that can happen at any time to anyone, people can **blame the victim** of bereavement and believe that the victim of bereavement was in some way responsible for the death—"If the individual had been a better parent, the child might not have been hit by the car," or "If I had been married to that person, I might also have committed suicide," or "No wonder that individual died of a heart attack, the spouse's cooking would give anyone high cholesterol." Therefore, bereaved persons are sometimes encouraged to feel guilt because they are subtly sanctioned by others' reactions.

Loss and Loneliness

Feelings of loss and loneliness creep in as denial subsides. The full experience of the loss does not hit all at once. It becomes more evident as bereaved individuals resume a social life without their loved one. They realize how much they needed and depended upon their significant other. Social situations in which we expected them always to be present seem different now that they are gone. Holiday celebrations are also diminished by their absence. In fact, for some, most of life takes on a "something's missing" feeling. This feeling was captured in the 1960s love song "End of the World."

> Why does the world go on turning?
> Why must the sea rush to shore?
> Don't they know it's the end of the world
> Cause you don't love me anymore?

Loss and loneliness are often transformed into depression and sadness, fed by feelings of self-pity. According to Kavanaugh (1972, p. 118), this effect is magnified by the fact that the dead loved one grows out of focus in memory—"an elf becomes a giant, a sinner becomes a saint because the grieving heart needs giants and saints to fill an expanding void." Even a formerly undesirable spouse, such as an alcoholic, is missed in a way that few can understand unless their own hearts are involved. This is a time in the grieving process when anybody is better than nobody, and being alone only adds to the curse of loss and loneliness (Kavanaugh, 1972).

Those who try to escape this experience will either turn to denial in an attempt to reject their feelings of loss or try to find surrogates—new friends at a bar, a quick remarriage, or a new pet. This escape can never be permanent, however, because loss and loneliness are a necessary part of the bereavement experience. According to Kavanaugh (1972, p. 119), the "ultimate goal in conquering loneliness" is to build a new independence or to find a new and equally viable relationship.

Relief

The experience of relief in the midst of the bereavement process may seem odd for some and add to their feelings of guilt. Michael Leming observed a friend's relief 6 months after her husband died. This older friend was the wife of a minister, and her whole life before he died was his ministry. With time, as she built a new world of social involvements and relationships of which he was not a part, she discovered a new independent person in herself whom she perceived was a better person than she had ever before been.

Relief can give rise to feelings of guilt. However, according to Kavanaugh (1972, p. 121): "The feeling of relief does not imply any criticism for the love we lost. Instead, it is a reflection of our need for ever deeper love, our quest for someone or something always better, our search for the infinite, that best and perfect love religious people name as God."

Reestablishment

As one moves toward reestablishment of a life without the deceased, it is obvious that the process involves extensive adjustment and time, especially if the relationship was meaningful. It is likely that one may have feelings of loneliness, guilt, and disorganization at the same time and that just when one may experience a sense of relief, something will happen to trigger a denial of the death.

What facilitates bereavement and adjustment is fully experiencing each of these feelings as normal and realizing that it is hope (holding the grieving person together in fantasy at first) that will provide the promise of a new life filled with order, purpose, and meaning.

Reestablishment occurs gradually, and often we realize it has been achieved long after it has occurred. In some ways it is similar to Dorothy's realization at the end of *The Wizard of Oz*—she had always possessed the magic that could return her to Kansas. And, like Dorothy, we have to experience our loss before we really appreciate the joy of investing our lives again in new relationships.

Four Tasks of Mourning

In 1982 J. William Worden published *Grief Counseling and Grief Therapy,* which summarized the research conclusions of a National Institutes of Health study called the Omega Project (occasionally referred to as the Harvard Bereavement Study). Two of the more significant findings of this research, displaying the active nature of the grieving process, are that mourning is necessary for all persons who have experienced a loss through death and that four tasks of mourning must be accomplished before mourning can be completed and reestablishment can take place.

According to Worden (1982), unfinished grief tasks can impair further growth and development of the individual. Furthermore, the necessity of these tasks suggests that those in bereavement must attend to "grief work" because successful grief resolution is not automatic, as Kavanaugh's (1972) stages might imply. Each bereaved person must accomplish four necessary tasks: (1) accept the reality of the loss, (2) experience the pain of grief, (3) adjust to an environment in which the deceased person is missing, and (4) withdraw emotional energy and reinvest it in another relationship (Worden, 1982).

Accept the Reality of the Loss

Especially in situations when death is unexpected and/or the deceased lived far away, it is difficult to conceptualize the reality of the loss. The first task of mourning is to overcome the natural denial response and realize that the person is dead and will not return.

Bereaved persons can facilitate the actualization of death in many ways. The traditional ways are to view the body, attend the funeral and committal services, and visit the place of final disposition. The following is a partial list of additional activities that can assist in making death real for grieving persons.

1. View the body at the place of death before preparation by the funeral director.
2. Talk about the deceased person and the circumstances surrounding the death.
3. View photographs and personal effects of the deceased person.
4. Distribute the possessions of the deceased person among relatives and friends.

Experience the Pain of Grief

Part of coming to grips with the reality of death is experiencing the emotional and physical pain caused by the loss. Many people in the denial stage of grieving attempt to avoid pain by choosing to reject the emotions and feelings that they are experiencing. As discussed by Erich Lindemann (1944), some do this by avoiding places and circumstances that remind them of the deceased. Michael Leming knows one widow who quit playing golf and quit eating at a particular restaurant because these were activities that she had enjoyed with her husband. Another widow found it extremely painful to be with her dead husband's twin, even though he and her sister-in-law were her most supportive friends.

Worden (1982, pp. 13–14) cites the following case study to illustrate the performance of this task of mourning:

One young woman minimized her loss by believing her brother was out of his dark place and into a better place after his suicide. This might not have been true, but it kept her from feeling her intense anger at him for leaving her. In treatment, when she first allowed herself to feel anger, she said, "I'm angry with his behavior and not him!" Finally she was able to acknowledge this anger directly.

The problem with the avoidance strategy is that people cannot escape the pain associated with mourning. According to Bowlby (cited by Worden, 1982, p. 14), "Sooner or later, some of those who avoid all conscious grieving, break down—usually with some form of depression." Tears can afford cleansing for wounds created by loss, and fully experiencing the pain ultimately provides wonderful relief to those who suffer while eliminating long-term chronic grief.

Assume New Social Roles

The third task, practical in nature, requires the griever to take on some of the social roles performed by the deceased person or to find others who will. According to Worden (1982), to abort this task is to become helpless by refusing to develop the skills necessary in daily living and by ultimately withdrawing from life.

An acquaintance of Michael Leming's refused to adjust to the social environment in which she found herself after the death of her husband. He was her business partner, as well as her best and only friend. After 30 years of marriage, they had no children, and she had no close relatives. She had never learned to drive a car. Her entire social world had been controlled by her former husband. Three weeks after his funeral she went into the basement and committed suicide.

The alternative to withdrawing is assuming new social roles by taking on additional responsibilities. Extended families who always gathered at Grandma's house for Thanksgiving will be tempted to have a number of small Thanksgiving dinners at different places after her death. The members of this family may believe that "no one can take Grandma's place." Although this may be true, members of the extended family will grieve better if someone else is willing to do Grandma's work, enabling the entire family to come together for Thanksgiving. Not to do so will cause double pain—the family will not gather, and Grandma will still be missed.

Reinvest in New Relationships

The final task of mourning is a difficult one for many because they feel disloyal or unfaithful in withdrawing emotional energy from their dead loved one. One of Michael Leming's family members once said that she could never love another man after her husband died. His twice-widowed aunt responded, "I once felt like that, but I now consider myself to be fortunate to have been married to two of the best men in the world."

Other people find themselves unable to reinvest in new relationships because they are unwilling to experience again the pain caused by loss. The quotation from John Brantner at the beginning of this chapter provides perspective on this problem: "Only people who avoid love can avoid grief. The point is to learn from it and remain vulnerable to love."

However, those who are able to withdraw emotional energy and reinvest it in other relationships find the possibility of a newly established social life. Kavanaugh (1972, pp. 122–123) depicts this situation well with the following description:

At this point fantasies fade into constructive efforts to reach out and build anew. The phone is answered more quickly, the door as well, and meetings seem important, invitations are treasured and any social gathering becomes an opportunity rather than a curse. Mementos of the past are put away for occasional family gatherings. New clothes and new places promise dreams instead of only fears. Old friends are important for encouragement and permission to rebuild one's life. New friends can offer realistic opportunities for coming out from under the grieving mantle. With newly acquired friends, one is not a widow, widower, or survivor—just a person. Life begins again at the point of new friendships. All the rest is of yesterday, buried, unimportant to the now and tomorrow.

Disenfranchised Grief

KENNETH J. DOKA

Introduction

Ever since the publication of Lindemann's classic article, "Symptomatology and Management of Acute Grief," the literature on the nature of grief and bereavement has been growing. In the few decades following this seminal study, there have been comprehensive studies of grief reactions, detailed descriptions of atypical manifestations of grief, theoretical and clinical treatments of grief reactions, and considerable research considering the myriad variables that affect grief. But most of this literature has concentrated on grief reactions in socially recognized and sanctioned roles: those of the parent, spouse, or child.

There are circumstances, however, in which a person experiences a sense of loss but does not have a socially recognized right, role, or capacity to grieve. In these cases, the grief is disenfranchised. The person suffers a loss but has little or no opportunity to mourn publicly.

Up until now, there has been little research touching directly on the phenomenon of disenfranchised grief. In her comprehensive review of grief reactions, Raphael notes the phenomenon:

> There may be other dyadic partnership relationships in adult life that show patterns similar to the conjugal ones, among them, the young couple intensely, even secretly, in love; the defacto relationships; the extramarital relationship; and the homosexual couple. . . . Less intimate partnerships of close friends, working mates, and business associates, may have similar patterns of grief and mourning.

Focusing on the issues, reactions, and problems in particular populations, a number of studies have noted special difficulties that these populations have in grieving. For example, Kelly and Kimmel, in studies of aging homosexuals, have discussed the unique problems of grief in such relationships. Similarly, studies of the reactions of significant others of AIDS victims have considered bereavement. Other studies have considered the special problems of unacknowledged grief in prenatal death, [the death of] ex-spouses, therapists' reactions to a client's suicide, and pet loss. Finally, studies of families of Alzheimer's victims and mentally retarded adults also have noted distinct difficulties of these populations in encountering varied losses which are often unrecognized by others.

Others have tried to draw parallels between related unacknowledged losses. For example, in a personal account, Horn compared her loss of a heterosexual lover with a friend's loss of a homosexual partner. Doka discussed the particular problems of loss in nontraditional relationships, such as extramarital affairs, homosexual relationships, and cohabiting couples.

This article attempts to integrate the literature on such losses in order to explore the phenomenon of disenfranchised grief. It will consider both the nature of disenfranchised grief and its central paradoxical problem: the very nature of this type of grief exacerbates the problems of grief, but the usual sources of support may not be available or helpful.

The Nature of Disenfranchised Grief

Disenfranchised grief can be defined as the grief that persons experience when they incur a loss that is not or cannot be openly acknowledged, publicly mourned, or socially supported. The concept of disenfranchised grief recognizes that societies have sets of norms—in effect, "grieving rules"—that attempt to specify who, when, where, how, how long, and for whom people should grieve. These grieving rules may be codified in personnel policies. For example, a worker may be allowed a week off for the death of a spouse or child, three days for the loss of a parent or sibling. Such policies reflect the fact that each society defines who has a legitimate right to grieve, and these definitions of right correspond to relationships, primarily familial, that are socially recognized and sanctioned. In any given society these grieving rules may not correspond to the nature of attachments, the sense of loss, or the feelings of survivors. Hence the grief of these survivors is disenfranchised. In our society, this may occur for three reasons.

1. The Relationship Is Not Recognized

In our society, most attention is placed on kin-based relationships and roles. Grief may be disenfranchised in those situations in which the relationship between the bereaved and deceased is not based on recognizable kin ties. Here the closeness of other non-kin relationships may simply not be understood or appreciated. For example, Folta and Deck noted, "While all of these studies tell us that grief is a normal phenomenon, the intensity of which corresponds to the closeness of the relationship, they fail to take this (i.e., friendship) into account. The underlying assumption is that closeness of relationship exists only among spouses and/or immediate kin." The roles of lovers, friends, neighbors, foster parents, colleagues, in-laws, stepparents and stepchildren, caregivers, counselors, co-workers, and room-mates (for example, in nursing homes) may be long-lasting and intensely interactive, but even though these relationships are recognized, mourners may not have full opportunity to publicly grieve a loss. At most, they might be expected to support and assist family members.

Then there are relationships that may not be publicly rec-ognized or socially sanctioned. For example, nontraditional relationships, such as extramarital affairs, cohabitation, and homosexual relationships have tenuous public acceptance and limited legal standing, and they face negative sanctions within the larger community. Those involved in such relationships are touched by grief when the relationship is terminated by the death of the partner, but others in their world, such as children, may also experience grief that cannot be acknowledged or socially supported.

Even those whose relationships existed primarily in the past may experience grief. Ex-spouses, past lovers, or former friends may have limited contact, or they may not even engage in inter-action in the present. Yet the death of that significant other can still cause a grief reaction because it brings finality to that earlier loss, ending any remaining contact or fantasy of reconciliation or reinvolvement. And again these grief feelings may be shared by others in their world such as parents and children. They too may mourn the loss of "what once was" and "what might have been." For example, in one case a twelve-year-old child of an unwed mother, never even acknowledged or seen by the father, still mourned the death of his father since it ended any possibil-ity of a future liaison. But though loss is experienced, society as a whole may not perceive that the loss of a past relationship could or should cause any reaction.

2. The Loss Is Not Recognized

In other cases, the loss itself is not socially defined as signifi-cant. Perinatal deaths lead to strong grief reactions, yet research indicates that many significant others still perceive the loss to be relatively minor. Abortions too can constitute a serious loss, but the abortion can take place without the knowledge or sanc-tions of others, or even the recognition that a loss has occurred. It may very well be that the very ideologies of the abortion con-troversy can put the bereaved in a difficult position. Many who affirm a loss may not sanction the act of abortion, while some who sanction the act may minimize any sense of loss. Similarly, we are just becoming aware of the sense of loss that people experience in giving children up for adoption or foster care, and we have yet to be aware of the grief-related implications of surrogate motherhood.

Another loss that may not be perceived as significant is the loss of a pet. Nevertheless, the research shows strong ties between pets and humans, and profound reactions to loss.

Then there are cases in which the reality of the loss itself is not socially validated. Thanatologists have long recognized that significant losses can occur even when the object of the loss remains physically alive. Sudnow for example, discusses "social death," in which the person is alive but is treated as if dead. Examples may include those who are institutionalized or

comatose. Similarly, "psychological death" has been defined as conditions in which the person lacks a consciousness of exis-tence, such as someone who is "brain dead." One can also speak of "psychosocial death" in which the persona of someone has changed so significantly, through mental illness, organic brain syndromes, or even significant personal transformation (such as through addiction, conversion, and so forth), that signifi-cant others perceive the person as he or she previously existed as dead. In all of these cases, spouses and others may experi-ence a profound sense of loss, but that loss cannot be publicly acknowledged for the person is still biologically alive.

3. The Griever Is Not Recognized

Finally, there are situations in which the characteristics of the bereaved in effect disenfranchise their grief. Here the person is not socially defined as capable of grief; therefore, there is little or no social recognition of his or her sense of loss or need to mourn. Despite evidence to the contrary, both the very old and the very young are typically perceived by others as having little comprehension of or reaction to the death of a significant other. Often, then, both young children and aged adults are excluded from both discussions and rituals.

Similarly, mentally disabled persons may also be disen-franchised in grief. Although studies affirm that the mentally retarded are able to understand the concept of death and, in fact, experience grief, these reactions may not be perceived by others. Because the person is retarded or otherwise mentally disabled, others in the family may ignore his or her need to grieve. Here a teacher of the mentally disabled describes two illustrative incidences:

> In the first situation, Susie was 17 years old and away at summer camp when her father died. The family felt she wouldn't understand and that it would be better for her not to come home for the funeral. In the other situation, Francine was with her mother when she got sick. The mother was taken away by ambulance. Nobody answered her questions or told her what happened. "After all," they responded, "she's retarded."

The Special Problems of Disenfranchised Grief

Though each of the types of grief mentioned earlier may cre-ate particular difficulties and different reactions, one can legiti-mately speak of the special problem shared in disenfranchised grief.

The problem of disenfranchised grief can be expressed in a paradox. The very nature of disenfranchised grief creates additional problems for grief, while removing or minimizing sources of support.

Disenfranchising grief may exacerbate the problem of bereavement in a number of ways. First, the situations mentioned tend to intensify emotional reactions. Many emotions are asso-ciated with normal grief. Bereaved persons frequently experi-ence feelings of anger, guilt, sadness and depression, loneliness, hopelessness, and numbness. These emotional reactions can be complicated when grief is disenfranchised. Although each of the situations described is in its own way unique, the literature uniformly reports how each of these disenfranchising circumstances can intensify feelings of anger, guilt, or powerlessness.

Second, both ambivalent relationships and concurrent crises have been identified in the literature as conditions that complicate grief. These conditions can often exist in many types of disenfranchised grief. For example, studies have indicated the ambivalence that can exist in cases of abortion, among ex-spouses, significant others in nontraditional roles, and among families of Alzheimer's disease victims. Similarly, the literature documents the many kinds of concurrent crises that can trouble the disenfranchised griever. For example, in cases of cohabiting couples, either heterosexual or homosexual, studies have often found that survivors experience legal and financial problems regarding inheritance, ownership, credit, or leases. Likewise, the death of a parent may leave a mentally disabled person not only bereaved but also bereft of a viable support system.

Although grief is complicated, many of the factors that facilitate mourning are not present. The bereaved may be excluded from an active role in caring for the dying. Funeral rituals, normally helpful in resolving grief, may not help here. In some cases the bereaved may be excluded from attendance. In other cases they may have no role in planning those rituals or in deciding whether even to have them. Or in cases of divorce, separation, or psychosocial death, rituals may be lacking altogether.

In addition, the very nature of the disenfranchised grief precludes social support. Often there is no recognized role in which mourners can assert the right to mourn and thus receive such support. Grief may have to remain private. Though they may have experienced an intense loss, they may not be given time off from work, have the opportunity to verbalize the loss, or receive the expressions of sympathy and support characteristic in a death. Even traditional sources of solace, such as religion, are unavailable to those whose relationships (for example, extramarital, cohabiting, homosexual, divorced) or acts (such as abortion) are condemned within that tradition.

Naturally, there are many variables that will affect both the intensity of the reaction and the availability of support. All the variables—interpersonal, psychological, social, physiological—that normally influence grief will have an impact here as well. And while there are problems common to cases of disenfranchised grief, each relationship has to be individually considered in light of the unique combinations of factors that may facilitate or impair grief resolution.

Implications

Despite the shortage of research on and attention given to the issue of disenfranchised grief, it remains a significant issue. Millions of Americans are involved in losses in which grief is effectively disenfranchised. For example, there are more than 1 million couples presently cohabiting. There are estimates that 3 percent of males and 2–3 percent of females are exclusively

homosexual, with similar percentages having mixed homosexual and heterosexual encounters. There are about a million abortions a year; even though many of the women involved may not experience grief reactions, some are clearly "at risk."

Disenfranchised grief is also a growing issue. There are higher percentages of divorced people in the cohorts now aging. The AIDS crisis means that more homosexuals will experience losses in significant relationships. Even as the disease spreads within the population of intravenous drug users, it is likely to create a new class of both potential victims and disenfranchised grievers among the victims' informal liaisons and nontraditional relationships. And as Americans continue to live longer, more will suffer from severe forms of chronic brain dysfunctions. As the developmentally disabled live longer, they too will experience the grief of parental and sibling loss. In short, the proportion of disenfranchised grievers in the general population will rise rapidly in the future.

It is likely that bereavement counselors will have increased exposure to cases of disenfranchised grief. In fact, the very nature of disenfranchised grief and the unavailability of informal support make it likely that those who experience such losses will seek formal supports. Thus there is a pressing need for research that will describe the particular and unique reactions of each of the different types of losses; compare reactions and problems associated with these losses; describe the important variables affecting disenfranchised grief reactions; assess possible interventions; and discover the atypical grief reactions, such as masked or delayed grief, that might be manifested in such cases. Also needed is education sensitizing students to the many kinds of relationships and subsequent losses that people can experience and affirming that where there is loss there is grief.

KEN DOKA, PhD, is a professor of gerontology at the College of New Rochelle in New York. He became interested in the study of death and dying quite inadvertently. Scheduled to do a practicum in a facility that housed juvenile delinquents, he discovered that his supervisor had changed the assignment. Instead, Doka found himself counseling dying children and their families at Sloan-Kettering, a major cancer hospital in New York. This experience became the basis of two graduate theses, one in sociology entitled "The Social Organization of Terminal Care in Two Pediatric Hospitals," and the other in religious studies entitled "Pastoral Counseling to Dying Children and Their Families." (Both were later published.) His doctoral program pursued another long-standing interest: the sociology of aging. In 1983, Dr. Doka accepted his present position at the College of New Rochelle where he specializes in thanatology and gerontology.

Active in the Association for Death Education and Counseling since its beginnings, Dr. Doka was elected its president in 1993. In addition to articles in scholarly journals, he is the author of *Death and Spirituality* (with John Morgan, 1993), *Living with Life-Threatening Illness* (1993) and *Disenfranchised Grief: Recognizing Hidden Sorrow* (1989), from which the following selection is excerpted. His work on disenfranchised grief began in the classroom when a graduate student commented, "If you think widows have it rough, you ought to see what happens when your ex-spouse dies."

From *Disenfranchised Grief: Recognizing Hidden Sorrow*, Lexington Books, 1989, pp. 3–11. Copyright © 1989 by Kenneth J. Doka. Reprinted by permission of the author.

Enhancing the Concept of Disenfranchised Grief

Doka (1989a, p. 4) defined disenfranchised grief as "the grief that persons experience when they incur a loss that is not or cannot be openly acknowledged, publicly mourned, or socially supported." He suggested that disenfranchisement can apply to unrecognized relationships, losses, or grievers, as well as to certain types of deaths.

This article contends that disenfranchisement in bereavement may have a potentially broader scope than has been hitherto recognized. That claim is defended by exploring further the implications of disenfranchisement and by suggesting ways in which certain understandings or misunderstandings of the dynamic qualities of grief, mourning, and their outcomes may be open to disenfranchisement or may participate in disenfranchisement.

The aims of this argument are to enhance the concept of disenfranchised grief in itself and to deepen appreciation of the full range of all that is or can be experienced in bereavement.

CHARLES A. CORR, PHD

In 1989 Doka (1989a) first proposed the concept of "disenfranchised grief." His suggestion had an immediate appeal to many and the concept of disenfranchised grief has since been widely accepted by practitioners, educators, and researchers in the field of death, dying, and bereavement. In particular, it has been applied in ways that seek to elucidate and validate the experiences of a broad range of bereaved persons.

In his initial proposal, Doka described the concept of disenfranchised grief, identified those aspects of the grief experience that he understood to have been subject to disenfranchisement, provided examples of many ways in which disenfranchisement has occurred, and indicated why attention should be paid to the concept of disenfranchised grief. This article seeks to enhance understanding of the concept of disenfranchised grief and by so doing to deepen appreciation of the full range of all that is or can be experienced in bereavement. The present analysis begins with a review of Doka's original description of the concept of disenfranchised grief. Thereafter, the inquiry is guided by two primary questions: 1) What exactly is meant by the disenfranchisement of grief?; and 2) What is or can be disenfranchised in grief? Responding to these questions may help to enrich understanding of Doka's seminal concept in particular, and of bereavement in general. On that basis, it may also be possible for helpers to identify better ways in which to assist grievers of all types, especially those whose experiences have been disenfranchised.

Disenfranchised Grief: The Original Concept

In his original work, Doka (1989a, p. 4) defined "disenfranchised grief" as "the grief that persons experience when they incur a loss that is not or cannot be openly acknowledged, publicly mourned, or socially supported." In addition, he suggested that grief can be disenfranchised in three primary ways: 1) the relationship is not recognized, 2) the loss is not recognized; or 3) the griever is not recognized. Some comments on each of these three types of disenfranchisement may help to clarify Doka's original proposal.

Disenfranchised Relationships

Why don't you just stop crying and grieving for that person who died. He wasn't even close to you.

I just don't see why you should be so upset over the death of your ex-husband. He was a bum, you hated him, and you got rid of him years ago. Why cry over his being gone for good?

With respect to a *relationship* that is disenfranchised, Folta and Deck (1976, p. 235) have noted that "the underlying assumption is that the 'closeness of relationship' exists only among spouses and/or immediate kin." Unsuspected, past, or secret relationships may simply not be publicly recognized or socially sanctioned. Disenfranchised relationships can include associations which are well-accepted in theory but not appreciated in practice or in particular instances, such as those between friends, colleagues, in-laws, ex-spouses, or former lovers. Disenfranchised relationships may also include nontraditional liaisons such as those involving extra-marital affairs and homosexual relationships. In referring to these as instances of disenfranchised grief, the implication is that such relationships have often been or may be deemed by society to be an insufficient or inappropriate foundation for grief.

Disenfranchised Losses

Why do you keep on moaning over your miscarriage? It wasn't really a baby yet. And you already have four children. You could even have more if you want to.

Stop crying over that dead cat! He was just an animal. I bet that cat wouldn't have been upset if you had been the one to die. If you stop crying. I'll buy you a new kitten.

In the case of a *loss* which is disenfranchised, the focus of the disenfranchisement appears to arise from a failure or unwillingness on the part of society to recognize that certain types of events do involve real losses. For example, until quite recently and perhaps still today in many segments of society, perinatal deaths, losses associated with elective abortion, or losses of body parts have been disenfranchised. Similarly, the death of a pet is often unappreciated by those outside the relationship. And society is only beginning to learn about grief which occurs when dementia blots out an individual's personality in such a way or to such a degree that significant others perceive the person to be psychosocially dead, even though biological life continues. As one husband said of his spouse with advanced Alzheimer's disease, "I am medically separated from my wife—even though she is still alive and we are not divorced." To say that loss arising from a "medical separation" of this type is disenfranchised is to note that society does not acknowledge it to be sufficient to justify grief—or at least not sufficient to justify grief of the type that society associates with a physical death.

Disenfranchised Grievers

I don't know why that old guy in Room 203 keeps moaning and whimpering about the death of his loud-mouthed daughter who used to visit him every week.

With his poor memory and other mental problems, he hardly even knew when his daughter came to visit anyway.

I told Johnnie he should grow up, be a man, and stop whining about his grandfather's death. He's too young to really remember much about his grandfather or even to understand what death really means.

In the case of a disenfranchised *griever,* disenfranchisement mainly has to do with certain individuals to whom the socially-recognized status of griever is not attached. For example, it is often asserted or at least suggested that young children, the very old, and those who are mentally disabled are either incapable

of grief or are individuals who do not have a need to grieve. In this case, disenfranchisement applies not to a relationship or to a loss, but to the individual survivor whose status as a leading actor or protagonist in the human drama of bereavement is not recognized or appreciated.

Disenfranchising Deaths

That teenager who killed himself must not have had all his marbles. His family is probably all screwed up, too. Don't be sorry for them. Just stay away from them.

It's just too bad that actor died of AIDS. God punished him for having all that sex. And now his boyfriends will probably wind up with all his money. They sure don't need us to feel sorry for them.

In his original concept, Doka (1989a) added that some types of deaths in themselves may be "disenfranchising." He offered as examples deaths involving suicide or AIDS. The point seems to have been that our society is repelled or turns away from certain types of death, mainly because their complexities are not well understood or because they are associated with a high degree of social stigma. As a result, the character of the death seems to disenfranchise what otherwise might have been expected to follow in its aftermath. But not all societies at all points in time would or have disenfranchised deaths associated with suicide or AIDS. In other words, what is disenfranchised in one social context may not be disenfranchised in another social context. This clearly recalls Doka's fundamental point that disenfranchised grief is always founded on a specific society's attitudes and values.

Why Pay Attention to Disenfranchised Grief?

The purpose of drawing attention to the meaning of disenfranchised grief and to the ways in which it can be implemented can be seen in Doka's (1989a, p. 7) observation that, "The very nature of disenfranchised grief creates additional problems of grief, while removing or minimizing sources of support." Additional problems arise that go beyond the usual difficulties in grief because disenfranchised grief typically involves intensified emotional reactions (for example, anger, guilt, or powerlessness), ambivalent relationships (as in some cases of abortion or some associations between ex-spouses), and concurrent crises (such as those involving legal and financial problems). In circumstances of disenfranchised grief there is an absence of customary sources of support because society's attitudes make unavailable factors that usually facilitate mourning (for instance, the existence of funeral rituals or possibilities for helping to take part in such rituals) and opportunities to obtain assistance from others (for example, by speaking about the loss, receiving expressions of sympathy, taking time off from work, or finding solace within a religious tradition).

Clearly, issues associated with disenfranchised grief deserve attention. They indicate that social outlooks often embody a judgmental element (whether explicitly articulated or not) and the short-term concerns of the group when dealing with some bereaved persons. That is, societies which disenfranchise grief appear to act on specific values or principles at the expense of an overarching interest in the welfare of all of their members. In these ways, disenfranchised grief can be seen to be an important phenomenon. It is also a phenomenon that is lived out in different ways in different societies, easily observed by those who pay attention to social practices, and hurtful to individual members of society if not to society itself. For all of these reasons, it is worth exploring further what is meant by saying that some grief is disenfranchised and what is or can be disenfranchised in grief.

What Is Meant by Saying That Some Grief Is Disenfranchised?

As has been noted, grief always occurs within a particular social or cultural context. The concept of disenfranchised grief recognizes that in various spoken and unspoken ways social and cultural communities may deny recognition, legitimation, or support to the grief experienced by individuals, families, and small groups.

It is important to recognize that the grief under discussion here is not merely silent, unnoticed, or forgotten. Any griever may keep silent about or decide not to reveal to the larger society the fact of his or her grief, or some of its specific aspects. Failing to disclose or communicate to others what one is experiencing in grief does not of itself mean that such grief is or would be disenfranchised. Society might be fully prepared to recognize, legitimize, and support grief that an individual, for whatever reason, holds in privacy and does not share.

Further, even when an individual is willing to share his or her grief, some grief experiences may still go unnoticed or be forgotten by society. Thus, Gyulay (1975) wrote of grandparents following the death of a grandchild as "forgotten grievers." She meant that all too often attention associated with the death of a child is focused on the child's parents or siblings to the exclusion of grandparents. In fact, however, bereaved grandparents often find themselves grieving both the death of their grandchild and the loss experienced by an adult who is simultaneously their own child (or son/daughter-in-law) and the child's parent (Hamilton, 1978). Typically, when this two-fold grief of grandparents is brought to the attention of members of society, it is not disenfranchised but acknowledged and respected.

In short, the concept of disenfranchised grief goes beyond the situation of mere unawareness of grief to suggest a more or less active process of disavowal, renunciation, and rejection. Not surprisingly, the word "disenfranchise" takes its origin from the term "enfranchise," which has two basic historical meanings: 1) "To admit to freedom, set free (a slave or serf)"; and 2) "To admit to municipal or political privileges" (*Oxford English Dictionary*, 1989, Vol. 5, p. 246). In the most familiar sense of this term, to enfranchise is to set an individual free from his or her prior condition by admitting that person to the electoral franchise or granting permission to vote for representatives in a government. Disenfranchisement applies to those who are not accorded a social franchise extended by society to individuals who are admitted to full participation in the community.

A more contemporary meaning of enfranchisement is to be granted a franchise or license to offer for sale locally some national or international product or service. For example, one might purchase or be awarded a franchise to sell a certain brand of fast food or automobile, or to advertise one's local motel as a member of a national chain of motels. Often one has to earn or somehow pay for the use of a franchise, and there may also be obligations to uphold certain service standards or to deliver a product of a certain type in a certain way. When the use of a franchise has not been earned or implemented properly, it may come into dispute or even be withdrawn by those in authority. In all of these examples, it is the permission to behave in a certain way (to vote, to act as a franchisee or agent of a franchise holder) that is central to both enfranchisement and disenfranchisement.

In the case of bereavement, enfranchisement applies in particular to those who are recognized by society as grievers. These are individuals who are free to acknowledge their losses openly, mourn those losses publicly, and receive support from others—at least within that society's accepted limits. Disenfranchised grief goes beyond the boundaries of what is regarded as socially accepted grief. It is therefore denied the legitimacy and freedom that comes with social sanction and approval (Doka, 1989b; Pine et al., 1990).

What Is or Can Be Disenfranchised in Grief?
Bereavement

Doka is clearly correct in recognizing that disenfranchisement can apply to relationships, losses, and grievers. These are, in fact, the three key *structural elements* that define the meaning of the term "bereavement." Thus, what Doka has really defined is "disenfranchised bereavement." For that reason, it may help to begin our exploration of how disenfranchisement applies to grief by reminding ourselves of how we understand the root concept of bereavement.

The word "bereavement" is widely understood to designate the objective situation of one who has experienced a significant loss. If there were no significant person or object to which an individual was attached, there would be no bereavement. For example, when a parent threatens to take away from a child a much-disliked serving of spinach as a "punishment" for the child's refusal to clean his or her plate at dinner, the child is not likely to experience a loss or to grieve. Further, if the object were a significant one to the child, but the child perceived (as a result of previous parental behavior patterns) that the threatened loss would not come about in fact, again there would be no bereavement or grief. Finally, if there were no individual to grieve a loss—as when someone threatens to or actually does take away a significant object, but the threat and the loss are not effectively communicated to the individual to whom they would presumably have been directed—again there is no bereavement or grief. A griever is effectively absent when the threat is merely an empty gesture made in his or her absence or when, for some other reason, there is no awareness or experience of a significant loss—as during the period between the death of a loved one in a far-off land and the communication of that fact to the survivor.

In short, the noun "bereavement" and the adjective "bereaved" only apply to situations and individuals in which there exists an experience such that one believes oneself to have been deprived of some important person or object. Both "bereavement" and "bereaved" (there is no present participial form, "bereaving," in standard English today) are words that derive from a verb not often used today in colloquial English. That word is "reave"; it means "to despoil, rob, or forcibly deprive" (*Oxford English Dictionary,* 1989, Vol. 13, p. 295). In short, a bereaved person is one who has been deprived, robbed, plundered, or stripped of something. This indicates that the stolen person or object was a valued one, and suggests that the deprivation has harmed or done violence to the bereaved person. In our society, all too many bereaved persons can testify that dismissal or minimization of the importance of their losses are familiar components of the experience of survivors, with or without added burdens arising from disenfranchisement.

We could explore further each of the central elements identified by Doka in describing his concept of disenfranchised grief. Such an exploration might produce: 1) a rich and varied portrait of the many types of *relationships* in which humans participate, including those fundamental relationships called "attachments" which serve to satisfy the basic needs of human beings; 2) a panorama of *losses* which may affect relationships involving human beings—some permanent, others temporary, some final, others reversible; and/or 3) a list of many different types of *grievers.* If we did this, it would become apparent (among other things) that loss by death is but one category of loss, and that certain types or modes of death are more likely to be disenfranchised than others. And we might also learn that while disenfranchising the bereaved involves costs of different types for individuals and societies themselves, enfranchising the disenfranchised might also involve costs of other types (Davidowitz & Myrick, 1984; Kamerman, 1993).

All of the above are ways to enrich appreciation of the concept of disenfranchised grief. Most involve simply accepting the conceptual scheme as it was originally proposed by Doka and applying it to specific types of relationships, losses, and grievers. Applications of this type have been prominent in written reports and conference presentations in recent years (e.g., Becker, 1997; Kaczmarek & Backlund, 1991; Schwebach & Thornton, 1992; Thornton, Robertson, & Mlecko, 1991; Zupanick, 1994).

In this article, it seems more useful to try to enhance or enlarge the concept of disenfranchised grief by examining it critically in relationship to the *dynamic components* of the bereavement experience, especially as it is related to grief, mourning, and their outcomes.

Grief

Stop feeling that way! You'll be better off if you just pack up all those bad feelings and throw them away with the garbage.

In reactions to being "reaved" or to perceiving themselves as having been "reaved," those who have suffered that experience typically react to what has happened to them. In normal circumstances, one would be surprised if they did not do so. Failure to react would seem to imply that the lost person or object was actually not much prized by the bereaved individual, that the survivor is unaware of his or her loss, or that other factors intervene. "Grief" is the reaction to loss. The term arises from the grave or heavy weight that presses on persons who are burdened by loss (*Oxford English Dictionary,* 1989, Vol. 6, pp. 834–835).

Reactions to loss are disenfranchised when they—in whole or in part; in themselves or in their expression—are not recognized, legitimated, or supported by society. How many times have grieving persons been told: "Don't feel that way"; "Try not to think those thoughts"; "Don't say those things (about God, or the doctor, or the person who caused the death)"; "You shouldn't act like that just because someone you loved died." Sometimes any reaction is judged to be inappropriate; in other circumstances, some reactions are accepted while others are rejected. In some cases, it is the existence of the reaction that is disenfranchised; in other examples, it is only the expression of the reaction that meets with disapproval. Through what amounts to a kind of "oppressive toleration" society often presses a griever to hold private his or her grief reaction in order not to trouble or disturb others by bringing it out into the open or expressing it in certain ways. The effect of any or all of these practices is to disenfranchise either some aspects of the grief or some modes in which they are manifested.

Grief as Emotions?

I can understand why you're feeling upset about your mother's death. You can be sad if you want to. But you've got to start eating again and getting a good night's sleep.

My co-worker used to be a such a great guy. But ever since his younger sister died, he comes to work and sometimes it's like he's wandering around in a fog and not concentrating on the job. I told him today that he needs to pull himself together and get focused on his work again.

My friend was always such a cheery person at the Senior Citizen's Center. But ever since her grandchild died, she keeps asking all those difficult questions about why God let such a bad thing happen to an innocent child. I told her that it was OK to be sad, but she just had to accept God's will and stop questioning it.

In each of these examples, feelings of grief are legitimized but other aspects of the grief reaction are disenfranchised. One might also argue that something very much like this form of disenfranchisement can be found in much of the professional literature on bereavement. For example, quite often grief is described or defined as "the emotional reaction to loss." On its face, a definition of this type is at once both obvious and inadequate. Clearly, bereaved persons may or do react emotionally to loss; equally so, they may not or do not merely react emotionally to loss. Careless, unintentional, or deliberate restriction of the meaning of grief to its emotional components is

146

an unrecognized form of disenfranchisement of the full grief experience.

In this connection, Elias (1991) reminded readers that, "Broadly speaking, emotions have three components, a somatic, a behavioral and a feeling component" (p. 177). As a result, "the term *emotion,* even in professional discussions, is used with two different meanings. It is used in a wider and in a narrower sense at the same time. In the wider sense the term *emotion* is applied to a reaction pattern which involves the whole organism in its somatic, its feeling and its behavioral aspects. . . . In its narrower sense the term *emotion* refers to the feeling component of the syndrome only" (Elias, 1991, p. 119).

The importance of feelings in the overall grief reaction to loss is undeniable. Equally undeniable is the importance of other aspects of the grief reaction. These include somatic or physical sensations and behaviors or behavioral disturbances, as Elias has indicated, as well as matters involving cognitive, social, and spiritual functioning. Establishing a comprehensive list of all of these aspects of the grief reaction to loss is not of primary importance here. What is central is the recognition that human beings may and indeed are likely to react to important losses in their lives with their whole selves, not just with some narrowly defined aspect of their humanity. Failure to describe grief in a holistic way dismisses and devalues its richness and breadth.

Grief as Symptoms?

As a psychiatrist and her son-in-law, I tried to talk to your mother about your father's death. She refused and got upset after I told her that her unwillingness to discuss with me her reactions to the death was a classic symptom of pathological grief. She said she had talked to her sister and just didn't want to talk to you or me or her other children about it.

Sadness and crying are two of the main symptoms of grief. Whenever we identify them, we should refer the individual for therapy.

Another form of depicting or categorizing grief in a limiting and negative way involves the use of the language of *symptoms* to designate both complicated and uncomplicated grief. In principal, grief is a natural and healthy reaction to loss. There can be unhealthy reactions to loss. One of these would be a failure to react in any way to the loss of a significant person or object in our lives. However, most grief reactions are not complicated or unhealthy. They are appropriate reactions to the loss one has experienced. In cases of uncomplicated grief—which constitute the vast majority of all bereavement experiences—we ought to speak of signs, or manifestations, or expressions of grief. And we ought to avoid the term "symptoms" in relationship to grief, unless we consciously intend to use the language of illness to indicate some form of aberrant or unhealthy reaction to loss. When we use the language of symptoms to describe all expressions of grief, we have pathologized grief and invalidated or disenfranchised its fundamental soundness as the human reaction to loss.

Mourning

OK, we've had our grief ever since Kerri died. Now that the funeral is over, that's it. There's nothing more we can do and nothing more we need to do. So, let's just put all this behind us and forget it.

Many aspects of what is called grief in bereavement are essentially reactive. They seek to push away the hurt of the loss with denial, or turn back upon it with anger, or reply to its implacability with sadness. Much of this is like a defensive reflex. But there is more to most bereavement experiences than this. The other central element in a healthy bereavement experience is in the effort to find some way to live with the loss, with our grief reactions to that loss, and with the new challenges that are associated with the loss. As Weisman (1984, p. 36) observed, coping "is positive in approach; defending is negative." In brief, coping identifies the efforts that we make to manage perceived stressors in our lives (Lazarus & Folkman, 1984). In the vocabulary of bereavement, this is "mourning"—the attempt to manage or learn to live with one's bereavement. Through mourning grievers endeavor to incorporate their losses and grief into healthy ongoing living.

If we fail to distinguish between grief and mourning in appropriate ways, we run the risk of ignoring the differences between reacting and coping, between seeking to defend or push away our loss and grief, and attempting to embrace those experiences and incorporate them into our lives. This is another form of disenfranchisement insofar as it blurs distinctions between two central aspects of bereavement, misconceives what is involved in mourning an important loss, and refuses to acknowledge and support both grief and mourning.

At the simplest level, the efforts that one makes to cope with loss and grief in mourning are frequently not understood for what they are and thus are not valued by society. For example, a griever will be told not to go over the details of the accident again and again, as if such filling in of the stark outlines of a death is not an essential part of the process of *realization* or making real in one's internal, psychic world what is already real in the external, objective world (Parkes, 1996). Another familiar way of disenfranchising mourning occurs when a bereaved person is advised that the proper way to manage a loss is simply to "put it behind you" or "get beyond it." This assumes that one can simply hop over a stressful event in life, ignore the unwelcome interruption, and go on living without being affected by what has happened. Sometimes, bereaved survivors are even counseled to "forget" the deceased person as if he or she had not been a significant part of their lives. None of these are appropriate elements in constructive mourning.

Note that mourning is a present-tense, participial word. As such, it indicates action or activities of the type expressed by verbs. In the language of nouns, this is "grief work" (a phrase first coined by Lindemann in 1944). Lindemann understood "grief work" in a specific way, but the central point is that the grief work at the heart of mourning is an active, effortful attempt to manage what bereavement has brought into one's life (Attig, 1991, 1996).

Moreover, since the consequences of bereavement typically include both primary and secondary losses, as well as grief and new challenges, there is much to cope with in the whole of one's mourning. Indeed, contrasting loss and grief with the new challenges of bereavement could be said to require an oscillation between "loss-oriented" and "restoration-oriented" processes in mourning (Stroebe & Schut, 1995).

In other words, in his or her mourning a bereaved person is faced with the tasks of integrating into his or her life three major elements: 1) the primary and secondary losses that he or she has experienced, 2) the grief reactions provoked by those losses; and 3) the new challenges involved in living without the deceased person. For example, if my spouse should die I would be obliged to mourn or try to learn to live in healthy ways with her loss (the fact that she has been taken away from me constituting my primary loss), with the secondary losses associated with her death (e.g., being deprived of her company or being without her guidance in some practical matters), with my grief reactions to those losses (e.g., my anger over what has been done to me or my sadness at the apparent barrenness of the life that is now left to me), and with my new situation in life (e.g., after years of marriage I may be unclear how to function as a newfound single person). If any aspect of my losses, grief, or new challenges is disenfranchised, then my efforts to mourn or cope with those aspects of my bereavement will also be disenfranchised.

Mourning: Interpersonal and Intrapersonal Dimensions

Because each human being is both a particular individual and a social creature or a member of a community, mourning has two complementary forms or aspects. It is both an outward, public, or *interpersonal* process—the overt, visible, and characteristically shared public efforts to cope with or manage loss and associated grief reactions—and an internal, private, or *intrapersonal* process—an individual's inward struggles to cope with or manage loss and the grief reactions to that loss. Each of these dimensions of mourning deserves recognition and respect. Much of what has already been noted here about mourning applies to its intrapersonal dimensions, but disenfranchisement is also frequently associated with the interpersonal aspects of mourning.

Interpersonal Dimensions of Mourning

Don't keep on talking about how he died. It's not going to make any difference or bring him back. Nobody wants to be around you when you keep going on about it.

What's the point of having a funeral, anyhow? Couldn't they just bury their child privately and leave us out of it? I don't want to get dragged into it.

Many people in contemporary society are unwilling to take part in the public or *interpersonal* rituals of mourning. Some of this has to do with a certain weakness or shallowness in many interpersonal relationships in contemporary society and a loosening of the bonds that formerly bound together families, neighbors, church groups, and other small communities. But it also appears to be linked to a discomfort with public ritual and open expression of strong feelings. Good funeral and memorial rituals are essentially designed to assist human beings in their need to engage in three post-death tasks: 1) to dispose of dead bodies appropriately; 2) to make real the implications of death; and 3) to work toward social reintegration and healthful ongoing living (Corr, Nabe, & Corr, 1994). Without indicating how these tasks will otherwise be met, many act as if society and individuals should do away with all public expressions of mourning. Young people in our society frequently state that when they die no one should be sad and that money that would otherwise be spent for a funeral should only be used for a party. Thoughts like this disenfranchise full appreciation of grief and the needs of individuals to mourn their losses within communities of fellow grievers.

This disenfranchisement of the interpersonal dimensions of mourning is not typical of all individuals in our society and is unacceptable to many ethnic or religious groups. Similarly, it does not apply to rituals following the deaths of public figures (e.g., a president) or very prominent persons (e.g., certain celebrities). In these instances, as well as in the very formal rituals of the armed forces which mandate specific conduct and ceremonial practice in a context of death and bereavement, or the informal but growing practice of members of sports teams wearing black bands on their uniforms or dedicating a game to the memory of someone who has died, the interpersonal needs of a community cry out for expression and guidance in public mourning practices.

In fact, formal or informal rituals—which are a prominent example of the interpersonal dimension of mourning—have been created by human beings as a means of helping to bring order into their lives in times of disorder and social disruption. Thus, Margaret Mead (1973, pp. 89–90) wrote: "I know of no people for whom the fact of death is not critical, and who have no ritual by which to deal with it." Bereavement rituals are intended precisely to give social recognition, legitimation, and support in times of loss and grief. Specific rituals may fall out of favor and no longer serve these purposes for the society as a whole or for some of its members. But to assume that such rituals can simply be abandoned without replacement, that society can satisfactorily conduct its affairs and serve its members without any ritual whatsoever in times of death, is to misconceive the needs of human beings and expose the dangers involved in disenfranchising mourning. As Staples (1994, p. 255) suggested, "The rituals of grief and burial bear the dead away. Cheat those rituals and you risk keeping the dead with you always in forms that you mightn't like. Choose carefully the funerals you miss."

Intrapersonal Dimensions of Mourning

I was proud of her at the funeral. She was so brave and she never cried. But now she's always crying and sometimes she just seems to be preoccupied with her inner feelings. I think she's just chewing on her grief like some kind of undigested food and simply won't let go of it. Last week, I told her that there were times when we all understood it was appropriate to grieve. But she's got to get over it and she just can't keep on gnawing at it when she thinks she's alone.

Why does she keep going back to the cemetary on the anniversary of her husband's death? That's morbid for her to keep on stirring up those feelings over and over again. She doesn't talk much to anyone else about it, but I think she needs to get on with her life without this behavior.

Some authors (e.g., *Oxford English Dictionary*, 1989, Vol. 10, pp. 19–20) seem to restrict the use of the term "mourning" to the expression of sorrow or grief, especially those expressions involving ceremony or ritual. For example, there is a traditional language that uses phrases like "wearing mourning" to refer to dressing in certain ways (e.g., in black or dark-colored garments) as a public expression of one's status as a bereaved person. Despite its historical justification, limiting the term mourning in this way leaves us without a term for the *intrapersonal* processes of coping with loss and grief.

Other authors (e.g., Wolfelt, 1996) maintain and emphasize the distinction between the intrapersonal and interpersonal dimensions of bereavement by using the term "grieving" for the former and reserving the term "mourning" for the latter. Again, there is justification for some linguistic distinction between intrapersonal and interpersonal aspects of coping with loss and grief. But the central point for our purposes is that this last distinction is a linguistic effort to fill out what is involved in both the intrapersonal and interpersonal realms when bereaved persons strive to cope with loss and grief. In this way, linguistic distinctions between intrapersonal and interpersonal aspects of mourning work to expand or enhance what is involved in coping with loss and grief, not to restrict or disenfranchise selected aspects of that coping.

Mourning: Outcomes

It's been almost three weeks and she's still not finished with her grieving. I told her she had to forget him and get on with her new life.

We invited John to come on a blind date with us and Mary's cousin, but he refused. Mary told him that he's got to stop wallowing in tears. He needs to get over his first wife and start looking around for someone new. Six months is long enough to mourn.

A final arena for possible disenfranchisement in bereavement relates to assumptions about the *outcomes* of mourning. This has been touched on above. If mourning is a process of coping with loss and grief, we can rightly ask: What are the results which it strives to achieve? Many would say "recovery," "completion," or "resolution." Each of these terms appears to imply a fixed endpoint for mourning, a final closure after which there is no more grieving and mourning. "Recovery," is perhaps the least satisfactory of the three terms, because it also seems to suggest that grief is a bad situation like a disease or a wound from which one must rescue or reclaim oneself (Osterweis, Solomon, & Green, 1984; Rando, 1993). Recovery is often implied in metaphors of "healing" from grief; talking in this

way may otherwise be quite helpful, but it tends to suggest a time at which one will be done with healing and after which one will apparently be back to one's former self essentially unchanged by the bereavement experience.

It has been argued earlier that it is not desirable to use symptom language to interpret grief and to impose disease models upon healthy experiences in bereavement. To that we can add here that there are no fixed endpoints in mourning. One can never simply go back to a pre-bereavement mode of living after a significant loss. In fact, there is ample evidence, for many at least, that mourning continues in some form for the remainder of one's life. Interpretations to the contrary disenfranchise processes related to loss and grief which take place after the assumed endpoint or completion of mourning. They also disenfranchise the life-changing power of significant losses and the ongoing need to continue to cope with loss, grief, and new challenges in life. The misconception that grief and mourning should be over in a short time or at some predefined point is what leads to the familiar experience of many bereaved persons that over time their grief appears to become disenfranchised (Lundberg, Thornton, & Robertson, 1987).

There are, in fact, different outcomes experienced by different individuals who are bereaved. That is not surprising. Individuals who live their lives in different ways may be expected to cope with loss and grief in different ways, and to come to different results in their coping work. Research by Martinson and her colleagues (McClowry, Davies, May, Kulenkamp, & Martinson, 1987) studied bereaved parents and other family members (mainly siblings) seven to nine years after the death of a child. Results suggested that different individuals and different families dealt with the "empty space" in their lives in different ways. Some worked diligently to "get over it," that is, to put the loss behind them and go on with their lives. Others sought to "fill the space" by turning their focus toward what they perceived as some constructive direction. This type of effort to find some positive meaning in an otherwise horrible event might be illustrated by those bereaved after automobile accidents associated with the use of alcoholic beverages who throw themselves into campaigns to prevent intoxicated drivers from driving motor vehicles or to take such drivers off the road when they have been identified. A third outcome identified in this research was that of "keeping the connection." This appeared in bereaved persons who struggled to maintain a place in their lives for the deceased individual, vividly illustrated by the mother who insists that she has two sons, despite her full awareness that one of them has died (e.g., Wagner, 1994).

The important point in this research is not to argue for one or the other of these three outcomes in mourning, or even to suggest that they are the only possible outcomes. The point is that mourning is a process of acknowledging the reality of a death, experiencing the grief associated with that loss, learning to live without the deceased, and restructuring one's relationship to the deceased in order that that relationship can continue to be honored even while the survivor goes on living in a healthy and productive way (Worden, 1991). This process can be carried out in different ways and it can be expected to have somewhat different results for different individuals. As one astute psychologist observed, it is not the time that one has to use but the use that one makes of the time that one has that makes all the difference in bereavement, grief, and mourning (S. J. Fleming, personal communication, 9/28/95).

Three widows in my own experience acted out their mourning in different ways. One removed her wedding ring after the death of her husband. She said, "I am no longer married to him." Another kept her wedding ring on the third finger of her left hand. She said, "We are still connected." A third removed her husband's wedding ring before his body was buried and had it refashioned along with her own wedding ring into a new ring which she wore on her right hand. She said, "I now have a new relationship with my deceased husband."

These and other possible variations identify alternative courses in bereavement and mourning. In each case, metaphors of healing or resolution are partly correct insofar as the survivor has found a constructive way in which to go forward with his or her life. The intensity of the bereaved person's grief may have abated, but many continue to experience grief and reoccurrences of mourning in some degree, in some forms, and at some times. Grief may no longer consume them as it seemed to do immediately after their loss. They have "gotten through" some difficult times in bereavement, but they are not simply "over" their grief. In fact, many bereaved persons report that their grief and mourning never completely end.

Outsiders must take care not to invalidate or disenfranchise the ongoing grief and mourning of the bereaved, as well as their healthy connectedness to the deceased, by speaking too facilely of closure and completion (Klass, Silverman, & Nickman, 1996; Silverman, Nickman, & Worden, 1992). Such language may speak not primarily about bereavement but about the time at which a helper judges that his or her role as a counselor or therapist is no longer required. Thus, when a bereaved child decides to leave one of the support groups at The Dougy Center in Portland, Oregon (because, as was once said, "he or she now has better things to do with his or her time"), he or she is given a drawstring pouch containing several small stones (Corr and the Staff of The Dougy Center, 1991). Most of the stones in the pouch are polished and thus serve to symbolize what the child has achieved in coping with loss and grief; at least one is left in a rough state to represent the unfinished work that always remains in bereavement.

Conclusion

What have we learned from this reflection on the concept of disenfranchised grief? First, it is a concept with immediate appeal. It resonates with the experiences of many bereaved persons and of many clinicians and scholars who have sought to understand experiences of bereavement or tried to be of assistance to bereaved persons. Second, disenfranchisement involves more than merely overlooking or forgetting to take note of certain types of bereavement and grief. It is more active than that in its nature and more determined in its messages, even if they are often conveyed in subtle and unspoken ways. Whatever is disenfranchised in grief is not free to experience or to express itself. It is prohibited, tied down, not sanctioned, and not supported by society.

Third, as Doka (1989a) originally pointed out, disenfranchisement can apply to any or all of the key structural elements in bereavement—relationships, losses, and grievers—as well as to certain forms of death. However, as this article has made clear, disenfranchisement can also be associated with the full range of the various reactions to loss (grief) and their expression, the processes of coping with or striving to manage loss, grief, and the new challenges which they entail (mourning), both the intrapersonal and the interpersonal dimensions of those processes, and various ways of living out their implications. In the aftermath of a death, the possible scope of disenfranchisement is not confined merely to the structural elements of bereavement or to grief understood in a kind of global way; it can extend to every aspect or dimension of the experience of bereavement and be applied to all of the dynamics of grief and mourning.

Enhancing our understanding of the concept of disenfranchised grief can contribute to improved appreciation of its breadth and depth. This same effort also provides an added way of drawing out some of the implications of the underlying concepts of bereavement, grief, and mourning. Further, attention to the enhanced concept of disenfranchised grief reminds helpers of the sensitivities they need to keep in mind in order not to devalue or rule out of bounds important aspects of the experiences of bereaved persons.

A caring society ought not incorporate within its death system—either formally or informally—thoughts, attitudes, behaviors, or values that communicate to bereaved persons inappropriate or unjustified messages such as: "Your relationship with the deceased person did not count in our eyes"; "Your loss was not really a significant one"; "You are not a person who should be grieving this loss;" "We do not recognize some aspects of your grief" or "Your grief is not acceptable to us in some ways;" "Your grief is in itself a symptom of psychic disorder or lack of mental health;" "Your mourning has lasted too long"; "You are mourning in ways that are publicly or socially unacceptable;" "You should not continue to mourn inside yourself in these ways"; or "Your mourning should be finished and over with by now."

Rather than the perspectives described in the previous paragraph, a caring society ought to respect the complexities and the individuality of each bereavement experience. While remaining sensitive to the deficits and excesses that define complicated mourning in a relatively small percentage of bereavement experiences (Rando, 1993), a caring society and its members ought to appreciate that healthy grief honors cherished relationships and that constructive mourning is essential for those who are striving to live in productive and meaningful ways in the aftermath of loss. Consider how different our society would be if it listened to and acted on comments such as the following from Frank (1991), who wrote: "Professionals talk too much about adjustment. I want to emphasize mourning as affirmation. . . . To grieve well is to value what you have lost. When you value even the feeling of loss, you value life itself, and you begin to live again" (pp. 40–41).

References

Attig, T. (1991). The importance of conceiving of grief as an active process. *Death Studies, 15,* 385–393.

Attig, T. (1996). *How we grieve: Relearning the world.* New York: Oxford University Press.

Becker, S. M. (1997, 26 June). *Disenfranchised grief and the experience of loss after environmental accidents.* Paper presented at the meeting of the Association for Death Education and Counseling and the 5th International Conference on Grief and Bereavement in Contemporary Society, Washington, DC.

Corr, C. A., and the Staff of The Dougy Center. (1991). Support for grieving children: The Dougy Center and the hospice philosophy. *The American Journal of Hospice and Palliative Care, 8*(4), 23–27.

Corr, C. A., Nabe, C. M., & Corr, D. M. (1994). A task-based approach for understanding and evaluating funeral practices. *Thanatos, 19*(2), 10–15.

Davidowitz, M., & Myrick, R. D. (1984). Responding to the bereaved: An analysis of "helping" statements. *Death Education, 8,* 1–10.

Doka, K. J. (1989a). Disenfranchised grief. In K. J. Doka (Ed.), *Disenfranchised grief: Recognizing hidden sorrow* (pp. 3–11). Lexington, MA: Lexington Books.

Doka, K. J. (Ed.) (1989b). *Disenfranchised grief: Recognizing hidden sorrow.* Lexington, MA: Lexington Books.

Elias, N. (1991). On human beings and their emotions: A process-sociological essay. In M. Featherstone, M. Hepworth, & B. S. Turner (Eds.), *The body: Social process and cultural theory* (pp. 103–125). London: Sage.

Folta, J. R., & Deck, E. S. (1976). Grief, the funeral, and the friend. In V. R. Pine, A. H. Kutscher, D. Peretz, R. C. Slater, R. DeBellis, R. J. Volk, & D. J. Cherico (Eds.), *Acute grief and the funeral* (pp. 231–240). Springfield, IL: Charles C. Thomas.

Frank, A. W. (1991). *At the will of the body: Reflections on illness.* Boston: Houghton Mifflin.

Gyulay, J. E. (1975). The forgotten grievers. *American Journal of Nursing, 75,* 1476–1479.

Hamilton, J. (1978). Grandparents as grievers. In O. J. Z. Sahler (Ed.), *The child and death* (pp. 219–225). St. Louis, MO: C. V. Mosby.

Kaczmarek, M. G., & Backlund, B. A. (1991). Disenfranchised grief: The loss of an adolescent romantic relationship. *Adolescence, 26,* 253–259.

Kamerman, J. (1993). Latent functions of enfranchising the disenfranchised griever. *Death Studies, 17,* 281–287.

Klass, D., Silverman, P. R., & Nickman, S. L. (Eds.) (1996). *Continuing bonds: New understanding of grief.* Washington, DC: Taylor & Francis.

Lazarus, R. S., & Folkman, S. (1984). *Stress, appraisal, and coping.* New York: Springer.

Lindemann, E. (1944). Symptomatology and management of acute grief. *American Journal of Psychiatry, 101,* 141–148.

Lundberg, K. J., Thornton, G., & Robertson, D. U. (1987). Personal and social rejection of the bereaved. In C. A. Corr & R. A. Pacholski (Eds.), *Death: Completion and discovery* (pp. 61–70). Lakewood, OH: Association for Death Education and Counseling.

McClowry, S. G., Davies, E. B., May, K. A., Kulenkamp, E. J., & Martinson, I. M. (1987). The empty space phenomenon: The process of grief in the bereaved family. *Death Studies, 11,* 361–374.

Mead, M. (1973). Ritual and social crisis. In J. D. Shaughnessy (Ed.), *The roots of ritual* (pp. 87–101). Grand Rapids, MI: Eerdmans.

Osterweis, M., Solomon, F., & Green, M. (Eds.) (1984). *Bereavement: Reactions, consequences, and care.* Washington, DC: National Academy Press.

The Oxford English Dictionary (1989). J. A. Simpson & E. S. C. Weiner (Eds.). 2nd ed.; 20 vols; Oxford: Clarendon Press.

Parkes, C. M. (1996). *Bereavement: Studies of grief in adult life* (3rd ed.). New York: Routledge.

Pine, V. R., Margolis, O. S., Doka, K., Kutscher, A. H., Schaefer, D. J., Siegel, M-E., & Cherico, D. J. (Eds.) (1990). *Unrecognized and unsanctioned grief: The nature and counseling of unacknowledged loss.* Springfield, IL: Charles C Thomas.

Rando, T. A. (1993). *Treatment of complicated mourning.* Champaign, IL: Research Press.

Schwebach, I., & Thornton, G. (1992, 6 March). *Disenfranchised grief in mentally retarded and mentally ill populations.* Paper presented at the meeting of the Association for Death Education and Counseling, Boston.

Silverman, P. R., Nickman, S., & Worden, J. W. (1992). Detachment revisited: The child's reconstruction of a dead parent. *American Journal of Orthopsychiatry, 62,* 494–503.

Staples, B. (1994). *Parallel time: Growing up in black and white.* New York: Pantheon.

Stroebe, M. S., & Schut, H. (1995, June 29). *The dual process model of coping with loss.* Paper presented at the meeting of the International Work Group on Death, Dying, and Bereavement, Oxford, England.

Thornton, G., Robertson, D. U., & Mlecko, M. L. (1991). Disenfranchised grief and evaluations of social support by college students. *Death Studies, 15,* 355–362.

Wagner, S. (1994). *The Andrew poems.* Lubbock, TX: Texas Tech University Press.

Weisman, A. D. (1984). *The coping capacity: On the nature of being mortal.* New York: Human Sciences Press.

Wolfelt, A. D. (1996). *Healing the bereaved child: Grief gardening, growth through grief and other touchstones for caregivers.* Fort Collins, CO: Companion Press.

Worden, J. W. (1991). *Grief counseling and grief therapy: A handbook for the mental health practitioner* (2nd ed.). New York: Springer.

Zupanick, C. E. (1994). Adult children of dysfunctional families: Treatment from a disenfranchised grief perspective. *Death Studies, 18,* 183–195.

The Increasing Prevalence of Complicated Mourning

The Onslaught Is Just Beginning

In this article, complicated mourning is operationalized in relation to the six "R" processes of mourning and its seven high-risk factors are identified. The main thesis is that the prevalence of complicated mourning is increasing today due to a number of contemporary sociocultural and technological trends which have influenced 1) today's types of death; 2) the characteristics of personal relationships severed by today's deaths; and 3) the personality and resources of today's mourner. Additionally, specific problems in both the mental health profession and the field of thanatology further escalate complicated mourning by preventing or interfering with requisite treatment. Thus, complicated mourning is on the rise at the precise time when caregivers are unprepared and limited in their abilities to respond. New treatment policies and models are mandated as a consequence.

THERESE A. RANDO, PHD

In the 1990s, the mental health profession (a term herein broadly used to encompass any caregiver whose work places him/her in the position of ministering to the mental health needs of another) and the thanatological community are at a crucial crossroads. Current sociocultural and technological trends in American society are directly increasing the prevalence of complicated mourning at the precise point in time at which the mental health profession is particularly both unprepared and limited in its abilities to respond to the needs created. Thanatology has a pivotal role to play in identifying this crisis, delineating the problems to be addressed, and advocating for the development of new policies, models, approaches, and treatments appropriate to today's grim realities. Failure of either profession to recognize these realities is bound to result not only in inadequate care for those who require it, but to place our society at greater risk for the serious sequelae known to emanate from untreated complicated mourning.[1]

After a brief review of complicated mourning, this article will: 1) identify the high-risk factors for complicated mourning; 2) delineate the sociocultural and technological trends exacerbating these factors, which in turn increase the prevalence of complicated mourning; 3) indicate the problems inherent in the mental health profession that interfere with proper response to complicated mourning and to its escalation; and 4) point out the pitfalls for addressing complicated mourning that reside in the field of thanatology today. The focus on this article is restricted to raising awareness of the problem and discussing its determinants.

Complicated Mourning

Historically, there have been three main difficulties in defining complicated mourning. The first stems from the imprecise and inconsistent terminology employed. The very same grief and mourning phenomena have been described at various times and by various authors as "pathological," "neurotic," "maladaptive," "unresolved," "abnormal," "dysfunctional," or "deviant," just to name some of the designations used. Communication has been hampered by a lack of semantic agreement and consensual validation. This author's preference is for the term "complicated mourning." Such a term suggests that mourning is a series of processes which in some way have become complicated, with the implication being that what has become complicated can be uncomplicated. It avoids the pejorative tone of many of the other terms. Additionally, there is no insinuation of pathology in the mourner. Heretofore, complications typically have been construed to arise from the deficits of the person experiencing the bereavement. The term "complicated" avoids the assumption that the complications necessarily stem from the mourner him or herself. This is quite crucial because it is now well-documented that there are some circumstances of death and some postdeath variables that in and of themselves complicate mourning regardless of the premorbid psychological health of the mourner.

A second difficulty stems from the lack of objective criteria for what constitutes complicated mourning. Unlike the analogous medical situation in which the determination of pathology is more readily discerned and defined (e.g., the diagnosis of a broken bone usually can be easily agreed upon by several physicians following viewing of an x-ray), the phenomena in mourning tend not to be so concrete or unarguable. For instance, a woman hearing her deceased husband's voice in some circumstances is quite appropriate, whereas in others it reflects gross pathology.

The third and related difficulty is found because mourning is so highly idiosyncratic. It is determined by a constellation of thirty-three sets of factors circumscribing the loss and its circumstances, the mourner, and the social support received. No determination of abnormality technically ever can be made without taking into consideration the sets of factors known to influence any response to loss.[2] What may be an appropriate response in one circumstance for an individual mourner may be a highly pathological response for a different mourner in other circumstances. For this reason, it appears most helpful to look at complications in the mourning processes themselves rather than at particular symptomatology.

With this as a premise, complicated mourning can be said to be present when, taking into consideration the amount of time since the death, there is a compromise, distortion, or failure of one or more of the six "R" processes of mourning.[1] The six "R" processes of mourning necessary for healthy accommodation of any loss are:

1. Recognize the loss
   • Acknowledge the death
   • Understand the death
2. React to the separation
   • Experience the pain
   • Feel, identify, accept, and give some form of expression to all the psychological reactions to the loss
   • Identify and mourn secondary losses
3. Recollect and reexperience the deceased and the relationship
   • Review and remember realistically
   • Revive and reexperience the feelings
4. Relinquish the old attachments to the deceased and the old assumptive world
5. Readjust to move adaptively into the new world without forgetting the old
   • Revise the old assumptive world
   • Develop a new relationship with the deceased
   • Adopt new ways of being in the world
   • Form a new identity
6. Reinvest

In all forms of complicated mourning, there are attempts to do two things: 1) to deny, repress, or avoid aspects of the loss, its pain, and the full realization of its implications for the mourner; and 2) to hold onto, and avoid relinquishing, the lost loved one. These attempts, or some variation thereof, are what cause the complications in the "R" processes of mourning.

Complicated mourning may take any one or combination of four forms: symptoms, syndromes, mental or physical disorder, or death.[1]

Complicated mourning symptoms refer to any psychological, behavioral, social, or physical symptom—alone or in combination—which in context reveals some dimension of compromise, distortion, or failure of one or more of the six "R" processes of mourning. They are of insufficient number, intensity, and duration, or of different type, than are required to meet the criteria for any of the other three forms of complicated mourning discussed below.

There are seven complicated mourning syndromes into which a constellation of complicated mourning symptoms may coalesce. They may occur independently or concurrently with one another. Only if the symptoms comprising them meet the criteria for the specific syndrome is there said to be a complicated mourning syndrome present. If only some of the symptoms are present, or there is a combination of symptoms from several of the syndromes but they fail to meet the criteria for a particular complicated mourning syndrome, then they are considered complicated mourning symptoms. The reader should be advised that a syndrome is not necessarily more pathological than a group of symptoms which clusters together but does not fit the description of one of the complicated mourning syndromes. Sometimes just a few complicated mourning symptoms—depending upon which they are—can be far more serious than the complicated mourning syndromes. With the exception of death, severity is not determined by the form of complicated mourning.

The seven syndromes of complicated mourning include three syndromes with problems in expression (i.e., absent mourning, delayed mourning and inhibited mourning); three syndromes with skewed aspects (i.e., distorted mourning of the extremely angry or guilty types, conflicted mourning, and unanticipated mourning); and the syndrome with a problem in ending (i.e., chronic mourning).

The third form that complicated mourning may take is of a diagnosable mental or physical disorder. This would include any DSM-III-R[3] diagnosis of a mental disorder or any recognized physical disorder that results from or is associated with a compromise, distortion, or failure of one or more of the six "R" processes of mourning. Death is the fourth form which complicated mourning may take. The death may be consciously chosen (i.e., suicide) or it may stem from the immediate results of a complicated mourning reaction (e.g., an automobile crash resulting from the complicated mourning symptom of driving at excessive speed) or the long-term results of a complicated mourning reaction (e.g., cirrhosis of the liver secondary to mourning-related alcoholism). The latter two types of death may or may not be subintentioned on the part of the mourner.

Generic High-Risk Factors for Complicated Mourning

Clinical and empirical evidence reveals that there are seven generic high-risk factors which can predispose any individual to have complication in mourning.[1] These can be divided into two categories: factors associated with the specific death and factors associated with antecedent and subsequent variables.

Factors associated with the death which are known especially to complicate mourning include: 1) a sudden and unanticipated death, especially when it is traumatic, violent, mutilating, or random; 2) death from an overly-lengthy illness; 3) loss of a child; and 4) the mourner's perception of preventability. Antecedent and subsequent variables that tend to complicate mourning include: 1) premorbid relationship with the deceased which has been markedly angry or ambivalent or markedly dependent; 2) the mourner's prior or concurrent mental health problems and/or unaccommodated losses and stresses; and 3) the mourner's perceived lack of social support.

To the extent that any bereaved individual is characterized by one or more of these factors, that individual can be said to be at risk for the development of complications in one or more of the six "R" processes of mourning, and hence at risk for complicated mourning.

Sociocultural and Technological Trends Exacerbating the High Risk Factors and Increasing the Prevalence of Complicated Mourning

Social change, medical advances, and shifting political realities have spawned the recent trends that have complicated healthy grief and mourning.

Social change, occurring at an increasingly rapid rate, encompasses such processes as urbanization; industrialization; increasing technicalization; secularization and deritualization (particularly the trend to omit funeral or memorial services and not to view the body); greater social mobility; social reorganization (specifically a decline in—if not a breakdown of—the nuclear family, increases in single parent and blended families, and the relative exclusion of the aged and dying); rising societal, interpersonal, and institutional violence (physical, sexual, and psychological); and unemployment, poverty, and economic problems. Consequences include social alienation; senses of personal helplessness and hopelessness; parental absence and neglect of children; larger societal discrepancies between the "haves" and the "have nots"; epidemic drug and alcohol abuse; physical and sexual abuse of children and those without power (e.g., women and the elderly); and availability of guns. All of these sequelae have tended to increase violence even more, to sever or severely damage the links between children and adults, and to expose individuals to more traumatic and unnatural deaths.

Medical advances have culminated in lengthier chronic illnesses, and increased age spans, altered mortality rates, and intensified bioethical dilemmas. These trends, plus those involving social change, accompany contemporary political realities of increasing incidence of terrorism, assassination, political torture, and genocide, which get played out against the ever-present possibility of ecological disaster, nuclear holocaust, and megadeath to impact dramatically and undeniably on today's mourner.[4-6]

Violence: A Particularly Malignant Trend

Any commentary on present-day trends would be negligent if it did not elaborate somewhat upon the phenomenon of violence in today's society. Violence contributes significantly to the increasing prevalence of complicated mourning, and is associated with most of its generic high-risk factors. One crime index offense occurs every two seconds in the United States, with one violent crime occurring every nineteen seconds.[7] Violent crime has risen to the extent that in April 1991 Attorney General Richard Thornburgh issued the statement that "a citizen of this country is today more likely to be the victim of a violent crime than of an automobile accident."[8] The U.S. Department of Justice estimates that five out of six of today's twelve-year-olds will become victims of violent crime during their lifetimes,[9] with estimates for the lifetime chance of becoming a victim of homicide in the United States ranging from one out of 133 to one out of 153 depending upon the source of the statistics.[10] One category of homicide—murder by juvenile—is increasing so rapidly that it is now being termed "epidemic" by psychologist and attorney Charles Ewing,[11] an authority on child perpetrators of homicide.

Other types of crime and victimization are on the rise in the United States. The National Victim Center Overview of Crime and Victimization in America[12] provides some of the horrifying statistics:

- Wife-beating results in more injuries that require medical treatment than rape, auto accidents, and muggings combined.
- More than one out of every 200 senior citizens are the victim of a violent crime each year, making a total of 155,000 elderly Americans who are attacked, robbed, assaulted, and murdered every year—435 each day.
- New York City has reported an eighty percent increase in hate-motivated crimes since 1986, with seventy percent of them perpetrated by those under age nineteen.
- One in three women will be sexually assaulted during her lifetime.
- Every forty-seven seconds a child is abused or neglected.

Certainly, society not only condones, but escalates, violence. Books, movies, music videos, and songs perpetuate the belief that violence is not merely acceptable, but exciting. Books focusing on real-life serial killers; escalating movie violence associated with anatomically precise and sexually explicit images; and music portraying hostility against women, murder, and necrophilia are routine. According to Thomas Radecki, Research Director for the National Coalition on Television Violence, by the age of 18 the average American child will have seen 200,000 violent acts on television, including 40,000 murders.[13] Children's programming now averages twenty-five violent acts per hour, which is up fifty percent from that in the early 1980s.[14]

The recently popular children's movie, *Teenage Mutant Ninja Turtles,* had a total of 194 acts of violence primarily committed by the "heroes" of the film, which was the most violent film ever to be given a "PG" rating.[15] In the week of March 11, 1990, *America's Funniest Home Videos* became the highest-rated series on television. Some of the stories on that program that viewers found particularly amusing included a child getting hit in the face with a shovel, seven women falling off a bench, a man getting hit by a glider, and a child bicycling into a tree.[15] All of this provides serious concerns given the twenty-year research of Leonard Eron and L. Rowell Huesmann, who found that children who watch significant amounts of TV violence at the age of eight were consistently more likely to commit violent crimes or engage in spouse abuse at age thirty.[13] These researchers determined that heavy exposure to media violence is one of the major causes of aggressive behavior, crime, and violence in society.

Other forms of violence are increasing as well. Reports of abused and neglected children continue to rise. They reached 2.5 million in 1990, an increase of 30.7 percent since 1986, and 117 percent in the past decade.[16] One out of three girls, and one out of seven boys, are sexually abused by the time they reach eighteen.[17] In the United States, when random studies are conducted without the inclusion of high-risk groups, one in eight husbands has been physically aggressive with his wife in the preceding twelve months.[18] At least 2,000,000 women are severely and aggressively assaulted by their partners in any twelve-month period.[18] It is a myth that what has been termed "intimate violence" is confined to mentally disturbed individuals. While ten percent of offenders do sustain some form of psychopathology, ninety percent of offenders do not look any different than the "normal" individual.[19]

Sequelae of the Trends Predisposing to Complicated Mourning

As a result of all the aforementioned sociocultural and technological trends, there have been changes in three main areas which have significantly increased the prevalence of complicated mourning:

1. the types of death occurring today
2. the characteristics of personal relationships that are severed by today's deaths
3. the personality and resources of today's mourner.

Each of these adversely impacts in one or more ways upon one or more of the high-risk factors for complicated mourning, thereby increasing its prevalence.

Types of Death Occurring Today

Contemporary American society is witnessing the increase in three types of death known to be at high risk for complicated mourning: 1) sudden and unanticipated deaths, especially if they are traumatic (i.e., characterized not only by suddenness and lack of anticipation, but violence, mutilation, and destruction; preventability and/or randomness; multiple death; or the mourner's personal encounter with death;[20] 2) deaths that result from excessively lengthy chronic illnesses; and 3) deaths of children. Each of these deaths presents the survivors with issues known to compromise the "R" processes of mourning, hence each circumstance is a high-risk factor for complicated mourning.

Sudden and Unanticipated Traumatic Deaths

Sudden and unanticipated traumatic deaths stem primarily from four main causes: 1) accidents; 2) technological advances; 3) increasing rates of homicide and the escalating violence and pathology of perpetrators; and 4) higher suicide rates. Although mortality rates for children and youth in the United States have decreased since 1900, the large proportion of deaths from external causes—injuries, homicide, and suicide—distinguishes mortality at ages one to nineteen from that at other ages; with external causes of death accounting for about ten percent of the deaths of children and youth in 1900 and rising to 64 percent in 1985.[21]

Current trends reveal that "accidents"—a term covering most deaths from motor vehicle crashes, falls, poisoning, drowning, fire, suffocation, and firearms—are the leading cause of death among all persons aged one to thirty-seven and represent the fourth leading cause of death among persons of all ages.[22] On the average, there are eleven accidental deaths and approximately 1,030 disabling injuries every hour during the year.[22] Accidents are the single most common type of horrendous death for persons of any age, bringing deaths which are "premature, torturous, and without redeeming value".[23]

Technological advances simultaneously have both decreased the proportion of natural deaths that occur and increased the proportion of sudden and unanticipated traumatic deaths. For instance, substantial improvements in biomedical technology have culminated in higher survival rates from illnesses which previously would have been fatal. This leaves individuals alive longer to be susceptible to unnatural death. Additionally, the increase in unnatural death is due to greater current exposure to technology, machinery, motor vehicles, airplanes, chemicals, firearms, weapon systems, and so forth that put human beings at greater risk for unnatural death. For example, prior to the advent of the airplane, a crash of a horse and buggy could claim far fewer lives and be less mutilating to the bodies than the crash of a DC-10.

The third reason for the increase in sudden and unanticipated traumatic deaths stems from the increasing rates of homicide and the escalating violence and pathology of those who perpetrate these crimes upon others. The increase in actual homicide incidence; the rising percentage of serial killers; and the types of violence perpetrated before, during, and after the final homicidal act suggest that there are sicker individuals doing sicker things. More than ever before, homicide may be marked by cult or ritual killing, thrill killing, random killing, drive-by shootings, and accompanied by predeath torture and postdeath defilement. The increasing pathology of those who commit violent crimes may be seen as the result of the previously mentioned sociocultural trends, especially but not exclusively the individual's decreasing social connections and sense of power; fewer social prohibitions, and increasing societal violence. It reflects the increasing number of individuals with impaired psychological development, characterized often by an absent conscience, low frustration tolerance, poor impulse control, inability to delay gratification or modulate aggression, a sense of deprivation and entitlement, and notably poor attachment bonds and pathological patterns of relationships.

The fourth reason for the increase in sudden and unanticipated traumatic deaths follows from the higher suicide rates currently found in Western society. As above, these types of death appear to derive from all of the aforementioned trends contributing to complicated mourning in general.

The reader will note that most of the sudden and unanticipated traumatic deaths in this category also are preventable. Given that the perception of preventability is a high-risk factor predisposing to complicated mourning, to the extent that a mourner maintains this perception as an element in his or her mourning of the death, that individual sustains a greater chance for experiencing complications in the process.

Long-Term Chronic Illness Death

This type of death is increasing in frequency because of biomedical and technological advances that can combat disease and forestall cessation of life. Consequently, today's illnesses are longer in duration than ever before. However, it has been well-documented that there are significant problems for survivors when a loved one's terminal illness persists for too long.[24] These illnesses often present loved ones with inherent difficulties that eventually complicate their postdeath bereavement and expose them to situations and dilemmas previously unheard of when patients died sooner and/or without becoming the focus for bioethical debates around the use of machinery and the prolongation of life without quality. With the increase in the Human Immunodeficiency Virus (HIV) and Acquired Immunodeficiency Syndrome (AIDS), significant multidimensional stresses arise which engender those known to complicate mourning in anyone (e.g., anger, ambivalence, guilt, stigmatization, social disenfranchisement, problems obtaining required health care, and so forth). The fact that an individual may be positive for the HIV virus for an exceptionally long period of time prior to developing the often long-term, multiproblemic, and idiosyncratic course of their particular version of AIDS, with all of its vicissitudes, gives new meaning these days to the stresses of long-term chronic illness.

Parental Loss of a Child

In earlier years, by the time an adult child died, his or her parents would have been long deceased. Today, with increases in lifespan and advances in medical technology, parents are permitted to survive long enough to witness the deaths of the adult children they used to predecease. Clinically and empirically, it is well-known that significant problematic issues are associated with the parental loss of a child—issues which when compared to those generated by other losses appear to make this loss the

most difficult with which to cope.[25] These problematic issues and complicated mourning are now visited upon older parents who remain alive to experience the death of their adult child. There is even some suggestion that additional stresses are added to the normal burdens of parental bereavement when the child is an adult in his or her own right.[26] It is a uniquely contemporary trend, therefore, that associated with all of today's deaths are a greater percentage of parents who, because of medical advancements, are alive to be placed in the high-risk situation for complicated mourning upon the death of their adult child. This is a population that can be expected to increase, and consequently swell the numbers of complicated mourners as well.

Characteristics of Personal Relationships Severed by Today's Deaths

As a consequence of societal trends, there has been an increase in conflicted and dependent relationships in our society. Both types are high-risk factors when they characterize the mourner's premorbid relationship with the deceased.[1] With more of these types of relationships than ever before, there is a relative increase in the prevalence of complicated mourning, which is predisposed to develop after the death of one with whom the mourner has had this type of bond.

In 1957, Edmond Volkart offered a classic discussion of why death in the American family tends to cause greater psychological impact than in other cultures, specifically causing the family to be uniquely vulnerable to bereavement.[6] The reasons he delineated are even more salient today, and are part of the trends already cited above. Among other trends, he noted that the limited range of interaction in the American family fosters unusually intense emotional involvement as compared to other societies, and that there is an exclusivity of relationships in the American family. Both trends breed overidentification and overdependence among family members, which in turn engender ambivalence, repressed hostility, and guilt that create greater potential for complications after the death. Adding fuel to this fire is the societal expectation that grief expression concentrates on feelings and expression of loss. There is a failure both to recognize and to provide channels for hostility, guilt, and ambivalence.

Problematic relationships are on the rise in our society for other reasons as well. Quite importantly, there is an overall increase in sexual and physical abuse of children, as well as other adults. Research repeatedly documents the malignant intrapsychic and interpersonal sequelae of abuse and victimization.[27,28] This leaves the victim susceptible to complications in mourning not only because of the myriad symptomatology and biopsychosocial issues they caused, but typically with significant amounts of the anger, ambivalence, and/or dependence known to complicate any individual's mourning. In addition, the victimization may interfere with the mourner permitting him or herself to mourn the death of the perpetrator—an often necessary task that many victims resist because of inaccurate beliefs about mourning in general and/or misconstruals of what their specifically mourning the perpetrator's death may mean.[1] This only further victimizes the person through the consequences of incomplete mourning.

These forms of victimization are not the only experiences which give rise to the conflicted and dependent relationships identified as predisposing to complicated mourning. Individuals raised in families with one or more alcoholic parents or a parent who is an adult child of an alcoholic (ACOA), or with one or more parents who are psychologically impaired, rigid in beliefs, compulsive in behaviors, codependent, absent, neglectful, or chronically ill are vulnerable too. As sociocultural trends escalate these scenarios, relationships characterized by anger, ambivalence, and dependency will become prevalent, and complicated mourning will, in turn, become more frequent.

The Personality and Resources of Today's Mourner

Current trends suggest that the personality and resources of today's mourner leave that individual compromised in mourning for three reasons. First, given the trends previously discussed, the personalities and mental health of today's mourners are often more impaired. These impaired persons—who themselves frequently sustain poor attachment bonds with their own parents because of these trends—typically effect intergenerational transmission of these deficits via the inadequate parenting provided to their own children and the unhealthy experiences those children undergo. Clinically, one sees more often these days impaired superego development, lower level personality organization, narcissistic behavior, character disorder, and poor impulse control. Given that one's personality and previous and current states of mental health are critical factors influencing any mourner's ability to address mourning successfully, a trend toward relatively more impairment in this area has implications for greater numbers of people being added to the rolls of complicated mourners.

Another liability for a mourner is the existence of unaccommodated prior or concurrent losses or stresses. In this regard, a second reason for the increased prevalence of complicated mourning comes from the presence of more loss and stress in the life of today's mourner as compared to times in the past. To the extent that contemporary sociocultural trends bring relatively more losses and stresses for a person, both prior to a given death (e.g., parents' divorce) and concomitant with it (e.g., unemployment), today's mourner is relatively more disadvantaged given his or her increased exposure to these high-risk factors.

The third reason for increased complications in mourning arises from the compromise of the mourner's resources. Disenfranchised mourning[29] is on the rise, and the consequent perceived lack of social support it stimulates is a high-risk factor for complicated mourning. It is quite evident that conditions in contemporary American society promote all three of the main reasons for social disenfranchisement during mourning, i.e., invalidation of the loss, the lost relationship, or the mourner.[29] Examples of unrecognized losses that are increasing in today's

society include abortions, adoptions, the deaths of pets, and the inherent losses of those with Alzheimer's disease. Cases of the second type of disenfranchised loss that are on the increase include relationships that are not based on kin ties, or are not socially sanctioned (e.g., gay or lesbian relationships, extramarital affairs), or those that existed primarily in the past (e.g., former spouses or in-laws). Increasingly prevalent situations where the mourner is unrecognized can be found when the mourner is elderly, mentally handicapped, or a child. The more society creates, maintains, or permits individuals to be disenfranchised in their mourning, the more those individuals are at risk for complicated mourning given that disenfranchisement is so intimately linked with the high-risk factor of the mourner's perception of lack of social support.

Problems Inherent in the Mental Health Profession which Interfere with Proper Response to Complicated Mourning and to Its Escalation

There are three serious problems inherent in mental health today that interfere with the profession's response to complicated mourning and its escalation. Each one contributes to increasing the prevalence of complicated mourning either by facilitating misdiagnosis and/or hampering requisite treatment. The three problems are: 1) lack of an appropriate diagnostic category in the DSM-III-R; 2) insufficient knowledge about grief, mourning, and bereavement in general; and 3) decreased funds for and increased restrictions upon contemporary mental health services.

In the DSM-III-R, there is the lack of a diagnostic category for anything but the most basic uncomplicated grief, with the criteria even for this being significantly unrealistic for duration and symptomatology in light of today's data on uncomplicated grief and mourning. If they want to treat a mourning individual, mental health clinicians are often forced to utilize other diagnoses, many of which have clinical implications that are unacceptable. Other diagnoses that clinicians employ to justify treatment and to incorporate more fully the symptomatology of the bereaved individual frequently include one of the depressive, anxiety, or adjustment disorders; brief reactive psychosis; or one of the V code diagnoses.

The second area of problems in the mental health profession is the shocking insufficiency of knowledge about grief and bereavement in general. Mental health professionals tend, as does the general public, to have inappropriate expectations and unrealistic attitudes about grief and mourning, and to believe in and promote the myths and stereotypes known to pervade society at large. These not only do not help, but actually harm bereaved individuals given that they are used to (a) set the standards against which the bereaved individual is evaluated, (b) determine the assistance and support provided and/or judged to be needed, and (c) support unwarranted diagnoses of failure and pathology.[30] Yet, the problem is not all in *mis*information. Too many clinicians actually do not even know that they lack the requisite information they must possess if they want to treat a bereaved person successfully. Without a doubt, the majority of clinicians know an insufficient amount about uncomplicated grief and mourning; and of those who do know an adequate amount, only a fraction of them know enough about complicated mourning. Clinician lack of information and misinformation is the major cause of iatrogenesis in the treatment of grief and mourning.

An overall decrease in funds permitted and an increase in third-party payer insurance restrictions mark contemporary mental health services and constitute the third problem in the field adding to the prevalence of complicated mourning. These changes occur at a time when it not only is becoming more clearly documented that uncomplicated grief and mourning is more associated with psychiatric distress than previously recognized[31] and that it persists for longer duration,[32] but precisely when the incidence of complicated mourning is increasing and demanding more extensive treatment for higher proportions of the bereaved. Consequently, at the exact point in time that the mental health community will have more bereaved individuals with greater complicated mourning requiring treatment for longer periods of time, mental health services will be increasingly subjected to limitations, preapprovals, third-party reviews by persons ignorant of the area, short-term models, and forced usage of inappropriate diagnostic classification. This scenario demands that the mental health professional working with the bereaved find new policies, models, approaches, and treatments which are appropriate to these serious realities. Failing to do so, the future is frightening as the current system simply is not equipped to respond to the coming onslaught of complicated mourners.

The Pitfalls for Addressing Complicated Mourning Residing in the Field of Thanatology Today

It is unfortunate, but true: Thanatologists are contributing to the rising prevalence of complicated mourning as are contemporary sociocultural and technological trends and the mental health profession. While it is not in the purview of this article to discuss at length the myriad problems inherent in our own field of thanatology that contribute to complicated mourning, it must be noted:

- A significant amount of caregivers lack adequate clinical information about uncomplicated grief and mourning, e.g., the "normal" psychiatric complications of uncomplicated grief and mourning.
- Many thanatologists, in their effort to promote the naturalness of grief and mourning and to depathologize the way they construe it to have been medicalized, maintain an insufficient understanding of complicated grief and mourning.

- There is nonexistent, or at the very least woefully insufficient, assessment conducted by caregivers who assume that the grief and mourning they observe must be related exclusively to the particular death closest in time and who do not place the individual's responses within the context of his or her entire life prior to evaluating them.
- The phenomenon of "throwing the baby out with the bathwater" has occurred regarding medication in bereavement. Out of a concern that a mourner not be inappropriately medicated as had been done so often in the past, caregivers today often fail to send mourners for medication evaluations that are desperately needed, e.g., antianxiety medication following traumatic deaths.
- The research in the field has not been sufficiently longitudinal and has overfocused on certain populations (e.g., widows), leaving findings that are not generalizable over time for many types of mourners, especially complicated mourners.
- Caregivers do not always recognize that any work as a grief or mourning counselor or therapist must overlay a basic foundation of training in mental health intervention in general. While education in thanatology, good intentions, and/or previous experience with loss may be appropriate credentials for the individual facilitating uncomplicated grief and mourning (e.g., a facilitator of a mutual help group for the bereaved), this is not sufficient for that person offering counseling or therapy.
- Given that thanatology itself is a "specialty area," thanatologists often fail to recognize that the field encompasses a number of "subspecialty areas," each of which has its own data base and treatment requirements, i.e., all mourners are not alike and caregivers must recognize and respond to the differences inherent in different loss situations (e.g., loss of a child versus loss of a spouse or sudden and unanticipated death versus an expected chronic illness death).
- Clinicians working with the dying and the bereaved are subject to countertransference phenomena, stress reactions, codependency, "vicarious traumatization",[33] and burnout.

This constitutes a brief, and by no means exhaustive, listing of the types of pitfalls into which a thanatologist may fall. Each "fall" has the potential for compromising the mourning of the bereaved individual and in that regard has the potential for increasing the prevalence of complicated mourning today.

Conclusion

This article has discussed the causes and forms of complicated mourning, and has delineated the seven high-risk factors known to predispose to it. The purpose has been to illustrate how current sociocultural and technological trends are exacerbating these factors, thereby significantly increasing the prevalence of complicated mourning today. Problems both in the mental health profession and in the field of thanatology further contribute by preventing or interfering with requisite intervention. It is imperative that these grim realities be recognized in order that appropriate policies, models, approaches, and treatments be developed to respond to the individual and societal needs created by complicated mourning and its sequelae.

Notes

1. T. Rando, *Treatment of Complicated Mourning,* Research Press, Champaign, Illinois, 1993.

2. T. Rando, *Grief, Dying, and Death: Clinical Interventions for Caregivers,* Research Press, Champaign, Illinois, 1984.

3. American Psychiatric Association, *Diagnostic and Statistical Manual of Mental Disorders,* (3rd ed. rev.), Washington, D.C., 1987.

4. H. Feifel, The Meaning of Death in American Society: Implications for Education, in *Death Education: Preparation for Living,* B. Green and D. Irish (eds.), Schenkman, Cambridge, Massachusetts, 1971.

5. R. Lifton, *Death in Life: Survivors of Hiroshima,* Random House, New York, 1968.

6. E. Volkart (with collaboration of S. Michael), Bereavement and Mental Health, in *Explorations in Social Psychiatry,* A. Leighton, J. Clausen, and R. Wilson (eds.), Basic Books, New York, 1957.

7. Federal Bureau of Investigation, U.S. Department of Justice, *Uniform Crime Reports for the United States,* U.S. Government Printing Office, Washington, D.C., 1990.

8. *Violent Crimes up 10%, Providence Journal,* pp. A1 and A6, April 29, 1991.

9. National Victim Center, *America Speaks Out: Citizens' Attitudes about Victims' Rights and Violence,* (Executive Summary), Fort Worth, Texas, 1991.

10. Bureau of Justice Statistics Special Report, *The Risk of Violent Crime,* (NCJ-97119), U.S. Department of Justice, Washington, D.C., May 1985.

11. Killing by Kids "Epidemic" Forecast, *APA Monitor,* pp. 1 and 31, April, 1991.

12. National Victim Center, *National Victim Center Overview of Crime and Victimization in America,* Fort Worth, Texas, 1991.

13. Violence in Our Culture, *Newsweek,* pp. 46–52, April 1, 1991.

14. J. Patterson and P. Kim, *The Day America Told the Truth,* Prentice Hall Press, New York, 1991.

15. National Victim Center, *Crime, Safety and You!,* 1:3, 1990.

16. Children's Defense Fund Memo on the Family Preservation Act, Washington, D.C., July 2, 1991.

17. E. Bass and L. Davis, *The Courage to Heal: A Guide for Women Survivors of Child Sexual Abuse,* Harper and Row Publishers, New York, 1988.

18. A. Brown, *"Women's Roles" and Responses to Violence by Intimates: Hard Choices for Women Living in a Violent Society,* paper presented at the conference on "Trauma and Victimization: Understanding and Healing Survivors" sponsored by the University of Connecticut Center for Professional Development, Vernon, Connecticut, September 27–28, 1991.

19. R. Gelles, *The Roots, Context, and Causes of Family Violence,* paper presented at the conference on "Trauma and Victimization: Understanding and Healing Survivors" sponsored by the University of Connecticut Center for Professional Development, Vernon, Connecticut, September 27–28, 1991.

20. T. Rando, Complications in Mourning Traumatic Death, in *Death, Dying and Bereavement,* I. Corless, B. Germino, and M. Pittman-Lindeman (eds.), Jones and Bartlett Publishers, Inc., Boston, (in press).

21. L. Fingerhut and J. Kleinman, Mortality Among Children and Youth, *American Journal of Public Health, 79,* pp. 899–901, 1989.

22. National Safety Council, *Accident Facts, 1991 Edition,* Chicago, 1991.

23. M. Dixon and H. Clearwater, Accidents, in *Horrendous Death, Health, and Well-Being,* D. Leviton (ed.), Hemisphere Publishing Corporation, New York, 1991.

24. T. Rando (ed.) *Loss and Anticipatory Grief,* Lexington Books, Lexington, Massachusetts, 1986.

25. T. Rando (ed.), *Parental Loss of a Child,* Research Press, Champaign, Illinois, 1986.

26. T. Rando, Death of an Adult Child, in *Parental Loss of a Child,* T. Rando, (ed.), Research Press, Champaign, Illinois, 1986.

27. C. Courtois, *Healing the Incest Wound: Adult Survivors in Therapy,* Norton, New York, 1988.

28. F. Ochberg (ed.), *Post-Traumatic Therapy and Victims of Violence,* Brunner/Mazel, New York, 1988.

29. K. Doka (ed.), *Disenfranchised Grief: Recognizing Hidden Sorrow,* Lexington Books, Lexington, Massachusetts, 1989.

30. T. Rando, *Grieving: How To Go On Living When Someone You Love Dies,* Lexington Books, Lexington, Massachusetts, 1988.

31. S. Jacobs and K. Kim, Psychiatric Complications of Bereavement, *Psychiatric Annals, 20,* pp. 314–317, 1990.

32. S. Zisook and S. Shuchter, Time Course of Spousal Bereavement, *General Hospital Psychiatry, 7,* pp. 95–100, 1985.

33. I. McCann and L. Pearlman, Vicarious Traumatization: A Framework for Understanding the Psychological Effects of Working with Victims, *Journal of Traumatic Stress, 3,* pp. 131–149, 1990.

This article is adapted from a keynote address of the same name presented at the 13th Annual Conference of the Association for Death Education and Counseling, Duluth, Minnesota, April 26–28, 1991 and from the author's book, *Treatment of Complicated Mourning,* Research Press, Champaign, Illinois, 1993.

Life Is Like the Seasons

Responding to change, loss, and grief through a peer-based education program.

ANNE GRAHAM

The experience of loss can place children and young people in a vulnerable position as it affects their development and overall emotional and social well-being (Davies, 1991; Tyson-Rawson, 1996). Situations that trigger feelings of loss can include family breakdown, the death of a relative or friend, parental unemployment, abuse, serious illness, injury, disability, loss of a pet, or imprisonment of a family member. Losses also can be the result of a change of house, school, neighborhood, community, friends, and financial security. For some children and young people, such experiences culminate with the loss of a dream or ideal, symbols, traditions, and routines.

The experience of loss can markedly influence young people's perceptions of themselves and their world. They may not trust the predictability of events, their self-image may be damaged, they may feel they no longer belong, their sense of fairness and justice may be compromised, and they may believe they have lost control over their lives (Worden, 1996). Facing such challenges during childhood and adolescence does not in and of itself predispose one to ongoing psychological or learning difficulties. However, it does raise pressing concerns about the most effective ways to support young people as they struggle to make sense of their experience and to respond constructively.

Children's Reactions to Divorce and Death

Divorce is now a commonplace reality for many Australian children. In 2001, 55,300 couples filed for divorce, involving 51,200 children under the age of 18 (Australian Bureau of Statistics, 2003). Since an increasing number of children are expected to experience such a family breakdown more than once, the number of children and young people experiencing loss as a result of changes in family structure alone is likely to continue to rise (Bagshaw, 1998). In the last few decades, many researchers have focused on the effects of separation, divorce, and remarriage on children (e.g., Pryor & Rodgers, 2001). While such research offers a range of insights into children's experiences, it also has been the subject of debate in relation to various ideological, methodological, and conceptual limitations. In considering how children fare with divorce, the debate is both "polarised and intense" (Pryor & Rodgers, 2001, p. 6), resulting in what Bagshaw (1998) argues are findings that are "inconclusive and to some extent ambiguous" (p. 2). Children's experiences are influenced by historical, social, cultural, economic, and legal issues, which invariably mean their experiences will differ over time and place. This being the case, Emery (1999) cautions that any discussion about the effects of divorce on children

should take into careful consideration "what we know, not just what we believe" (p. 1).

Significant research suggests that losing a parent through death does not confer the same degree of risk as parental separation (Amato, 2000; Pryor & Rodgers, 2001). However, such contentions should not detract from the fact that the death of a parent or other significant person is a very distressing event for a child or adolescent (Fleming & Balmer, 1996). Although we have no reliable data on children affected by the death of a family member in any given year, the numbers are clearly high enough to warrant greater efforts to understand and respond to the effect such loss has on the young person (Clark, Pynoos, & Goebel, 1996). Worden (1996) suggests that children experiencing divorce do face a number of challenges that distinguish the reaction from that resulting from the death of a parent or other significant person. These challenges include fantasies of reunion, difficulties in mourning, pre-loss conflict, loyalty conflicts, ongoing parent-child relationships, feeling responsible for the breakup, less community support, struggles over finances, fears about the future, parental dating behavior, and family restructuring. While some of these issues will be evident following a death, others are distinctly identified with adjustment following separation and divorce.

General consensus exists in the literature that a child's capacity to recognize the finality of death, and to express his or her grief, varies with age or stage of development (Bagshaw, 1998). From this developmental perspective, the death of a parent or other significant person is often a challenge to the adaptive capacities of the child or adolescent (Clark et al., 1996), a fact recognized by many teachers. Findings from studies such as Brown's (1999) and Graham's (2003) suggest that teachers are increasingly aware of the impact that significant change and loss has on children's performance and their overall social and emotional well-being.

Children, Loss, and Resilience

A focus on the importance of supporting children as they adapt to the adverse circumstances associated with a death or divorce in their family is consistent with research regarding childhood resilience. Resilience is defined by Masten, Best, and Garmezy (1990) as "the process of, capacity for, or outcome of successful adaptation despite challenging or threatening circumstances" (p. 426). Resilient children tend to have the personal resources or capacities to cope effectively with and overcome adversity. These include personality features ("I am"), family and external structures ("I have"), and the child's own social and interpersonal skills ("I can") (Barnard, 1997). These protective factors also have been described in terms of social competence, problem-solving skills, autonomy, and a sense of purpose (Masten & Coatsworth, 1998). Death, separation, and divorce can pose a serious challenge to these protective factors.

Such research points to the potential contribution of school-based loss and grief education interventions that focus on problem solving, self-esteem, and peer support. While there has been widespread recognition of the potential value of peer support groups for children coping with death (Smith & Pennells, 1995), there also exists an emerging body of research, particularly in the United States, that identifies the need for education programs for both parents and children experiencing divorce (Arbuthnot & Gordon, 2000). As Bagshaw (1998) points out, however, many such initiatives are court-mandated educational programs that "rarely address issues of grief and loss in children, or provide educational instruction . . . directly to the children involved" (p. 13). Since children gradually come to make sense of their world and their experiences through their conversations and social interactions with adults and peers, it would seem that prevention programs that capitalize on these dynamics while specifically targeting issues of change, loss, and grief are worthy of closer attention. The following section provides an overview of one such intervention, the Seasons for Growth program (Graham, 1996, 2002).

Seasons for Growth

The Seasons for Growth education program has the broad aim of promoting the social and emotional well-being of children and young people, ages 6–18, who have experienced significant change and loss as a result of death, separation, or divorce. First developed in 1996, evaluated in 1999, and revised in 2002 to reflect developments in research and practice, Seasons for Growth has been implemented in approximately 3,000 schools and community agencies in Australia, New Zealand, England, Ireland, and Scotland. The program is a not-for-profit initiative sponsored in Australia by the MacKillop Foundation and is made available at low cost to enable provision to any child or adolescent who may benefit from it. Seasons for Growth was developed in consultation with teachers, mental health experts, bereavement specialists, academics, parents, and young people to ensure the program was educationally and psychologically sound, user-friendly, and based on a broad range of relevant multidisciplinary evidence and practice.

The Seasons for Growth program focuses on understanding the effects of change, loss, and grief and is aligned with key research on social and emotional education that promotes mental health and contributes to childhood resilience (Masten, Best, & Garmezy, 1990). Seasons for Growth is best understood in terms of prevention through education and skills building. The program specifically targets skills in communication, decision making, and problem solving. The approach to the program is consistent with a growing body of evidence that mental health-related initiatives can help students and schools to achieve desired outcomes (Weist, Sander, Lowie, & Christodulu, 2002).

The broad objectives of the Seasons for Growth program are to:

- Support young people as they work to understand and manage the issues they experience when death, separation, or divorce occurs in their families
- Help young people understand that their reactions to the changes in their lives are normal
- Educate about change, loss, and grief
- Develop skills for coping, problem solving, and decision making
- Build a peer support network
- Help restore self-confidence and self-esteem.

Seasons for Growth is based on a cognitive-behavioral approach that explores feelings, values, and beliefs, and encourages new ways of thinking and behaving. Such an approach has been shown to enhance self-esteem and self-concept (Burnett, 1994, 1995); more specifically, programs using this approach have been associated with an increase in positive self-talk and a decrease in negative self-talk in children and adolescents (Burnett, 1996). In this way, the learning processes encourage young people to value who they are and the particular "story" they have; to modify their thinking, attitudes, beliefs, and constructs about life; and to take charge of their behaviors.

Seasons for Growth is designed as a small-group peer process for between 4 and 7 participants. Each group is facilitated by a teacher or volunteer (known as a "Companion"), who participates in a mandatory 10 hours of training. The advantages of group work in maximizing learning for children in areas relating to mental health are well-known. Group work can encourage change, parallel the experience of the group with the wider social environment, provide a sense of belonging, address common needs, and provide a cost-effective response to psychosocial support (Geldard & Geldard, 2001). It seems that the reason most children participate in a group is not because they are clinically depressed or suicidal, but because they wish to learn how to cope with change, both internally and externally (Wolfe, 1995). The learning processes underpinning the Seasons for Growth program promote the development of new understandings, skills, attitudes, and ideas that the participants will take with them beyond the group experience.

As the name of the program implies, the different seasons of the year provide a rich symbolic framework in which to explore issues of change and loss. Drawing on the wide variation in the seasons, in Australia and elsewhere, the metaphor addresses the "ups and downs" of life. Each of the eight weekly sessions, the final celebration session, and two subsequent reconnector sessions (which range from 40 minutes to an hour, depending on the participants' ages) explore a concept such as I Am Special; Life Changes Like the Seasons; My Story Is Special; Feelings, Memories, Choices; and Support Networks. Each concept is linked not only to the imagery of one of the seasons but also to one of the tasks of grief as theorized by Worden (1991, 1996). The tasks are to:

- Accept the reality of the loss
- Work through the pain of grief
- Adjust to an environment in which the significant person or thing is no longer present
- Relocate the person or thing emotionally and move on with life.

The program has a sound curriculum structure and utilizes a wide range of age-appropriate creative learning activities, including art, mime, role-play, stories, discussion, play dough, music, and journaling. These strategies are consistent with research that highlights the value of creative, play-based, physical, and discussion activities that enable young people to express their feelings and help normalize their experiences (Gordon, Farberow, & Maida, 1999; Smith & Pennells, 1995).

Each session lists learning outcomes that guide the process of the session and indicate what the children will explore. To facilitate these outcomes, a range of activities are provided across each level of the program. For example, in Session 4 of the program, the outcomes are concerned with acknowledging and naming feelings and identifying reactions and behaviors linked to feelings. Level 1 of the program (for 6- to 8-year-olds) involves the children in coloring in and making a "feelings cube"; each face of the cube has a picture and word (e.g., "silly," "happy," "proud," "mad," "scared," "sad"). The children play a game with the cube, and each child thinks about the feeling word that lands face up and gives an example of a time when he/she had experienced that feeling. The Companion then uses this discussion to explain that feelings sometimes make us feel different in our bodies (e.g., "When I feel scared, I get butterflies in my tummy"). The Companion also uses this exercise to emphasize that feelings change, just like the seasons do; that we all have feelings and they are OK; and that these feelings won't last forever.

Among other activities, they learn the words and actions to a song, "I'm Boss of All My Feelings." The song provides an opportunity for the children to think about how being a "boss" means they are in charge of how they act in response to how they feel. They are encouraged to share ideas about what they do when they feel sad, angry, lonely, and so forth. They learn from each other that there are many ways to express what they feel without hurting themselves or others.

In Level 2 of the program (for 9- to 10-year-olds), the session on feelings involves the children taking turns to choose a feelings mask (representing, for example, happiness, sadness, surprise, fright, anger), holding it to their faces, and sharing a situation or event that prompted this feeling (e.g., "I feel happy when Grandma comes to visit"). The children gather around a life-size outline of a child's body shape, drawn on flip-chart paper. They brainstorm all the feeling words associated with change and loss, and then write these words inside the body shape. The children then play a game in which they throw a button on the body map and note the word closest to where it lands. They share with the group what they do when they experience this feeling (e.g., "When I feel sad, I cuddle my teddy"). The Companion affirms the idea that although we experience many feelings when changes occur in our families, these feelings are normal and are shared by others in similar and different ways.

Another important aspect of the Seasons for Growth program concerns the concept of choice. The desired outcomes for this session (Session 7) include being able to discuss why it is important to make good decisions and being able to identify some choices they can make in difficult situations. Again, the activities that facilitate this learning differ across the five levels of the program to take account of age, developmental abilities, and interests. They include a memory card game in which the children match problems and choices and are given an award badge at the end of the session that reads "(name of child) makes terrific choices" (Level 1); a balloon activity wherein children write on an inflated balloon an "I can" choice they take home to try in the coming week (Level 2); a "goal kicking" activity in which children discuss what it feels like to score a goal in their favorite sport and then use this experience to learn about the importance of setting realistic and achievable goals (Level 3: 11–12 years); a STOP, THINK, DO strategy for effective problem solving (Level 4: 13–15 years); and developing a "Guide to Quality Decisions," based on an activity that explores the "I cans" and "If onlys" experienced following a significant change or loss (Level 5: 16–18 years).

The Seasons for Growth program is accompanied by a comprehensive set of resources: a trainer's manual for those accredited to train other teachers and volunteers; a handbook for school coordinators, which provides a step-by-step process and support materials for planning, implementing, and evaluating the program; Companion manuals with comprehensive session notes and resources for both the primary school (6 to 12 years old) and secondary school (13 to 18 years old); five levels of student journals; imagery folios; music CDs and cassettes; regular newsletters; and professional development opportunities for staff involved in delivering the program on an ongoing basis.

Does Seasons for Growth Work?

In 1999, the Australian government funded an extensive qualitative and quantitative evaluation (see Muller & Saulwick, 1999) of the program that included 197 interviews and survey data from 220 randomly selected sites in four states. The results suggest that the program has a strong positive effect for both primary and secondary participants. For example, the data indicate that primary-age participants finish the program with a "more positive attitude" towards themselves and their circumstances than they started with. In response to the statement, "The Seasons for Growth program helped me to feel good about

myself," over 80 percent of respondents answered either 4 or 5 on a 5-point Likert scale, on which 1 represented "Strongly Disagree" and 5 represented "Strongly Agree." This survey finding was consistent with interview data that elicited such responses as:

It was very helpful to me because of the anger I had and the sadness. It was just like carrying a lot of weight on my back. . . . It's made me a lot happier. It was good to let the pain out. (Male, 11 years)
It helped me. You learned there's a lot of families it happens to. There's not just you. (Male, 8 years)
I felt happier, yes. I'm not feeling so sad anymore and I'm happy I told someone about how I was feeling. I was the same as my friends. (Female, 12 years)

The findings were similar for the secondary-age participants who were asked to rate the effect of the program on a number of measures, using a 5-point scale on which 1 was the most negative and 5 the most positive. They rated the program as having a positive effect on their confidence (a mean of 4.1), ability to talk about their feelings (4.2), ability to get along with other people (4.1), understanding of personal issues (4.1), and general feelings of happiness (3.9). This survey data was borne out through such comments as:

I suppose I'm now a bit more honest with myself. Like what I'm actually thinking and feeling. I learnt a lot about myself and what I was feeling inside. (Male, 17 years)
I can talk to my mother now . . . because I know she probably feels like I do. (Female, 13 years)
It was good. I didn't feel pushed but each week I found I was saying a bit more, you know, thinking "Well, at least I'm not the only one." (Male, 16 years)
When you're having one of those winter days, it helps you to know everything is not really bad. Like you need to find some good things to look forward to. (Female, 14 years)

The majority of responses from participants suggested that the program had "removed their sense of isolation, allowed them to express their feelings without being ashamed of them, enabled them to see that other young people had challenges and circumstances not unlike their own and helped them to develop trust in others" (Muller & Saulwick, 1999, p. 11). As a result of such learning, many participants indicated they had been able to:

- Seek support, when necessary, from the Companion outside the formal processes of the program
- Form friendships and support networks with others in the program
- Communicate better with their parents or siblings
- Understand that life moves on and that change does happen
- Cope better with their feelings.

These findings indicate a strong link between program outcomes and the key protective factors for resilient children and young people outlined earlier. In particular, it is evident that many of the participants grow in their social competence through being involved in a like-to-like peer group process, develop problem-solving skills as they try out new ideas and share these with the group, demonstrate autonomy in seeking out support networks, and develop a stronger sense of purpose through realistic goal setting (i.e., through focusing on the issues and circumstances they can influence rather than those they can't).

Parents, Companions, school principals, and agency managers also reported that the program benefited participants:

You can see that strength of the ego starting to come through. . . . She finally realized Dad wasn't going to come home and her destiny was in her hands. It was really empowering. I can still see the look on her face. (Companion)

My son would go to his mother's grave and he would not cry. Now he knows it's OK to cry. This program has shown him you can let it out, you have to let it out. (Parent)

It's achieved here what it set out to achieve, and probably more than we hoped for. So in terms of my expectations, probably 100% plus. In terms of a cure-all, no. But it is an avenue. Some kids have zoomed as a result of it; others are still walking slowly, but perhaps with more direction. (School Principal)

Conclusion

Teachers, parents, and caregivers agree that children and young people may not necessarily have either the innate capacities or the supportive relationships to assist them with the social and emotional challenges that they face when death, separation, or divorce occurs in their families. Such awareness begs further attention to education interventions that promote understandings, attitudes, and skills that enable young people to cope with present challenges and have hope for the future. The Seasons for Growth program is one example of a small-group process that accomplishes these goals through its normalizing emphasis on change and loss as an inevitable part of life. In educating children and young people in this way, we might expect they will be somewhat better equipped for a world marked by the challenges of unemployment, family breakdown, threats of terror, transient lifestyles, job insecurity, and fragmented communities.

More information on the Seasons for Growth program is available at www.goodgrief.aust.com.

References

Amato, P. (2000). The consequences of divorce for adults and children. *Journal of Marriage and the Family, 62,* 1269–1287.

Arbuthnot, J., & Gordon, D. (2001). *What about the children: A guide for divorced and divorcing parents* (5th ed.). Athens, OH: Center for Divorce Education.

Australian Bureau of Statistics. (2003). *Australian social trends.* Family and community: National summary tables. www.abs.gov.au/ausstats/abs%40.nsf

Bagshaw, D. (1998, October). Determining the best interests of the child—A grief and loss perspective. Paper presented at the Third National Family Court Conference, Melbourne, Australia.

Barnard, B. (1997). Fostering resiliency in children and youth: Promoting protective factors in the school. In D. Saleebey (Ed.), *The strengths perspective in social work practice* (2nd ed., pp. 167–182). New York: Longman.

Brown, E. (1999). *Loss, change & grief.* London: David Fulton.

Burnett, P. C. (1994). Self-concept and self-esteem in elementary school children. *Psychology in the Schools, 31,* 164–171.

Burnett, P. C. (1995). Cognitive behaviour therapy vs rational-emotive education: Impact on children's self-talk, self-esteem and irrational beliefs. *Australian Journal of Guidance Counselling, 5,* 59–66.

Burnett, P. C. (1996). Children's self-talk and significant others' positive and negative statements. *Educational Psychology, 16,* 57–68.

Clark, D., Pynoos, R., & Goebel, A. (1996). Mechanisms and processes of adolescent bereavement. In R. Haggerty, L. Sherrod, N. Garmezy, & M. Rutter (Eds.), *Stress, risk, and resilience in children and adolescents* (pp. 100–146). Cambridge: Cambridge University Press.

Davies, B. (1991). Long-term outcomes of adolescent sibling bereavement. *Journal of Adolescent Research, 6*(1), 70–82.

Emery, R. (1999). *Marriage, divorce and children's adjustment* (2nd ed.). Thousand Oaks, CA: Sage.

Fleming, S., & Bahner, L. (1996). Bereavement in adolescence. In C. A. Corr & D. E. Balk (Eds.), *Handbook of adolescent death and bereavement* (pp. 139–154). New York: Springer Publishing.

Geldard, K., & Geldard, D. (2001). *Working with children in groups. A handbook for counsellors, educators and community workers.* Hampshire, UK: Palgrave.

Gordon, N., Farberow, N., & Malda, C. (1999). *Children and disasters.* Philadelphia: Brunner/Mazel.

Graham, A. (1996, 2002). *Seasons for growth; Loss and grief education program.* Sydney: MacKillop Foundation.

Graham, A. (2003). *Teacher perspectives on mental health issues.* Unpublished report. Lismore: Southern Cross University.

Masten, A., Best, K., & Garmezy, N. (1990). Resilience and development: Contributions from the study of children who overcome adversity. *Development and Psychopathology, 2,* 425–444.

Masten, A., & Coatsworth, J. (1998). The development of competence in favourable and unfavourable environments: Lessons from research on successful children. *American Psychologist, 53,* 205–220.

Muller, D., & Saulwick, I. (1999). *An evaluation of the Seasons for Growth program.* Consolidated report. Canberra: Commonwealth of Australia.

Pryor, J., & Rodgers, B. (2001). *Children in changing families: Life after parental separation.* Oxford, UK: Blackwell.

Smith, S., & Pennells, M. (1995). *Interventions with bereaved children.* London: Jessica Kingsley.

Tyson-Rawson, K. (1996). Bereavement in adolescence. In C. A. Corr & D. E. Balk (Eds.), *Handbook of adolescent death and bereavement* (pp. 312–328). New York: Springer Publishing.

Weist, M. D., Sander, M. A., Lowie, J. A., & Christodulu, K. V. (2002). The expanded school mental health framework. *Childhood Education, 78,* 269–273.

Wolfe, B. (1995). Group interventions with bereaved children five to seventeen years of age. In C. Smith & M. Pennells (Eds.), *Interventions with bereaved children* (pp. 296–320). London: Jessica Kingsley Publishers.

Worden, J. W. (1991). *Grief counselling and grief therapy* (2nd ed.). New York: Springer.

Worden, J. W. (1996). *Children and grief: When a parent dies.* New York: Guildford Press.

ANNE GRAHAM is Director, Centre for Children & Young People, School of Education, Southern Cross University, Lismore, New South Wales, Australia.

Counseling with Children in Contemporary Society

This article examines elements related to children's developmental understandings of death, ways to talk to children about death, a broad understanding of the nature of children's grief and bereavement, recognition of the common characteristics of grieving children, and useful interventions for the bereaved child by mental health counselors.

LINDA GOLDMAN

This article examines elements related to children's developmental understandings of death, ways to talk to children about death, a broad understanding of the nature of children's grief and bereavement, recognition of the common characteristics of grieving children, and useful interventions. The research related to the child grief process and the intrinsic value of therapeutic and educational supports in working with grieving children are discussed through case studies, the professional literature, and practical interventions that support the process of grief therapy for mental health counselors and the bereaved child.

Grief counseling with children in contemporary society is a complex enterprise for mental health counselors (MHCs). Today's children are bombarded with loss in a way that many adults did not experience growing up. Common childhood losses are amplified by a world filled with terrorism, war, bullying, drugs, violence, sexuality, gender issues, and fear of nuclear or biological annihilation. Grief counseling with children benefits from the creation of a community grief team, whereby the parent or guardian, the school system, and the mental health counselor are part of an integral group that nurtures and supports the grieving child in an often confusing and unpredictable world. The purpose of this article is to address children's grief, focusing on their developmental understandings of death, ways to talk to children about death, the nature of children's bereavement, and the implications for mental health counselors. The research related to the child's grief process and the intrinsic value of supports through counseling and education in working with bereaved children is woven into this material. This information is presented through case studies, research, and intellectual understandings to support the process of grief therapy for mental health professionals and their clients.

Bereaved Children

It is essential when working with children who have experienced the death of someone close to them to be aware of the many childhood losses incurred. Often there are secondary losses for bereaved children. The death of a loved one can be the catalyst creating many secondary losses including loss of friends, home, schools, neighborhoods, self-esteem, and routines. Angela was a 7-year-old in a single parent home. She rarely saw her dad after her parent's divorce. Mom had died in a plane crash. Within a week she moved to another state to live with her dad and a stepmother and stepbrother she barely knew. Angela began to do poorly in school and said she "couldn't concentrate." She told her dad that she had no energy to play soccer anymore. She felt different now that her mom had died, and she "didn't want to talk about it with anyone." Within a short time she had lost her mom, her home, her school, her friends, her neighborhood, her ability to learn, and her day-to-day life as she knew it. These are multiple childhood losses that can occur due to the death of a parent.

MHCs' awareness of the following common losses experienced by children (Goldman, 2000b) can give insight into the complexities of children's grieving process. In addition to the types of losses that come easily to mind, like the loss of a family member or friend, children experience more subtle or less obvious losses. Other relationship losses include the absence of teacher or a parent being unavailable due to substance abuse, imprisonment, or divorce. Children experience loss of external objects through robbery or favorite toys or objects being misplaced. Self-related losses include loss of a physical part of the body or loss of self-esteem perhaps through physical, sexual, emotional, or derivational abuse. Many children live with loss in their environment including fire, floods, hurricanes, and other natural disasters. A primary death can often create the secondary loss of a move, change of school, change in the family structure, or family separation. Other childhood losses are loss of routines and habits and loss of skills and abilities after the death of a close loved one. Lastly, the loss of a future and the protection of the adult world are common experiences for the grieving child, causing them sometimes to exhibit a lack of motivation and an inclination to choose violence as a way of solving problems.

Children's Developmental Understanding of Death

A child's understanding of death changes as he or she develops, as explained by Piaget's (Ginsberg, & Opper, 1969) cognitive stages of development. Gaining insight into children's developmental stages allows the MHC to predict and understand age-appropriate responses. During the pre-operational stage, usually ages 2–7, magical thinking, egocentricity, reversibility, and causality characterize children's thinking. Young children developmentally live in an egocentric world, filled with the notion that their words and thoughts can magically cause a person to die. Children often feel they have caused and are responsible for everything (Ginsberg, & Opper). For instance, 5-year-old Sam screamed at his older brother, "I hate you, and I wish you were dead!" He was haunted with the idea that his words created his brother's murder the following day. Due to Sam's age-appropriate egocentrism and magical perception, he saw himself as the center of the universe, capable of creating and destroying at will the world around him. Reversibility also characterizes children's grieving. For example, Jack, a 5-year-old first grader, was very sad after his dad died in a plane crash. Age-appropriately, he perceived death as reversible and told his friends and family that his dad was coming back. Jack even wrote his dad a letter and waited and waited for the mailman to bring back a response. Alice, age 7 years, who told me that she killed her mother, exemplifies the common childhood notion of causality in the following story. She was 4 years old when her mom died. When I asked how she killed her, she responded, "My mom picked me up on the night she had her heart attack. If she hadn't picked me up, she wouldn't have died; so I killed her."

Piaget's next stage of development, concrete operations, usually includes ages 7–12 years (Ginsberg, & Opper, 1969). During this stage the child, in relation to death, is very curious and realistic and seeks information. Mary, at age 10, wanted to know everything about her mother's death. She stated that she had heard so many stories about her mom's fatal car crash that she wanted to look up the story in the newspaper to find out the facts. Jason, age 11, wondered about his friend who was killed in a sudden plane crash. "What was he thinking before the crash, was he scared, and did he suffer?" Tom age-appropriately wondered at age 9 if there was an after-life and exactly where his dad was after his sudden fatal heart attack. These examples illustrate that, at this stage of development, children commonly express logical thoughts and fears about death, can conceptualize that all body functions stop, and begin to internalize the universality and permanence of death. They may ponder the facts about how the terrorists got the plane to crash, wanting to know every detail. When working with this age group, it is important to ask, "What are the facts that you would like to know?" and to assist children in finding answers through family, friends, media, and experts.

Adolescents' (age 13 and up) concept of death is often characterized in accord with Piaget's prepositional operations, implications, and logic stage of development (Ginsberg, & Opper, 1969). Many teenagers, being self-absorbed at this age, see mortality and death as a natural process that is very remote from their day-to-day life and something they cannot control.

Teenagers are often preoccupied with shaping their own life and deny the possibility of their own death. Malcolm, 16 years old, expressed age-appropriate thoughts when he proclaimed, "I won't let those terrorists control my life. I'll visit the mall in Washington whenever I want. They can't hurt me!"

Children can misinterpret language at different developmental stages. The young child can misunderstand clichés associated with grieving, and these clichés can actually block the grieving process. Sammy, at age 6, began having nightmares and exhibited a fear of going to sleep after he was told that his dog Elmo died because "the vet put him to sleep." Alice was told it was "God's will" that her grandmother died because "God loved her so much." Alice questioned, "Why would God take Grandma away from me, doesn't God love me, and will God take me too?" Tom, age 9 years, continually heard the message that dad was watching over him. One day he asked the mental health clinician, "Do you really think my dad is watching over me all of the time? That would be very embarrassing."

Talking to Children about Death

Sudden or traumatic deaths, divorce and abandonment, the death of a grandparent, and the loss of a pet are a few of the many grief issues that children face (Goldman, 2000b). These losses shatter the emotional and physical equilibrium and stability a child may have had. The terror, isolation, and loneliness experienced by too many of today's children after a death leave them living in a world without a future, without protection, and without role models. Children normally and naturally assume the adult world will care for them, support them, and nurture them. When Grandpa has a sudden fatal heart attack, Dad dies in a car crash, Mom dies of suicide, or sister Mary overdoses on drugs, a child's world is shattered. "How could this have happened to me?" is the first question.

Children need to know the age-appropriate truth about a death (Goldman, 2000b). They often have a conscious or unconscious knowing of when they are being lied to, and this knowing can create a secondary loss of the trust of their emotional environment. In talking with children, mental health counselors, parents, and teachers can define death as "when the body stops working." In today's world we need to provide specific definitions for children for different kinds of death. Suicide is when "someone chooses to make his or her body stop working," and homicide is "when someone chooses to make someone else's body stop working." MHCs can say, "Sometimes people die when they are very, very, very old or very, very, very sick; or they are so, so, so injured that the doctors and nurses can't make their bodies work any more." It is important to know that children ask questions such as "Will I die too?" The common questions that children ask about death and grieving give the MHC an insight into their process. The questions serve as a mirror to reflect the child's inner thoughts and feelings that might be otherwise hidden. By responding to questions like the following, the mental health professional or other adult can create an openness to grieve: (a) Who will take care of me if you die too?, (b) Will you and daddy die too?, (c) What is heaven?, (d) Can I die if I go to sleep?, (e) Where did grandpa go?, (f) Will it ever stop hurting?, (g) Why did God kill my mom?, (h) Will Grandpa come back?, (i) Will I forget my person?, (j) Did my person suffer?, and (k) Was it my fault?

Understanding the Nature of Children's Bereavement

Fox (1988) explained that one useful way to help bereaved children and monitor their ongoing emotional needs is to "conceptualize what they must do in order to stay psychologically healthy" (p. 8). Fox emphasized that, in order to assure children's grief will be good grief, they must accomplish four tasks: understanding, grieving, commemorating, and going on. Each child's unique nature and age-appropriate level of experience can influence how he or she works through these tasks. The specific cause of death can also influence the way a child accomplishes these tasks. A dad's death by suicide may create significantly different issues than an anticipated grandfather's death from pneumonia.

Bereaved children may not process grief in a linear way (Goldman, 2000b). The tasks may surface and resurface in varying order, intensity, and duration. Grief work can be "messy," with waves of feelings and thoughts flowing through children when they least expect it to come. Children can be unsuspectingly hit with these "grief bullets" in the car, listening to a song or the news, seeing or hearing an airplane overhead, reading a story in school, or watching the news about a terrorist attack. A fireman's siren, a jet fighter, a soldier in uniform, a postal letter, or a balloon bursting can trigger sudden and intense feelings without any warning, and often without any conscious connection to their grief and loss issue.

Common characteristics of grieving children. Children in the 21st century experience grief-related issues involving safety and protection that many adults may not have had as children. Whether children ever really enjoyed the protection of the adults in their lives is a debatable question, but the perception of that safety seems to have existed in previous generations. Although grief-related issues have always existed through time, today's children are exposed to an extraordinary visual and auditory barrage of input. The news, the World Wide Web, music, and videos are constantly bombarding children with sounds and images of school shootings, killings, violence, and abuse. Children are left with feelings of vulnerability and defenselessness. Either by real circumstances or vicariously through media reports, young people are inundated with issues such as murder, suicide, AIDS, abuse, violence, terrorism, and bullying that often hinder their natural grief processes. This disruption is an overlay for other interactive components that may affect a child's grief process.

Three categories of interactive components can be examined in assessing the grieving child (Webb, 2002):

- Individual factors
- Death-related factors
- Support system factors

The flowing and overlapping of these components create a complex world for the grieving child. Individual factors include cognitive and developmental age; personality components; past coping mechanisms in the home, school, and community environments; medical history; and past experience with death. Death-related factors involve the type of death, contact with the deceased such as being present at death, viewing the dead body, attending funerals and gravesite, expressions of "goodbye," and grief reactions. The third group of variables concerns the child's support system including grief reactions of the nuclear family and extended family; school, peer, and religious recognition and support of the grief process; and cultural affiliation including typical beliefs about death and the extent of a child's inclusion. Other factors related to a death that may increase complications for the grief process include suddenness and lack of anticipation, violence, mutilation, and destruction, preventability and/or randomness, multiple death, and personal encounter of the mourner such as a threat or shocking confrontation.

As noted by Webb (2002), "although virtually any death may be perceived by the mourner as personally traumatic because of the internal subjective feeling involved . . . circumstances that are objectively traumatic are associated with five factors known to increase complications for mourners" (p. 368). Learning to recognize the signs of grieving and traumatized children is essential to normalizing their experience of grief and trauma. A mental health counselor needs to be educated in these common signs in order to reinforce for bereaved children, families, and educators that these thoughts, feelings, and actions are natural consequences in the child's grief process. This reassurance helps to reduce anxiety and fear.

Children may experience the following physical, emotional, cognitive, and behavioral symptoms common in the grieving process: The child (a) continually re-tells events about his or her loved one and their death; (b) feels the loved one is present in some way and speaks of him or her in the present tense; (c) dreams about the loved one and longs to be with him or her; (d) experiences nightmares and sleeplessness; (e) cannot concentrate on schoolwork, becomes disorganized, and/or cannot complete homework; (f) finds it difficult to follow directions or becomes overly talkative; (g) appears at times to feel nothing; (h) is pre-occupied with death and worries excessively about health issues; (i) is afraid to be left alone; (j) often cries at unexpected times; (k) wets the bed or loses his or her appetite; (l) shows regressive behaviors (e.g., is clingy or babyish); (m) idealizes or imitates the loved one and assumes his or her mannerisms; (n) creates his or her own spiritual belief system; (o) becomes a class bully or a class clown; (p) shows reckless physical action; (q) has headaches and stomach aches; and (r) rejects old friends, withdraws, or acts out.

Complications in children's grief. In addition, children's grief can be complicated, and common signs include withdrawal, sleep disorders, anxiety, difficulty in concentration, and regression. The common signs associated with children's bereavement may become heightened by their intensity, frequency, and duration. The term disenfranchised grief is used by Doka (1989) to refer to losses that cannot be openly acknowledged, socially sanctioned, or publicly mourned. Five categories of situations may create complications for the bereaved child (adapted with permission from Goldman, 2001). These categories are:

- Sudden or traumatic death
- Social stigma and shame
- Multiple losses
- Past relationship with the deceased
- The grief process of the surviving parent or caretaker

They explain circumstances that can create complications leading to obstructions in the child's grief process. Awareness of the commonality of feelings and thoughts surrounding these situations can aid the mental health counselor in normalizing what may seem so unfamiliar for the children.

Sudden or traumatic death can include murder, suicide, a fatal accident, or sudden fatal illness. With a sudden or traumatic death, an unstable environment is immediately created in the child's home. Children feel confusion over these kinds of death. A desire for revenge often is experienced after a murder or fatal accident. Rage or guilt, or both, emerge against the person who has committed suicide. A terror of violence and death unfolds, and the child feels shock and disbelief that suddenly this death has occurred.

Social stigma and shame frequently accompany deaths related to AIDS, suicide, homicide, terrorist attacks, or school shootings. Children as well as adults often feel too embarrassed to speak of these issues. They remain silent out of fear of being ridiculed or ostracized. These suppressed feelings get projected outward in the form of rage or inward in the form of self-hatred. Often times these children feel lonely and isolated. They cannot grieve normally because they have not separated the loss of the deceased from the way the deceased died.

Multiple losses can produce a deep fear of abandonment and self-doubt in children. The death of a single parent without a partner is a good example of a multiple loss. When the only parent of a child dies, the child can be forced to move from his or her home, the rest of his or her family and friends, the school, and the community. The child is shocked at this sudden and complete change of lifestyle and surroundings, and may withdraw or become terrified of future abandonment. Nightmares and/or bed-wetting could appear.

The past relationship to the deceased can greatly impact the grieving child. When a child has been abused, neglected, or abandoned by a loved one, there are often ambivalent feelings when the loved one's death occurs. A 5-year-old girl whose alcoholic father sexually abused her may feel great conflict when that parent dies. Part of her may feel relieved, even glad, to be rid of the abuse yet ashamed to say those feelings out loud. She may carry the secret of the abuse and become locked into that memory and be unable to grieve. Children often feel guilt,

fear, abandoned, or depressed if grief for a loved one is complicated by an unresolved past relationship.

The grief process of the surviving parent or caretaker greatly affects children. If the surviving parent is not able to mourn, there is no role model for the child. A closed environment stops the grief process. Many times the surviving parent finds it too difficult to watch his or her child grieve. The parent may be unable to grieve him or herself or may be unwilling to recognize the child's pain. Feelings become denied and the expression of these feelings is withheld. The surviving parent may well become an absentee parent because of his or her own overwhelming grief, producing more feelings of abandonment and isolation in the child. Children often fear something will happen to this parent or to himself or herself and, as a result, become overprotective of the parent and other loved ones (Goldman, 2001).

Implications for Mental Health Counselors

There are important general purposes for the MHC when working with grieving children. A major purpose is allowing children freedom to express emotion. This expression of emotion is an integral component of counseling and includes interventions with writing, drawing, poetry, projective techniques, and dream work. Support groups for children enhance the expression of emotions with peers who are working through similar situations. Allowing children to connect to and maintain memories serves as another important purpose for the MHC professional. Through remembering and sharing with others, the bereaved child can maintain a continuing bond with the person who died. Educating grieving children and the adults around them underscores another purpose for the mental health counselor: To create common thoughts and practices that harmoniously integrate the network of support surrounding the bereaved child.

Identifying At-Risk Children

Grieving children wonder if the pain will ever stop hurting. As Celotta, Jacobs and Keys (1987) identified, two questions that at-risk children respond to 100% of the time are: "Do you feel hopeless?" and "Do you feel sad?" These responses were part of a checklist given to elementary school children to identify depression. Mental health counselors can create simple tools to help target children who are traumatized and may be at-risk. Asking them to write or draw in response to questions such as "What makes you the most sad?," "What makes you the angriest?," or "What makes you feel the loneliest?" can provide useful information. Jim, a 10-year-old student from China, explained his picture showing a boy with his soul next to him. His older brother had recently died of suicide. Jim explained, "This is me, and this is my soul. Sometimes I feel like killing myself so I won't feel all of the pain. Sometimes I wish I would just disappear." This simple intervention created the identification of an at-risk child and pointed out the need for further exploration and evaluation.

Interventions for Individual Counseling

"The goal of helping children of all ages to cope with death is to promote their competence, facilitate their ability to cope, and recognize that children are active participants in their lives" (Silverman, 2000, p. 42). Mental health counselors need to be prepared to respond to children's questions. Grieving children are becoming a larger and larger, growing segment of our youth; and their grief issues arise at younger and younger ages. Not that long ago, parents were advised to exclude their children from memorials and not talk to them about death or about feelings about their loved one. Today, mental health professionals can emphasize the importance of seeing children as recognized mourners and as an integral part of the family system's bereavement process. Mental health counselors can speak, share, and create a space for young people to freely participate in the family's mourning. The MHC's goal is to allow safe expression of children's grief responses in a respectful environment. Grief-resolution techniques are important to create and stimulate discussion and exploration of thoughts and feelings, because bereaved children cannot always integrate their emotions and their intellect. While the MHC is building a relationship of trust, children also experience support and affirmation in an atmosphere that honors and respects them. The following techniques allow them to spontaneously and safely work through difficult spaces at their own comfort level. Healing is promoted when children put their feelings outside of themselves (Goldman, 1998a).

Expression of feelings. There are several interventions that are useful for helping children to express themselves. Worry lists, letter writing, reality checks, worry and safe boxes, drawing, and poetry are all valuable interventions with children. Projective techniques and dream work are interventions that allow release of thoughts and feelings in verbal and nonverbal ways.

One of the common signs of grieving children is that they worry excessively about their health and the health of the surviving parent or guardian. Roxanne, 10 years old, had multiple deaths in her family and worked in grief therapy for many months. In one counseling session, she seemed worried and agitated. When asked to list her five greatest worries, her first was a concern she had never mentioned until that moment: "I'm so scared my dad will die too! He smokes and I want him to stop." She burst into tears. Roxanne decided to write her dad a letter to express her feelings; and after being given the choice to send it or not, she decided to give it to him. Her anger and frustration are obvious in the letter:

> Dear Dad, You know how I feel about you smoking right now. You know how many losses I've had already . . . I don't want you to go next. I really worry about you; so please stop smoking. I feel like ripping your head off to make you stop. Think before you buy so many cigarettes. Love, Roxanne P.S. Write me back. (Goldman, 2000b, p. 69)

Seven-year-old Brian's dad died in a sudden car crash. He confided during one session, "I'm worried my mom will die too. I think about it at school and before I go to bed." An intervention Brian found comforting was a reality check at mom's doctor.

She had a complete check up and asked the doctor to write a note to Brian to reassure him that mom seemed healthy. This note provided a concrete and tangible linking object that comforted his worry about his mom's health. The letter read, "Dear Brian, I wanted to let you know that your mom had a complete physical exam and she seems to be very healthy. Dr. Jones."

Margie's dad was killed in the Pentagon attack. She began having nightmares and had great difficulty sleeping. She decided to create a safe box, with objects inside that made her feel safe and peaceful. She decorated her box in grief therapy, using magazines and stickers, to create images that were calming to her. Inside her box, she put a favorite stuffed animal; her dad's medal from the military; a picture of her dog, Snuffy; and a bracelet her best friend Tanya had given her. Margie put her safe box on her dresser in her bedroom where it made her feel better whenever she went to it.

Adam, a 13 year old, witnessed his brother being killed in a ride-by shooting. He was bombarded with stimuli that re-triggered his panic about the violent way his brother died. Loud noises, sirens, and even the burst of a balloon could immediately begin difficult feelings of panic and anxiety for him. One intervention that he found soothing was the creation of a worry or fear box in which he could place his fears. Adam drew pictures and found slogans that illustrated things that made him scared. Drugs, guns, and terrorists were a major theme. He cut a hole in the top of his box and began placing little notes, his own private fears, inside. Sometimes he shared them, but other times he did not. Writing down his fears was a first step for Adam to begin to identify and cope with them.

Writing, drawing, and poetry are useful interventions for expression of feelings for the bereaved child. They serve to allow safe release of often hidden feelings. Writing was useful for 8-year-old Julia whose best friend, Zoe, and Zoe's family died in the terrorist attack. The following is a part of a poem she created as a tribute to her friend in her memory book. "Julia. Remembers by memories and hearing her name. Who wishes for peace and unity. Strong" (Goldman, 2003, p.146). Tyler's best friend Juan was killed in a car crash. He drew a picture of one of his favorite memories with his friend Juan. They were playing soccer at the park and fell, and they both burst into laughter. Tyler said that, when he looked at his picture, he felt happy. Andrew was 16 years old when his grandfather and his favorite aunt died. His grief was coupled with his sadness as he watched family members grieve too. He expressed his grief through poetry in the following way: "Tears flow—As time passes—The relatives grieve—In love for the deceased" (Andrew Burt, personal communication, December 11, 2001).

Middle and high school students may successfully respond to writing in locked diaries. Melissa was a teenager who came to counseling after the suicide of her older brother Joey. The shame she felt about the way her brother Joey died made it difficult to discuss complex feelings openly. She mentioned in session that she loved her diary, and kept it under her bed locked, safe, and private. She wrote her "sacred" thoughts and feelings in her diary. She used her diary not only as a safe receptacle for feelings, but also as an avenue for expression she could choose to use according to her readiness.

Projective play and dream work are grief interventions that allow children to use their unconscious mind and their imagination to safely express thoughts and feelings (Goldman, 2001). Young children learn through play, and they also grieve through play. Role-playing, puppets, artwork, clay, and sand table work are a few of the many ways that they can imagine, pretend, and engage in meaningful activities that allow them to act out or project their grief feelings without having to directly verbalize them. Play therapy is especially useful with bereaved children. Children have a limited verbal ability for describing their feelings and a limited emotional capacity to tolerate the pain of loss, and they communicate their feelings, wishes, fears, and attempted resolutions to their problems through play (Webb, 2002). Projective play allows many young children to work through difficult times. Having props such as helping figures, puppets, costumes, and building blocks allows children to recreate their experience and role-play what happened and ways to work with what happened. Bereaved children feel empowered when they can imagine alternatives and possible solutions, release feelings, and create dialogue through projective play.

Sometimes, what may appear as a frivolous play activity can be an extremely meaningful outlet for children to recreate an event and safely express conflicting ideas. For example, 6-year-old Jared was very sad in a beginning grief therapy session. He missed his dad, who was killed in a car accident. He walked around the office, talking about how much he missed Dad and that he wished he could talk to him. Jared picked up a toy telephone and followed the mental health professional's suggestion that he call and tell him how he feels. Jared sat down on the floor, dialed the number, and began an ongoing, very present conversation with his dad including "Hi Dad. I love you and miss you so much. Are you ok? Do you miss me? I hope heaven is fun and you can play baseball there. Let me tell you about my day." Children may commonly reach out to initiate a connection to their deceased parent. Through projective play, Jared was able to feel he could communicate in a satisfying way with his father. Alex, who was bereaved in the Sept. 11th terrorist attack, spontaneously built towers of blocks to represent the Twin Towers, and then knocked them down with an airplane. When replaying the attack and the falling of the towers, Alex explained, "Airplanes make buildings go BOOM!" Allyson, a kindergartner, suffered the tragic death of her mom at the Pentagon. She created a cemetery out of blocks and explained what was bothering her through the use of toy figures. She reported, "When me and Daddy visit the cemetery I wonder about Mommy. There was no coffin or body at the cemetery. I wonder where my Mommy's body is now." Play allowed the expression of deep concern about her mom's body and opened communication about this in the therapeutic environment. Allyson agreed to share her block cemetery and questions about mom with dad, as a way to begin to answer them. Michael, age 5 years, recreated the disaster setting of his dad's death. Dad was inside his office when a tragic fire took his life. Using toy doctors, nurses, fireman, and policeman as props, he pretended to be a rescue worker and saved his dad. Then he put on a fire hat and gloves and shouted, "Don't worry I'll save you. Run for your life."

Puppets and stuffed animals are also a safe way for children to speak of the trauma through projecting thoughts and feelings onto props, and dream work is another tool allowing children to process difficult feelings. For example, the MHC might inquire of a bereaved child, "I wonder what Bart (the dog puppet) would say about the trauma. Let's allow Bart to tell us about his story." In addition, children often feel survivor guilt after a sudden death (Worden, 1991). In dreams, sadness and depressing thoughts and feelings surface, accompanied by guilt that the child has survived, another person has died, and the child did not or could not help the deceased. Justin, a 10-year-old, explained a common theme in his dream. Justin continually revisited a nightmare after Uncle Max suddenly died during his military deployment. He shared his dream with his mental health professional and drew a picture showing his uncle calling out for help and Justin being unable to reach him.

Connecting to and maintaining memories. Silverman, Nickman, & Worden (1992) found that it was normal for children "to maintain a presence and connection with the deceased and that this presence is not static" (p. 495). The bereaved child constructs the deceased through an ongoing cognitive process of establishing memories, feelings, and actions connected to the child's development level. This inner representation leads to a continuing bond to the deceased, creating a relationship that changes as the child matures and his or her grief lessens. There are five strategies of connection to a deceased parent: (a) making an effort to locate the deceased, (b) actually experiencing the deceased in some way, (c) reaching out to initiate a connection, (d) remembering, and (e) keeping something that belonged to the deceased.

Those MHCs who work with bereaved children "may need to focus on how to transform connections and place the relationship in a new perspective, rather than on how to separate from the deceased" (Silverman et al., 1992, p. 503). In locating the deceased, many children may place their loved one in a place called "heaven" (p. 497). Michelle was 7 years old when she began in counseling. Her mom had died in a sudden car crash. One day Michelle asked in session, "What do you think heaven is?" Reflecting Michelle's question, the mental health professional asked, "What do you think it is?" Both began to draw a picture of their image of heaven. This intervention helped Michelle reflect on her own question, and she was able to remember her mother by sharing the place where she thought Mom was. It was also a way to honor Mom, express things about Mom, and symbolically again tell Mom how much she loved her. In addition, Michelle wrote the following story about heaven:

> What is heaven? This is what heaven is to me. It's a beautiful place. Everyone is waiting for a new person, so they can be friends. They are also waiting for their family. They are still having fun. They get to meet all the people they always wanted to meet (like Elvis). There are lots of castle where only the great live, like my Mom. There's all the food you want and all the stuff to do—There's also dancing places, disco. My mom loved to dance. I think she's dancing in heaven. Animals are always welcome. (My Mom loved animals.) Ask her how Trixie is. That's her dog that died. Tell her I love her. (Goldman, 2000b, pp. 79–80).

169

Memory books, memories boxes, and memory picture albums can all be used to address bereaved children's questions of "Will I forget my person?" Memory work is an important part of the therapeutic process. Children often fear they will forget their person who died, and memory work can provide a helpful tool to safely process the events of their grief and trauma. Memory books store pictures and writings about loved ones; memory boxes hold cherished objects belonging to a special person; and memory picture albums hold favorite photographs. Mental health counselors can ask children the following questions as a foundation for discussion and processing memories after a death: (a) Where were you when your person died?, (b) What was your first thought?, (c) What are the facts about how your person died?, (d) What makes you sad, happy, angry, frustrated?, (e) What sticks with you now?, (f) Did you do anything wrong?, (g) What is it you still want to know?, (h) What scares you the most?, (i) What makes you feel peaceful?, and (j) What can you do to feel better?

Memory books are extremely useful tools to allow children to express feelings and complete unfinished business, including feelings and thoughts that boys and girls were unable to communicate at the time of their person's death. Inside a memory book, grieving children can use stars, stickers, photographs, and other decorations to expand their own writings and drawings about their person. These are a few suggestions about various themes for memory book work: (a) The most important thing I learned from my person is . . . , (b) What was life like before your person died?, (c) What is life like now?, (d) My funniest memory is . . . , (e) My most special memory is . . . , (f) If I could tell my loved one just one more thing, I would say . . . , and (g) If I could say one thing I was sorry for it would be . . . (Goldman, 2000b). For example, Alfred, age 10, made a memory book page illustrating the events of September 11, 2001. It was his attempt to make sense of his world after the disaster. His memory page was a picture that helped him release feelings, tell stories, and express worries and concerns. The picture he drew showed where he was and what was happening at his New York school situated so close to ground zero. His only message was "Run for your life." With this memory book page, Alfred was able to begin to release some of the terror he felt that day at being so close to the Twin Towers as he also told his story.

Memory boxes are an excellent craft project for grieving children. They can be used to hold special articles, linking objects that are comforting because of belonging to or being reminders of the person who died. These objects can be put in a shoebox and decorated by the child as a valuable treasure of memories, which is also a tool for stimulating conversation. Memory boxes serve as a linking object by holding something that belonged to the deceased. These linking objects help the child maintain his or her connection or link to his or her loved one (Silverman et al., 1992). For instance, Tanya, an 8-year-old, made a memory box with pictures and special objects that reminded her of her friend Angie who died in a sudden plane crash. Tanya included pictures, stuffed animals, a list of her top favorite memories, and a bracelet her friend had given her. She explained that it made her "feel good" whenever she held it and she loved to share it with her friends and family. The memory box created a place where Tanya could "be with her friend Angie."

Creating memory picture albums with children titled "My Life" is often an extremely useful tool in creating dialogue and sharing feelings. Henry's dad died of cancer when he was 11. Henry created his memory album by choosing pictures he loved to make an album about his life before and after dad died. He placed each picture in his book and wrote a sentence telling about it.

Children love to express memories through artwork. Memory murals and memory collages are examples of memory projects that are helpful therapeutic interventions for grieving children. Children can creatively express feelings and thoughts about their loved ones. Fifteen-year-old Megan prepared a collage of magazine pictures that reminded her of her best friend, Ashley, who had recently died of cancer. She included Ashley's favorite foods, favorite clothes, favorite music, and favorite movie stars. Zack, age 9 years, was a best friend to Andrew, who had died when he was 6. Zack drew a picture for the cover of Andrew's third memorial booklet, "On the Occasion of Andrew's Third Anniversary." He explained that his drawing showed Andrew "shooting hoops in heaven." He felt in the few years since Andrew's death, he had been playing basketball, and assumed Andrew was doing the same in heaven. By participating in the memorial booklet, and being given a voice to explain his work, Zack was able to continue to actively remember his friend and participate in ongoing involvement with memory work.

Memory e-mails are a creative example of memory work and computer use. After 14-year-old Donald's classmate Ethan got killed in a car crash, Donald and his classmates decided to create a chat room only for e-mail memories about Ethan. They also created a memory video of Ethan, using a popular rock group as a background for a montage of pictures of Ethan from birth until he died, including friends, pets, and family.

Using children's grief and loss resources is an excellent technique to allow discussion and expression of sometimes hidden feelings. It's often reassuring to bereaved children to read words that speak of the loss they have experienced and the many new feelings they have associated with grief. Children's resources can become a helpful tool for parents. These books create meaningful discussion and often allow adults to dialogue about their common loss issues (Goldman, 2000b). A few examples of useful books for children on grief are: *When Dinosaurs Die* (Brown & Brown, 1996), *When Someone Very Special Dies* (Heegaard, 1988), *Bart Speaks Out: Breaking the Silence on Suicide* (Goldman, 1998a), *Honoring Our Loved Ones: Going to a Funeral* (Carney, 1999), and *After a Murder: A Workbook for Kids* (The Dougy Center, 2002). Suggestions for useful books for grieving teens include: *Death Is Hard to Live With* (Bode, 1993), *When a Friend Dies* (Gootman, 1994), *Facing Change* (O'Toole, 1995), and *Fire in My Heart, Ice in My Veins* (Traisman, 1992). Readers can contact the author for a more complete list.

Support Groups

Many bereaved children feel alone and find peers and family members so often want them to move on and stop talking or even thinking about their person (Goldman, 2000b). They wonder who they can really talk with about their mom or dad or sister who has died. Often they feel different and choose not to share. Grief support groups can provide a safe haven for them to explore their overwhelming and often confusing feelings with others that understand because they are going through a grief process also. Becoming a member of an age-appropriate grief support group allows children and teens a safe place to share with others and create friendships.

Education

If mental health counselors can join together with parents, educators, therapists, and other caring professionals to create a cohesive unit, sharing similar thought forms, supports, resources, and information, a child's grieving experience becomes more congruent. Usually when children grieve, their world feels fragmented. The more consistency MHCs can create within children's lives, the more solid and secure their world will become. The role of mental health counselors as liaisons to parents, educators, and community members is an important aspect of children's grief therapy. Educating caring adults provides a united multiple support system for the grieving child.

Mental health professionals can educate surviving parents and guardians on common signs of grieving children and coach the adults on how to reduce the children's fear and anxiety about new thoughts and feelings. This education helps adults reduce their own anxieties that can unconsciously be projected onto their children. MHCs can provide age-appropriate words to help family members create open dialogue and identify their own unresolved grief and the impact of their grieving process on their children. For example, 15-year-old Mark lived with his grandmother after his mom's death. Grandma often told the mental health professional that she was concerned because Mark "doesn't seem to be grieving." One day in a seemingly unrelated conversation, she mentioned that Mark takes a nap every day on his mother's bed. Grandma was unaware that grieving teens commonly reach out to initiate a connection with their person who died (Silverman et al., 1992). That connection may well be taking a daily nap on mom's bed.

The MHC can also be an advocate for the grieving child in the school system. This advocacy can offer suggestions to educators, who are working with bereaved children, as a support after their person's death. Because children are sometimes flooded with feelings and are not immediately able to verbalize them, MHCs can work with educators in developing strategies for children to follow when they feel upset. In doing so, MHCs can emphasize the importance of the child being part of the decision-making process in choosing appropriate people or places they are comfortable with to be used to implement these strategies. These ideas can be implemented throughout the school year and continued for the next year if necessary. Suggestions include any or all of the following (Goldman, 1998b). The child (a) has permission to leave the room, if needed, without explanation, (b) can choose a designated adult or location within the school as a safe space, or (c) can call home if needed. Amy, who worried about Mom after Dad died, provides an example of how this might occur. She thought about her Mom a lot in the mornings and chose to call home at that time to make sure she was all right. Other strategies include the child's having (a) permission to visit the school nurse if needing a reality check, (b) a class helper, (c) private teacher time, (d) some

modified work assignments, and (e) school personnel inform faculty, PTA, parents, and children of the loss. In addition, it may be useful to give the child more academic progress reports such as was done for Henry who had a hard time concentrating after his brother Sam died (Goldman, 2000a). Henry could not remember as well and found his test scores declined. Having frequent progress reports helped him keep his studies on track.

The MHC serves as a liaison to the school system to inform those involved that there is a grieving child in the school. Presenting a loss inventory (Goldman, 2000a) that can be shared with educators is a helpful tool for communication within the school. All too often school systems do not communicate to their entire staff that a child has experienced the death of a close loved one. This lack of knowledge can create trauma and an added layer of sadness for students. Liam was a fifth grader who was star athlete for the soccer game. Many parents and friends had gathered to watch the team in their tournament finals. Coach McGuire approached Liam before the game and asked, "Is your dad here today?" "No," Liam grumbled. "He had to work." Liam played his worst game. Coach McGuire was unaware that Liam's dad had died recently; there was no written record to communicate this within the school. If this school system had an established practice of using a loss inventory, this lapse in communication and its devastating impact on Liam may not have occurred.

A grief therapy homework assignment, which can be used even in educational or advocacy situations, can help children and teens identify their individual support systems. Children can be asked to create a "circle of trust," placing a picture of themselves in the center and three trusted people with their phone numbers that they can call for support. They can create a second circle for people they would call next. They may even create a third circle for people they know they cannot trust. Their circle of trust can stimulate dialogue in therapy as well as serve as a tool for recognition of those they can and cannot count on for support during their present loss (Goldman & Rosenthal, 2001).

Childhood Commemoration

Children become recognized mourners when adults create ways for bereaved children to ask questions and share thoughts and feelings about death. Adults can also prepare and invite children to participate in funerals, memorials, and other rituals. When children can attend a memorial service they gain a great gift, the gift of inner strength (Goldman, 1996). It assists their grief process to be included in the funeral and other rituals associated with the death of a loved one (Rando, 1991). Knowing they could participate and be present with adults in a community remembrance of a friend or family member gives them awareness of how people honor a life, come together for each other as a community, and say good-bye. Honoring a life gives children a way to value and respect their own lives. They become identified mourners and an ever present and integral part of the grief process. Research indicates that children who were allowed to attend the funeral of a loved one later expressed positive feelings about going and about the meaning they attached to their attendance (Silverman & Worden, 1992). Children in the study felt "it was important to them that they had attended. Attendance helped them to acknowledge the death, provided an occasion for honoring their deceased parent, and made it possible for them to receive support and comfort" (p. 319). This nurturing environment supports their emotional and spiritual growth as human beings. So often caring adults are too uncomfortable talking to children about death. They may not have the words to use, may feel powerless when children are sad or cry, and ultimately may inhibit tears and stop the grief process.

Bereaved children can actively commemorate their loss by participating in safe and comfortable processes that allow for the expression of grief (Goldman, 1996). The following are age-appropriate ways children and teens can give meaning to their many thoughts and feelings. They can plant a flower or tree, send a balloon, blow bubbles, or say a prayer. Bereaved children might light a candle or write a poem, story, or song about their loved one and share it. Some boys and girls find talking into a tape recorder or creating a video of memories is helpful. Others enjoy (a) making cookies or cakes and bringing them to the family of the person who has died, (b) creating a mural or collage about the life of the person who has died, or (c) drawing a picture or making a memory book. Christina and Christy were two young children who were prepared, invited, and given choices about joining in a memorial service for their friend, Andrew. They were an active part of the service, sitting with family members, blowing bubbles, sharing, listening, and drawing pictures for their friend.

Conclusion and Recommendations

Research suggests that certain mental health outcomes may emerge for grieving children (Lutzke, Ayers, Sandier, & Barr, 1997). Bereaved children may show (a) more depression, withdrawal, and anxiety; (b) lower self-esteem; and (c) less hope for the future than non-bereaved children. Adults who were bereaved children tend to exhibit higher degrees of suicide ideation and depression and are more at risk for panic disorders and anxiety. Support for bereaved children is essential in helping to reduce negative outcomes related to unresolved or unexplored grief during childhood. The findings suggest that, although trauma associated with death-related situations could not always predict later symptom formation, therapeutic intervention at the time of the death may help to reduce or extinguish future anxiety that could escalate without intervention.

A key debilitating factor creating ongoing trauma for grieving children is often a sense of loss of control in their lives. Early interventions through counseling and grief support groups can help boys and girls regain their sense of control and reduce the stress associated with the death of a friend or family member. Early interventions may also support children in their grief by providing a meaningful relationship with at least one caring adult (e.g., the MHC). Mishara (1999) reported that children with strong social supports have a reduced presence of suicide ideation. Another study (U.S. Secret Service, 2002) clearly indicates "the importance of giving attention to students who

are having a difficult coping with major losses . . . particularly when feelings of desperation and hopelessness are involved" (p. 14). The report suggests that an important aspect in prevention may be to allow young people the opportunity to talk and connect with caring adults.

The MHC needs to view him or herself not only as a therapist, but also as an advocate for bereaved children. MHCs' role as an ally and friend creates a link to the child's larger community that extends to parents, clergy, educators, physicians, and other health care professionals. Educating members of these supportive networking systems in the common signs of bereaved children and suggesting age-appropriate interventions can extend the boundaries of mental health services into the child's home, school, and community. MHCs are trained to see the child in the present and to view changes in behaviors as a cry for help. Using therapeutic interventions such as projective techniques, sharing, and listening allows children to work through their grief. Active involvement in commemoration, rituals, and support groups facilitates the healing process of the bereaved child. Giving boys and girls the opportunity to release their emotions within a safe haven is the underlying thread inherent in counseling grieving children.

References

Bode, J. (1993). *Death is hard to live with.* New York: Dell.

Brown, L., & Brown, M. (1996). *When dinosaurs die.* New York: Little, Brown.

Carney, K. L. (1999). *Honoring our loved ones: Going to a funeral.* Wethersfield, CT: Dragonfly.

Celotta, B., Jacobs, O., & Keys, S. (1987). Searching for suicidal precursors in the elementary school child. *American Mental Health Counselors Association Journal, 9,* 38–48.

Doka, K. J. (Ed.). (1989). *Disenfranchised grief: Recognizing hidden sorrow.* New York: Lexington Books.

Dougy Center. (2002). *After a murder: A workbook for kids.* Portland, OR: Author.

Fox, S. S. (1988). *Good grief: Helping groups of children when a friend dies.* Boston, MA: The New England Association for the Education of Young Children.

Ginsberg, H., & Opper, S. (1969). *Piaget's theory of intellectual development.* Englewood, NJ: Prentice Hall.

Goldman, L. E. (1996). We can help children grieve: A child-oriented model for memorializing. *Young Children: The National Association for the Education of Young Children, 51,* 69–73.

Goldman, L. E. (1998a). *Bart speaks out: Breaking the silence on suicide.* Los Angeles, CA: Western Psychological Services.

Goldman, L. E. (1998b). Helping the grieving child in the school. *Healing Magazine, 3,* 15–24.

Goldman, L. E. (2000a). *Helping the grieving child in the school.* Bloomington, IN: Phi Delta Kappa International.

Goldman, L. E. (2000b). *Life and loss: A guide to help grieving children* (2nd ed.). New York: Taylor & Francis.

Goldman, L. E. (2001). *Breaking the silence: A guide to help children with complicated grief suicide, homicide, AIDS, violence and abuse* (2nd ed.). New York: Taylor & Francis.

Goldman, L. E. (2003). Talking to children about terrorism. In M. E. Eicht & K. J. Doka (Eds.), *Living with grief, coping with public tragedy* (pp. 139–149). Washington, D.C. Hospice Foundation of America.

Goldman, L. E. (2001). *Circle of trust: Support for grief.* In H. G. Rosenthal (Ed.), Favorite counseling and therapy homework assignments (pp. 108–110). New York: Taylor & Francis.

Gootman, M. (1994). *When a friend dies.* Minneapolis, MN: Free Spirit.

Heegaard, M. (1988). *When someone very special dies.* Minneapolis, MN: Woodland.

Lutzke, J. R., Ayers, T. S., Sandler, N. S., & Barr, A. (1997). *Risk and interventions for the parentally bereaved child.* In N. Sandier. & S. Wolchik (Eds.), *Handbook of children's coping: Linking theory and intervention* (pp. 215–242). New York: Plenum.

Mishara, B. (1999). Conceptions of death and suicide in children ages 6–12 and their implications for suicide prevention. *Suicide and Life-Threatening Behavior, 29,* 105–118.

O'Toole, D. (1995). *Facing change.* Burnsville, NC: Compassion Books.

Rando, T. (1991). *How to go on living when someone you love dies.* New York: Bantam.

Silverman, P. (2000). *Never to young to know: Death in children's lives.* NY: Oxford University.

Silverman, P., Nickman, S., & Worden, J. W. (1992). Detachment revisited: The child's reconstruction of a dead parent. *American Journal of Orthopsychiatry, 62,* 494–503.

Silverman, P., & Worden, J. W. (1992). *Children's understanding of funeral ritual.* Omega, 25, 319–331.

Traisman, P. S. (1992). *Fire in my heart: Ice in my veins.* Omaha, NE: Centering.

U.S. Secret Service. (2002). Preventing school shootings: A summary of U. S. Secret Service Safety school initiative. *National Institute of Justice Journal, 248,* 10–15.

Webb, N. B. (Ed.). (2002). *Helping bereaved children: A handbook for practitioners* (2nd ed.). New York: Guilford.

Worden, J. W. (1991). *Grief counseling and grief therapy: A handbook for the mental health practitioner.* New York: Springer.

Lɪɴᴅᴀ Gᴏʟᴅᴍᴀɴ, CLPC, CT, is a grief therapist, author, and adjunct faculty at John Hopkins University, Baltimore, MD. E-mail: lgold@erols.com.

From *Journal of Mental Health Counseling,* October 1998. Copyright © 1998 by American Mental Health Counselors Association. Reprinted by permission.

Test-Your-Knowledge Form

We encourage you to photocopy and use this page as a tool to assess how the articles in *Annual Editions* expand on the information in your textbook. By reflecting on the articles you will gain enhanced text information. You can also access this useful form on a product's book support Web site at *http://www.mhcls.com*.

NAME:

DATE:

TITLE AND NUMBER OF ARTICLE:

BRIEFLY STATE THE MAIN IDEA OF THIS ARTICLE:

LIST THREE IMPORTANT FACTS THAT THE AUTHOR USES TO SUPPORT THE MAIN IDEA:

WHAT INFORMATION OR IDEAS DISCUSSED IN THIS ARTICLE ARE ALSO DISCUSSED IN YOUR TEXTBOOK OR OTHER READINGS THAT YOU HAVE DONE? LIST THE TEXTBOOK CHAPTERS AND PAGE NUMBERS:

LIST ANY EXAMPLES OF BIAS OR FAULTY REASONING THAT YOU FOUND IN THE ARTICLE:

LIST ANY NEW TERMS/CONCEPTS THAT WERE DISCUSSED IN THE ARTICLE, AND WRITE A SHORT DEFINITION:

We Want Your Advice

ANNUAL EDITIONS revisions depend on two major opinion sources: one is our Advisory Board, listed in the front of this volume, which works with us in scanning the thousands of articles published in the public press each year; the other is you—the person actually using the book. Please help us and the users of the next edition by completing the prepaid article rating form on this page and returning it to us. Thank you for your help!

ANNUAL EDITIONS: Dying, Death, and Bereavement 09/10

ARTICLE RATING FORM

Here is an opportunity for you to have direct input into the next revision of this volume.
We would like you to rate each of the articles listed below, using the following scale:

1. **Excellent: should definitely be retained**
2. **Above average: should probably be retained**
3. **Below average: should probably be deleted**
4. **Poor: should definitely be deleted**

Your ratings will play a vital part in the next revision.
Please mail this prepaid form to us as soon as possible.
Thanks for your help!

RATING	ARTICLE	RATING	ARTICLE
	1. Death, Dying, and the Dead in Popular Culture		18. Death and the Law
	2. Dealing with the Dead Patient at the Intensive Care Unit		19. What Living Wills Won't Do: The Limits of Autonomy
	3. How Much Is More Life Worth?		20. Ethics and Life's Ending: An Exchange
	4. Confronting Death: Perceptions of a Good Death in Adults with Lung Cancer		21. Suicidal Thoughts among College Students More Common than Expected
	5. Estimating Excess Mortality in Post-Invasion Iraq		22. When Students Kill Themselves, Colleges May Get the Blame
	6. The Sociology of Death		23. The Tuneful Funeral
	7. Rituals of Unburdening		24. How Different Religions Pay Their Final Respects
	8. To Live with No Regrets		25. The Arlington Ladies
	9. "Cast Me Not Off in Old Age"		26. Green Graveyards—A Natural Way to Go
	10. Caregiving Systems at the End of Life: How Informal Caregivers and Formal Providers Collaborate		27. Social Workers' Final Act of Service: Respectful Burial Arrangements for Indigent, Unclaimed, and Unidentified People
	11. Needs of Elderly Patients in Palliative Care		28. The Grieving Process
	12. Altered States: What I've Learned about Death & Disability		29. Disenfranchised Grief
	13. Life after Death		30. Enhancing the Concept of Disenfranchised Grief
	14. The Comfort Connection		31. The Increasing Prevalence of Complicated Mourning: The Onslaught Is Just Beginning
	15. Are They Hallucinations or Are They Real? The Spirituality of Deathbed and Near-Death Visions		32. Life Is Like the Seasons
	16. Dying on the Streets: Homeless Persons' Concerns and Desires about End of Life Care		33. Counseling with Children in Contemporary Society
	17. Aging Prisoners' Concerns toward Dying in Prison		

ABOUT YOU

Name

Date

Are you a teacher? ❏ A student? ❏
Your school's name

Department

Address

City

State

Zip

School telephone #

YOUR COMMENTS ARE IMPORTANT TO US!

Please fill in the following information:
For which course did you use this book?

Did you use a text with this ANNUAL EDITION? ❏ yes ❏ no
What was the title of the text?

What are your general reactions to the Annual Editions concept?

Have you read any pertinent articles recently that you think should be included in the next edition? Explain.

Are there any articles that you feel should be replaced in the next edition? Why?

Are there any World Wide Web sites that you feel should be included in the next edition? Please annotate.

May we contact you for editorial input? ❏ yes ❏ no
May we quote your comments? ❏ yes ❏ no